D1106181

A History and Bibliography of American Magazines 1810-1820

by

NEAL L. EDGAR

The Scarecrow Press, Inc.

Metuchen, N.J.   1975

PN 4877
E 3
1975

Library of Congress Cataloging in Publication Data

Edgar, Neal L   1927-
    A history and bibliography of American magazines,
1810-1820.

        Bibliography: p.
        Includes index.
        1. American periodicals--History. 2. American
periodicals--Bibliography. I. Title.
PN4877.E3   016.051   75-11882
    ISBN 0-8108-0821-8

Printed in the United States of America

For the memory of
Rudolph Gjelsness
who provided the original idea
and to my wife
Susanna
who provided the oomph

CONTENTS

PART I

HISTORY
OF
AMERICAN MAGAZINES
1810-1820

1

PREFACE

I always, Sir, detested prefaces; I never read them, and I will not write one. --But ..., said my obstinate advisor in your work a preface is essentially requisite: to apoligize (!) for its numerous errors. Again Sir, I cannot coincide with you, for, in my opinion, an apology for an error, is but a repetition of the fault, and a tacit insult to the reader's candor and information, forwhose (!) memory cannot recall the hackneyed line,

Who're expects a faultless work to see, &c.

And trust me, dear Sir, if the liberality of my readers cannot extenuate the errors in the Regale; the weak powers of my pen will be ineffectual, therefore, I will not write a preface.

--Intellectual Regale, I (1814) i.

INTRODUCTION

The landmark history of American magazines is Frank Luther Mott's A History of American Magazines. Mott's work is selective, covering only the more important titles. One famous smaller study is Albert Smyth's The Philadelphia Magazines. A few of the other books and articles on American magazines and related topics are listed in the bibliography. The reasons for this book are two. The major, important gap in American bibliography was 1800-1820. Books are covered to some extent by the Shaw-Shoemaker American Bibliography and some other tools, but magazines are not. This gap needed to be filled. The second basic reason is that Benjamin Lewis completed A History and Bibliography of American Magazines, 1800-1810 in 1955. The second decade needed to be done, and this book attempts to do just that.

The major research on this book was completed in 1965. For this reason, the bibliography does not include more recent publications. Many items have appeared in the interval, but none has added substantially to the information in this book, so the bibliography has not been revised.

One of the essential tools in literary research is the bibliography. Many items referred to in this study are bibliographies themselves, and three of them should be mentioned as indispensable. The Union List of Serials provides the most comprehensive list, but its alphabetical arrangement limits its use for chronological investigation. The entire set was read, entry by entry, and in this way titles not mentioned in more specialized bibliographies were discovered. Clarence Brigham's History and Bibliography of American Newspapers provided many details, and it remains the best source

3

for those publications which fall between the magazine and the news-
paper--the literary newspaper.

The third "bibliography" to mention is the American Periodical Series. This microfilm project published by Xerox-University
Microfilms provided runs of many of the titles. Some libraries
have sets which vary in some bibliographic details from the set
filmed for the APS; the series is by no means complete; and in a
few instances the periodical actually filmed is not the title claimed
by the APS. Despite this, and some other inconsistencies in film-
ing and quality, the APS remains the single best source for magazines in early America.

One problem in limitation is to discover what a magazine
really is. The broadest term is serial, and this is usually considered to be any publication issued in parts, in some sort of sequence, and with a stated or implied intention to continue indefinitely.
Somewhat more refined is the term periodical which is differentiated
as a type of serial in that it is generally not a monograph, but in
that it has the other features of a serial. The two most frequently
found forms of periodicals are newspapers and magazines. A newspaper is a serial whose periodicity is usually stated, and whose
primary intention is to relate the current news. Frequently, newspapers will prefer one side of an issue, and they have frequently
tried to add an element of entertainment as a means of attracting
readers. A magazine is a periodical publication, usually appearing
regularly, containing articles written by several people, and intended
to include material which may be descriptive, critical, narrative,
biographical, or literary. At times the literary material includes
stories, poems, and other literary genres, often serialized. A
magazine may either be designed to entertain the general public, or
it may be intended for a specialized group, either a subject-related
one, or one associated by age, education, religion, political belief,
or some other common factor.

The limitation that a magazine must contain articles written
by several people cannot be adhered to very rigidly. William Tudor
wrote almost every word of the first two volumes of the North
American Review, and to exclude this magazine would be to remove

one of the very few really important titles. Nor can the irregularity of a given magazine exclude it since many magazines fluctuated in their issuance, and many of the more interesting but minor items known as magazines were virtually unpredictable in their periodicity.

This book is divided into three sections. The first is an attempt to point briefly to some of the major aspects of the American magazines which existed during the second decade of the nineteenth century. The second part is an alphabetically arranged series of annotations which reveal the major bibliographic features of each title. In general, the more important the title, the more extensive the annotation. The third section is a group of three appendices which attempts to make this a more useful tool for the student of American cultural history.

Appendix A covers ninety-two titles divided into ten groups. For several reasons, these titles were not included in the main part of the bibliography, but each of the titles has an annotation. Appendix B is a chronological list arranged by the date of first appearance. Some idea of the growth pattern of magazines in this period is one of the values of such a list. The third appendix is a register of printers, publishers, editors and engravers. It is hoped that this register will add some pertinent information about some of the men and women involved with early American intellectual life.

The American Periodical Series claims 195 titles for the period from 1810 to 1820. Four of these, Militia Reporter, The Mirror of Literature, The Truth, and Watchman, are not magazines. The reasons are given in the appendix of exclusions. Two others excluded are: Christian Observer and The Journal of Science and the Arts. Both are English, but both are included in the appendix of exclusions.

To the remaining 189 titles, sixty-eight others were added. Nineteen of these are not listed in the Union List of Serials. This new total, 257, is considered to be the number of magazines which existed at one time or another during the decade covered in this bibliography. Of these, seven were in French or German, and thirteen were conceived for children. No copies could be found for fourteen. These are noted, however, since some evidence, however slim, supports the titles as having lived.

A comprehensive and entirely satisfactory history of magazines probably cannot be achieved since the magazines are so diverse and the aspects of them which can be studied are so numerous and miscellaneous. American magazine publishing began in January 1741 with the first issue of William Bradford's American Magazine. Despite frequent claims to the contrary, Benjamin Franklin had nothing whatever to do with the Saturday Evening Post, which first appeared in August 1821, not 1728 as the magazine itself claimed. Nonetheless, between the two, and since, a remarkable record of cultural history can be found on the pages of magazines. This book is intended to unlock some of this material.

CHAPTER 1

THE MAGAZINES AND THEIR STRUCTURE

Magazines have become a common feature of American life.
They fulfill many needs, appear in a variety of shapes and sizes,
and may be found nearly anywhere. But there was a time when
editors were less secure about their subscriptions and were just
beginning to develop an audience.

> Magazines, by what name soever distinguished, have given
> rise to a new epoch in the history of intellectual improve-
> ment. They come to the purchasers on terms so reason-
> able, and at periods so regularly distant, as to render the
> procuring of them a circumstance unattended with incon-
> venience. ... They portray and transmit characters and
> events as they daily occur.... Many young authors, who
> have risen to considerable eminence, have here made their
> first attempt in composition. They convey information
> through regions which larger publications cannot reach. [1]

Although somewhat optimistic and no doubt written to encourage subscriptions to the magazine in which it appeared, this statement conveys something of the feeling editors had about the publications they worked so hard to produce.

Many factors entered into the make-up of magazines in the
early nineteenth century, and many factors came to bear on their
production, contents, distribution, and success. A brief examination
of some of these precedes a discussion of the magazines' influence
in American life.

Statistics

Only a few American cities produced magazines in the eighteenth century. In the next ten years, forty cities in fifteen states
and the District of Columbia could claim magazines. [2] The nineteenth
century's second decade experienced a similar but ever greater

7

increase as indicated in the following table.

State	Places	Titles
Connecticut	3	9
District of Columbia	3	6
Georgia	2	2
Kentucky	3	8
Maine	2	2
Maryland	1	21
Massachusetts	8	43
Missouri	1	1
New Hampshire	3	5
New Jersey	3	4
New York	13	76
North Carolina	2	2
Ohio	3	4
Pennsylvania	10	64
Rhode Island	1	3
South Carolina	2	6
Tennessee	2	2
Vermont	6	7
Virginia	5	7

Publishing Centers	Titles
New York City	52
Philadelphia	52
Boston	35
Baltimore	21
Albany, N. Y.	7
New Haven, Conn.	6
Lexington, Ky.	5
Charleston, S. C.	5
Washington, D. C.	4
Hudson, N. Y.	4
Four cities with three titles	12
Ten cities with two titles	20
Forty-nine cities with one title	49

Seventy-three cities and towns in eighteen states and the District of Columbia printed magazines in the second decade of the nineteenth century. Of the states added to the Union before 1820, only Alabama, Illinois, Indiana, and Mississippi printed no magazines until after 1820. The total number of titles in both tables is 272, and this is fifteen higher than the number of titles covered in this study, 257. This difference results from ten magazines having been printed in more than one place; these titles are:

American Law Journal	2 places
Cricket	4 places
Churchman's Magazine	2 places
Emporium of Arts and Sciences	2 places
Gospel Visitant	3 places
Herald of Gospel Liberty	4 places
Le Médiateur	2 places
Quarterly Theological Magazine	2 places
Scientific Magazine	2 places
The Sunday Visitant	2 places

Each of these titles, by changing location once or more, adds something to the magazine total in the early United States. This statistical swelling is out of proportion with its importance, however, since new titles were not added, and not one of the above is of primary importance.

A new publishing center, Baltimore, had appeared between 1810 and 1819. Nearly one-tenth of the decade's magazines originated here; and the four largest centers, Baltimore, Boston, New York, and Philadelphia, accounted for nearly three-fourths of all the magazines. With perhaps the single exception of the Western Review, which came from Lexington, Kentucky, every really important magazine started in the decade came from one of these centers.

The fastest growing city in terms of population was Baltimore, and her magazine contribution became important. Three important magazines, Portico, Niles' Weekly Register, and The American Farmer were started in Baltimore, but even these could not compare with the product of the three larger cities which formed the intellectual axis of early America.

	Population		Printers	
	1810[3]	1820[4]	1810	1820
Baltimore	35,583	62,738	27[6]	29[6]
Boston	33,250	43,940	60[7]	82[7]
New York[5]	96,373	123,706	95[8]	164[8]
Philadelphia	53,583	63,802	168[9]	207[9]

From the beginning in 1741 through 1799, about one hundred
magazines appeared in the United States. Only four of these were
still alive in 1800. and only two, The Ladies' Weekly Museum and
Medical Respository, lasted past 1810. During the first decade of
the nineteenth century, about 138 magazines appeared of which
thirty-four were still alive on January 1, 1810.[10] The table below
indicates something of the manner in which magazines increased
from 1810 to 1820. The increase was erratic, especially from 1815
to 1817, but the number rose steadily until 1819 when ninety magazines were alive at one time or another during the course of the
year.

Magazine Totals

Year	Extant	New	Omitted*	Total	Died
1810	32	21	8	61	22
1811	39	19	3	61	27
1812	34	17	2	53	14
1813	39	17	6	62	16
1814	46	18	1	65	24
1815	41	12	5	58	14
1816	44	19	1	64	17
1817	47	16	3	66	18
1818	48	24	2	74	15
1819	59	28	3	90	20

The number of magazines extant in 1810, plus all the
new magazines which appeared from 1810 through 1819 is 223.
Each of these is covered by a full-length annotation. The thirty-
four omissions, giving a total of 257, will be found in Appendix A.
The "Total" column in the preceding table represents the full number of magazines for which at least one issue appeared in that year.
The year 1820 dawned with seventy magazines on the American
scene. This number rapidly changed, however, since The Ladies'
Port Folio, which superseded the Boston Kaleidoscope, issued its
first number on the cold dawn of January 1, 1820.

In 1812 the United States suffered a depression which served
to decrease the total number of magazines somewhat. Fewer were

---

*For an analysis of titles omitted from this study, see Appendix A.

started, and more died. Again in 1815 the total number dropped because of postal restrictions. But nearly every other year saw a larger number of magazines. Increased stability, better distribution, and improved format overcame the 1818-1819 depression, and magazines were again on the increase. The number of magazines in America has continued to rise ever since.

Editors, Printers, and Publishers

A magazine's success depends largely upon the ability of its editor, and its pages reflect his personality, character, and individuality. Some of the more important editors are mentioned later in this study, but it should be noted that many of the more able men in the United States during the decade under study were associated with a magazine. That these men chose this means to disseminate their ideas testifies to their belief in the magazine as a potentially powerful weapon for intellectual activity and for the encouragement of American nationalism.

The printers and publishers of magazines were often the more prominent ones, especially in the large cities. The printers especially saw the advantage of a magazine as an advertising medium for books, and many hoped to use a magazine to diversify their output and to make money at the same time. Seldom, except for the religious magazine, was a title produced as a public service.

The apprentice system was still common in early nineteenth century America, especially in a trade like printing. The staffs of these magazines are seldom identified in their pages, and only when a man like Joseph Buckingham writes an autobiography[11] do the names of some of them become known.

Since printing was frequently a family business, several women had been printers in the eighteenth century.[12] At least six women were directly connected with magazines of the decade 1810-1820. Margaret Harrison in New York served as both printer and publisher for The Ladies' Weekly Museum from February 15, 1806 to March 26, 1808. The public printer in Frankfort, Kentucky in 1814 was Mrs. William Gerard, and she printed the Kentucky

Missionary and Theological Magazine in that year. Lydia Bailey
printed the New Jerusalem Church Repository in Philadelphia from
1817 to 1818. Mrs. Mary Carr, also of Philadelphia, acted as
both editor and printer for the Intellectual Regale during its whole
life from 1814 to 1815.

Two women, Miss O. White in 1819 and Miss A. Hall in
1819, produced illustrations for the Port Folio. Miss Hall, although
the identification is not definite, probably was a member of the Hall
family which had four brothers working with the Port Folio at this
time.

While most of these women probably became involved for
family reasons, they nonetheless did become active in a business at
a time when working outside the home was generally frowned upon.
As these women became active in publishing, they helped to lay the
groundwork for others of their sex to work for magazines, and indeed in many other areas of public life.

Printing

It does not appear that any magazine of this period was
printed other than by hand-set type and hand-operated presses.
Stereotyping, it is true, was introduced to America between 1811
and 1813.[13] Books were produced by this method, but no record
exists of a magazine or newspaper being stereotyped before 1820.
The first mention of a machine press involves a book produced in
1823,[14] and also "America's adaptation of the cylinder press actually began when Major Mordecai Noah imported a Napier from
England in 1829."[15]

This laborious method of printing certainly affected the number of magazines which could be produced, and it limited other
physical aspects as well. Magazines were nearly always quarto in
size, and nearly always appeared in multiples of four pages.
Printing methods made this necessary, and the time allowed for
printing limited the length of issues except when they came from
very large printing establishments which had a number of presses
and a fairly large number of printers working at any one time. An

additional problem was the inclusion of illustrations. At times
small wood-cuts were used for decoration and to break up a solid
type-page, but nearly always the illustrations were engravings which
were produced separately and inserted, or even sent later to subscribers with instructions for binding them in the magazines. This
may account for the varying placement of engravings in bound sets
of early magazines which are still in American libraries.

Illustrations

Several hundred engravings appeared in the magazines in the
decade under study. Executed by many of America's best artists,
their quality constantly improved. The single most lavishly illustrated magazine was the Port Folio, but others like the Analectic
and Emporium of Arts and Sciences contributed to magazine illustration by experimenting with new techniques and by broadening the
subjects of these illustrations. Several new techniques appeared in
the period, and others were continued and refined. Aquatinting was
introduced by John Hill,[16] J. Kidder,[17] and William Strickland.[18]
An etching on glass, made with "fluoric acid," was done by Cornelius Tiebout.[19] The first roulet engraving in an American magazine was also done by Tiebout.[20] Two color plates were also
found, both unsigned, and both of scientific subjects.[21] They were
handcolored, a process that was both time-consuming and costly.

Perhaps the most important single illustration in the period
was America's first magazine lithograph, an untitled country scene
which appeared in the Analectic for July 1819, as executed and
signed by Bass Otis. This method of illustration proved less expensive than engraving, and it led to more frequent illustrations in
all forms of printing.

Publication Problems

One of the principal problems for magazines remained the
financial one. Publishers trustingly sent magazines on credit, and
readers, more frequently than not, avoided remitting the requested
price. Yet the subscription was sorely needed to cover costs, since

little income resulted from advertisements. Time after time, notices
like this one appear:

> The deficiency of our subscription list has made it con-
> venient to our publisher, that the present number be the
> last of the Harvard Lyceum. [22]

"Convenient" was hardly the word. "Necessary" or "impera-
tive" would have been better. Most of the magazines which failed
did so because the collection of subscriptions proved to be impossible.

A further problem was the inability of the editors to obtain
material:

> Previous to its commencement, several gentlemen had
> volunteered to write for it, which subsequent circum-
> stances prevented. [23]

This type of notice lies behind the second most frequent reason for
magazine failure--the lack of worthwhile articles to print.

Distribution was also a problem. Roads were very few in
America in the early nineteenth century, and the time taken to
travel from one town to another was too long to allow for rapid
delivery. For a stagecoach to average only two miles an hour was
not unusual, and in 1802 the journey from Boston to New York took
four days of riding from three in the morning until eight at night
with stops in Worcester, Hartford, and Stamford. [24] Even within
the cities themselves, no regular distribution system existed, and
magazines often had their own employees who delivered copies by
hand. Several broadsides describe this aspect of magazine publishing, such as the "Address of the Carriers of the Philadelphia
Repertory to their Patrons on the Commencement of the year
1811." [25] The long and wordy poem describes the hardships of a
carrier, his faithfulness, and his hopes that payment will be forthcoming.

Postal delivery was another problem. Before 1810, no official sanction nor federal enforcement existed for postal delivery. [26]
With no regulations, bulk mail was at the mercy of individual post-
masters, and delivery conditions were haphazard. This lack of
consistency resulted in irregular delivery, the loss of dependable

income and circulation, the lack of a national coverage, and the final demise of many of the magazines. Not until 1814 was regular service instituted from Albany to Buffalo, and St. Louis obtained a weekly mail delivery from the East only in 1816.[27] As early as 1792 the postmaster had ruled that magazines should be carried at a letter rate, but in 1815 Return Jonathan Meigs, Jr., then the Postmaster, decided that pamphlets and magazines interfered with the mail, and these items, except for religious publications, were excluded from the mail.[28] The objections raised to the decision caused Congress to pass an act in 1816 which readmitted magazines at from one to two cents per sheet according to the distance carried. Four folio, eight quarto, or sixteen octavo pages were considered a single sheet. Even this regulation limited distribution because it was costly to send a very large magazine through the mail, and although more and more magazines appeared, they continued to have distribution problems.

Most magazines in this decade were locally distributed. This both avoided the cost of the mails and the regulations which hampered sending magazines to distant communities. Religious magazines, perhaps because they were generally exempted from the postal regulations, and especially those in New England, were exceptions. The scattered subscription lists published in the magazines indicate subscribers who lived in several states. Some few magazines like the Port Folio and Niles' Weekly Register were apparently successful in reaching national circulation; but generally speaking, magazines of this period were published with a local audience in mind, and they usually did not attempt to go beyond city limits. Probably the first magazine which achieved national importance and circulation was the North American Review, but this was not until after 1820.

Prices

The difficulty magazine publishers had in collecting subscriptions was one matter; the rates charged was another. Prices ranged from that of a book catalog, New England Literary Herald,

which was distributed free, to an incredible $12.00 for the Journal
of Musick.   No prices were printed on seventy of the magazines,
but others have a wide range.   Fifty-nine cost up to two dollars,
eighty-five cost between two and five dollars, and nine were priced
above that.   The average price probably was about three dollars.

By way of comparison, the prices below, taken from the
General Shipping and Commercial List, show the costs of a few
necessities in the same period.

Product	August 1, 1815[29]	August 3, 1819[30]
American cheese (pound)	10-13 ¢	8-11 ¢
Coffee (pound)	25-28 ¢	24-25 ¢
Sea Island Cotton (pound)	36-42 ¢	33-42 ¢
Superfine flour (barrel)	$8.00-8.75	$6.25-6.50
Ham (pound)	18-19 ¢	14-15 ¢
Honey (pound)	18 ¢	15-16 ¢
Molasses (gallon)	80-83 ¢	36-42 ¢
Sugar (cwt.)	$26.00-27.00	$15.00-16.00
Virginia tobacco (pound)	12-15 ¢	7-8 ¢
Madeira wine (gallon)	$3.37-4.00	$2.25-2.50

Even as late as 1825, a worker in a cotton mill earned
about five cents an hour, or between fifty-five and sixty cents a
day.[31]   Working every day of the year, an annual income of little
more than $200 could be expected.   On another part of the scale,
Washington Irving was paid about $1,500 for editing the Analectic
Magazine[32]--hardly a lordly stipend for a man so famous.   A brief
consideration of these prices and wages indicates that the magazine
was a luxury item in this period.

A second problem lies in the fact that at least three-fourths
of the population was rural, and many of these people lacked hard
cash.   Even if they had it, it may have been state bank money
which was frequently difficult to spend outside the bank's area.

Not only was the population limited in numbers and in magazine buying power, but also the individual's daily work schedule of
ten or twelve hours left little time for leisure reading--provided,
of course, he could read at all.

Finally, nearly every magazine which changed its price in

the period raised it, thus making magazine purchase for the average man even more of a luxury.

Contents

The magazines as a whole follow a standard pattern. Biography, book reviews, serialized fiction, the miscellaneous essay, sermons, and poetry were standard items. Some local and summarized national news, marriage and death notices, and advertisements completed the array of materials. In the over-all view, little difference existed among the magazines, with one exception. This was the period of the appearance of the special subject magazine--a magazine devoted to the interests of a special audience, generally professional, and usually centered in the cities. In this period, magazines first appeared for educators, lawyers, mathematicians, and scientists. They were of varying quality, but some became important. The first really significant literary review, the North American Review, appeared in 1815. And in religion, the first magazines for Catholics appeared.

CHAPTER 2

THE MAGAZINES AND AMERICAN LITERATURE

American nationalism and the creation of an indigenous
literature inextricably compound one intellectual problem which not
only defies separation but which also creates difficulties of definition
and clarification. One study which has helped to identify the birth
of American literature is that of William Cairns.[1] Two companion
studies which have dealt with literary nationalism are those by
James Coberly[2] and Henry Birnbaum.[3] All three of these neatly
enclose the period covered by this study, and all have been used,
in part, as a basis for some of the comments and conclusions
which follow.

Nearly all studies recognize four periodicals as the best
early American literary magazines. These are Port Folio, Monthly
Anthology, Analectic, and North American Review. No quarrel is
made with this conclusion, but some investigation of the lesser magazines is necessary to discover what, if anything, other magazines had
to contribute to a slowly developing trend toward a native literature
in America.

That these other magazines at least attempted to supply some
impetus toward a native literature was well stated by Robert Walsh:

> Another topic ... is, the apparent necessity for some
> such enterprize (as this periodical) with a view to the
> promotion of the literary fame of this country.
> . . . .
> If the foundations were once settled, there remains no
> doubt but that with the scaffolding of English literature,
> a fabric of literary reputation might be ere long erected,
> of materials which both for their variety and excellence
> would delight and surprise the nations of Europe. It is
> certain that our means are not duly appreciated abroad;--
> that we ourselves have not done justice to our resources,

either of genius or learning.   Whatever may be said by
the prejudiced or the uninformed critics of Europe, there
is, nevertheless, among us an ample portion of the 'ethe-
real spirit, ' and an abundant store of erudition, competent
to extend the limits of human knowledge and to shed lustre
on the national character.... [4]

The attempt to initiate some momentum in literary nationalism had been tried by magazines nearly 400 times over two decades.
No matter how frequently failure occurred during these twenty years,
another optimist was bound to say:

> Periodical works, however numerous, can scarcely be
> productive of injurious consequences to the public, and
> are almost necessarily beneficial, at least in a degree, as
> they excite discussion, and, by multiplying the number of
> writers, are the means of saving facts which might other-
> wise be lost. [5]

Problems were recognized and frankly stated:

> There is in the situation of countries newly settled, pe-
> culiar circumstances, which must for a long time retard
> the progress of the human mind, and the liberal culture
> of science and literature. [6]

At the end of the second decade, one editor could mournfully, but
accurately, state that:

> It has been the misfortune of our country, that efforts
> made to establish, and conduct periodical publications,
> especially those of a religious character, have been di-
> vided.   These publications have, therefore, received but
> a partial support, have been of circumscribed usefulness,
> and of short continuance. [7]

However, the optimists were still to be found:

> It shall be a primary object to gain for our paper a
> literary character; and to diversify it with reviews of
> literature, accounts of books and authors, history and
> biography, scientific and philosophic intelligence; and
> agriculture and manufacturers shall have a liberal share
> of attention. [8]

How successful were the men who tried and tried again?   Not
very.   But without adumbrating the end of the chapter, a brief survey of some of the literary magazines will serve to provide an understanding of what was available to the reader of periodicals in the
early nineteenth century.

Miscellaneous Magazines

Over seventy-five periodicals of a highly miscellaneous nature
appeared in the decade 1810-1820. Four categories of these seem
fairly convenient, and the groups each have some broadly based common characteristics. The largest group, called the Literary Miscellany, had about thirty titles typical of which would be Polyanthos,
Monthly Anthology, General Repository and Review, Rhode Island
Literary Repository, Literary and Musical Magazine, Boston Kaleidoscope, and Journal of Belles Lettres.

A second group which had a much broader concept is called
the General Miscellany. Included here are Port Folio, Analectic,
American Magazine, Parterre, Portico, New England Galaxy, and
Saturday Magazine. About twenty-five of these general miscellanies
appeared, and each, while placing some emphasis on literature, included many other materials.

A group of about fifteen Humorous Miscellanies can be
counted. They are given this name because they were satirically
critical, or because they were predicated upon some base which was
other than serious. Typical titles are: Something, Tickler, Beacon,
Cynick, Hive, Satirist, Corrector, and Red Book.

One final group is the Special Miscellanies. The Freemason's Magazine, while not wholly aimed at Masons, included
material for them. So, incidentally, did the New England Galaxy.
Noah Webster's Friend of Peace could be called a pacifist magazine, as could Theophilanthropist. The True Briton had the Anglophile for an audience; and the inveterate chance-taker might have
found solace in the pages of Cohen's Gazette and Lottery Register.

The possible groupings of the magazines in this period is
endless. These divisions are suggested as one possible way to
make a broad grouping of the more literary magazines. The brief
examination of some of the "literature" which appeared in them will
be, in part, based on the fact that these magazines, at least, tried
to offer something like original work.

One other group suggests itself--and this is possibly the
least important of all. Some eighteen Literary Newspapers are

identified in the annotations which follow. These range from Boston Mirror, Rural Visiter (!), Independent Mechanic, and Bureau to National Museum, Weekly Recorder, Philanthropist, and Villager. A typical issue might be one of the Philanthropist for December 12, 1817.[9] In eight pages, one could read a very brief notice of fashions, an extracted sermon, a poem, "The Horrors of War," an article on war and peace, something about Indian treaties, a few anecdotes, some moralistic passages, announcements of local meetings, a condemnation of slavery, and a series of small advertisements. All in all, the contents represented a mishmash of ephemera. Any issue of any other literary newspaper would be little different. Sampling here and there, a combination of them all, if such an issue can be imagined, would include at least some of the following: religious news, moralistic columns, a column covering the arts and sciences, publication notices, a geography column, new inventions, national and local news, and a page or two of advertisements.

The religious news often concerned the Bible societies, their meetings and activities. These columns contain names, statistics, and details of the activities of these groups which frequently cannot be found elsewhere.

Articles on education and the methods used in teaching were common. The geographical descriptions, the articles on "natural philosophy," biographies, and the other features give the magazine something of the appearance of a teaching tool. Poetry and agricultural paragraphs were occasionally printed. From 1812 to 1815, war news appears, nearly always taking the form of summaries of battles, especially the naval ones.

Joseph Tinker Buckingham brought some good things to his magazines. He was associated with six magazines in the period, and he used them for many purposes. In his words, "My first attempt to amuse, instruct, and edify the public, was the publication of The Polyanthos."[10] Buckingham had specific views on nationalism, and his magazines reflect his reputation as a hard fighter against anything he felt to be false. This type of advocacy, in fact,

differentiates his and other literary magazines from the more excellent papers of the period.   The editors had political, economic, or
religious views which interfered with their search for literature.
Certainly, if they found any literature, precious little found its way
into print in these pages.

But what did find its way into the literary magazine?   The
next pages will point to some of the examples of criticism, novelettes, essays, biography, drama, poetry, and humor which are to
be found.   In addition, a word or two will be said of Negro and
foreign literature, and about the literary clubs which were behind
most of the better magazines.

Criticism

From before the Revolution, American writers had been pre-
occupied with the problems of freedom and generally had not developed belles lettres.   While political separation began in 1776 and
continued to develop through the nineteenth century's first decade,
lasting independence proved difficult to secure, and American authors
continued to concentrate on the concept of full political freedom.
This goal was not to come within America's grasp until after the
second war for independence which ended in 1815.   And now came
the matter of intellectual and literary independence, a difficult matter considering linguistic and cultural ties to the motherland as well
as an almost total lack of precedents in America for authors who
would write with other than religious or political purposes in mind.

The opportunity for a beginning was offered even before the
War of 1812 by the great influx of foreign visitors, many of whom
wrote letters, diaries, or travel books in which they recalled their
contacts in this new country.   The reactions to America in these
writings were not all favorable, and American editors, essayists,
and critics answered back, defending American customs and ideas,
trying to show there was an indigenous culture which could reasonably
be expected to act as a springboard for literature.

With this exchange of opinions there began America's "third
war of independence," the so-called Paper War.   The story of this

has already been told,[11] and there is no need to repeat it here, except to mention the barest outline.   The third war between America
and Great Britain has had far-reaching cultural influences and is
still going on, although the shots are now generally less vitriolic.
Starting in 1810 with Charles Jared Ingersoll's Inchquin, the
Jesuit's Letters, During a Late Residence in the United States of
America,[12] the shots of the first battle flew back and forth at
least until William Tudor's The United States and England, Being
a Reply to Criticism on Inchquin's Letters Contained in the Quarterly Review for January 1814.[13]   The squabbling had existed before, but this series of articles seemed to have created a storm,
aggravated by the shooting war; and the pitched battle on this one
issue continued until well after the decade.

    Interestingly enough, reviews of British books continued to
appear in American magazines throughout the decade, even in the
midst of the shooting war which many magazines managed to avoid
covering.   Possibly the author to receive the most attention was
Byron--at least until 1816--although an actual count of reviews
would be needed to prove this assumption.

    Politics, government, social customs, living habits, dress,
food, transportation, and other similar aspects of American life
were at issue, and the attacks and defenses are strongly worded and
to some extent amusing to the modern reader.   To the contemporary,
they were serious and answers to them were deeply motivated.

    Among the better magazines was Samuel Ewing's Select Re-
views.   About two-thirds of the contents were borrowed outright
from English sources.   An early example of the eclectic miscellany,
this title serves to forecast a type of magazine which was to come
later in great numbers.   But here, most of the material was
British, and this was true throughout most of the magazine's life.
Often the reviews were interesting and witty; but they were concerned with British books.

    Almost at the end of the decade, William Gibbs Hunt tried
his hand by issuing the Western Review.   Hunt was a Harvard
graduate, a member of all the right clubs and societies, and an

urbane intellectual. Lexington, Kentucky was the western frontier,
but it was close to Transylvania University. Hunt no doubt felt that
an academic atmosphere, added to an area without a good magazine,
would be an ideal combination for success. Although designed as a
review, and serving this purpose well, the magazine also preserves
historic and anthropological material of value. John D. Clifford,
the author of the series "Indian Antiquities," held memberships in
both the Philadelphia Academy of Natural Sciences and the American
Antiquarian Society. Fully half the total pages of all four volumes
consist of reviews--nearly 770 pages in two years. Much of this
was copied from English magazines with some emphasis on Scott
and Byron. Little was said of American poetry "for the plain reason
that but little American poetry existed in 1819."[14]

    At least two religious magazines concentrated on the review.
The Christian Register, edited in New York by Thomas Y. How,
and the Quarterly Theological Review, edited in Philadelphia by Ezra
Styles Ely, both frequently devoted almost all the space in an issue
to long, scholarly, omnibus reviews--but almost always of religious
books with little lasting merit. These were the two best religious
reviewing media in the decade, and the search in them for important
reviews by literary critics is in vain.

    The pages of the North American Review provide the best
source of American literary criticism in the years 1810-1820.
Started in 1815 by William Tudor and a group from the Anthology
Society in Boston, the North American Review used a patriotic desire for things American as one of its foundation stones. Tudor advocated 100 per cent Americanism, and he called for a truly American literature based on American traits and involved with American
ideals. But the aim was easier to state than to realize. For two
years, Tudor was forced to write nearly every word in the North
American Review, and many of the books he reviewed, even through
1819, were European. But the reviews were American, and some
of them deserve to be remembered.

    In 1815, Tudor produced reviews of Lydia Huntley's Moral
Pieces in Prose and Verse[15] and Walter Scott's The Lord of the

Isles.[16] Edward Everett's review of Goethe's Aus Meinem Leben: Dichtung und Warheit appeared in 1817.[17] Two samples from 1818 might include Edward T. Channing's review of Walter Scott's Rob Roy[18] and William Cullen Bryant's review of Solyman Brown's An Essay of American Poetry.[19] Richard Henry Dana contributed at least two long reviews in 1819: of William Hazlitt's Lectures on the English Poets[20] and Washington Irving's Sketch Book.[21]

These are but a sampling. The importance of them is that they demonstrate America did have at least some competent reviewers, and as far as the North American Review was concerned, the best was yet to come.

Novelettes

Despite the early and continuing popularity of such novels as The Power of Sympathy and Charlotte Temple, novel reading had not become universally accepted by 1810, and in fact, most readers were limited to women. Opinion about novels was not always good. Many sermons thundered against them, and magazines frequently repeated a somewhat dour opinion by saying things like:

> ... the attachment which young females exhibit to novel reading must originate in the weakness of their minds, resulting from a deficiency in their education; ... A young girl accustomed or addicted to novel reading opens wide the two great avenues to seduction, vanity and suscepti- bility.[22]

Herbert Ross Brown's The Sentimental Novel in America[23] carefully investigates the place of one form of literature in America, but few of the novelettes which appeared in magazines were discussed in this study. Many magazines published these stories, almost always in serial form, and most of these magazines were indeed aimed at least partially toward women. The man who read novels habitually was still scarce, and no wonder when the novels were written to attract a female audience anyway.[24]

The magazine fiction of the eighteenth century was classified in four ways by Effie Jane Wheeler.[25] She identifies the domestic and social instructive tale of contemporary life, the philosophical

reflective tale with exotic setting, the thrilling and amusing tale,
and the hybrid. Her investigation also shows that "in all the categories the bulk of the stories will be discovered to be mediocre
and frankly imitative of the magazine tales of British origin."[26]
The fiction also produced "adequate prototypes"[27] for nineteenth
century stories. These types include the romantic-realistic tale
of Irving, the reflective romance of Hawthorne, and the exotic fan-
tasy of Poe. The fiction in American magazines of the second
decade of the nineteenth century is a part of this development, not
only in the generally mediocre and imitative quality of the stories,
but also in the possibility that magazine fiction of this decade provided further prototypes for the century's later novelists and short
story writers.

An 1810 magazine, Emerald, printed Mary, a True Story.[28]
Anonymous, centered around a woman, and based on "facts," the
novelette typifies what women were supposed to like and what was
good for them to read. Interestingly, the second part of "Mary"
is followed by "Conjugal Celibacy" by An Old Bachelor,[29] which is
a satirical criticism of married bliss, and number one of "The
Monitor," devoted to seduction.[30] The conclusions which could be
drawn from this juxtaposition lead to the assumption that Emerald's
Peter Pleasant had a rather sharp tongue.

> Mary was the daughter of a gentleman of moderate for-
> tune, who dwelt on the borders of Cumberland; she was
> his favourite child, and he took a pride in bestowing on
> her every advantage of education. Alas! how often does
> it happen that an unjust partiality is punished by the dis-
> grace of the beloved object! so it was with the old man.
> His darling Mary was no longer innocent![31]

Mary's adventures, her dangers, illnesses, abductions, and
the loss of her virtue are all boiled down into a dozen pages of
moralistic, romantic drivel which was not only unoriginal but also
short-lived in value as literature.

The mention of Cumberland in the passage from "Mary" may
indicate its English origin, but more positive evidence of a de-
pendence on England for material shows up early since 1810 had
hardly begun when Mistrust; or, Blanche and Osbright, a Feudal

Romance by Matthew G. Lewis was serialized.[32] This romantic
story is somewhat Gothic in structure, rather strained in syntax,
and guaranteed to bring a catch to many throats. Typical of the
entire tone is the last sentence:

> Here every day they met to indulge their common sorrows:
> here every night they joined in prayer for the eternal hap-
> piness of those dear ones: here during many years of un-
> availing anguish they bathed with tears the marble tablet,
> on which stood engraven these words, so mournful, so
> fatal, and so true,
> -'Here rest the Victims of Mistrust'[33]

One year later, the Baltimore Repertory offered Agrarius
Denterville; or, The Victim of Discontent.[34] Against this man,
the fates must have been working over-time:

> 'The Heavens are against me,' exclaimed Agrarius, re-
> tiring into his house with his rake over his shoulder,
> 'the heavens are unpropitious, and my hay will be spoiled.
> My ground never afforded so large a crop of grass; how
> eagerly have I anticipated the sum it would produce, and
> to what advantage has my imagination disposed of the
> money, and now to behold my prospects blasted--surely
> 'tis unsupportable.'[35]

The literary merit of this aside, a farmer who uses vocabu-
lary like "unpropitious" stretches the imagination somewhat; an
audience which would be attracted to this would be difficult to locate.

England as the source of these novelettes appears again with
the Monk of the Grotto, the first episode of which was printed in
January 1811 in The Lady's Miscellany.[36] This was not Matthew
Lewis' Monk, but probably based on Pigault Lebrun's The Monk of
the Grotto; or, Eugenio & Virginia.[37] Quickly following this in the
same magazine were the episodes of The Spaniard; or, The Pride
of Birth.[38]

Still another example, also from a New York magazine, is
Self-Indulgence; a Tale of the Nineteenth Century.[39] Turning to
Philadelphia, and a little later in the decade, another woman's maga-
zine prints the chapters of Clermont Herbert; or Presentment.[40]
Eloisa, an orphan, tries to live by "her imagination rather than her
judgment," meets the expected problems, winds her way through

over fifty installments, and finally she and several of the other
characters who almost lose the gallant struggle in tear-filled incidents marked with death and insanity, wind up the improbable events
in an emotional scene marked by marriage and families. Quite a
tale! Mary Carr, the magazine's editor, printed each episode as
a paragraph regardless of sense, but here lies an unrecognized
sentimental novelette which typifies the fiction presented in early
magazines in America.

Another Philadelphia magazine, produced a few examples
which appeared at the decade's end. Sophis; or, The Dangerous
Indiscretion, [41] also English in origin, but anonymous, was one
such example. The same magazine later printed The Female War-
rior; or, Fortunio and The Modern Griselda; or, A Lesson to
Wives.

Georgia's first magazine for women, and one of the first
good magazines from the deep South, began in March of 1819 and
continued for five issues to publish Elizabeth Yeames' Julia Pal-
mira. [43] Intended as what might be called biographical fiction, the
novelette is also highly moralistic.

Each of the above points to one or more of the obvious
features of these stories. They were written with women in mind,
and frequently featured a woman. Her adventures were usually
complex, hair-raising, and usually emotional. They claimed they
were based on "facts." The magazines of the period contained
many more of these tales, and a complete catalog would probably
comprise at least fifty titles. Some of these would be reprinted
English stories, thus evading royalty payments. Some would be
original material. Nearly all would exemplify the early sentimental
novelette.

Essays

Early in the period an anonymous editor expressed his
feelings about essays in magazines:

> No paper possessing the constituents of the genuine peri-
> odical essay, has as yet been attempted in the United

States. Our periodical publications are either exclusively
political, or theologic, or issued upon the plan of a review; or lastly they consist of a variety of subjects, but
without unity of design, dramatic incident, or development
of human passion and character. [44]

The same man listed as essential to a periodical essay "variety of
topic, brevity of execution, unity of design, dramatic effect, and
classical expression. "[45] This definition obviously was not original
to the Literary Visitor because the exact words were used, probably
by David Graham, in The Pioneer about a year earlier. [46] But
quibbling about originality is not the point; the words are accurate
and applicable to early American magazines. The magazines are
almost rampant with items like "Observations on the Nature and
Cause of Certain Accidents that have Usually Been Ascribed to the
Wind of a Ball. "[47] Literally thousands of brief "essays" on thousands of "topics" appear in the magazines as leading features, as
regular columns, as occasional pieces, and as filler material. They
were usually hack work, more often than not borrowed--especially
from the newspapers, and seldom written with any level of compe-
tence. Among all the names, three stand out in the literary area,
historical and scientific essays being another matter.

One of these is Joseph Tinker Buckingham. In the second
decade, he had some associations with at least five magazines. [48]
Of these he was the publisher of three, one of which was religious
and largely written by men like Noah Worcester and Henry Ware.
The others were Polyanthos and New England Galaxy. (The sixth
title may never have been published.)

The first issue of the Polyanthos' new series, aside from a
biography of Samuel Harris, contained number one of the Examiner,
devoted to a review of "Monody on the Victims and Sufferers by the
Late Conflagration in Richmond, Virginia. "[49] More of an explication
than a criticism, the essay was intended to point to the poem's in-
adequacy. Also in this issue were eleven paragraph-length bits which
Buckingham apparently wished known as essays. A longer essay on
the alphabet also began in this issue, [50] and was continued. Although
rather interesting in a superficial way, it was English and written in

the eighteenth century--hardly a native American product. Many of
the other miscellaneous essays were borrowed, and the others were
original. Nearly all were little unimportant bits like "On the Use of
Snuff."[51] These paragraphs discuss a possible social evil, but do
so with no particular brilliance or care for style. The arguments
are based on emotional rather than logical grounds. Although anonymous, Buckingham probably was the author since the essay uses
ridicule--Buckingham's favorite weapon.

Buckingham's other journal was New England Galaxy and
Masonic Magazine. In it, Buckingham published material of interest
to him, and one thing was social life and customs in Boston. Subscription to this journal may have been a personal favor since the
essays were subjective and opinionated. Although the subjects included insane asylums, literary and theatrical reviews, legal trials,
and the Masons, Buckingham's chief interest seems to have been
manners and morality. His essays may be social documents, but
they do not qualify as literary essays.

One literary essayist who remains a small giant is Washington
Irving. His Sketch Book began to appear in 1819, but this is not a
periodical. The magazine essays he produced were in connection
with his editorship of the Analectic, a post Irving held from 1813 to
1815. Irving wrote two or three reviews in some of the issues, and
he possibly contributed some of the "original" essays. In 1816 the
Naval Chronicle was added, but this was not Irving's work since it
began after Irving left the magazine. Some of the previous biographies were done by Irving, but while excellent by comparison with
other biographical material, they were not purely literary essays.

The most famous essayist in the early 19th century was
Joseph Dennie. The Lay Preacher Essays had been run in newspapers, and Dennie also used some of them in the Port Folio.
Dennie wrote on fine arts and travel, and he may have written at
least a part of the series "The Table d'Hote."[52] When Dennie died
in 1812, the Port Folio changed, but it didn't improve. It had
reached its zenith, especially in the essay, when Dennie was the
editor.

One final echo of Dennie may be found in the Villager for
May of 1819. Here begins a series called "The Lay Preacher,"
but it was a hollow imitation of the real Dennie. In American
literature, the essay was yet to come--at least as far as the magazine essay was concerned.

Biography

Biography appeared more frequently than any feature except
book-reviews and poetry. Nearly every magazine used this form,
and during the period the great majority of persons so eulogized
were ministers or naval heroes.

The Port Folio published an engraving with nearly every
biography, and many of these have become famous by use in other
biographies of the same people. Brief, concise, and frequently
timely pieces were done on William Burrows, Alexander Murray,
Richard Dale, Lewis Warrington, Duncan Elliot, and more familiar
names like Meriwether Lewis and Oliver Perry. Possibly the most
popular biographical subject in the years of the War of 1812 was
Lieutenant James Lawrence. His biography is quite long, and there
are two portraits. [53]

An example among many from Polyanthos might be the
"Sketch of the Life and Character of Mr. Samuel Harris." [54] The
unsigned engraving showing a profile likeness may have been a self-
portrait. Samuel Harris was the engraver who had contributed frequently to the earlier series of the magazine, and Buckingham
thought this tribute the best way to begin his second attempt at the
title.

Buckingham, among other editors, often used biographies of
famous Europeans. They were well known, and their examples
might have been used to stir some feelings in America to create
artistic efforts which would be native. Just one example would be
the "Life of Haydn" [55] which occupies three and a half columns on
the front page of a literary newspaper, and was, according to an
appended note, from the Edinburgh Encyclopaedia.

The famous series started by Irving and published in the
Analectic was noted, copied, and frequently criticized:

> ... we have never been pleased with the sentiments, en-
> lightened by the genius, or charmed by the philosophy of
> the Analectic Magazine. On the contrary, the style of its
> original matter (we mean of those delectable pieces of
> Biography) is, in our opinion, at once affected, puerile,
> and pedantic - full of laboured ease, and mighty pretti-
> nesses. The prevailing sentiment, is, to our taste, sickly
> and mawkish, and the philosophy altogether too liberal,
> too magnanimous. We cannot therefore help wishing that
> the deeds of our infant, but glorious navy, should be
> chronicled by other pens. [56]

This particular criticism is not unfair when applied to most
of the biographies in question.

Drama

Theatrical periodicals provide a basis for history of the
American drama, but in the period 1810-1820 they provide no plays.
Actors' biographies, schedules of the theatres, and reviews of American productions of plays, both native and foreign, were all reported
in several of the magazines. But in the decade, no American play
appears to have been printed in an American magazine. The payment of royalties to a playwright was almost unheard of in this era,
and many authors were unwilling to risk non-existent capital by
printing a work with no promise of financial gain. Why should he
print in a magazine with even less chance to make money?

The major theatrical magazines of the period were Mirror of
Taste, Rambler's Magazine, and Whim. Some theatrical material
appears in many other magazines such as American Monthly Magazine, Boston Weekly Magazine, Cabinet, Christian Monitor, Comet,
Cynick, Monthly Recorder, and New England Galaxy. Most of the
articles, such as one from Polyanthos, [57] list coming productions and
briefly review productions on the boards at the time. The announcements were not always limited to the city in which the magazine was
printed, and with transportation difficulties as bad as they were,
this is a bit of a mystery. After all, how could someone plan to
run up to Boston from New York for a theatre party when the trip,
under favorable conditions, took four days?

Ten plays were printed in two magazines in the decade, and
every one of them is British. Many were eighteenth century in
origin, and surely were available in other editions. These plays
probably were printed for two reasons which recur with solemn
monotony. British material could be printed without paying royalty;
and there was a lack of anything American to print. Buckingham
ran a theatre column for two years in New England Galaxy, and not
once did he mention a Boston production of an American play.

Poetry

The problem of locating contributions to American poetry in
early magazines has been investigated before, and the results are
unrewarding. The choice generally must be made between long,
polemic, moralistic verse and material of which each of the following is an example.

The first representative is an eight stanza poem, of which
these are the first and the last:

On Seeing Mira Weeping
Near a Withered Rose Tree[58]

Charles J. Cox

But late I saw, that faded rose,
    So bright in morning's tremb'ling dew
I saw a tear-drop there repose
    Its beauty glow'd--It look'd like you.
. . . .
Then would our thoughts and wishes wreathe
    Like sister buds of one dear tree
In one fond gale their perfume breathe,
    Then flee to heav'n in ecstacy.

A shorter example, of only two stanzas, is:

To Anna[59]

My dearest Anna why these sighs,
That throb beneath that panting breast,
Ah tell me where your sorrow lies?
That I may ease and give you rest.

Why let those beauteous charms decay--
Some hidden grief I can discover;
Why throw life's pleasure all away,
Come and confide in me your lover?

The punctuation in that poem is curious to say the least, but the author's lack of confidence is easier to understand than why the author of the next selection said so little.

> Maria was handsome, in prime of her youth,
> Maria had feeling and taste--
> For a chaste education directed by truth
> Her native endowments had grac'd. [60]

And then there is this charming little ode:

Kissing [61]

> Thanks to my gentle absent friend
> A kiss you in a letter send,
> But oh! the thrilling charm is lost
> In kisses which arive by post
> That fruit alone can tasteful be,
> When gather'd melting from the tree.

The authors seem to have been consistent in choice of theme, at least in the samples here and in others seen in the magazines. And these samples represent American poetry in magazines during the decade 1810-1820. Original poetry for the magazines was not done by skillful hands, and the men who could and did write poetry seem to have printed in book form. Hymns and translations were printed in some of the magazines, especially the ones in the Cambridge-Boston area, but this was not original poetry, and samples of this would not give a true picture of what the magazines could offer in American verse.

During the entire period, only two samples stand out, and they are head and shoulders above all the rest. The first of these is William Cullen Bryant's "Thanatopsis."[62] Enough has been said elsewhere about this poem to obviate any comment except the reminder that American literature had little to offer until this appeared.

The second example is one of the few things which did come before Bryant. The first known printing of "The Star Spangled Banner" in an American magazine occurred in 1814.[63] In this printing the poem was anonymous, and the title was given as "Defense of Fort M'Henry." The poem also appeared a little more than

two years later in The War.[64] Here the note is added that it should
be sung to the tune of "Anacreon in Heaven." Francis Scott Key may
have known this tune and similar ones published in a war-song contest run by the Port Folio in 1813, but there is no evidence that
Key's words were sent to the contest.

If poetry inspired by the War of 1812 can be counted as poetry of the second decade, the most famous (or perhaps infamous)
example is Richard Emmons' The Fredoniad, or Independence Preserved. Finally published in 1826, the work requires four volumes,
covers forty cantos, and runs to over 40,000 lines.

> The Doctor's poetic feet stretch out to miles and leagues,
> but not a single verse do I find that prompts to quotation;
> though I am free to confess that I have not read them all,
> and much doubt if anyone, save the infatuated author, and
> perhaps a long-suffering proofreader, ever did read the
> whole of 'The Fredoniad.'[65]

The same comment may be made, in general, of poetry in
American magazines for the period 1810-1820. American poetry in
periodicals as a literary genre, like the essay, had not yet appeared.

Humor

American magazines printed humorous essays, anecdotes,
poetry, and even some short stories. The humor naturally rests on
somewhat different standards than present-day humor, and the puns
frequently remain obscure to the reader lacking an intimate knowledge of contemporary social life and mores. However, a few examples are mentioned to give the general tone and level of early nineteenth-century magazine humor.

The "farmer's daughter" story probably became almost a
type by itself long before printing could spread the endless variations on this ribald theme. In 1810, "The Squire and the Farmer's
Daughter" crops up in a magazine[66] when the editor had previously
promised that his pages would contain "nothing inconsistent with the
purest virtue." Indeed the farmer's daughter maintains her mar-
riageability throughout, and possibly the story is seriously intended
as a moral lesson. But it is hard to resist the feeling that the

anonymous author merely has his fun with a bumbling squire whose
servants substitute an ass for the lass at the sacrificial feast and
prepare the squire for an evening in bed with the same mistake.
Sex frequently finds a close second in religion for off-color
stories. Such is the case with the essay "A Petition of the Genteel
and Fashionable for the Repeal of the Ten Commandments"[67] of
which this is but a sample:

> The seventh is such a dashing prohibition, and the thing
> itself would lose so much of its zest if it were not for-
> bidden, that I am almost inclined to let it remain. Were
> it taken away, indeed, where would be the gusto of our
> picnic parties; nay une affaire bien arrangée would be-
> come so tiresome and insipid, that I doubt not we should
> soon have husbands making love to their own wives, by
> way of novelty; a coach box would lose its charms, and
> landladies would give over peeping.

Another play, this time on a religious custom, was made
with the Baptists in this riposte:

> Some females discoursing of the vices of a certain man,
> one of them observed that in the early part of her ac-
> quaintance with him, he was a respectable member of the
> baptist society, and had been dipped. Another replied, it
> had not cleansed him much. No, said a girl of about
> sixteen years of age, he should have been put to soak
> over night. [68]

Poetry could also be rather humorous, and frequently played
on a theme of morality.

To Laura[69]

My lovely girl, you've often said
And swore that you would die a maid;
Listen not then to vows, my dear,
Fond Strephon breathes for you to hear;
Lest in some sanguine moment he
May find a way to perjure thee.

The newspapers which gave current prices were a natural
target for satire, and one Abram Abrahams compiled this list:

Prices Current For July, 1813[70]

Honesty . . . . None in Market
Patriotism first quality. . . . . . . No Demand

[Patriotism] sec. quality	Principally bought up by speculators
Prudence	At par. (all held by <u>old</u> stockholders)
Modesty	None but damaged parcels in market
Vice	Large quantities held, no sales
Pride.	Markets glutted
Politeness	Very cheap, but the owners appear indifferent about the disposal of it
Wit.	All bought up for the New York market
Scandal.	None offered at wholesale - The article altogether engrossed by hawkers, and pedlars
Religion.	When brought into market, it is generally highly adulturated. Sales nominal
Love	None offered, except for real estate
Coquetry	Very little offered, in consequence of the difficulty of managing the sales
Talents.	A cash article. No credit allowed
Sincerity	Out of season

Foreign Literature

Interest in German culture was apparently slow to develop until after the War of 1812. Various internal problems as well as a shooting war tended to take precedence over an investigation of German literature which had begun to develop in the eighteenth century. That American magazines printed little about Germany and even less in German up to about 1817 indicates that this low-keyed interest affected periodical publications.[71]

After 1817, however, interest in German civilization and literature increased greatly. Factors leading to this included: the continued influence in America of English magazines which now turned to Germany to investigate her newly appearing literature; the return to America of the first men educated in Germany and attracted to the German literary developments; and the dawn of the

"Era of Good Feelings" which encouraged an interest in European influence.

Among the men educated in Germany were Edward Everett and George Ticknor, both of whom had future roles to play in the production of American magazines, especially the North American Review after 1820, when Everett became its editor.

Reviews of German literature had appeared before the War, for example, Goethe's Die Wahlverwandtschaften;[72] and there had been a consideration of other foreign literature such as an article on Asiatic literature in the Monthly Recorder for June 1813.

However, the magazines' reflection of serious consideration remained slight until the end of the decade. The Journal of Belles Lettres published articles on French, German, and Italian literature as well as a few on what the editors referred to as the "North of Europe." The Western Gleaner added Spanish to the list, and there had been material on the classics in collegiate magazines. But like so much else in magazines, major consideration of foreign literature was yet to come.

Negro Literature

The literature of the American Negro was almost wholly ignored by early American magazines. White men controlled the outlets and made up by far the greater share of the reading public. And then there was the matter of slavery.

Perhaps the first work by an American Negro reviewed in an American magazine was Price Saunders' A Memoir to the American Convention for Promoting the Abolition of Slavery, and Improving the Condition of the African Race,[73] published in 1818 by Philadelphia's Dennis Heartt.

Phillis Wheatley, the most popular early American Negro woman writer, was not reviewed until 1834.[74]

Interest in Negro affairs was usually limited to a few comments on slavery and to the colonization movement. Abolition, rather than emancipation or manumission, took the forefront. Political, ideological, moral, religious, and sectional matters were pretty generally ignored. People knew about the Negro, but they did not express themselves about him in the magazines.

Literary Clubs

As early as 1721 a manuscript magazine written by Ebenezer Turell may have circulated among the members of a literary club in Cambridge, Massachusetts.[75]

An organization known as The Knights of the Round Table came into being in Hartford, Connecticut in 1819.[76] In August of that year, the club issued the first number of The Round Table, and eventually produced at least seven other pamphlet-like publications called The Candle, The Extinguisher, The Magpie, The Parterre, The Retort, The Square Table, and The Stand.

In Philadelphia, The Tuesday Club had a hand in the Port Folio, and other groups like The Ugly Club and The Bread and Cheese Club may have had indirect magazine connections.

A literary and social organization known as the Delphian Club was founded by and for the literati of Baltimore. It met in a house behind Barnum's Hotel, and its members included: Tobias Watkins and Paul Allen[77] as well as Francis Scott Key, John P. Kennedy, John Neal, John Pierpont, Jared Sparks, Rembrandt Peale, William Gwynn, and Edward Pickney.[78] Some of the society's minutes were published in the Red Book, which had somewhat the same relationship to the Delphian Club as the Monthly Anthology had to the Anthology Society in Boston.

> This little work comes before the publick eye the careless offspring of chance, unsupported by patronage, and unadorned by the tinsel of name or fashion.
> . . . .
> It possesses this advantage, that let the world slight it as it may, it will always be red - a greater favor, surely, an author could not wish.[79]

Tobias Watkins, the founder of the Delphian Club, was one of the co-founders with Stephen Simpson of the Portico. Simpson was nationalistic, and he used this magazine to further his ideas.[80] He attacked Robert Walsh, a Federalist, and his well-formulated

ideas expressed in the Portico played a role in a growing movement
for a national literature.

John Neal, also a member of the Delphian Club, lent his
talents to the Portico "because the magazine provided an outlet for
an editor willing to crusade for a national literature."[81]

The Portico, however, held two views. One was that British
literature was of first quality and should not be imitated but should
be reproduced. The other was that an American literature must be
created out of whole cloth. Thus, while the Portico hoped for a
native literature, it still supported a foreign one.

Another current runs through the pages of the Portico,
namely, that while Americans were slow to start, they had the
background and historical experience to produce literature with an
American basis; and this was indeed different from the view of a
magazine like the North American Review which would agree that
American literature was, in fact, the literature of the American
Indians.

The early history of The Monthly Anthology has been told by
Louis P. Simpson,[82] and this account covers the history of this
interesting magazine. The editors hoped to include "every art and
science," as well as politics, and hoped to print critical opinions
of "important literary productions" appearing in America. Here
was an early forecast of an American literature, and to judge by
the pages, the editors succeeded, at least to a small degree.

But the important fact is that The Monthly Anthology really
produced the Anthology Society, and not the other way around. And
the Anthology Society was searching for a way to establish a national
literature the necessity for which had been made obvious through the
instinct and intellectual acumen of the members. The magazine
gave these men the chance to establish a rationale for such a literature; the magazine was a sounding board for their ideas; and the
magazine encouraged the members in their search.

That this search did not bear real fruit until the founding of
the North American Review is only a testimony to this early effort
in the search for a national literature. It is interesting that a

magazine, The Monthly Anthology, encouraged a group of men, the Anthology Society, to make the effort.   It is further interesting that many of these men, including William Tudor, were the very men who were able to establish the magazine which actually made possible the early growth of an indigenous American literature.

Summary

After all this wandering through the obviously trivial magazines which came into being in the nineteenth century's second decade, what has been discovered?   Very little.   Except for the literary clubs just mentioned, even the contemporaries recognized the lack and were honest enough to say that the literature did not exist:

> Another cause impeding Science in her march is, the little encouragement given to literary works; as a palpable instance of which, we may mention, the numerous unsuccessful efforts made, to publish Scientific as well as Miscellaneous Journals, in this country.   That this neglect is not attributable to the want of intrinsic merit in the works themselves, may be proved, by comparing them, as far as they have been published, with those of a similar kind, which have an extensive circulation in the trans-atlantic states: indeed, although our literary productions are comparatively few, I will be bold to say, that among the few, there are some, which lose nothing when contrasted with those of Europe, either for genuine wit, correct taste, or for chaste and classic style.[83]

Perhaps the very men who most hoped to see the creation of American literature were the most lax by encouraging the proliferation of second rate material.

> Instead of our critics being too severe, they are, in many instances, not severe enough; they praise where praise is not due; they pour the broad sunshine on the plant that is too tender to bear the blaze, and it is scorched, and withers away: whereas, had only one ray been permitted to visit it at a time, the young plant would have gradually shot forth, and the same light that blasted it before, would now add vigor to the stalk, and bid it bloom in all the beauty of perfection.
> At some more convenient season the subject shall be enlarged; I now conclude with this brief assertion, viz. There never will be a truly excellent American poet, until American critics shall be more severely just.[84]

But there was one exception. To the four magazines mentioned at the outset should be added one more, the Portico.

Naval victories in the War of 1812, especially the conquest of the Guerrière by the Constitution, gave rise to an increased American self-confidence in her ability to develop a literature. [85] Many of the magazines, at least those which had Democratic rather than Federalist editors, printed long and effulgent articles[86] which openly declared the necessity for America to become culturally as well as politically independent.

The correlation of naval victories with a growing American literature was one contribution of American magazines in general, and of the Portico in particular. For example, the editors of the Portico felt that naval victories were sufficient reason to encourage native American authors to take a chance on adverse criticism by producing original material which would help to advance the cause of an indigenous literature. [87]

This cause was closely allied to freedom in the mind of the Portico's editor when he wrote that "the importance of improving the literature of America should be realized by every American or they ought to relinquish their title to freedom and forego their pretensions to valor. "[88]

The Portico took many occasions to express the need for a national literature. Many articles, and the very choice of these articles, argue for a native American literary output and the arguments are as varied as they are colorful. Reading was encouraged as the best method to spread intellectual appreciation. Authorship was encouraged by pointing out that literature was an excellent path upward for the ambitious who could share in the establishment of American literature.

Many reviews of American literary works appear in the Portico's pages, and the reviews were generally as favorable as reviews of English writers were unfavorable; and this despite the quality of the work involved. The Portico suggested many themes for material, among them a history of the War of 1812 and a biography of George Washington, both of which would appeal to the growing instinct of nationalism.

Also treated extensively in the Portico was the American
Indian. Perhaps Henry Schoolcraft in his later magazines and in
his work in Michigan received inspiration from the 1818 volume of
the Portico which was replete with material on these people who it
feared would be extinct in a few generations.

And at the period's end, Joseph Buckingham was still optimistic enough to say:

> ... there is in this country, enough of mind and genius;
> --if it is well brought out, and skillfully managed and
> made the most of, to create a national literature, which
> should be, and deserve (!) to be immortal.[89]

CHAPTER 3

THE MAGAZINES AND AMERICAN SOCIETY

The aspects of American society revealed in American magazines from 1800 to 1810 have been discussed by Benjamin Lewis.[1]
Many of these trends are much the same for the second decade.
One major difference lies in the greater number and variety
of special subject magazines. At least five agricultural, four legal,
ten medical, four scientific, and nine women's magazines existed at
one time or another in the decade. Well over fifty other magazines
had some special emphasis.

When the War of 1812 broke out, the United States consisted
of eighteen individualistic, independent entities each of which watched
out for its own welfare and cared little for benefits to the Union as
a whole. In addition to the original thirteen, Vermont, Kentucky,
Tennessee, Ohio and Louisiana were the states which made up the
loosely-bound nation.

Just before the War, America's troubles at sea had led to
the Embargo Act of 1807, which was not successful in terminating
various shipping troubles. The embargo was discussed at length
in some magazines and hardly mentioned by others. The same holds
true for impressment and other factors leading to the War which at
times occupied magazine space; and at times, not. The material
printed in magazines differed from what was to be read in newspapers, and its presence in magazines follows a geographic pattern.

"The eastern states as a rule opposed the war; the western
states were all for it, with the southern and middle states divided."[2]
The exception to "split" votes was Vermont, whose senators and
representatives in Congress all voted in favor of the War.

The interesting phenomenon which connects all these facts

44

and magazines is related to membership in political parties and the
printing of periodicals.   Political parties in this period had comparatively sharp geographical divisions, frequently coinciding with
state lines.   The publishers in the various areas nearly always had
some political connection, generally with that of the majority party;
and as a consequence magazines tended to reflect the political interests or prejudices of the area in which the magazines were published.

The majority party in the East was Federalist, and these
men regularly opposed the War as ruinous to business and a complete folly.   Rather than print diatribes against the War, the magazine publishers seem to have risen above this squabble by choosing
to ignore the War in their publications.   Strangely, then, in the
northeast, the section which opposed the War most strongly, the
magazines printed the least about the War, frequently ignoring even
the greatest victories like the sinking of the Guerrière by Commodore Hull and the most disastrous defeats like the surrender of
Detroit by General Hull.

But coverage of the War did exist.   Thomas O'Connor, who
later issued The Shamrock, edited the magazine which offered the
fullest account of the War of 1812.   Called simply The War,[3] it
appeared largely between June 1812 and September 1814, with one
concluding issue appearing in 1817.   Over 460 pages report official
communications, quote documents, relate battles, refight naval en-
gagements, and detail a myriad of facts about people, places, and
things.   In many ways it remains the single most valuable contemporary periodical source.

A second periodical issued by O'Connor was The Military
Monitor and American Register.   Why O'Connor issued two magazines with such similar contents remains a mystery, but issue them
he did.   About one-third of the war-account material was borrowed,
about one-third of the space given over to current congressional
debates and hearings, and another third quoted official documents.

A favorite item in all the magazines which did any reporting
at all was called something like "Chronological Table of the Most

Remarkable Events Connected with the Present War Between the
United States and Great Britain. "[4]   This same type of reportorial
coverage appeared in other magazines and often was short and
borrowed from a local newspaper or the National Intelligencer, a
perennial favorite.

In September 1812, the Port Folio included the first of a
series called "American Gallantry--For the Port Folio" which
would report "such incidents, in our military annals, as, from
their minuteness, have escaped the general historian..."[5]   This
first article dealt with Revolutionary War heroes.   After this, the
Port Folio added frequent articles on the War and allied topics.
A naval song contest was begun in 1813,[6] a review of a naval history,[7] a description of new firearms,[8] and articles on "military
and naval gallantry"[9] and "American heroism"[10] are some examples.   Dozens of others like book reviews and biographies appeared
in practically every war-time issue.   In February 1815 the series
"Naval and Military Chronicle of the United States" first appeared.[11]
Nearly every article included a well-executed plate,[12] and while
biographies were most frequent, accounts of battles and other descriptive items also appeared.

Although better known, the reputation of "The American
Naval Chronicle" which appeared in the Analectic[13] probably depends
on its innovator, Washington Irving.[14]   Irving hoped it would be:

> ... a record whence the future historians may perhaps
> gather materials that would otherwise be either lost, or
> only found through the medium of much laborious re-
> search.[15]

The material is much the same as that found in the Port
Folio, and there is little doubt that the two magazines borrowed
each other's ideas and competed for readers on the basis of the
two series.   Taken together they form a different approach from
that of The War, and one which results in far more rewarding
reading.

Some other magazines included material, but seldom as complete.   The Christian Observer included about ten articles in two
years.   The Examiner made the rather acid comment that "the

present war was unnecessarily commenced, and is, now at least,
most unnecessarily continued. "[16] The editor later added:

> After the disgraceful termination of the campaign of 1812,
> and especially at the commencement of the autumn of
> 1813, it became palpable to every man whom undue preju-
> dice and passion had not blinded to the perception of plain
> truth and fact, that the administration of the general
> government was as incapable of devising any thing like a
> skilful (!) and successful plan of territorial warfare, as
> its commanding generals were, for the most part, unquali-
> fied to execute it. [17]

Later, this same magazine modified to a degree its dissatisfaction
in reporting the treaty by saying that:

> ... the treaty is honourable to the country: inasmuch as
> none of its real rights have been sacrificed or abandoned;
> but disgraceful to the administration: inasmuch as not a
> single matter set forth in Mr. Madison's declaration of
> war, is so much as even mentioned in the treaty. [18]

One minor result of the War was the establishment of a
large number of Peace Societies. Noah Worcester, under the
pseudonym of Philo Pacificus, wrote A Solemn Review of the Custom of War which appeared in the Connecticut Evangelical Magazine[19]
before it was issued as a part of the Friend of Peace, Worcester's
own magazine. This largely Congregational movement achieved
momentary popularity when men like Jedidiah Morse, who helped
establish the Massachusetts Peace Society, endorsed its ideals.

Many magazines ignored the war entirely. Very few magazines considered themselves news organs, in the modern sense of
that term, and many editors could not bring themselves to report
the unpopular. They simply avoided reporting events so as not to
antagonize patrons who might cancel subscriptions desperately needed
to survive.

Another factor in the magazines' value as repositories of
history is this very survival. Few had much continuity, and without
this span of coverage, they possess little value. True, the New
York Historical Society, founded in 1804, began to publish its Collections in 1811, but this and similar serial publications with some
longevity can hardly be considered as magazines.

The War of 1812 caused the newspapers to find ways to increase service and to make the service more secure.[20] The lack of late news made the newspapers barren; they needed a consistent and trustworthy source of contemporary information, and the War offered the opportunity to develop means of providing them with such a source. Also, the haphazard coverage of the War of 1812 continued the policy of publishing more foreign than American news in papers. A growing feeling of nationalism forced this change, and to change meant increased and more efficient local and national news coverage. But this was true only for the newspapers.

Another reason for the lack of magazine information was that the present-day system of correspondents did not exist. Reporters were not sent out to cover events; and even if they had been, the general state of communications and transportation would have prevented any rapid means of transmitting information back to the place of publication.

The single magazine source of most value is Niles' Weekly Register.[21] Niles became a leading proponent of nationalism, and used the magazine to promote this idea. He noted and did not like America's lack of solidarity and her lack of a unifying purpose. The use of the word "national" became more and more frequent, and this is obvious when he changed the title of his periodical to Niles' National Register. Niles asked for American publications of all sorts, and he promoted the idea of a national literature. He printed other items which support a free press based on the idea that a free press is essential to a democracy.

Hezekiah Niles made several contributions by means of his journal which is possibly the only memorable magazine news medium of the early nineteenth century. Niles attempted a national publication with a national coverage, assuming that such a publication was needed in a nation. He also attempted to establish some firm publishing ethic by the example of his own excellent work and by his coverage of all sides of burning issues. He also attempted to promote an increased feeling of American nationalism in literature and publishing as well as in politics and public life.

William Cobbett comes to light as an unusual source of improved magazine journalism in the United States.   Cobbett came to
the United States as early as 1792[22] when he published several
pamphlets as Peter Porcupine, quarreled with Thomas Paine, advocated the Federalist side in public issues, and returned to England leaving a reputation as an advocate of reform.   His reform
activities in England forced him to return to America, where he
issued his already existing Political Register as Cobbett's American
Political Register.   The first American issue, printed here on
September 21, 1816, had been written in England on January 6th,
and it is numbered as number one of volume thirty.   The earliest
American issues are letters to people in England and America
examining various facets of government in both countries.

One issue[23] includes a letter "To Mr. Niles" in which Cobbett discusses "Piracies of the English Press."   He says:

> There are, perhaps, 400 or 500 proprietors of periodical
> publications in your Republic; and though to become a
> beggar in that country would be dreadful to think of, I
> verily believe, that there is not one out of the 500, who
> would not rather beg his bread from door to door, than
> to gain it by means like those by which these men are
> gaining their bread from me. [24]

Perhaps Cobbett referred to plagiarism, and if so, it is amazing
he had so small an understanding of where editors gained most of
their material in America.   The 500 proprietors he refers to must
have included newspaper publishers, and it would be unusual to find
so large a group in one profession all of whom maintained the integrity and ethics which Niles was working so hard to develop.

An interesting comment, which is as timely as any comment
in all of the magazines of the period, is also made to Niles:

> ... I hope you will not forget to build ships and cast
> cannons; for, I am well convinced, that to build ships
> and to cast cannons, are the best if not the only, security
> that you can have for lasting peace. [25]

Robert Walsh was the third fairly important editor in America who attempted to bring news to magazines.   He issued three
magazines in the period, and at least three magazines or newspapers

after 1820.   But he was unable, at least before 1820, to gather
enough current material to compete with the contemporary newspapers.

The pattern is also seen in the issues of Journal of the
Times edited by Paul Allen in Baltimore.   He hoped to make the
Journal a record of passing events, but he very soon found that in
such a publication all events were forestalled by the early papers,
and that when they appeared in his columns at the end of a week,
curiosity was cold and indifferent, and he was compelled to become
a dull and uninteresting echo of intelligence already communicated.
Like an echo, he soon faded away.

To the eighteen pre-War states, Indiana, Mississippi,
Illinois, and Alabama were added before 1820.   During these few
years a great deal was happening inside the United States.   Mech-
anization was altering manufacturing with the power loom and
farming with the cotton gin.   Road building was starting, and the
Erie Canal got its first "low bridge" in 1817.   The first National
Bank sank into obscurity in 1811, and the second appeared in 1816.
Few of these are really discussed in the magazines.   Amazingly,
most of these important social changes were passed over by editors
who remained fixed in the old pattern of obvious articles.   The
bank did receive some attention.   Throughout 1819, the Literary
Cadet published a series of articles with the almost oratorical
title: "An Essay on Banks, In which the benefits and evils of
banking, the power of the legislature over the banks existing in
this state, and the measures of relief proper to be adopted at the
next session, are discussed and demonstrated."   But the articles
carry little real information, and the newspapers seem to have had
the audience and the better material.

But two issues which later proved to be major social prob-
lems come to light in the magazines of this period--the American
Indian and the slave.   The first of these appeared only at the very
end of the decade, and primarily in the Western Review.   John D.
Clifford began a five-part series, "Indian Antiquities in the Western
Country,"[26] and a second series recalled "Heroic and Sanguinary

Conflicts with the Indians."[27] These were both a possible forecast
of Henry Schoolcraft's material on the Indian which came in his
magazine The Muzziniegun, but they barely hinted at the problems
which were to develop around these tribes. The articles on Indians
which the Analectic contains did not begin to appear with any regularity until after 1820.

The second of these problems, slavery, was noted more
frequently and with some heat despite the silence of the pro-slavery
faction. The New York State law which abolished slavery in that
state was passed in 1817,[28] but many editors had been plain-spoken
before this eventful day--and not just in the "northern" states were
they to print statements like these:

> The editors will pay particular attention to a certain
> tribe of men, who, are either themselves engaged, or
> are the panders of some secret and informal agents in
> the traffic of HUMAN FLESH; buying and selling their
> fellow Man, and transporting him into slavery;--wresting
> the parting wife from the fond embraces of a husband and
> children--parting, never to meet until they appear before
> the high chancery of heaven, to confront those who led
> and sold them into distant bondage and misery.[29]

> The disgraceful and inhuman manner in which some per-
> sons, calling themselves Christians, treat those inheritors
> of misery and pain, is almost enough to shock the adaman-
> tine heart of unrelenting Cruelty ...[30]

> A crime, which not only involves the slave holders, but
> church and state, and will, if there is any justice in
> Heaven, ere long draw down the heaviest judgments of
> Almighty God, not only upon the heads of the barbarous,
> inhuman monsters, who hold the people in bondage, but
> upon all the inhabitants of the beautiful, flourishing coun-
> try, for all must be considered as guilty, who set (!) and
> look quietly on, and do not take some effectual measures
> to put down such a crying sin, such an overwhelming
> disease, such cruelty, wickedness, folly, and shame.[31]

After the passage of the law, the statements continue, and
at times they became even more blunt.

> There is a law, it is true, prohibiting the importation of
> slaves into the United States; but to what effect?... We
> do not think it improbable that some of the slave vessels
> now engaged, are owned by Americans....

> We are not guiltless of the blood and wrongs of these
> murdered and enslaved men. Whilst slavery exists in
> this land, it is the solemn duty of every good man, con-
> stantly and steadily to press for its abolition. --But at a
> time like this, when those demons in human form, are
> pushing this Hellish traffic in human blood, to the utmost
> of their power, the duty becomes imperious that the
> benevolent every where should arouse from their slumbers,
> and unite their efforts in defense of the violated rights of
> man. [32]

> We consider the voluntary enslaving of one part of the
> human race by another, as a gross violation of the most
> precious and sacred rights of human nature; as utterly
> inconsistent with the Law of God, which requires us to
> love our neighbors as ourselves; and as totally irrecon-
> cilable with the spirit and principles of the Gospel of
> Christ, which enjoin that all things whatsoever ye would
> that men should do to you, do ye even so to them. [33]

The Quakers had long opposed slavery, and other groups were
slowly following suit, but slavery had become a political and a sectional issue more than a social one. The eventual pressure magazines were to bring to bear had only just begun, and the first signs
of it only began to appear by 1819.

The development of American science is most clearly reflected in the pages of several journals, among them the first
purely scientific magazine in America, the American Mineralogical
Journal, edited by Archibald Bruce from 1810 to 1814.

The object of this magazine was "to collect and record such
information as may serve to elucidate the Mineralogy of the United
States."[34] Descriptions of native American ores, experiments to
identify them, and general information on geological formations are
among the subjects of the articles. Correspondence between Bruce
and Benjamin Silliman, and material by Samuel L. Mitchell and
Samuel Akerly all appear.

Second in time was John Redman Coxe's Emporium of the
Arts and Sciences. Coxe was Professor of Chemistry at the University of Pennsylvania, just as Silliman was at Yale.

> The Emporium professes to be a source of practical in-
> formation in the various branches of scientific research,
> and is intended to convey the rich harvest of facts,

> contained in foreign valuable papers on Chemistry, Mine-
> ralogy, Natural Philosophy, Arts, Sciences, and Agricul-
> ture, with the proper cultivation of which, undoubtedly the
> truest interests of every country, but especially our own,
> are clearly connected. [35]

The important words here are "foreign valuable papers"--a
tacit admission that the foreign material was valuable and an impli-
cation that Coxe found no native material worth the printing.

The new series, edited by Thomas Cooper, included three
volumes only, but there is an immediate change. Number one,
for June 1813, opened with the first part of an article on iron, 155
pages long. The rest of the 183 pages were devoted to a miscellany.
Number two, for August, continued the article on iron. Seventy-four
pages were added. Five plates were included. This may well have
been the longest and most comprehensive treatment on the subject
ever to appear in a magazine.

In number two, the article on iron is followed by one on
steel which ran to over 120 pages in two consecutive numbers.
Taken together, they form a compendium of what was known on the
topic and provide much insight into contemporary metal-working
techniques.

Nearly all of the second volume is devoted to the steam
engine. Other articles appeared, but they were short and of
secondary importance. Most of the plates in this single issue
were of various steam engines, their parts, and applications.

The majority of the next issues are devoted to copper, lead,
and tin--the ores, smelting, refining, and various uses of these
metals. This volume is a virtual text on these metals, since it
summarizes most of the important knowledge then available.

The new series was intended to encourage domestic manufactures, pointing out that Americans had become independent from
Great Britain, and that America now had both the skill and the raw
materials to produce those articles which she had previously purchased from the mother country.

Teaching mineralogy and geology, and having the primary
responsibility for the Yale Medical School, where he taught chemistry,

Benjamin Silliman over the years amassed a reputation as a bril-
liant public lecturer.   No doubt this added to the spread of the
American Journal of Science, which he started in 1818 in New
Haven, Connecticut.   For over one hundred years this magazine
remained in Silliman's immediate family.   The story of this magazine, a real landmark in American science, culture, history, and
magazine publishing, has not yet been adequately told.

Although not America's first scientific magazine, it was the
most important.   Intended to cover all scientific topics, not in every
issue, but as material became available, the later proliferation of
scientific literature in serial form points to the awesome responsibility of such a journal.

The centennial number, published in July, 1918, points to
Silliman's problems, to the early history of the journal, and to the
contributions made to it.   The first article in 1818 was an "Essay
on Musical Temperament."[36]   It was not the last material on music,
but it implies the scope laid out for the magazine.

Silliman and the members of his family who edited the
journal for over a century carried out the prospectus by covering
material on every phase of scientific investigation, discovery, and
advancement.   The American Journal of Science lives today as
America's oldest magazine with an uninterrupted publishing history.

Five magazines covered agricultural matters.   The first of
these was the Agricultural Museum begun in 1810 by David Wiley.
Designed for both the farmer and the manufacturer, the division of
these occupations is not clear in its pages.

Articles included extracts from other magazines, "addresses"
made to meetings, material on sheep, mineral black, manufacturers
in various areas, roads, navigation on canals, cider, butter, and
making gunpowder.   One typical article, "Indian Corn,"[37] describes
planting methods here and abroad, advantages of various ways of
improving the yield, dangers to prepare against, and a word on
crop rotation.   The material, although sound enough in theory, is
rather superficial.

Of far more importance is the American Farmer, first issued

in 1819 by John Stuart Skinner. The contents were largely borrowed
and frequently rather dull, [38] but the magazine started a trend. A
notable difference between this and subsequent farm magazines, and
even other contemporary magazines, was that it contained no advertisements. Poetry, news, humor, home cures, temperance articles, marriages, and deaths are all found. But the magazine was
able to catch on and firmly established the concept of agricultural
journalism.

Many magazines included occasional mathematical puzzles
or articles on curiosities such as the mathematical wizard, Zerah
Colburn. [39] The Scientific Journal, begun in 1818 by W. Marrat,
was devoted largely to mathematical problems. Solving of these
was accomplished by nothing more complicated than quadratics.
Robert Adrian's Analyst was begun in the previous decade and appeared erratically. Not enough men were trained in mathematics
to support such a specialized magazine, and the real possibilities
of theoretical and applied mathematics had not yet been realized.

Some ten magazines published material on medicine. Medical
Repository had begun in 1797 and was to last until 1824. The New
England Journal of Medicine and Surgery appeared in 1812, and although it has undergone several name changes and mergers, it is
still published today. Eight other journals, many ephemeral and
short-lived, attempted to supply doctors with case studies which
could be of use in practice. Doctors possibly comprised the largest
single professional group in America of the time, and they easily
and freely exchanged ideas and knowledge of new techniques.

Medicine seriously inquired about women's diseases, cata-
racts, communicable diseases, and insanity. Mercury was a favorite
drug, and many medicines were exotic and unusual. Some magazines were prone to include articles on lightning rods and other
curiosa, but a typical issue would also cover spotted fever, enteritis,
drinking water analysis, catalepsy, and Benjamin Rush's doctrine of
disease. [40] A typical article might be Horace H. Hayden's "Anatomical and Pathological Observations on the Teething of Infants, and
on the Analogy Between Infantile Dentition and Some Other Diseases. "[41]

In the Medical and Surgical Register of May 11, 1818, Valentine
Mott reports the attempt to tie the innominate artery--a feat apparently no one had ever done before. [42]

The absence of a well-developed experimental method, and
the lack of clinical, laboratory, and chemical technique and knowledge resulted in some blind stabbing in medicine which seems crude
and even silly by modern standards. However, this groping was
done by men of great skill and daring, men who were highly perceptive and ingenious in diagnosis, men who had integrity and ethical
standards, and men who had the heart and stamina to try. At
times they failed; but often they succeeded, and the foundations of
an American medicine, based in part on suspicion of tradition, were
set down firmly and well.

The business world began to receive recognition in magazines and newspapers. Several publications, really newspapers,
regularly listed the prices of wholesale and retail commodities, the
prices of stocks, insurance rates, and other commercial information.
The most important of these was General Shipping and Commercial
List. Mahlon Day and Charles Turner established this journal in
1815 and managed to keep their information accurate and timely. On
September 10, 1819, the paper was purchased by Charles Turner and
John Johnston who continued to publish long after 1820. Some other
magazines at times published prices in their own speciality, for
example, the prices of drugs in London appeared in the New England
Journal of Medicine and Surgery. [43]

Descriptive articles on inventions like the cotton gin were
frequently published, but almost no material on contemporary industry, labor, manufacturing techniques, or other aspects of American commercial life appeared.

Some of the farm magazines were concerned with internal
improvements. Skinner's American Farmer frequently had short
articles devoted to improved transportation because "he felt that
roads, canals, and railroads not only contributed largely to the
national wealth, but expedited transportation and lowered the costs
which influenced agricultural prosperity."[44]

The Plough Boy was similarly concerned, and published many short items promoting new roads in New York. But this was the period just before railroads began, and the canals in New York were either still under construction or consideration. The need for improved transportation had not yet really become apparent, and the advocacy of these facilities did not appear in the magazines to any great extent.

The first substantial educational periodical was John and Albert Picket's Academician. Many of the articles describe and evaluate the teaching innovations of Andrew Bell, Philipp Fellenberg, Joseph Lancaster, and Johann Pestalozzi. These methods were being tried in America, and some attention to the expanding needs of schools prompted the Pickets to offer many new theories as well as suggestions for teaching in several specific areas. Although short-lived, the magazine opened the way to a whole new area of investigation.

Many other magazines offered "departments" or columns devoted to educational problems and to the need for children's reading matter. Among these were Omnium Gatherum, Christian Herald, Parterre, and Inquisitor. Frequent articles on education appeared in isolated instances in magazines whose primary concern lay in other directions. An "Essay on Education,"[45] and articles "On the Prevailing Systems of Education,"[46] and "The Advantages of the Lancastrian System of Education"[47] are but a few among the many.

Children's magazines, which began in 1789, offer another area of interest for educational historians. A list of those which existed from 1810 to 1820 appears in Appendix A.

About five magazines produced by college undergraduates demonstrate, through their exceptional quality, the possibilities of educated journalism. The best of these, from the viewpoint of education, was the Harvard Lyceum. Material on the history of schools, classes in education, the study of a few subject fields, education in France and England, and the education of women all find some close analysis. A series of five "Letters to a Student"[48] cover practical advice and even have a word to say on the subject of book selection.

Three law magazines began to publish abstracts of court cases, reports of state supreme court cases, reviews of law books, and articles on British law as it applied to America. Chief among these, the American Law Journal, was designed to serve as a case-book for lawyers who might be practicing without the benefit of a library. The Carolina Law Repository and the New York City Hall Recorder were published on the same plan but were more locally concerned in their coverage. Supreme Court decisions as they affected the country as a whole sometimes appeared in other magazines. The Dartmouth College case, although only briefly noted,[49] was apparently not recognized for its future importance.

One decision which did receive somewhat more attention was John Marshall's ruling in McCulloch vs. Maryland which was handed down on March 6, 1819. In it, the U.S. Constitution is supported as being supreme, and laws of the United States are held superior and not controlled by the constitutions and laws of the states which are a part of the Union. In John Marshall's words, the Court held:

> ... a conviction that the states have no power, by taxation, or otherwise, to retard, impede, burden, or in any manner control the operations of the constitutional laws enacted by congress to carry into execution the powers vested in the general government.[50]

Music had always played a part in American life. The Puritans enjoyed both singing and dancing, and the first book printed in the United States, The Bay Psalm Book, although it lacked printed notes, could be considered a music book since its contents were intended to be sung. Most music publishing appeared in song books, but there had been a few early music magazines,[51] and between 1810 and 1820 the Journal of Musick and Pelissier's Columbian Melodies both appeared briefly.

Another music magazine deserves some brief mention as probably being the first American magazine to alter completely its format, contents, and purpose to maintain its readers and to attempt an expansion of its subscription list. The Literary and Musical Magazine began as a woman's magazine in 1817, but on January 1, 1819 became a music magazine. The change didn't help, but the innovation was interesting and original.

At least nine magazines began their lives with the intention
of serving the needs and interests of the distaff side. Nearly all
contained serialized fiction which was romantic and sentimental,
one or two popular articles, news summaries, poetry, and advertisements. The early magazines for women were patterned after
British counterparts, but the money was not available for dress
patterns, engravings, and music, which were all found in the English periodicals. [52]   In 1814, the first woman's magazine since before 1810 appeared in Philadelphia, Intellectual Regale, edited by
Mrs. Mary Clarke Carr. It was like the other in contents, but
more personal.

> A ladies' magazine ... did not mean pages of patterns,
> columns of advice to the lovelorn, nor even bright fashion
> plates and pretentious embellishments.... But a ladies'
> magazine was primarily, a periodical in which humble
> readers were offered a share in the cultural life of the
> country, and in which a woman might find a place as a
> contributor and editor. [53]

These magazines were not remarkable nor were they successful. They came and went almost unnoticed. But they all had
one important success. Each of the magazines had at least a few
readers; and all of them together helped to produce a reading public
which was prepared to support the more interesting and important
magazines which were to come later in the century.

CHAPTER 4

THE MAGAZINES AND RELIGION

America's cultural ties to religion make any examination of
America's society almost impossible unless the influence of religion
is considered. At the same time, the religious patterns of American life can be so complex that a brief consideration of one aspect
of this life may lead to dangerous oversimplification and unaccept-
able generalization. During the decade 1810-1820, magazines
formed one part of religious activity, and the magazines illuminate
to some degree a newly developing religious diversity in the United
States which was both a result and a cause of a changing America.

By 1810, the Second Awakening in the first decade of the
nineteenth century had not created the vast surge toward religion
which was hoped for.[1] Timothy Dwight, despite his firm resolves,
was bound by the intellectually centered traditions of institutions
like Yale, whose president he was, and he was either unable or unwilling to face the reality of America's refusal to accept a wholly
organized religion. This indifference was to change, but the in-
transigently independent American people refused to become swayed
to any one viewpoint, and this may have been especially true when
the words came from an intellectual center and were directed
toward an America largely rural, backward, under-educated, and
unrefined.

The magazines which typify the various viewpoints tended to
be lofty, rather philosophical, superficially learned, and dull. The
endlessly reiterated arguments in their pages talked down to people,
and the magazines seldom appealed to more human instincts.

The religious magazines, frankly, were inadequate. America
was changing more quickly than the religious leaders were willing to

admit. American religion aimed itself toward the Evangelical movement, and the magazines were, as yet, not reflecting this trend very
strongly. What was good in the religious magazines was not religious, and the religious material failed to reflect the full aspects
of American culture.

In the first decade of the century, some thirty-four religious
magazines appeared, [2] and in the second decade, about sixty-five can
be counted. The number is difficult to pinpoint since many magazines were partly religious, and at least twelve of them were
avowedly non-denominational. An exact specification of denomination is often difficult except for the expert. One of the better aids
in the solution of this problem is the bibliography by Gaylord Albaugh. [3] This is but one part of a larger study which will identify
all religious periodicals published in America from 1730 to 1830.

The three largest and most active religious groups in
America at this time were the Presbyterians, Baptists and Methodists.

> ... Not far from the beginning of the nineteenth century,
> doubtless influenced by the political freedom in state af-
> fairs, Methodists in the South became impatient with the
> Methodist hierarchy, and Presbyterians of the West wrote
> the 'Last Will and Testament' of their presbytery. Bap-
> tists of the North also broke with their Church exclusive-
> ness, and all came out of their respective denominations
> endeavoring to form Churches of greater fraternity and
> more harmony with republican institutions. [4]

This activity led to added magazines, and to somewhat different material. The West saw many revival and missionary activities which were led by men with less education, since the mi-
grating Americans began to associate education with leisure. They
wanted entertainment, not homiletics.

Anti-slavery sentiment appeared quickly and vehemently in
religious magazines. [5] Much of what appeared took a moral tone
rather than using political or legal arguments which other magazines
favored. The early magazines probably helped to keep abolitionist
sentiments alive, but it is somewhat surprising that the effect of
these statements was so slight for so long a time. Assuming that

the followers of the various sects really predicated their actions on
the tenets of the various faiths, it must be assumed that the magazines were not read. In practice, this seems to have been the case
since circulations were so low, and since so many magazines disappeared so quickly from the American scene.

Religious activity included many intra-denominational and
independent groups, especially those formed by women, whose purpose was to carry on missionary and reform activities.

> Among the auspicious occurrences of the present day,
> perhaps the most important, are the establishment and
> wonderful progress of Bible Societies. The good which
> these institutions have already produced is incalculable,
> and suited to call forth expressions of joy and gratitude... [6]

And these groups were formed in many places. One contemporary list includes thirty-one societies from Maine to Georgia,
and from Rhode Island to Ohio. [7] They were not limited to any one
denomination and frequently based their operations on cooperation.

These societies raised contributions for publishing and dis-
tributing the Bible in many languages and in all parts of the world.
Perhaps the most active groups belonged to the Baptists who established the American Baptist Foreign Mission Society in 1814 for
just this purpose. Many of these groups supported magazines, and
many published annual reports in the magazines as a means of
spreading word about their activities. Although established for
many purposes, at least half were connected with religious activity
in some way, and this connection was usually for missionary work
or for the dissemination of the Bible.

But the magazines also had a role to play in this activity.
Merely by reporting activities, magazines could and did encourage
the work of religious groups. The Christian Monitor editorialized
that:

> The Bible Society of Virginia has recommended the intro-
> duction of the Bible into the schools in our State, and has
> promised to afford all the aid in its power for the pro-
> motion of a scheme so laudable. [8]

Other contents of the religious magazines follow a set pattern.

Historical and background articles, sermons, explications of religious
teaching and scriptures, book reviews, and reports of missionary and
revival activities were combined with hymns, reports of deaths and
ordinations, and miscellaneous religious news.

At times the background material presented unusual features
of American religious activity. A "History of the Shakers" was reported with no criticism of the group, [9] and was made to give the
magazine's readers a greater understanding of other religious practice.

One interesting magazine of a different sort was the Evangelical Repository, published in Philadelphia in 1816. The entire first
issue was a "Biographical Memoir of the Messiah, "[10] and a similar
biography appeared in each issue during the year. Saint John was
there, but so was Alexander Hamilton. Jonathan Edwards was
covered in two issues, as were several other historically prominent
men. The material may not have been new, but these biographies,
along with hundreds of others in similar magazines, appear to be
forgotten, are not listed in any readily available source, and have
seldom been used by the biographers of these men.

At least twelve religious groups supported magazines from
1812-1820. In addition to the three largest denominations of Protestants, some publishing was done by Catholics, the Christian Denomination, Congregationalists, Deists, Episcopalians, Lutherans,
the New Jerusalem Church, Unitarians, and Universalists. A brief
analysis of each of these titles accompanies the annotation for that
title, but some mention of a few of these magazines will indicate
their basic content and purpose.

The Presbyterians published at least sixteen magazines in
the second decade of the nineteenth century. [11] The Evangelical
Recorder, published in Auburn, New York from 1818-1821, may serve
as a typical example. Dirck Lansing included several articles explaining the Presbyterian doctrine as well as the denomination's position in many social areas. Slavery was criticized, and the need
for missionary activity among American Indians was described. The
Massachusetts Peace Society and the American Colonization Society

were both described, and Lansing reprinted reports by these groups
in an attempt to advocate their positions.   Many other church-related activities, such as Sunday Schools, were described, and material was printed for their use.

The Rev. Joshua T. Russell, a Presbyterian minister, began
the Christian Messenger in Baltimore in 1817.   While Russell published theological articles which advocated his position, he also made
the magazine available to other denominations by printing news of
their activity.   In this aspect the magazine was typical of others in
the period.   Little interest could be aroused, and the editors attempted to attract readers by an appeal to all sects.   The printing
of very standard material, much of which was borrowed from other
magazines and newspapers, did not make the magazine other than
ordinary.

Occasionally, Presbyterian material appeared in nonreligious
magazines.   In October 1812, an engraving of the Presbyterian
Meeting House, which for years stood on Federal Street in Boston,
appeared in Polyanthos.[12]   But this type of material was printed
for historical reasons and with no idea of propagating religion.

The autonomous nature of Baptist congregations created problems for any magazine this group may have wished to make national.
Nearly every Baptist congregation issued minutes of its annual
meeting which recorded conversions, ordinations, donations to missionary work, and other similar material.   However, some forward-
thinking men managed to try magazines intended for general use.
Obed Warren, a minister in Rutland, Vermont, was among those
who started the Vermont Baptist Missionary Magazine.   As its name
implies, it was intended to report Baptist missionary activity and to
create interest in the denomination.   Like all other such sects, the
Baptists felt they had the best answer to the problems of organized
religion, and the pages contain many articles which advocate this
particular viewpoint.   Warren hoped to make the magazine miscellaneous in nature, and divided the contents among news of revivals,
anecdotes, "inspired" essays, reports of "extraordinary" events,
missionary accounts, and countless homilies on such things as "The

Vanity of Mere Speculative Knowledge,"[13] and "The Wilful Liar's Dreadful Appeal."[14]   A topic which attracted a great deal of attention was the death of Thomas Paine on June 8, 1809.   The magazine published an account of his death which it hoped would teach a lesson:

> ... As his name has acquired some distinction by the virulence with which he attacked the Christian religion, it may not be unprofitable to survey his conduct in the last moments of his death.[15]

Perhaps the most important Baptist magazine of the period was Thomas Baldwin's American Baptist Magazine.   In one way or another this magazine lasted throughout the entire century and is a repository of early American Baptist history with its hundreds of biographies and reports of missionary activity, most of which mention names and give associated places and dates.   This title is a continuation of the Massachusetts Baptist Missionary Magazine which Baldwin had started in 1803, and the series of titles carries down to the recent Baptist periodical, Missions.   There is a possibility that this magazine had the largest circulation of any magazine in America at the time, since it claimed to have printed 134,000 copies of the twelve issues for 1818.[16]   Certainly this is an amazing figure, but there is no reason to doubt it.

In January 1818 Joshua Soule opened the Methodist Magazine. In later years, this publication became known as the Methodist Review and lasted until 1931.   Joshua Soule was an extraordinary man, and his connection with the Methodist Magazine marked one of those happy coincidences of history which juxtapose a good idea with the exact man needed to bring the concept to fruition.   Soule, although raised a Presbyterian, was admitted to the Methodist Church in 1799 and twenty-five years later was made a bishop of that denomination.[17]   Meantime, he had served as a book agent, worked with the American Bible Society, and helped to establish the Missionary and Bible Society of the Methodist Episcopal Church in America. All of these activities added strength and background for his work with the Methodist Magazine, and it became one of the few really worthwhile early religious publications.

The nine divisions of each issue were designed to teach and were often quite well written.

1. Divinity
2. Biography
3. Scripture Illustrated
4. The Attributes of God Displayed in the Works of Creation and Providence
5. The Grace of God Manifested
6. Miscellaneous
7. Religious and Miscellaneous Intelligence
8. Obituary
9. Poetry

These sections followed one another regularly. Some of the material was borrowed, and this was usually shortened to fit the brief article idea which Soule wished to maintain. The printing was of high calibre, and the pages had a neat, clean appearance. Revivals and conversions were reported frequently. Importantly, the magazine produced what was promised, and was not inaccurate when it printed:

> Let parents consider the Methodist Magazine as a legacy for their posterity, and as soon as the last number for the year is received, have the whole bound together and carefully preserved.[18]

A wide gap separates this magazine and four other Methodist magazines of the period. Typical was the New England Missionary Magazine, which appeared in Concord, New Hampshire in 1816. Martin Ruter, also an extraordinary man, spent a full life largely concerned with education and made many contributions in this area. He was not able to do what Joshua Soule had done with the Methodist Magazine, however, and instead produced a polemical and dogmatic tract-like publication which lasted for four issues. The contrast between the two magazines may not seem pertinent, but it was a typical picture--one towering magazine of excellent quality, and on the other side, a host of unimpressive attempts.

The Universalist position was most typically represented by Hosea Ballou. His first magazine, the Gospel Visitant, while not the first Universalist magazine, reflected clearly Ballou's ideals and his ability to organize his opinions in a clear, strongly reasoned

manner. Ballou was involved in many controversies, not the least
of which was carried on with the Boston Kaleidoscope and his own
second magazine, the much improved Universalist Magazine. Ballou
was editor of this journal for ten years, and he contributed enough
strength and wisdom to its pages to enable it to last nearly sixty
years, thus making it one of the ten or so really durable magazines
to appear in the period 1810-1820.

The Congregational viewpoint was held by three or four magazines, at least two of which lasted more than a century. The Congregationalist and Herald of Gospel Liberty, which has been con-
fused with other publications with a similar name, appeared in
Boston in January 1816. The editors remain anonymous, but groundwork was well laid by them. In the beginning, the publication was
designed like a newspaper, both in format and content. The reasons
for this may have included the postal regulations which limited the
distribution of magazines as well as the editors' knowledge that a
newspaper could attract readers while a magazine could, and often
did, die unnoticed. The Congregationalist opened with a series
called "A Brief Historic View of the Progress of the Gospel, in
Different Nations, Since Its First Promulgation." This helped to
establish the tone of the paper and led naturally to many questions
and answers easily turned into other columns.

More important as a publication was the magazine which
began as the Panoplist and later became known as Missionary
Herald at Home and Abroad. The 146 years of life for this magazine were sparked by "the most indefatigable defender of orthodoxy
in New England, Jedidiah Morse, pastor of the Congregational
Church in Charlestown, Massachusetts."[19] The views Morse had
were orthodox and opposed to the more liberal views held by some
compatriots. Although he edited the Missionary Herald for only
five years, he barely entered the second decade as an editor. But
he left his impression, and his magazine continued. Morse's activities also included at least three religious societies. He aided
in the establishment of the New England Tract Society, the American
Bible Society, and the American Board of Commissioners for Foreign

Missions. The latter two of these issued annual reports of various kinds, and Morse probably practiced his skills as a writer on these publications. Later in his life, Morse took an active interest in American Indians,[20] and while this interest is not directly related to magazines, he may have had some knowledge of Indian interests represented in earlier magazines.

Noah Worcester, perhaps best known for his A Solemn Review of the Custom of War and for the Friend of Peace, had other magazine connections stemming from his Universalist views. Worcester's friends in Boston helped to establish the Christian Discipline in May 1813:

> Its immediate purpose was to furnish a mouthpiece for Noah Worcester, who had, a few years before, lost his pulpit at Thornton, N.H., through advocacy of the Unitarian cause.[21]

The magazine had Boston-Cambridge connections and seems to have enjoyed some affiliation with Harvard-trained men who contributed material. This might be called the key to a New England magazine's success, since the Christian Disciple not only had a better appearance but also more readable contents than the majority of the other religious magazines.

The Episcopalians managed to produce five magazines at one time or another in the period. Perhaps the best of these was the Christian Register, issued in New York from July 1816 to July 1817. Its editor was Thomas How, the assistant rector of Trinity Church, then as now one of the more famous churches of that denomination. The magazine really attempted to be a book review, and many of its reviews were well written commentaries on secular titles. For some reason none of the Episcopalian magazines was able to attract a wide audience. As a group, they have a higher tone, are more polished, and seem to be aimed at a more intellectual audience. Perhaps this was paradoxically their drawback. An early attempt at "snob" appeal was simply premature.

Roman Catholic interests were served by at least three magazines in this period. The first of these, Journal des Dames, not only was written in French but also was produced by what amounted to a parochial school, since the girls who attended its classes were almost all Catholic. The second chronologically was the Shamrock, a New York literary newspaper begun in December 1810 and continued intermittently through 1817. The third was the Globe, which lasted six months in 1819.

The Shamrock was probably the first Catholic, adult magazine in the United States. Although a newspaper in appearance, its purpose was the continuation of Irish nationalism in America, and its contents went far beyond the reporting of news. Aside from the news, the lists of immigrants, pro-Irish articles, and religious contents served to introduce the Irish to America and New York City to the Irish.

Thomas O'Connor joined Edward Gillespy as publisher of the Shamrock, and his connection with this magazine led him to attempt a magazine of his own, the Globe. This magazine was designed to digest news of interest to the Irish with biographical and narrative material about Ireland. The purely religious material was kept to a minimum, some issues barely mentioning the Catholic faith at all. Together these two magazines represent Catholic periodical publishing for adults in early America before the 1830's, and the content was quite different from the Protestant magazines in that neither attempted polemical, evangelical, or missionary material.

America did not have a magazine devoted to the interests of the Jewish population until later. The Jew had been in the Americas since about 1655, [22] but the first magazine for Jewish interests seems to have been attempted only in 1823 by Solomon Brown. [23]

The other religious magazines of the period 1810-1820 were all generally of far less interest, worth, and importance. They were very similar in appearance, and all contained extracted sermons, moralistic essays and "intelligence" which generally involved missionary activity, revival meetings, conversions, "remarkable occurrences," and the like. Many were tract-like publications and seem to have been produced to serve as Sunday-School texts.

The typical magazine also contained other quite predictable and often similar items. Biography, generally of a religious nature;

poetry; and a miscellaneous group of less valuable material made
up the bulk. Only the exceptional magazine included a book review,
and then these were frequently included so that denominationally
slanted doctrinal arguments could be reinforced.

The effect and importance of these magazines is difficult to
judge. A non-religious magazine like the Floriad could print "The
Influence of Religious Opinion on Our Happiness,"[24] but the specifically religious magazines seemed, in general, to have failed to
find the proper formula for influencing great numbers of people with
the beneficence of their opinions. The problems of printing and
distribution, lack of an audience, lack of material, and the absence
of promotional ability are all applicable to the failure of religious
magazines; but so also are the facets of another complex of conditions.

American Protestantism was becoming diversified. Migration was spreading a population thinly in unsettled areas where
organized, formal religion as yet had no place. These two factors
alone made finding a magazine audience difficult, and when it is
considered that nearly every religious magazine of the period was
such an inadequate production, it is no wonder that few of them,
no matter how honestly conceived, could continue to live.

Religious activity was an important factor in the development
of American culture in the early nineteenth century, but the magazines are not the best source of information on this trend simply
because the magazines do not reflect the intricacies of an expanding
country experiencing both the diversification of religion and the
problems and profits of a newly awakening nationalism.

CONCLUSION

The selection of magazines available at a modern American magazine rack or in many libraries suggests the possibility that earlier publications would reveal interactions of many aspects of life in that earlier period. A detailed look at magazines of the decade 1810-1820 demonstrates that this assumption is not as fruitful as the cultural historian would wish.

The number of magazines rose steadily throughout the period with thirty-two alive on January 1, 1810 and seventy ready to greet the New Year on December 31, 1819. The only magazine alive at both times was the Medical Repository, and to be inferred from this is the transitory nature of these early magazines. The physical appearance of the magazines had not greatly improved from the previous decade except in illustration. The printing was often good; but equally often, it was careless and unattractive; and this probably resulted from the magazines being printed from hand-set type and from hand-operated presses which had both seen better days. The illustrations, however, greatly multiplied in both number and quality. New techniques, such as lithography, were brought to bear, and many skilled engravers worked to improve the quality and appearance of the engravings which are often marvels of detail and artistic subtlety.

The problems facing the magazines surpass what modern publishers would accept as reasonable. Distribution was hampered by poor roads and unfavorable postal regulations. Payment for subscriptions was frequently not made. And perhaps most important, the editors searched in vain for quality material to publish.

Six of the magazines lasted more than a century; and two of them, about seventy-five years. But the rest lived, on the average,

71

between one and two years, with many surviving only one or two
issues. Standing out from the rest, the following titles, with their
dates of establishment, appear to be the decade's ten most important: Port Folio (1801), Monthly Anthology (1811), Niles' Weekly
Register (1811), Analectic (1813), North American Review (1815),
Portico (1816), American Baptist Magazine (1817), American Journal
of Science (1818), Methodist Review (1818), and American Farmer
(1819).

Two of these ten, Monthly Anthology and North American
Review, represent the Boston-Cambridge literary strength and are
an indication that America's literary center was about to shift from
Philadelphia to the northern pole of America's cultural axis. Philadelphia's strength in magazines still included Port Folio, Analectic,
and Portico; and the first two of these influenced intellectual life
until after 1820.

These five magazines were the decade's most important
literary periodical publications, and not one of them could regularly
print indigenous American literature. One or two poems, the essays of Joseph Dennie and Washington Irving, and a series of war-
inspired biographies stand nearly alone. The one exception to the
paucity of literary material resulted from the influence which the
literary club brought to bear. The Anthology Society and the Delphian Club insisted that criticism might inspire the creation of
original work; but in both cases, at least at the start, many of the
reviews they published were either borrowed or were written about
foreign books.

Very few magazines seriously reported news. Very few attempted to act as repositories of historical information. The one
exception was Niles' Weekly Register which almost alone began two
traditions now common in the news magazine: to report all sides
of an issue, and to serve as a source of contemporary information
for the future historian.

The religious magazines of the second decade clearly reflect
America's burgeoning religious pattern. The fractionization of denominations, the spread of the evangelical movement, the political

necessity for disestablishment of church-state relationships, the first glimmers of some aspects of the reform movement, and the reaction against firmly established hierarchies and formally educated clergy are all at least implied in numerous, short-lived, religious magazines. Most were also biased, polemic, and overly moralistic. Only the Baptists and the Methodists could inspire magazines which were to have long lives, and both were started by men who understood that for success it was necessary to avoid the parochial.

The decade did produce America's first specialized magazines for fields like law, veterinary medicine, education, and science. The professions were expanding in size and number and needed information sources unique to their fields. The best example, and one which reflects America's widening interests and ability in the development of science and industry is the American Journal of Science. In its pages, Benjamin Silliman hoped to cover all fields of science with scholarly, authoritative, well-written articles. That this magazine, alone among all others in the period, enjoys a continuous publishing history, stands testimony to his success and to America's awakening interest and ability in all areas of science.

Over 530 men and women spent some of their energies on these magazines. Among the names which still have firm places in American history are: Washington Irving, Benjamin Silliman, David Edwin, Archibald Bruce, Joseph Tinker Buckingham, and William Tudor. These men and others are identified in Appendix C. It indicates that many of America's best printers, publishers, editors, and engravers held some faith that the magazine held an important cultural position.

The nineteenth century's second decade was a period of American transition. Finally achieving economic and political independence in 1815, America was attempting to find literary and intellectual independence as well. The road from neoclassicism to Romanticism, from diversity to union, and from colonial status to nationalism had been filled with trials, and more were yet to come. The success of magazine publication was also, as yet, an unfulfilled

dream; but the magazines from 1810 to 1820 did leave some lega-
cies which, although somewhat ephemeral, were the ground on which
future seed was to prove fertile.

The important things are these. It was not what the magazines printed, but rather the attitude taken about what they wanted
to print--an indigenous, American literature. The magazines
helped to create an audience which may not have supported magazines from 1810 to 1820, but which would support later ones. The
period produced the first important scientific and reviewing journals
in America--prototypes of those alive today. And although generally
unsuccessful and failing to make any lasting contribution to American culture, history, and literature, the magazines did firmly establish a trend which resulted in the magazine's later becoming an
invaluable and important social document.

NOTES TO PART I

Introduction

1. Samuel Joseph Marino, The French Refugee Newspapers and
   Periodicals in the United States, 1789-1825 (Ph.D. dissertation, University of Michigan, 1962).
   Karl J. R. Arndt and May E. Olson, German-American Newspapers and Periodicals, 1732-1955, Deutsche Presseforschung, Bd. 3 (Heidelberg: Quelle & Meyer, 1961).

Chapter 1

1. "Introduction," The Latter Day Luminary, I (1818), iv-v.

2. Benjamin Morgan Lewis, A History and Bibliography of American Magazines, 1800-1810 (Ph.D. dissertation, University
   of Michigan, 1955), p. 9.

3. U.S. Census Office. 3d Census, 1810. Aggregate Amount of
   Each Description of Persons Within the U.S.A., and the
   Territories Thereof ... in the Year 1810 (Washington,
   1811), passim.

4. _____. _____. 4th Census, 1820. Census for 1820
   (Washington: Gales and Seaton, 1821), passim.

5. New York City at this time was only what is now Manhattan
   Island.

6. Number obtained from Rollo G. Silver, The Baltimore Book
   Trade, 1800-1825 (New York: New York Public Library,
   1953), passim.

7. Number obtained from Rollo G. Silver, The Boston Book
   Trade, 1800-1825 (New York: New York Public Library,
   1949), passim.

8. Harry B. Weiss, "The Number of Persons and Firms Connected with the Graphic Arts in New York City, 1633-1820,"
   New York Public Library, Bulletin, L (October 1946), 785.

9. _____, "The Growth of the Graphic Arts in Philadelphia, 1666-1820," New York Public Library, Bulletin, LVI (February 1952), 83.

10. For the names of these magazines, see Appendix B, infra.

11. Joseph Tinker Buckingham, Personal Memoirs and Recollections of Editorial Life (Boston: Ticknor, Reed, and Fields, 1852).

12. Frank Luther Mott, American Journalism; A History 1690-1960, 3d ed. (New York: Macmillan, 1962), p. 25.

13. Rollo Gabriel Silver, "Problems in Nineteenth Century American Bibliography," Bibliographical Society of America, Papers, (First Quarter, 1941), pp. 39-40. Also North American Review, I (May 1815), 133.

14. Ibid., p. 35.

15. Ibid., p. 39.

16. "View of Richmond Virginia," Analectic, IX (June 1817).

17. "Boston Common," Polyanthos, 3d series, II (June 1813).

18. "View on the Susquehanna," Port Folio, 4th series, VI (November 1815).

19. Untitled view, The Emporium of Arts and Sciences, I (July 1812).

20. "Cottage Scene," Port Folio, 3d series, III (April 1810).

21. "Kalmia Latfolia," Port Folio, 5th series, VI (July 1818). "Tropacolum Majus," The Monthly Preceptor, I (March 1815).

22. Harvard Lyceum, no. 18 (March 9, 1811), 429.

23. Theophilanthropist, no. 9 (September 1810), 382.

24. Alice Morse Earle, Stage-Coach and Tavern Days (New York: Macmillan, 1922), pp. 371-2.

25. Bound with Philadelphia Repertory, II (1811). APS reel 186.

26. Pao Hsun Chu, The Post Office of the United States, 2d ed. (New York: Columbia University Press, 1932), p. 32.

27. Wesley Everett Rich, The History of the United States Post Office to the Year 1829 (Cambridge: Harvard University Press, 1924), p. 183.

28. Ibid., p. 145.

29. General Shipping and Commercial List, I (August 1, 1815).

30. Ibid., V (August 3, 1819).

31. Robert G. Layer, Earnings of Cotton Mill Operatives, 1825-
     1914 (Cambridge: Committee on Research in Economic
     History, 1955), pp. 18-21.

32. Stanley T. Williams, The Life of Washington Irving (New
     York: Oxford University Press, 1935), I, p. 136.

Chapter 2

1.   William B. Cairns, On the Development of American Litera-
     ture from 1815 to 1835; with Especial Reference to Periodi-
     cals. (Madison: Published by the University, 1898).

2.   James H. Coberly, The Growth of Nationalism in American
     Literature, 1800-1815 (Ph.D. dissertation, George Washing-
     ton University, 1950).

3.   Henry Birnbaum, American Literary Nationalism After the
     War of 1812: 1815-1825 (Ph.D. dissertation, George
     Washington University, 1954).

4.   American Review of History and Politics, I (1811), iv-v.

5.   New York Medical and Philosophical Journal, II (1810), 285.

6.   The Western Gleaner, I (December 1813), 1.

7.   Quarterly Christian Spectator, I (1819), iii.

8.   New England Galaxy, II (October 1819), 1.

9.   Philanthropist, I (December 12, 1817), 105-112.

10. Buckingham, op. cit., pp. 53-4.

11. H. Lloyd Flewelling, "Literary Warfare," in his Literary
     Criticism in American Magazines, 1783-1820 (Ph.D. dis-
     sertation, University of Michigan, 1931), pp. 179-221.

12. New York: I. Riley, 1810.

13. North American Review, I (May 1815), 61-89.

14. William Henry Venable, "Early Periodical Literature of the
     Ohio Valley," Magazine of Western History, VIII (June
     1888), p. 103.

15. North American Review, I (May 1815), 111-21.

16. Ibid., I (July 1815), 275-84.

17. Ibid., IV (January 1817), 217-62.

18. Ibid., VIII (July 1818), 149-84.

19. Ibid., VII (July 1818), 198-211.

20. Ibid., VIII (March 1819), 276-322.

21. Ibid., IX (September 1819), 322-56.

22. Something, no. 26 (May 12, 1810), 403-4.

23. New York: Pageant Books, 1959.

24. For information leading to this conclusion see the first chapter
     of Herbert Ross Brown, The Sentimental Novel in America
     (New York: Pageant Books, 1959).

25. Effie Jane Wheeler, Narrative Art in the Prose Fiction of
     Eighteenth Century American Magazines (Ph.D. dissertation,
     University of Michigan, 1942).

26. Ibid., p. 5.

27. Ibid., p. 433.

28. Emerald, no. 1 (November 3, 1810), 10-11.

29. Ibid., no. 2 (November 10, 1810), 18-21.

30. Ibid., pp. 21-2.

31. Ibid., no. 1 (November 3, 1810), 10.

32. Huntingdon Literary Museum, I (January-December 1818),
     passim.

33. Ibid., I (December 1810), 535-6.

34. Baltimore Repertory, I (January 1811), 7-10, et seq.

35. Ibid., p. 7.

36. The Lady's Miscellany, XII (January 5, 1811), 166-7.

37. London: Minerva Press, 1800. 2 vols.

38. Ibid., XIII (September 21, 1811), 337-40, et seq.

39. The Olio, I (January 27, 1813), et seq.

40. Intellectual Regale, I (November 19, 1814), 2-6, et seq.

41. The Inquisitor, I (December 30, 1818), 1-3, et seq.

42. London: Longmans, Hurst, Rees, Orme and Brown, 1818.
    3 vols.

43. Ladies Magazine, nos. 6-10 (March 2-April 24, 1819).

44. The Literary Visitor, I (no month 1813), 165.

45. Ibid., p. 156.

46. The Pioneer, I (February 28, 1812), 7.

47. The American Magazine, I (June 1815), 8-17.

48. For a list of these, see Appendix C.

49. Polyanthos, new series, I (February 1812), 15-22.

50. Ibid., pp. 35-46.

51. Ibid., (September 1812), 258-61.

52. Port Folio, new series, I (January 1810), 60-4, et seq.

53. Ibid., 4th series, II (September 1813), 235-55.

54. Polyanthos, new series, I (February 1812), 3-15.

55. New England Galaxy, I (December 19, 1817), 1.

56. Corrector, no. 1 (July 1815), 32-3.

57. Polyanthos, I (February 1811), 58-69.

58. Huntingdon Literary Museum, I (August 1810), 377-8.

59. Emerald, I (February 23, 1811), 206.

60. Something, no. 15 (February 24, 1810), 239.

61. Inquisitor, I (April 7, 1819), 60.

62. North American Review, V (September 1817), 338-40.

63. Analectic Magazine, IV (November 1814), 433-4.

64. The War, III (August 24, 1817), 54.

65. Frank Hayward Severance, "The Periodical Press of Buffalo,
     1811-1915, " Buffalo Historical Society, Publications XIX
     (1915), 209-10.

66. The Massachusetts Watchman, I (April 1810), 128-31.

67. Emerald, I (December 22, 1810), 87-90.

68. Intellectual Regale, I (December 10, 1814), 43

69. Emerald, I (November 3, 1810), 14.

70. Stranger, I (July 17, 1813), 22.

71. Scott Holland Goodnight, German Literature in American Maga-
     zines Prior to 1846 (Madison: University of Wisconsin,
     1907), pp. 34-9.

72. American Review of History and Politics, III (January 1812),
     51-69.

73. Analectic, XIII (April 1819), 276-94.

74. Julian Dewey Mason, The Critical Reception of American
     Negro Authors in American Magazines, 1800-1900 (Ph.D.
     dissertation, North Carolina, 1962), p. 21.

75. For details of this magazine, see the annotation for the Har-
     vard Lyceum.

76. Connecticut Historical Society, Bulletin VII (October 1940), 2-4.

77. John C. McCloskey, "A Note of the Portico, " American
     Literature VIII (November 1936), 300.

78. Marshall W. Fishwick, "The Portico and Literary Nationalism
     After the War of 1812, " The William and Mary Quarterly,
     3d series, VIII (April 1951), 240.

79. Red Book, I (1819), ix.

80. McCloskey, op. cit. , p. 300.

81. Fishwick, op. cit. , p. 241.

82. Louis P. Simpson, "A Literary Adventure of the Early Re-
     public: The Anthology Society and The Monthly Anthology, "
     New England Quarterly, XXVII (June 1954), 168-90.

83. Journal of the Times, I (November 28, 1818), 181.

84. Honey Bee, no. 2 (December 25, 1819), 5-6.

85. John C. McCloskey, "The Campaign of Periodicals after the War of 1812 for National American Literature," PMLA, L (March 1935), pp. 262-73.

86. "Biographical Memoire of Commodore Perry," The Analectic Magazine, II (December 1813), 494-510.

87. Portico, II (August 1816), 111-2.

88. Ibid., p. 119.

89. New England Galaxy, III (December 31, 1819), 46.

Chapter 3

1. Lewis, op. cit., pp. 29-53.

2. Nicholas Murray Butler, The Effect of the War of 1812 upon the Consolidation of the Union (Johns Hopkins University, "Studies," series 5, no. 7) (Baltimore: Johns Hopkins, 1927), p. 22.

3. Strangely, this title seems to have been omitted from the American Periodicals Series.

4. Polyanthos, new series, I (March 1813), 333-4.

5. Port Folio, 3d series, VIII (September 1812), 245.

6. Ibid., 4th series, I (June 1813), 636-7.

7. Ibid., II (June 1813), 38-51.

8. Ibid., II (October 1813), 401-3.

9. Ibid., IV (August 1814), 231-3.

10. Ibid., IV (October 1814), 326-31.

11. Ibid., V (February 1815), 105-9.

12. A list of these and all other illustrations in the Port Folio as well as other magazines is in Appendix E.

13. Analectic, VI (September 1815), 231-57, et seq.

14. For one contemporary opinion, see the quotation in Chapter Two under "Biography," supra.

15. Analectic, VI (September 1815), 235.

16. Examiner, I (October 25, 1813), 1.

17. Ibid., II (May 14, 1814), 1.

18. Ibid., III (February 25, 1815), 341.

19. VIII (April-May 1815), 120-31, 160-71.

20. For a general discussion of this development, see especially:
     Frank Luther Mott, American Journalism ..., 3d ed. (New
     York: Macmillan, 1962).

21. Norval Neil Luxon, Niles' Weekly Register: News Magazine of
     the Nineteenth Century (Baton Rouge: Louisiana University
     Press, 1947).

22. Factual material is based on the DAB, XI, pp. 142-5.

23. Cobbett's American Political Register, XXX (May 28, 1816),
     cols. 79-88.

24. Ibid., col. 82.

25. Ibid., col. 87.

26. Western Review, I (September 1819), 96-100, et seq.

27. Ibid., I (August 1819), 46-53, et seq.

28. Port Folio, 5th series, III (June 1817), 530.

29. Scourge, I (June 2, 1810), 5.

30. Hive, no. 11 (July 6, 1811), 81.

31. Ibid., no. 15 (September 7, 1811), 114.

32. Philanthropist, I (December 19, 1817), 113.

33. Religious Intelligencer, III (June 27, 1818), 56.

34. American Mineralogical Journal, I (1810), iii.

35. Emporium of Arts and Sciences, I (1812), vi-vii.

36. American Journal of Science, I (July 1818), 9-35, et seq.

37. Agricultural Museum, II (September 1811), 73-81.

38. Claribel R. Barnett, "The Agricultural Museum ...,"
     Agricultural History, II (April 1928), 99.

39. New York Medical Magazine, III (no month 1811), 19-23.

40. American Medical and Philosophical Register, I (July 1810).

41. Medical Repository, XIII (January 1810), 217-25.

42. Myrl L. Ebert, "Rise and Development of the American Medical Periodical, 1797-1850," Medical Library Association, Bulletin XL (July 1953), 25.

43. V (October 1816), 413-5.

44. Albert Lowther Demaree, The American Agricultural Press, 1819-1860 (New York: Columbia University Press, 1941), p. 32.

45. Panoplist, V (April 1810), 517-21.

46. Christian Observer, XI (July 1812), 424-31.

47. Almoner, I (September 1811), 145-7.

48. Harvard Lyceum, no. 7 (October 6, 1810), 156-8, et seq.

49. American Monthly Magazine, IV (March 1819), 390.

50. Weekly Register, XVI (March 20, 1819), 76.

51. Charles Edward Wunderlich, A History and Bibliography of Early American Music Periodicals, 1782-1852 (Ph.D. dissertation, University of Michigan, 1962).

52. Bertha Monica Stearns, "Early Philadelphia Magazines for Ladies," Pennsylvania Magazine of History and Biography LXIV (October 1940), 480.

53. _____. "Southern Magazines for Ladies, 1819-1860," South Atlantic Quarterly, XXI (January 1932), 87.

Chapter 4

1. The general information in these pages is based on studies like: George Dangerfield, The Era of Good Feelings (New York: Harcourt, Brace, 1952).

2. Lewis, op. cit., p. 75.

3. Gaylord P. Albaugh, "American Presbyterian Periodicals and Newspapers, 1752-1830, with Library Locations," Journal of Presbyterian History, XLI (September 1963), 165-87; (December 1963), 243-62; XLII (March 1964), 54-67; (June 1964); 124-44.

4. "Centennial of Religious Journalism," Independent, LXV (October 1, 1908), 801.

5. For fuller comment, see Chapter Three, supra.

6. Missionary Herald at Home and Abroad, new series, V (June 1812), 1.

7. Weekly Recorder, I (July 5, 1814), 2.

8. Christian Monitor, I (August 13, 1815), 48.

9. Evangelical Record and Western Review, I (March 1812), 82-9.

10. Evangelical Repository, I (January 1816), 1-26.

11. The bibliography by Gaylord Albaugh identifies a greater number, but many of these titles were newspapers, and others were not wholly Presbyterian and are not included in this count.

12. Polyanthos, 3d series, I (October 1812), front.

13. Vermont Baptist Missionary Magazine, I (April 1811), 50.

14. Ibid., pp. 62-3.

15. Ibid., I (August 1811), 85.

16. American Baptist Magazine, II (January 1819), 30.

17. DAB, XVII, p. 404.

18. Methodist Magazine, I (January 1818), 6.

19. Oliver Wendell Elsbree, "The Rise of the Missionary Spirit in New England, 1790-1815," The New England Quarterly, I (July 1928), 304.

20. DAB, XIII, p. 246.

21. "The Christian Disciple and the Christian Examiner," New England Quarterly, I (April 1928), 197.

22. Bernard Postal, "The Early American Jewish Press," Reflex, II (April 1928), 68.

23. The Jew. New York. Vols. 1-2 (March 1823-March 1825). See ULS, p. 1409.

24. Floriad, I (September 27, 1811), 145-8.

PART II

BIBLIOGRAPHY
OF
AMERICAN MAGAZINES

INTRODUCTION

The 223 bibliographical descriptions in this section are arranged alphabetically by title. The title used in each entry is generally its latest or most important form.

Bibliographic details are limited to the chronological period covered by this study. When pertinent, titles and dates were carried out to include the entire run of the magazine if it lasted after December 31, 1819. The basic rule, however, has been to leave the last name or detail as an open entry.

The form of personal names given in these annotations is, with the exception of pseudonyms, as it is found in or on the magazines themselves. A fuller form of the name and a street address where it has been possible to locate this information have been supplied in the Register of Printers, Publishers, Editors and Engravers.

The designation for "type" of magazine is frequently an arbitrary decision, and this classification results from an over-all view of the contents. Few of the magazines, by their very nature, can be neatly classified; but some differentiation seems necessary.

The terms Frequency, Price, Size, and Length apply to individual issues. For example, when "16 pp." appears after the word "Length" this should be taken to mean that each issue contained that number of pages. When this information varies from issue to issue, that is indicated in some way for the individual magazine.

"Availability" of the magazines does not include a finding list. Only those titles not in the American Periodicals Series (here designated as APS) have a location indicated. All but nineteen of the titles are included in the Union List of Serials (here designated as ULS), and most of this small group may be found in Brigham's bibliography where locations are given.

The indexing of these magazines is included since the value of such publications is severely limited where no indexing exists. Shown within the annotations are: cumulative self-indexing, inclusion in Poole's Index to Periodical Literature, and representation in the Index to Early American Magazines which has been issued in part by the Readex Microprint Corporation as American Periodical Index to 1850.

The entries under "References" are given only for a significant article or book about a title. For the most frequently cited works, only the author's last name appears. Details will be found in the Selected Bibliography.

Just after the section of remarks, a section called "Notes" is added for some titles. This section contains what normally would appear as footnotes. This arrangement brings the citations close to the annotations themselves rather than placing them apart from the magazine to which they apply.

The information included here varies from title to title simply because the magazines themselves vary and because the information is not always available. For most of the titles the information here is greater than in any other single source.

1. ACADEMIC RECREATIONS

Title: Academic Recreations
Place: New York   Dates: February-July 1815
Editor: By the Columbian Peitho-Logian Society of Columbia College
Publisher: Eastburn, Kirk & Co.
Printer: Forbes & Co.
Type: Collegiate
Frequency: Monthly   Price: Not given
Size: ca. 8 x 5   Length: 48 pp.
Motto: Conamur tenues grandia.
Availability: Not in APS or ULS.   Microfilm obtained from Brown
        University.

Remarks: The students of Columbia College were not to be outdone
by Harvard and Yale and produced this undergraduate magazine.   As
was the case with most such magazines, the best printers did the
work, and it was excellent.
        The essays were to be original and were to cover all aspects
of literature.   History and biography were to receive little emphasis, and science and math were seldom mentioned.   Original poetry
and translations appear in each issue.
        Throughout the six issues, a series on the origin, progress,
and profection of romantic fiction, both in prose and verse appeared.
These may have been the results of reworking lecture notes since
they seem to follow a careful outline.
        One article, "On the Advantages of Science to the Cause of
Christianity," states:

> ... We see that science, instead of shewing the falsehood
> of Christianity, has served most strongly to convince men
> of its truth, and to promote its promulgation...[1]

A rather unusual statement considering religious opinions in 1815.

Notes: 1.   Academic Recreations, I (April 1815), 1056.

2. ACADEMICIAN

Title: The Academician, Containing the Elements of Scholastic
        Science, and Outlines of Philosophic Education, Predicated
        on the Analysis of the Human Mind, and Exhibiting the Im-
        proved Methods of Education
Place: New York   Dates: January 7, 1818-January 29, 1820

Editor: Albert Picket; John W. Picket
Printer: S. Marks (January 7, 1818-July 10, 1819); Charles Bald-
          win (September 25, 1814-January 29, 1820)
Type: Education
Frequency: Semi-monthly   Price: $3.00
Size: 9 x 5 1/2   Length: 16 pp.
Motto: Doctrina sed vim promovet insitam
          Rectique cultus pectora roborant.
Availability: APS reel 47
Indexed: Cargill

Remarks: The title of this magazine was repeated as the title of a
brief series of articles devoted to methodology which appeared in
the first few issues of what is probably America's first magazine
devoted to education.   The early issues were divided into sections
or "Departments" called Philological, Geographical, Mathematical,
and Arithmetical. Book reviews, a miscellany of news, and poetry
concluded each number.
        Various educational systems, especially those of Lancaster,
Bell, Pestalozzi, and Fellenberg, were outlined and explained.   For
example, "The New School; or Lancasterian System" discussed the
basics of a system which Picket felt to be noteworthy for what might
now be called reinforcement.[1]
        Other articles make fascinating reading.   They are interesting
from the viewpoint of the history of education and as studies in
teaching methods, some of which are quite acceptable by modern
standards.   The last numbers ran a long series concerned with the
philosophy of education which form a milestone in American education.   They indicate a real interest in pupil involvement and the
transfer of training, although the terms are not used.
        Twenty-five issues of The Academician appeared before the
Picket brothers felt the burden of producing a magazine by themselves too great.   Their ideas were good, but perhaps they were
too advanced for an American educational system which was relatively underdeveloped.

Notes: 1.   The Academician, no. 5 (April 30, 1818), 68-70.

3. ADVISOR

Title: The Advisor; or, Vermont Evangelical Magazine
Place: Middlebury, Vt.   Dates: January 1809-November/Decem-
        ber 1815
Editor: Asa Burton and a varying committee of the Congregational
        Church.   In 1815, John Hough
Publisher: William Hooker (1810); Samuel Swift (1811-1814); Tlmo.
        C. Strong (1815)
Printer: Joseph D. Huntington (1810); T. C. Strong (1811-1814);
        Tlmo. C. Strong (1815)
Type: Religious - Congregational

Frequency: Monthly   Price: $1.00
Size: 8 x 5   Length: avg. 32 pp.
Availability: APS reels 1, 47
Reference: Lewis, p. 99

Remarks: The pattern of religious journals--to include biography,
"religious communications," news of churches, book reviews, and
sermons, all with a denominational, pious slant--was followed by
Asa Burton. He was a Congregational minister, and he let this
view-point slant much that was published.
      The advocacy of Bible societies and a pro-British attitude
frequently found in New England during the War of 1812 are both
reflected in the rather stolid pages of a magazine whose main purpose was to extend missionary work.
      The Advisor was well printed and care was taken with ap-
pearance. The type was of good quality; and some design experiments were made, apparently to attract subscribers. Despite the
pages' lack of interest and originality, The Advisor had somewhat
longer than an average life.

4. AERONAUT

Title: The Aeronaut: A Periodical Paper
Place: New York   Dates: May 18, 1816-September 30, 1822
Editor: An Association of Gentlemen (May 18-July 26, 1816); A
         Literary Association (August 1, 1816-   )
Printer and Publisher: None - a manuscript magazine
Type: Miscellany - Literary
Frequency: Irregular   Price: None given
Size: ca. 9 1/4 x 5 1/4   Length: 8-16 pp.
Motto: Aetatis cojusque notandi sunt tibi mores.
Availability: APS reels 48-9

Remarks: Although this periodical was not printed, was irregular,
and its issues were apparently each written by an individual, it can
be called a magazine in the sense that it was distributed in the
same way The Cricket was. The first issue states the purpose by
saying:

          The essays are to be confined to no particular subject
          within the range of general literature. Polemical des-
          criptions and party politics must be interdicted from our
          pages for ever; the hydra of fiction must not there be
          permitted to shew her head.[1]

      The Literary Society met once a week to read the prepared
essay and discuss its merits. The copy book containing the essays
was handed to another member who prepared the next week's material. The handwriting is frequently poor and varies from issue to
issue as much as the contents. Poetry appeared, some "title pages"

are decorated, and single initials are used as signatures.

The issues were each numbered, but not all were dated. About 190 issues appeared through 1819, and the periodical continued erratically thereafter. None of the material is of great importance although it does reveal something of literary taste in New York after the War of 1812.

Notes: 1. The Aeronaut, I (May 18, 1816), 10.

5. AGRICULTURAL MUSEUM

Title: The Agricultural Museum: Designed to be a Repository of Valuable Information to the Farmers and Manufacturers and the Mean (!) of a Free Communication of Sentiment, and General Interchange of Ideas, on the Important Subjects of their Occupations
Place: Georgetown, D.C.   Dates: July 4, 1810-May 1812
Editor: David Wiley
Publisher and Printer: W. A. Rind
Type: Agriculture
Frequency: Bi-weekly (1810); Monthly (1811-12)
Price: $2.50 for 24 issues
Size: 8.6 x 5.2   Length: 16-32 pp.
Motto: Omnis feret omnia tellus.
Availability: APS reel 49
Reference: Barnett, Claribel R., "The Agricultural Museum; "An Early American Agricultural Periodical," Agricultural History, II (April 1928), 99-102.

Remarks: This was probably the first American periodical devoted to agriculture, and it acted as an unofficial organ of the Columbian Agricultural Society for the Promotion of Rural and Domestic Economy. Wiley was the principal and librarian of the Columbian Academy in Georgetown and the secretary of the Columbian Agricultural Society. In addition, he served as superintendent of a turnpike road, and was a postmaster, merchant, miller, and preacher. After 1810 he was elected mayor of Georgetown. Added evidence that Wiley was an American renaissance man was his launching of a subject magazine.

Much of the contents lacked originality, and most of the material written for the magazine was somewhat strained and artificial. Extracts of the proceedings of United States and foreign agricultural societies took up many pages and several items were borrowed from newspapers; very few worthwhile ideas for farm improvement were offered. The single series of real value is one on wheat.

An attempt to attract contributions resulted in an article by John Taylor of Caroline published on September 12, 1810.

6. ALLEGHANY MAGAZINE

Title: Alleghany Magazine; or, Repository of Useful Knowledge
Place: Meadville, Pa.   Dates: July 4, 1816-November 1817
Editor: Timothy Alden
Printer: Thomas Atkinson
Type: Miscellany - General
Frequency: Monthly - Irregular   Price: $2.00
Size: 8 1/4 x 5 1/4   Length: ca. 30 pp.
Availability: Not in APS.   Copy examined at the American Anti-
     quarian Society.

Remarks: This title is noted by Albaugh as a Presbyterian magazine,[1] and he gives additional locations of files.   Although much of
the religious material may have had a Presbyterian view-point, the
major share of material is of a general nature.
     The circulation was expected to be limited to the Alleghany
valley.   The last issue lists 189 subscribers--hardly enough to support a magazine.   Had all these people paid for the magazine, less
than $400 would have been received, and it is doubtful that a maga-
zine could carry on on this income.
     Much historical material on Alleghany College was printed;
religious and agricultural articles; obituaries; and a series on "dead
languages" are the major contents.   Several Bible societies were
described.   One of them, named for a local lady, Mrs. Harriet
Newall, was called The Newall Memoriter Bible Society.
     Little bits and pieces on dozens of subjects from archaelogy
to zoology appeared.   Lacking a definite purpose and a strong subscription list, the magazine had a typically short life.

Notes: 1.   Albaugh, op. cit., p. 170.

7. ALMONER

Title: The Almoner, a Periodical Religious Publication
Place: Lexington, Ky.   Dates: April 1814-May 1815
Editor and Publisher: Thomas T. Skillman
Type: Religious - Presbyterian
Frequency: Monthly   Price: Not stated
Size: 6 1/2 x 4   Length: 50-64 pp.
Motto: Let thy work appear unto thy servants, and thy glory unto
     their children.
Availability: APS reel 51

Remarks: Thomas Skillman's printing and publishing activities in
Kentucky were wide-spread; and this magazine, despite a short life,
was well produced and skillfully printed.   Although the specific price
is not stated, Skillman wrote that "... the Almoner is the cheapest
book that ever has been printed, or proposed to be printed in the
Western country."[1]

The contents are entirely typical, consisting of sermons, commentaries on scripture, news of religious activity, and the like. Biography of men like John Huss and discussions of educational developments like the Lancastrian plan add something of a more general interest than a narrow, polemic viewpoint.

Although Skillman also published the Evangelical Record, no connection between this and The Almoner directly existed.

Notes: 1.   The Almoner, I (July 1814), 116.

8.   AMERICAN BAPTIST MAGAZINE

Title: The American Baptist Magazine and Missionary Intelligencer
Place: Boston   Dates: January 1817-November 1824
Editor: Thomas Baldwin
Publisher: Baptist Missionary Society of Massachusetts
Printer: James Loring and/or Lincoln & Edmands
Illustration: One plate of Rev. Andrew Fuller in May 1819
Type: Religious - Baptist
Frequency: Bi-monthly   Price: 75¢
Size: 8 3/4 x 5 1/2   Length: 40 pp.
Availability: APS reel 71
Indexed: Baptist Missionary Magazine has an index volume covering
            the years 1803-1883 which include The American Baptist
            Magazine and The Massachusetts Baptist Missionary Magazine.
Reference: Mott, I, pp. 251-2
History: Supersedes: The Massachusetts Baptist Missionary Maga-
            zine.   Later: Baptist Missionary Magazine until 1909.   In
            1910, united with Baptist Home Mission Monthly, and Good
            Work to become Missions.

Remarks: This title is considered separately although it was a continuation of The Massachusetts Baptist Missionary Magazine.   In January 1817 a new series started with volume one, although the publisher and editor were the same as for the previous magazine.

If dating were to begin in 1803, this is certainly the first American magazine to last one hundred years; and it was old when other venerable magazines began.   This is a tribute to Thomas Baldwin and to the force of the Baptist missionary movement in the United States.   In early volumes Baldwin was assisted by Daniel Sharp and Thomas M. Winchell.

Biography usually opened each issue; this was followed by a variety of religious articles, reviews, news of ordinations, obituaries, and poetry.   A heavy emphasis was placed on articles about missionary work, and these were polemic and dogmatic in tone. Nearly every article, review, and piece of news was Baptist-related in some way, other sects seldom being mentioned.

In September 1817, the editor claimed a circulation of 10,000; and at the close of 1818, a claim was made to have printed 134,000 copies of the twelve issues.[1]   If this were even close to

being true, this magazine may have had the largest circulation in
America at the time.

The early issues are an important source of nineteenth century church history, especially in the mission field, since literally
hundreds of reports appear in its pages.

The Library of Congress card for the APS series incorrectly calls this title: American Baptist Missionary Magazine and
Missionary Intelligencer.

Notes: 1. American Baptist Magazine, II (January 1819), 30.

9. AMERICAN FARMER

Title: The American Farmer, Containing Original Essays and Se-
          lections on Rural Economy and Internal Improvements, with
          Illustrative Engravings and the Prices Current of Country
          Produce
Place: Baltimore, Md.   Dates: April 2, 1819-February 1897
Editor: John S. Skinner (April 2, 1819-   )
Printer: Ebenezer French (April 30-September 10, 1819); Joseph
          Robinson (September 17, 1819-   )
Illustrations: In 1819, mostly small wood-cuts printed with text.
Type: Agriculture
Frequency: Weekly   Price: $4.00
Size: 7 x 5 1/2   Length: 8 pp.
Motto: O fortunatas nimium sua si bona norint agricolas.
Availability: APS reel 51
Reference: Brigham, p. 225

Remarks: Although the closing date is given here as 1897, The
American Farmer underwent several changes in title and ownership
after 1834, and these may have brought changes in policy.

During 1819, the contents included descriptions of inventions
and techniques of use to farmers, tips on when and how to plant
various crops, seasonal news, and continued articles meant to be
an agricultural text. Two special departments appeared sporadically
--a woman's page, and sporting news. Poetry, news summaries,
humor, home cures, temperance articles, marriages and deaths
were used when space allowed. Advertising was accepted and usually
limited to the final page.

John Skinner felt that internal improvements like roads and
canals added to national wealth, lowered costs, and helped the
farmer transport his produce. All of this influenced agricultural
prosperity.

10. AMERICAN JOURNAL OF SCIENCE

Title: The American Journal of Science, more especially of

Mineralogy, Geology, and the other branches of natural his-
tory; including also agriculture and the ornamental as well as
useful arts
Place: New Haven   Dates: July 1818-present
Editor: Benjamin Silliman (July 1818-April 1838)
Publisher: James Eastburn and Co., New York (July 1818-   );
    Howe and Spaulding, New Haven (July 1818-   )
Printer: Abraham Paul, New Haven (July 1818-   )
Illustrations: Several miscellaneous plates are scattered throughout
    each early volume.
Type: Science
Frequency: At start, irregular   Price: Not given
Size: 8 1/2 x 5   Length: 104-32 pp.
Availability: APS reel 53
Indexed: Poole
    Volume 50 (1849) contains an index of volumes 1-49.
Reference: Mott, I, pp. 302-5

Remarks: Although volume one started in July 1818 and was completed in July 1819, the first number of volume two did not appear
until April 1820. A stumbling start was not an accurate forecast of
what was to come from America's oldest magazine in continuous
publication without a change in title.
    The plan for the magazine, printed in volume one, promised
articles on natural history, mineralogy, biology, zoology, chemistry,
natural philosophy, mathematics, agriculture, manufactures, domestic economy, music, sculpture, engraving, printing, military and
civil engineering, navigation, review of books, biographical and
obituary notices, comparative anatomy and physiology, and other
minor items. The scope of the articles eventually added "and the
Arts" to the basic title, but this phrase has since been dropped.
    The first article dealt with music, and the first volume very
nearly exactly fulfilled the promise made at the start. Benjamin
Silliman managed to gather a wide range of material, written and
signed by the best brains in America, and frequently well illustrated.
    Although some of the material was European, most was
American in origin - the result of experiments and discoveries by
Americans, described by Americans. The geology and mineralogy,
the maps, and the inventions were American. This, combined with
the word "American" in the title, gave rise to pride in and conse-
quent support of a first-rate magazine devoted to scientific and artistic progress in America. Growing nationalism and an increasing
security in America's ability to contribute to Western culture enabled this magazine to discover the nearly unobtainable formula for
success.

11. AMERICAN LAW JOURNAL

Title: The American Law Journal and Miscellaneous Law Repertory
    Sometimes cited as Hall's American Law Journal

Place: Philadelphia and Baltimore
Dates: January 1810-December 1817. Not issued 1811-1812, and
          1815-1816.
Editor: John Elihu Hall
Publisher: Farrand and Nicholes (1810); Moses Thomas (1813);
          Edward J. Ceale (1814); Harrison Hall (1817)
Printer: Fry and Krammerer (1810); Sergeant Hall (1813); William
          Fry (1814); James Maxwell (1817)
Type: Law
Frequency: Quarterly   Price: $4.00
Size: 8 1/2 x 4 3/4   Length: About 100 pp.
Motto: Seu linguam causis acuis, seu civica jura respondere paras.
Availability: APS reels 1, 53
Reference: Lewis, pp. 101-2
Superseded by: Journal of Jurisprudence

Remarks: Intended to serve as a library of legal information, this
magazine digested important state laws relating to such things as
money, legal instruments, and domestic relations; it summarized
major English and American court cases; and contained lists of new
statutes and legal publications.
       Probably America's first periodical devoted to law, it pio-
neered in making works like Cornelius van Bynkershoek's Treatise
on the Law of War available to the profession;[1] and it placed an
emphasis on scholarship and clear, forceful writing.
       Three of the Hall brothers were connected with this title,
and their dealings with magazines became widespread, partly as a
result of their experience on this journal. Harrison Hall became
one of the more important names in early nineteenth century printing.

Notes: 1.   The American Law Journal, III (1810), 251.

12.   AMERICAN MAGAZINE

Title: The American Magazine, A Monthly Miscellany, Devoted to
         Literature, Science, and the Arts, Including also State Pa-
         pers and Public Documents, with Intelligence, Domestic,
         Foreign, and Literary, Public News, and Passing Events:
         Being an Attempt to form a Useful Repository for Every
         Description of American Readers
Place: Albany   Dates: June 1815-May 1816
Editor: Horatio Gates Spafford
Printer: E. & E. Hosford
Illustrations: Plates of buildings and scenery are scattered irregu-
         larly in some issues.
Type: Miscellany - General
Frequency: Monthly   Price: $2.50
Size: 8 x 5   Length: 48 pp.
Availability: APS reel 53

Remarks: This periodical was as general and as miscellaneous as any magazine of the period containing, at times, even more variety. than the title would indicate. Some news was to be found, and even marriages and deaths appear.

Some articles perpetuated strange ideas, as one which attributed accidents to the "wind" of passing objects. Other articles discussed: divining rods, newspapers, the Lancastrian teaching method, and numismatics.

Although no reasons for the death of the magazine are stated, they may be assumed to include the lack of support, the necessity of paying higher postage rates, and other Albany competition.

Publication was begun on June 16th;[1] and, in his note about the magazine, the editor of The Corrector felt The American Magazine was none too important a contribution.

Notes: 1. The Corrector, no. 1 (July 1815), 37.

13. AMERICAN MEDICAL AND PHILOSOPHICAL REGISTER

Title: American Medical and Philosophical Register; or, Annals of
        Medicine, Natural Science, Agriculture, and the Arts
Place: New York   Dates: July 1810-April 1814
Editor: Conducted by a Society of Gentlemen. Probably: David
        Hosack and John Wakefield Francis.
Publisher: Ezra Sargeant (1810-1813); Van Winkle and Wiley (1814)
Illustrations: Most issues have at least one plate. These are por-
        traits of doctors, views of medical buildings, and scientific
        subjects.
Type: Medical and general science
Frequency: Quarterly   Price: $2.00
Size: 7 1/2 x 4 1/2   Length: 100-144 pp.
Availability: APS reel 54

Remarks: The scope of this magazine was quite broad, and included in the first volume material on: Lightning rods, spotted fever, enteritis, drinking water analysis, catalepsy, and Benjamin Rush's "doctrine" of disease.

One early announcement by a rival said: "The principal object of the editors, is ... to advocate the foreign origin of yellow fever."[1]

Although articles on this subject appear, the magazine by no means limits itself to this discussion. Not only are the articles wide-ranging in subject, but also two other parts of the periodical regularly appear. Book reviews, generally of a medical nature; and Philosophical and Literary Intelligence both form important aspects of the contents.

This title has some importance if only because it was a part of the new trend in periodical publishing--the subject periodical. The greatest weakness in the early years of this development was material.

When the death of the magazine was announced in April 1814, the
reason given was not money but rather the impossibility of acquiring
sufficient original material to keep the magazine alive. An important reason to remember the title is the fairly large number of contemporary biographies, usually accompanied by an engraving.

Notes: 1. New York Medical and Philosophical Journal, II (1810),
             285.

14. AMERICAN MEDICAL RECORDER

Title: The American Medical Recorder, of Original Papers and In-
        telligence in Medicine and Surgery
Place: Philadelphia   Dates: January 1818-July 1829
Editor: Conducted by Several Respectable Physicians of Philadel-
        phia (1818); John Eberle (1819-   )
Publisher: James Webster (1818-   )
Printer: William Brown (1818-   )
Illustrations: Each issue planned one or more plates which were of
        portraits, buildings, and diseased anatomy.
Type: Medical
Frequency: Quarterly   Price: Not given
Size: 8 1/4 x 4 3/4   Length: 150 pp.
Motto: Nullius addictus jurare in verba magistri.
Availability: APS reel 55

Remarks: The first two years of this journal were not marked by
any great magazine innovations. Many distinguished contributors
like John Dorsey, William Harner, and James Mease sent case
studies which they frequently had published previously. Only one
plate appeared in each issue of volume one, and these were not always of medical subjects. Each issue contained about twenty articles, half American and half foreign; and these reports usually were
of positive results obtained with drugs and treatment.
     As is true of other medical journals in this period, the re-
ported techniques are somewhat crude and naive by modern standards. However, these men were skillful, daring, perceptive, and
ethical. They were attempting to raise the standards of a profession clouded with quackery and incompetence. By contributions to
another medical journal they added to growing literature and to an
improved education of American doctors.

15. AMERICAN MINERALOGICAL JOURNAL

Title: American Mineralogical Journal: Being a Collection of Facts
        and Observations Tending to Elucidate the Mineralogy and
        Geology of the United States of America. Together with

other Information Relating to Mineralogy, Geology, and
Chemistry, Derived from Scientific Sources
          Sometimes referred to as: Bruce's American Mineralogi-
cal Journal.
Place: New York   Dates: January 1810-January 1814
Editor: Archibald Bruce
Printer: Collins & Co.
Illustrations: Only two plates were found in the file, both of
          minerals.
Type: Science
Frequency: Annual   Price: Not given
Size: 9 x 5   Length: 62 pp.
Availability: APS reel 57
Reference: New York Medical and Philosophical Journal, II (1810),
          107-8. Eclectic Repertory, II (January 1812), 210-8.

Remarks: No future historian of American science will fail to com-
          memorate this work as our earliest purely scientific
          Journal, supported by original American Communications. [1]
     A secure place in magazine history should be guaranteed this
title, although only four brief annual volumes appeared, thus making
the magazine's contents relatively unimportant. About forty articles
appeared, and all deal with American mineral deposits.
     The stated object of describing the United States was only
partly realized, since roughly half the articles are devoted to such
non-American geology as a discussion of Mount Vesuvius. Most of
the articles are quite brief, many running only a paragraph or so.
The book reviews are much longer, and they generally evaluate as
well as summarize.
     Bruce discontinued the magazine when he realized he could
not obtain enough material to fill its pages. He could not agree
merely to reprint foreign items and was unsuccessful in an attempt
to obtain original articles.

Notes: 1. "Introductory Remarks," The American Journal of
          Science, I (July 1818), 3.

16. AMERICAN MONTHLY MAGAZINE

Title: The American Monthly Magazine and Critical Review
Place: New York   Dates: May 1817-April 1819
Editor: H. Biglow (May-October 1817); H. Biglow and Orville Luther
          Halley (November 1817-October 1818); Orville Luther Halley
          (November 1818-April 1819)
Publisher: Kirk & Mercein (May 1817-April 1818); subsequent pub-
          lisher not named.
Printer: T. & W. Mercein (May-October 1817); D. Fanshaw (Novem-
          ber 1817-April 1818); Benjamin G. Jansen (May 1818-April
          1819)
Illustrations: Occasional small wood-cuts, some the work of A.
          Anderson.

Type: Miscellany - General
Frequency: Monthly.   Volumes: May-October, November-April
Size: 8 1/4 x 5   Length: 80 pp.
Availability: APS reel 58
Indexed: Cargill
Reference: Mott, I, pp. 297-8

Remarks: This magazine included a little of almost everything.
Each issue opened with reviews, and continued with: literary, philosophical, and religious "intelligence"; poetry; drama reviews and
notices and announcements; an annual report of diseases treated at
the New York public dispensary; other medical articles; and to cap
it off, a miscellany.   In July of 1817, mathematical puzzles appeared and were continued throughout each volume.
     The first item reviewed was the third canto of Byron's
Childe Harold's Pilgrimage; and it is interesting to note that the
critical view of Byron was attuned to his personal life, which the
reviewer was quick to attack.
     Interesting items are frequently buried and found in brief
paragraphs.   The Dartmouth College Case's Supreme Court decision
was reported in fewer than fifty words,[1] commendable brevity considering later discussions.
     Contributors included important men of letters and leaders
in many fields, not the least of whom were Samuel L. Mitchell,
James K. Paulding, and De Witt Clinton.   It is rather unusual that
most of them signed the articles, since anonymity was generally the
rule.

Notes: 1.   The American Monthly Magazine, IV (March 1819), 390.

17.   AMERICAN REGISTER

Title: The American Register: or, General Repository of History,
         Politics, and Science
Place: Philadelphia   Dates: No months, 1807-1810
Editor: Robert Walsh (1809-1910)
Publisher: C. and A. Conrad
Printer: A. Small
Type: History
Frequency: Semi-annual   Price: $ 3.25
Size: 8 5/8 x 5 1/8   Length: 500 pp. per vol.
Availability: APS reels 2, 59
Indexed: Cargill
Reference: Lewis, pp. 105-107
Followed, but not superseded by: American Review of History and
         Politics (q.v.).

Remarks: Charles Brockden Brown started this magazine, and he
remained its editor through 1809.   Each volume contained about 500

pages devoted to annals of Europe and America, foreign state papers,
American state papers, a "chronicle" of sixty-odd pages, and several
miscellaneous articles.

Although much verbatim material appeared, Walsh was not
above editorializing. He accused Congress of being "a specimine(!)
of incoherency and incongruity of legislation," and chose his state
papers to suit his own pronationalistic leanings.

This was the first of a series of short-lived papers the purpose of which was to preserve important speeches and other documents. Frequently material in this magazine can be used as a convenient source of contemporary thought and political action.

The poetry and miscellaneous articles lacked originality and
acted as filler material. They were largely eclectic and not, in
1810, what Charles B. Brown would desire as an example of his
work. Robert Walsh's editorial skill improved with his later efforts.

18. AMERICAN REGISTER

Title: American Register; or, Summary Review of History, Poli-
       tics, and Literature
Place: Philadelphia   Dates: February-August 1817
Editor: Robert Walsh
Publisher: Thomas Dobson and Son
Printer: William Fry
Type: Miscellany - General
Frequency: Semi-annual   Price: $6.00
Size: 9 x 5 1/2   Length: 450 pp.
Availability: APS reel 59
Indexed: Cargill

Remarks: This title could easily be called a historical magazine
as are the other publications of Robert Walsh, but it was more
general in nature. Several articles on international affairs open
each issue. These are followed by: speeches, literary essays, reviews of continental literature, articles on finance, and articles
summarizing scientific progress.

Much of the material was gathered from other magazines and
even newspapers. An article "Of Libraries" was extracted from the
European Magazine for March of 1816,[1] and other sources were frequently continental in origin.

A treatment of American literature promised for volume two
never appeared, but Walsh substituted other material which appeared
"to deserve preference." Possibly Walsh could find nothing which
he felt to be worthy.

Notes: 1. American Register, I (February 1817), 319-27.

19. AMERICAN REVIEW OF HISTORY

Title: American Review of History and Politics, and General Re-
       pository of Literature and State Papers
Place: Philadelphia   Dates: January 1811-October 1812
Editor: Robert Walsh
Publisher: Ferrand and Nicholas
Printer: Fry and Krammerer
Type: History
Frequency: Quarterly   Price: $6.00
Size: 9 1/4 x 5 1/4
Length: 200 pp. plus 100 pp. appendix
Availability: APS reel 60
Indexed: Cargill; Poole
Reference: Select Reviews, V (April 1811), 217-24.

Remarks: This title was preceded by but did not supersede The
American Register--a magazine of similar purpose. The chief aims
were "the propogation of sound political doctrines, and the direction
and improvement of the literary taste of the American people."[1]
Plans were made to include a review of European news, Congressional history, domestic policy, European literature, and state documents.
      Much space was devoted to diplomacy, biography, and geo-
graphical articles. Foreign literature was reviewed in nearly every
issue.
      This title was part of an unconnected series of early Ameri-
can magazines the purpose of which was to publish material on
contemporary trends and yet to remain neutral. These early experiments were too eclectic to succeed, and until the techniques of publishing would make this material of great enough value and interest
not one was destined to succeed.

Notes: 1. American Review, I (January 1811), i.

20. AMERICAN WEEKLY MESSENGER

Title: American Weekly Messenger; or, Register of State Papers,
       History, and Politics
Place: Philadelphia   Dates: September 25, 1813-September 17,
        1814
Editor: John Conrad
Publisher: John Conrad
Printer: Dennis Heartt
Type: News
Frequency: Weekly   Price: $5.00
Size: 9 3/4 x 5 3/4   Length: 16 pp.
Quotation: The common and continual mischiefs of the spirit of

party are sufficient to make it the interest and duty of
wise people to discourage and restrain it.
Washington
Availability: Not in APS. Microfilm obtained from the American
Antiquarian Society.

Remarks: Many aspects of a newspaper are present, but "The
sole object (of this magazine) is to seize important political facts
for the purpose of establishing them on permanent record."[1] The
concept of a record of events belongs to the magazine and not the
newspaper.
The issues contained: domestic and political news; domestic
papers and documents; legislative debates; articles on arts, manufactures, agriculture, and commerce; legal information; foreign
news; and miscellaneous articles which included much original material.
An important aspect of the paper was its emphasis on documents relating to the War of 1812. Connected with this material
were the Congressional summaries and reports of important European activities.

Notes: 1. American Weekly Messenger, I (March 19, 1814), 401.

21. ANALECTIC

Title: The Analectic Magazine, Containing Selections from Foreign
Reviews and Magazines and Such Articles as are Most Valu-
able, Curious, or Entertaining (1813-1815); Analectic Maga-
zine and Naval Chronicle (1816-1817); The Analectic Maga-
zine (1817-1821)
Place: Philadelphia   Dates: January 1813-December 29, 1821
Editor: Washington Irving (1813-1815); Thomas Isaac Wharton
(1815-   )
Printer: Moses Thomas (1813-1819). Rogers and Ester printed
many of the plates.
Illustrations: A profusely illustrated magazine, with emphasis on
portraits and scenery.
Type: Miscellany - General
Frequency: Monthly (1813-1820)   Price: Not given
Size: 8 x 5   Length: 86 pp.
Motto: The wheat from these publications should be winnowed.
Availability: APS reels 61, 62, 63
Indexed: Cargill; Poole
Reference: Mott, pp. 279-83
Superseded: Select Reviews of Literature (1809-1812)
Superseded by: Literary Gazette (January-December 1821)

Remarks: The first issue began with "Select Reviews," and this
feature continues as an important part of the magazine. Other sections included: "Spirit of the Magazines," selected poetry, and

publishers' announcements. Later in 1813, original articles were
added. In 1814, science appears as do retrospective reviews of important books. Many reviews of English literature seem to reveal
the feeling that similar American literature did not exist. In September 1815 the introductory essay to "An American Naval Chronicle"
appeared, and the magazine's own title changed in January 1816 to
accommodate this material. By 1817 the general format had changed,
perhaps in imitation of the North American Review.

Illustrations include the first known lithograph to appear in an
American magazine. Designed and executed by Bass Otis, this un-
dated work appeared in July 1819.

Many interesting miscellaneous essays brought to the Analectic
a well-founded publication policy seen in few other magazines of the
period. No subject escaped attention; and many, such as descriptive
natural history, appeared frequently.

Literature was a major emphasis. A quick glance through
the volumes brings many reviews of Byron's works to light, and the
discussions seem to reveal the embryonic power of criticism which,
although on the wane in Philadelphia, was to achieve full flower in
later nineteenth-century Boston as a result of the inspiration and
leadership of the North American Review.

Biography nearly always began an issue. These sketches, reflecting contemporary interests, included reports on naval heroes
written by Washington Irving, or even an inventor when some mechanical device was in the news.

Travel drew attention to new places, and articles about them
offered a chance for nationalistic material in which comparisons
were made with American institutions and ideas.

22. ANALYST

Title: The Analyst; or Mathematical Museum, Containing New Eluci-
        dations, Improvements and Discoveries, in Various Branches
        of the Mathematics, with Selections of Questions Proposed and
        Resolved by Ingenious Correspondents
Place: Philadelphia   Dates: 1808-1814
Editor: Robert Adrian
Publisher: William P. Farrand and Co. (1808-1811)
Printer: Fry and Krammerer (1808-1811)
Printer and Publisher: New Series, I (1814) George Long
Type: Mathematical
Frequency: Quarterly; irregular   Price: $1.00
Size: 8 1/4 x 4 3/4   Length: 48 pp.
Motto: Utile dulci.
Availability: APS reel 64
Reference: Lewis, p. 111

Remarks: The promise of the title was not fulfilled since this is a
largely ephemeral and rather irregular publication. The pages contained problems and trick questions, but Louis Karpinski calls one

article on probability of error in observations "the most important
mathematical article in America before 1850."[1]
   Although mathematical problems had appeared in many magazines before, this was probably the first American publication devoted wholly to the subject.   This one-man production with five regular issues is not of first importance.

Notes: 1.   Louis Charles Karpinski, Bibliography of Mathematical
         Works Printed in America Through 1850.   (Ann Arbor: Uni-
         versity of Michigan Press, 1940), p. 581.

23.   ARCHIVES OF USEFUL KNOWLEDGE

Title: Archives of Useful Knowledge, A Work Devoted to Commerce,
         Manufactures, Rural and Domestic Economy, Agriculture and
         the Useful Arts
Place: Philadelphia   Dates: July 1810-April 1813
Editor: James Mease
Publisher: David Hogan
Printer: Thomas T. Stiles
Illustrations: Nearly a dozen engravings of a scientific nature ap-
         peared.   Most are unsigned, and no portraits are included.
Type: Miscellany - General
Frequency: Quarterly   Price: Not given
Size: 8 x 5   Length: 124 pp.
Availability: APS reel 65

Remarks: Calling this magazine a general miscellany is a slight
misnomer since no literature appeared; however the scope of the
contents is wide enough to have appealed to a variety of interests.
   Perhaps a modern parallel would be Popular Science.
Grafting trees appears along with an article advocating glass manufacturing as an American industry.   In this sense, Archives may be
taken as a magazine of nationlistic leanings since it frequently advocated an independence from abroad in the areas of manufacturing
and economy.
   The printing quality is average for the period and the solid,
unrelieved, block page also typical.   The quality of the articles is
not particularly high, and the writing style is a little too stilted in
its ornate syntax.
   No complaints were made about subscription nonpayment, but
the magazine died in less than two years.   Presumably the lack of
material--original or otherwise--simply prevented gathering a sufficient number of articles to make publishing worthwhile.

24.   ATHENEUM

Title: Atheneum

Place: New Haven, Conn.   Dates: February 12-August 6, 1814
Editor: Members of the Senior Class (1814) of Yale
Printer: Oliver Steele
Type: College publication
Frequency: Bi-weekly   Price: $1.00
Size: 8 1/4 x 5   Length: 8 pp.
Availability: APS reel 65; copy consulted at Trinity College, Hart-
        ford, Conn. Listed in ULS as Athenaeum.

Remarks: Those responsible for the magazine may have been: W.
B. Calhoun, D. Lord, G. E. Spruill, W. L. Storrs, and L. Withing-
ton. A note in the Trinity College copy says that Spruill wrote its
prospectus, but this was not found. A notice of publication refers
to the Atheneum as a literary paper and says it was intended to improve the students' writing.
        The lead of each issue was "The Vagrant," and other cynical
articles appear such as "Miseries of a College Life." Conditions
haven't changed much in 150 years. Other articles emphasize serious literary criticism and book reviews, and original poetry ends
each issue.
        Despite a brief eight pages, the printing, content and format
maintain high quality. College publications had been issued before
this one, and the Atheneum demonstrated again that able men with
good ideas could produce interesting and valuable magazines.

25. ATHENEUM

Title: The Atheneum; or, Spirit of the English Magazines
        Issue title: Spirit of the English Magazines
Place: Boston   Dates: April 1, 1817-March 1832
Editor: Not given
Publisher: Munroe and Francis
Illustrations: Three architectural frontispieces
Type: Miscellany - General
Frequency: Semi-monthly
Price: $2.50 (1817); $5.00 (1818-   )
Size: 8 1/4 x 5   Length: 40 pp.
Availability: APS reel 66
Indexed: Cargill

Remarks: The editor, who may have been either Edmund Munroe
or David Francis, felt that English magazines contained much of
interest to Americans and much which would be of little value. By
careful selection a magazine consisting entirely of English material
should have an attraction for a United States audience. Since this
magazine lasted fifteen years, it must have been a sound idea.
        The contents ranged far and wide. Biography; short stories;
letters; news and miscellaneous pieces on literature, the arts, and
science; drama notices; material about literary and philosophical societies; and any number of miscellany and curiosa fill the pages.

This was a true eclectic miscellany, and certainly helped to establish the tradition of a type of magazine which still flourishes.

26. BALANCE

Title: The Balance, and Columbian Repository (1802-1807); The Balance (1808); The Balance, and New York State Journal (1807-1810); The Balance and State Journal (January 1-December 24, 1811)
Place: Albany   Dates: January 5, 1802-December 24, 1811
Editor: Henry Croswell (?)
Publisher: Henry Croswell and Jonathan Frary (through June 1810); Croswell alone (July 3, 1810-December 24, 1811)
Illustrations: Only a few small wood-cut decorations appeared as column headings and in a few advertisements. These seem to have come from stock and were frequently repeated.
Type: Literary newspaper
Frequency: Bi-weekly (1810); weekly (1811)
Price: $3.00 (1810); $4.00 (1811)
Size: Varies, but usually large quarto.
Length: 4 pp. (1810); 8 pp. (1811)
Masthead: Hand holding a weight balance which encloses the amersand in the title.
Availability: APS reel 70
Reference: Lewis, pp. 114-5

Remarks: Prior to 1810, The Balance appeared in Hudson, New York. The move was made to Albany on the chance of larger circulation, and it had all the marks of a newspaper since it was published in four pages of five columns.
    In 1811 four pages were added, and original essays made a large part of the paper. Political and religious news; agricultural, legal, and literary information; and miscellaneous short articles and poetry were all added in greater numbers. A real attempt was made to appeal to both audiences, or to create an audience for a paper with both aspects--a magazine with local news. Albany had at least two regular newspapers in publication at the time,[1] and perhaps the stage was not right for a literary magazine. The Balance disappeared with a mass of debts at the end of 1811.

Notes: 1. These were the Albany Gazette and the Albany Register. Details are given by Brigham.

27. BALTIMORE MEDICAL AND PHILOSOPHICAL LYCAEUM

Title: Baltimore Medical and Philosophical Lycaeum
Place: Baltimore

Dates: January/March-October/December 1811
Editor: Nathaniel Potter
Publisher: George Hill
Printer: B. Edes
Illustrations: The copy in the APS has only two plates, both placed
          as frontispieces.   Other plates may have been issued.
Type: Medical
Frequency: Quarterly   Price: $2.00
Size: 8 1/4 x 5   Length: 100 pp.
Availability: APS reel 71

Remarks: The prospectus said: "As it is highly problematical
whether the subscription will ever be sufficient to encounter the ex-
pense, any effort can be considered only as an experiment."[1]   Potter
was right--his magazine lasted only four issues.
        One purpose was to describe and evaluate dissections in an
attempt to solve the problem of disease and to investigate the reasons for death.   Regrets were expressed that dissections were difficult in the South because specimens could not be preserved.
        The lead article concerned scrofula--the identification, treat-
ment, prevention, possible cure, and residual effects.   Humphrey
Davy's experiments in electrochemistry were dutifully reported--as
they were in nearly every other American magazine which was even
vaguely scientific.   The only illustration in the file examined was of
Davy's apparatus.
        Most of the articles were from other sources, and the re-
views were mediocre.   Baltimore was not yet ready for a medical
magazine, and lack of support killed another potentially good magazine.

Notes: 1.   Baltimore Medical and Philosophical Lycaeum, I (January/
        March 1811), 1.

28.   BALTIMORE REPERTORY OF PAPERS

Title: Baltimore Repertory of Papers on Literary and Other Topics,
        Including a Selection of English Plays
Place: Baltimore   Dates: January-June 1811
Editor: A Society of Gentlemen
Printer and Publisher: Joseph Robinson
Type: Miscellany - Literary
Frequency: Monthly   Price: Not given
Size: 8 x 4 3/4   Length: 60 pp.
Availability: APS reel 71

Remarks: Short fiction, miscellaneous essays, reviews, and poetry
form the bulk of this title.   Summaries of activity in Congress and
the Maryland legislature also appear.   Also carried was a literary
column called "The Vigil" which contained biography and literary
criticism.   Four English plays were bound as a supplement.

One interesting feature was "Antiquarian Bibliography; or, Accounts of Old and Scarce Books"[1] in which three seventeenth-century books were given critical attention. This series added to the one which had already appeared in the <u>Monthly Anthology</u> and it forecast William Tudor's series to appear in the <u>North American Review</u>.

In an early issue, the editor regretted the past and accurately predicted his own future by saying:

> In the city of Baltimore so many abortive attempts have been made to establish a literary miscellany, that Experiment and Disappointment have become synonymous terms.[2]

Three earlier magazines which failed, one which never even appeared, and <u>Emerald</u> are cited as examples of the inability of Baltimore literaries to live. But at least the attempts were made, and sooner or later someone would make the grade.

Notes: 1. <u>Baltimore Repertory of Papers</u>, I (January-June 1811), 68, 226, 325.
       2. <u>Ibid.</u>, I (January 1811), p. 5.

29. BALTIMORE WEEKLY MAGAZINE

Title: Baltimore Weekly Magazine, and Ladies Miscellany
Place: Baltimore   Dates: May 2-October 24, 1818
Editor and Publisher: Alvan Munroe
Type: Woman's magazine
Frequency: Weekly   Price: $3.00
Size: ca. 8 x 5   Length: 4 pp.
Availability: Not in APS or ULS. Microfilm obtained from the Maryland Historical Society.

Remarks: Only one volume of twenty-six weekly issues of this magazine seem to have appeared, and only the last sixteen of these were available. Alvan Munroe's subscriber list was probably quite small, and circulation may have been limited to the city of Baltimore.

The average issue contained short fiction, several essays, poetry, marriage and death notices, short news summaries, and a few anecdotes. One essay, "Thoughts on Marriage. Addressed to a Young Lady," hinted that Munroe had women's features in mind. His series called "Corsets" included ideas on a wide range of topics, and certainly never mentioned underwear. Articles on London and American fashions, a few religious essays, and an assortment of news presumably interesting to women appeared.

No central theme or idea runs throughout the issues. The format varied, apparently not to create interest but from a lack of material. The factor which differentiates this magazine is that it was one of a growing group aimed exclusively toward women.

30. BEACON

Title: The Beacon, Erected and Supported by Lucidantus and his
        Thirteen Friends
Place: Philadelphia   Dates: November 27-December 11, 1811
Editor: Lucidantus, pseud.
Publisher: W. Brown
Illustrations: Title page is engraved; there are no plates.
Type: Humor
Frequency: Bi-weekly   Price: Not given
Size: 7 1/2 x 4 1/4   Length: 10 pp.
Availability: Not in APS or ULS. Microfilm obtained from The
        Historical Society of Pennsylvania.
References: Smyth, p. 184
            Seilhamer, p. 274

Remarks: Only two numbers of this title have been discovered.
The identity of Lucidantus remains unknown, as do the real names
of his thirteen friends. The publisher, W. Brown, may have been
responsible for editing The Beacon. The pattern of having the same
man as editor and publisher was common in early magazines.

    Whoever the editor may have been, he wrote "we propose to
develop to our readers the machinery and composition of our Philadelphia Society."[1] In the two numbers issued most space was devoted to establishing this purpose by use of Johnson's definition of
a beacon, and to describing the editor's position as a retired man
in Philadelphia.

    The Society divided, he said, "... into male and female.
Under the former I shall consider, 1. Merchants, 2. Physicians,
3. Lawyers, and 4. Idlers"[2] It is a pity he did not define "female"
and did not continue his examination of Philadelphia Society. The
basis of some excellent satire was laid but nothing else appeared.

Notes: 1. The Beacon, no. 2 (December 11, 1811), 11.
        2. Ibid., p. 14.

31. BEAU

Title: The Beau; or, The Polite Intelligencer
Place: New York   Dates: July 27, 1814 / / ?
Editor: Will Watchful, Esq., pseudonym of John Mein
Publisher: John Mein
Type: Miscellaneous - Humor
Frequency: Only one known issue   Price: Not given
Size: 6 x 3 3/4   Length: 10 pp.
Quotation: Sweet Cupid, and ye graces three,
                    attend our court;
            Ye Nine, with finest melody
                to us resort.

Availability: Not in APS. Microfilm obtained from The Library
          Company of Philadelphia.

Remarks: Only one issue of this title was located, but it is both
numbered and dated, and there may have been an intention to continue.
          The magazine was to entertain the ladies with a series of
"breezy and bubbly" essays. This may have been only a hope of
John Mein's when he issued what easily could be considered a pamphlet. Many publications of this nature appeared in this decade,
and most seem to have been what in more modern times would be
called "vanity" publications.
          The introductory essay--the entire contents of the one issue--
roundly attacked New York's Moralist as a waste of time, and called
R. H. Carroll a traitor. The editor promised to expose foolishness
and immorality and to have his "Robin Goodfellow" attend and report
on meetings of the Tammany and Washington Benevolent Societies.
He also hoped to advocate moderation in style and fashion in dress.

32. BEREAN

Title: The Berean; or, An Appeal to the Scriptures on Questions
          of Utmost Importance to the Human Race (no. 1); The Berean,
          or Scripture Searcher (nos. 2-6)
Place: Boston   Dates: April 1802-1810
Editor: The Berean Society
Printer: v. 1, Munroe and Francis; v. 2, S. G. Snelling
Type: Religious - Universalist
Frequency: Irregular   Price: Not given
Size: 8 3/8 x 4 7/8   Length: 40-48 pp.
Availability: APS reels 6, 72
Reference: Lewis, p. 124

Remarks: This title can be questioned as a magazine since it was
not a regular, numbered series. Only one issue appeared in 1810,
and its entire contents were devoted to an attack on Jacob Norton,
Pastor of the First Church in Weymouth, Massachusetts.
          On December 18, 1808, Norton preached "The Will of God
Respecting the Salvation of All Men ... " The Berean Society answered Norton in a tract which Norton in turn answered from the
pulpit. This 1810 issue of The Berean is an answer to Norton's
answer. How long this bickering actually continued is not known,
although another issue was promised. Apparently this seventh number never appeared.
          The type style is old-fashioned; the page is cramped; and
this semi-magazine, pamphlet series is of secondary importance.
Several magazines issued by Universalists appeared later in the
decade 1810-1820, and all of them were of more value as expressions of the Universalist view-point.

33. BOSTON KALEIDOSCOPE

Title: The Kaleidoscope (November 28, 1818-January 9, 1819);
        Boston Kaleidoscope and Literary Rambler (January 16?-
        November 27? 1819)
Place: Boston
Dates: November 28, 1818-November 27? 1819
Editor: Nathaniel H. Wright (through May 8, 1819). No name given
        after this date.
Publisher: Abraham Hews and Sylvester T. Goss (November 28,
        1818-July 10, 1819); Sylvester T. Goss (July 17-November
        27? 1819)
Type: Miscellany - Literary
Frequency: Weekly   Price: $2.00
Size: ca. 10 x 6   Length: 4 pp.
Availability: Not in APS. Microfilm obtained from the American
        Antiquarian Society.
Reference: Brigham, p. 314
Absorbed: The Idiot on January 9, 1819
Superseded by: The Ladies Port Folio (?)

Remarks: The arrangement, scope, and format of this title were
those of a newspaper. The large size and three columns to a page
made it seem like the average four-page, quarto news sheet; but its
contents were those of a magazine.
    Serialized fiction, brief miscellaneous essays, and poetry
were the backbone; brief news summaries, and marriage and death
notices were added on the back pages as filler and to attract those
interested in these events.
    On January 9, 1819, The Kaleidoscope absorbed The Idiot,
changed its name, and attempted to become a humor magazine.
Women's features were added, but neither became dominant. Sylvester Goss proposed a new magazine, The Ladies' Port Folio, in
the issue of November 6, 1819. The first issue of this title appeared on January 1, 1820 and it may have been designed to supersede the Boston Kaleidoscope.

34. BOSTON MIRROR

Title: The Boston Mirror
Place: Boston   Dates: October 22, 1808-July 21, 1810
Editor: "A Gentleman of Education and Talents"
Publisher: Edward Oliver
Type: Literary newspaper
Frequency: Weekly   Price: $3.00
Size: 17 1/2 x 11   Length: 8 pp.
Availability: Not in APS. Microfilm obtained from the American
        Antiquarian Society.
Reference: Lewis, p. 128

Superseded: Times

Remarks: A connection also exists with The Emerald, a Boston
magazine of the decade 1800-1810.[1]   "Essays, poetry, biography,
tales, anecdotes, and some advertising"[2] were the major contents.
The miscellaneous humor, news briefs, theatrical announcements,
and speeches added to the general appearance of a newspaper.

> ... we shall endeavor to hold up a faithful mirror, which
> shall reflect the "manners living as they rise," to pre-
> sent to our readers the most important news of the day,
> and to comment as much on public men and measures as
> is consistent with a paper intended to be literary, rather
> than political.[3]

At its demise, the editor referred readers to the Harvard
Lyceum as a magazine which would offset the loss of The Boston
Mirror.

Notes: 1.   Lewis, op. cit., p. 128.
         2.   Ibid.
         3.   The Boston Mirror, I (October 22, 1808), 1.

35.   BOSTON SPECTATOR

Title: The Boston Spectator; Devoted to Politicks and Belles-Lettres
Place: Boston   Dates: January 1, 1814-February 28, 1815
Editor: John Park
Printer: Munroe, Francis and Parker
Type: Literary newspaper
Frequency: Weekly   Price: $3.00
Size: 12 x 8 3/4   Length: 4 pp.
Availability: APS reel 74
Reference: Brigham, p. 346

Remarks: The general index lists large categories of articles such
as: political, literary, miscellaneous, and poetry.   One other type
should have been added.   News articles, for example, are a large
share of each issue.   These generally take the form of summaries
as does most news at the time.
       The War of 1812 was treated with indifference.   A few
factual articles, and eventually the Treaty of Ghent appear, but
this is not a strong repository of source material.   And even in
Federalist, anti-war, Anglophile Boston it is surprising, in February 1814, to read of the "Close of Lord Nelson's Glorious Life."
       The literary aspects of The Boston Spectator were varied.
Serialized fiction, essays almost as varied as they were numerous,
and poetry are the bulk.   But the material was not first-rate, and
the printing quality was not as good as it could have been in Boston.

Money did not come in to pay the printer, and the paper ceased after
sixty-one issues.

36. BOSTON WEEKLY MAGAZINE

Title: Boston Weekly Magazine (October 12, 1816-October 4, 1817);
        Weekly Magazine and Ladies Miscellany (October 11-December
        27, 1817); Semi-Weekly Magazine and Mercantile Advertiser
        (January 3, 1818); Boston Weekly Magazine and Ladies' Mis-
        cellany (January 10-April 4, 1818); Weekly Magazine and
        Ladies' Miscellany (May 16-November 7, 1818); Boston Weekly
        Magazine and Ladies Miscellany (November 14, 1818-May 8,
        1819; March 20-December 25, 1824)
Title pages: All have: The Boston Weekly Magazine - Devoted to
        Polite Literature, Useful Science, Biography, and Dramatic
        and General Criticism. Sub-titles varies slightly.
Running title: Boston Weekly Magazine (October 12, 1816-April 4,
        1818) except: Semi-Weekly Magazine (January 3, 1818);
        Weekly Magazine (May 16, 1818-   )
Editor: Ezra B. Tileston and James Parmenter
Publisher: Parmenter and Norton (October 12, 1816-April 4, 1818);
        Henry Bowen (May 16, 1818-   )
Type: Miscellany - General
Frequency: Weekly   Price: $2.50
Size: 12 1/2 x 9 3/4   Length: 4 pp.
Motto: Born to No Master-Of No Sect are We.
Masthead: Cut of woman seated in bower surrounded by symbols of
        the arts. Engraved by Howen. Used on title pages of vols.
        2 and 3, also October 11-December 27, 1817; May 16-Novem-
        ber 7, 1818 in period when title was Weekly Magazine.
Availability: APS reel 74

Remarks: A brief break from April 4 to May 16, 1818 was the
only publishing hiatus until May 1819; and this break probably was
allowed to effect the transfer of ownership.
        The contents generally included "polite" literature, natural
or scientific developments, biography, agricultural articles, drama
listings and criticism, and news summaries. At irregular intervals law cases were reported, and several novels were serialized.
The drama department generally limited coverage to Boston, and
the performances were frequently reviewed with some care and evident theatrical knowledge.
        The exact format tended to vary from time to time, and the
material also changed. Despite the intention to attract women,
little of direct interest to them, except literature, was included.
But the magazine was one of wide general appeal and helped to establish the norms of coverage used by later popular miscellanies.

37. BUREAU

Title: The Bureau; or, Repository of Literature, Politics, and In-
    telligence
Place: Philadelphia   Dates: March 28-November 14, 1812
Editor: S. C. Carpenter
Printer: Dennis Heartt
Type: Literary newspaper
Frequency: Weekly   Price: $5.00
Size: 12 x 9   Length: 8 pp.
Availability: Not in APS or ULS. Microfilm obtained from The
    Library Company of Philadelphia.
Reference: "Proposals, " Philadelphia Repertory, II (May 2, 1812),
    400.
Superseded: Philadelphia Reportory

Remarks: The proposal for The Bureau claimed it as "a work
which is to be published in successive parts, " and hoped it would
unite a review, a magazine, and a newspaper. The object was to
present information on serious topics, something for the mass of
the readers, and some aspects of important daily news. Added to
all of this, a Congressional Register, speeches, political articles,
and a chronology were all planned.
    The "review" section of The Bureau included articles such as
a "History of British Poetry, "[1] which was continued throughout
several issues. Some attention was paid to the theatre; and after
June, to the War of 1812.
    The pattern was fairly consistent throughout all thirty-four
numbers; an essay or two, some serialized fiction, a poetry page,
political news, and brief news items often of the unusual rather than
the day-to-day.
    No mention of discontinuance appeared in the known issues,
but it may be assumed that the magazine's death resulted from lack
of support.

Notes: 1. The Bureau, I (April 18, 1812), 26-7.

38. CABINET

Title: The Cabinet; A Repository of Polite Literature
Place: Boston   Dates: January 5-March 23, 1811
Editor, Publisher, Printer: Not given
Illustrations: One plate of George Frederick Cooke is included in
    the first issue.
Type: Miscellany - Literary
Frequency: Weekly   Price: $2.00 per vol., $4.00 per year
Size: 9 x 5 1/4   Length: 16 pp.
Availability: APS reel 75
Indexed: Cargill

Remarks: Only ten numbers appeared of The Cabinet. The film copy available for this study does not indicate the editor, printer, or publisher; and no clues seem to exist in the contents which will reveal their identity.

The first number set the pattern for the following issues. Included were biographical and critical material about George Frederick Cooke, one of the more popular actors of his day. Cooke's portrait is the only illustration in the series. Other items were a brief anecdotal story about Peter the Great, and a number of miscellaneous articles, some on the Boston theatre.

Short fiction and poetry rounded out each issue, and Cargill thought highly enough of this material to include the title in his Index to Early American Magazines.

Although no definite reasons for the cessation of this magazine were given, lack of support and material probably contributed their usual burden.

39. CAROLINA LAW REPOSITORY

Title: The Carolina Law Repository, Containing Biographical Sketches of Eminent Judges; Opinions of American and Foreign Jurists, and Reports of Cases Adjudged in the Supreme Court of North-Carolina

Place: Raleigh, N.C.   Dates: March 1813-September 1816
Editor: Not given
Printer: Joseph Gales
Type: Law
Frequency: Semi-annual   Price: Not given
Size: 8 3/4 x 5 1/4   Length: 140 pp.
Availability: APS reel 75

Remarks: The tpyical issue contained a biography, half a dozen law opinions, and about twenty adjudged cases. Added space was granted to articles and "extracts" dealing with politics and law.

Increased legal activity produced a natural audience for law journals since cases were being decided on constitutional as well as common law grounds, and lawyers needed help in keeping track of decisions. In 1813 and 1814, cases of treason, marital law, and similar war-time topics were reported. Many cases involving Negro slaves were extracted, and these decisions may have provided arguments and precedents to those who wished to continue slavery. Other property cases and decisions on wills are quite frequent subjects. Most cases adjudged in the U.S. Supreme Court from 1811 to 1816 are also reported.

That such a magazine could be produced in a state apart from the main cultural centers, and that it lasted for over three years indicates a growing need for the specialized magazine.

40. CASKET

Title: The Casket
Place: Hudson, N.Y.   Dates: December 7, 1811-May 30, 1812
Editor: Charles Candid
Printer and Publisher: Caleb N. Bement
Illustrations: One plate of a romantic and moralistic scene recommending knowledge and learning to youth.
Type: Humor
Frequency: Weekly   Price: $1.00
Size: 7 3/4 x 4 1/2   Length: 12 pp.
Masthead: Title is divided by a round, woven basket filled with flowers.
Motto: With sweetest flowers enrich'd
       From various gardens cull'd with care.[1]
Availability: APS reel 75
Superseded by: The Lounger (A27). No copy found.

Remarks: The motto chosen for The Casket is the same as that used by The Ladies' Weekly Museum, although this may have been merely coincidence.
       The editor announced he was aware of possible hard times, but continued: "Let every tub stand upon its own bottom ... my business is to print and publish every Saturday a pamphlet of twelve pages--the business of the men, women, boys, and girls is to subscribe for this paper and to read it carefully when published."[2]
       That was rather outspoken in its bluntness. So also was the satire of the "Apollonian Wreath," a series appearing in most numbers. Eventually, the editor, probably Bement, announced with his usual candor that support was not sufficient; and The Casket disappeared.

Notes: 1. This motto was also used by The Ladies Weekly Museum.
       2. The Casket, no. 1 (December 7, 1811), 1.

41. CASTIGATOR

Title: The Castigator
Place: Lexington, Ky.   Dates: November 19? 1818-
Editor: Not given
Publisher: Xenophon J. Gaines
Type: Literary newspaper
Frequency: Weekly?   Price: $2.00
Size: 11 x 8 1/2   Length: 4 pp.
Motto: Castigatio sine ira.
Availability: Not in APS or ULS. Photocopy obtained from the Lexington (Kentucky) Public Library.
Reference: Brigham, p. 162.

Remarks: April 14, July 24, 1819, and January 22, 1820 are the dates of the only three issues of this title located in any American library. These issues are battered and incomplete, and lack the information necessary to identify the editor and printer.

Despite the three-column appearance of a newspaper, this item should be considered a magazine since its main contents seem to have been essays, letters, and commentaries. Many of these deal with contemporary affairs, especially politics, and with the currently held ideas on banking, both nationally and in Kentucky. Some local interest prevails as in one article which sharply criticizes the paintings in the Representatives Chamber in Frankfort, Kentucky.

42. CHRISTIAN CHRONICLE

Title: Christian Chronicle
Place: Bennington, Vt.   Dates: February 7-December 26, 1818
Editor: Not given
Publisher: Anthony T. Haswell
Printer: Darius Clark
Type: Religious - Non-denominational
Frequency: Bi-weekly   Price: $1.50
Size: 8 x 4 1/2   Length: 16 pp.
Availability: APS reel 77

Remarks: The denominational influence of this title is difficult to determine, especially since the articles deal with many religious groups in Vermont. Nearly all the activity reported deals with this state, and the issues contain information valuable to early religious history in Bennington and other Vermont communities.

Topics include: Bible societies, religious revival, missionary activity, religious readings, commentaries on scripture, and poetry. Much of this material was borrowed, not always with credit given, and many articles appear to have been shortened to fit the magazine's pages.

One article, "A concise descant, upon the Majesty, Excellence, and Preciousness of the Scriptures"[1] sets the tone of the magazine and could serve as the theme of all its pages.

Notes: 1. Christian Chronicle, I (April 25, 1818), 81-3.

43. CHRISTIAN DISCIPLE

Title: The Christian Disciple (1813-1818); The Christian Disciple and Theological Review (1819-1823)
Place: Boston   Dates: May 1813-November/December 1823
Editor: Noah Worcester (1813-1818); Henry Ware, Jr. (1819-1823)

Publisher: Cummings and Hilliard (1813-1815); Wells and Lilly
‾‾‾‾‾‾‾‾‾ (1816); Joseph T. Buckingham (1817-1818); Wells and Lilly
(1819-   )
Printer: Hilliard and Metcalf (1813-1815); same as publisher?
‾‾‾‾‾‾ (1816-   )
Type: Religious - Unitarian
Frequency: Monthly (1813-1818); bi-monthly (1819-1823)
Price: $1.75
Size: 8 1/4 x 4 3/4
Length: 32 pp. (1813-1818); 88 pp. (1819-   )
Motto: Speaking the Truth in Love.
Availability: APS 77, 78
Indexed: Poole
Reference: Mott; I, pp. 284-92
Continued as: The Christian Examiner and Theological Review

Remarks: This magazine has some of the good qualities of other
magazines from the Boston-Cambridge complex. The printing was
excellent, and the editorial ability of its founders enabled it to continue after 1823 under a different title.
    Essays on or explications of scripture or doctrinal teaching
contained suggestions for living or maintaining a pious life. Some
poetry, most of it borrowed, filled in the last part of the issues.
Most of the news was of ordinations, deaths, Bible societies, conversions, and missionary activity.
    The magazine was established by Unitarians--including Chan-
ning, Lowell, and Parkman--so that Noah Worcester would have a
vehicle from which to advocate peace and his opposition to the War
of 1812. Worcester's Friend of Peace carries on these ideas.
    In 1819, when the editorship changed, reviews were added;
and these, along with the social, philosophical, and educational commentaries, give the magazine retrospective value.

44. CHRISTIAN HERALD

Title: The Christian Herald (March 30, 1816-April 2, 1821); The
‾‾‾‾ Christian Herald and Seaman's Magazine (April 16, 1821-
December 18, 1824)
Place: New York   Dates: March 30, 1816-December 18, 1824
Editor: John Edwards Caldwell (through March 1819)
Publisher: John E. Caldwell (March 30, 1816-March 21, 1818);
‾‾‾‾‾‾‾ W. B. Gilley (April 4, 1818-March 6, 1819); John Gray
(April 17, 1819-   )
Printer: J. Seymour (March 30, 1816-March 21, 1818); J. Gray
‾‾‾‾‾‾ & Co. (April 17, 1819-   )
Type: Religious - Presbyterian (?)
Frequency: Weekly (thru April 1818); bi-weekly (May 1818-   )
Price: $4.00
Size: 8 x 5   Length: 16 pp.; 32 pp. (1818)
Availability: APS reels 493, 494

Remarks: In 1821 the magazine was published "under the patronage"
of the Port of New York Society for Promoting the Gospel Among
Seamen. Previously the magazine did not have this purpose, although
it was designed to aid in the spread of Christianity.
     Material on Sunday schools, missionary activity, and Bible
societies form a major part of the essays. A juvenile department
presented news of religious activities and publications which were
designed for young people.
     The periodicity and price were changed in April 1818; and a
notice in the magazine says the editor died on March 9, 1819. No
new editor's name appears. A change in the quality of the magazine
makes it more loosely organized, added poetry and biography, but
makes no marked change in the literary content. The new audience
found for the magazine kept it alive for a few years.

45. CHRISTIAN HERALD

Title: The Christian Herald; Containing Subjects Historical, Experi-
     mental, Biographical, Miscellaneous and Poetical
Place: Portsmouth, N.H.   Dates: May 1818-March? 1835
Editor: Robert Foster
Printer: At the Gazette office. Gideon Beck and Daniel C. Foster
Type: Religious - Christian Church
Frequency: Bi-monthly   Price: Not given
Size: 9 3/4 x 5 3/4   Length: 24 pp.
Availability: APS reel 79 (through 1819)
Superseded: Herald of Gospel Liberty (1810-1817)
Superseded by: Christian Journal

History: The Herald of Gospel Liberty (q.v.) ceased publication in
1817. In May 1818 Robert Foster, using the same facilities and
with the same editorial ideas started a new magazine called The
Christian Herald which lasted until 1835 when the paper was purchased by the Eastern Christian Publishing Association which began
to publish Christian Journal edited by Elijah Shaw. In 1839 this
became Christian Herald and Journal. Numerous other changes were
made in name, ownership, and publisher until March 13, 1851, when
the old name Herald of Gospel Liberty was adopted. This second
Herald united with the Congregationlist in 1930 to become Congregationlist and Herald of Gospel Liberty (q.v.). This latter title bore
no direct relationship to the first Herald of Gospel Liberty.
     This history is outlined by John Barrett[1] and his evidence
shows the real bibliographical relationship. Neither the Herald of
Gospel Liberty nor The Christian Herald had long lives.

Remarks: Poetry, news of religious and church-related nature, and
many types of religious activity formulate the basis of this paper.
The editor felt the times were such that another religious journal
was needed to give the people a new direction and purpose.
     Although nominally an organ of the Christian Church, this
paper is editorially non-sectarian. Equal weight is given to all

religious news. The paper had a twenty-four page, two-column magazine format and was interesting enough to achieve a fairly wide New Hampshire audience.

Notes: 1. John Pressley Barrett, The Centennial of Religious
Journalism, 2d ed. (Dayton, Ohio: Christian Publishing Association, 1908), pp. 37-75.

46. CHRISTIAN JOURNAL

Title: The Christian Journal, and Literary Register
Place: New York   Dates: January 22, 1817-December 1830
Editor: John Henry Hobart and Benjamin T. Onderdonk (1817-1819);
        T. & J. Swords (1819-1830)
Publisher: T. & J. Swords (1817-1830)
Illustrations: Volume one title-page vignette of St. John's Church,
        Canandaigua, New York
Type: Religious - Episcopal
Frequency: Bi-weekly (1817-1818); monthly (1818)
Price: $1.00
Size: 8 1/2 x 5   Length: 1817-18, 16 pp.; 1819, 32 pp.
Availability: APS reel 80
Indexed: Cargill

Remarks: This was the fourth Episcopal magazine to exist sometime between 1810 and 1820. While no more successful than the
others, it was similar in scope and content as well as in a generally high quality of material.
        The scope and content of most religious magazines was the
same, and this was no exception. Miscellaneous theological and
religious essays are the backbone, and they are supported by biography, obituaries, poetry, and explication of scripture.
        The issues were shorter than many religious magazines.
They may have been used in Sunday schools, and certainly the magazine experienced financial problems since it first became a monthly,
and then ceased when support could not be raised.

47. CHRISTIAN MESSENGER

Title: The Christian Messenger
Place: Baltimore, Md.   Dates: May 10, 1817-May 1, 1819
Editor and Publisher: Joshua T. Russell
Printer: Pomeroy and Toy (May 10-August 16, 1817); John D. Toy
        (August 23, 1817-May 1, 1819)
Type: Religious - Presbyterian
Frequency: Weekly   Price: $4.00
Size: ca. 8 x 5   Length: 16 pp.

Motto: God forbid that I should glory, save in the cross of our
         Lord Jesus Christ.
Availability: APS reel 82
Superseded by: The Christian Traveller (A38)

Remarks: The first issue announced the publication as one which
would be available to any Christian denomination, and indeed material of interest to many sects appeared. The magazine is called
Presbyterian because Albaugh's bibliography includes the title and
because much of the theological material advocated this view-point.
     The magazine was originally announced by the firm of Allen
and Edes; but no connection was found in the actual issues. Pomeroy and Toy were able to introduce some variety--especially by
changing the order of the contents from issue to issue. The material is standard, however, including: biography; articles on Bible,
missionary, and other societies; explications of scripture, and
poetry. One topic which raised the magazine above the ordinary
was African colonization for Negroes which Russell advocated at
length and at times with some heat.

48. CHRISTIAN MESSENGER

Title: The Christian Messenger, Being a Miscellaneous Work;
         Directed to the Improvement of the Human Mind.   In Prose
         and Verse
Place: Pittsford, N.Y.   Dates: November 1815-March 1816
Editor and Printer: Luscomb Knap
Type: Religious
Frequency: Monthly   Price: Not given
Size: 7 1/2 x 4 1/2   Length: 24 pp.
Quotation: As various are the tastes of men,
             As natures golden stores;
             Let then each Philosophic pen,
             Extract from every pore.
Availability: APS reel 82

Remarks: To which denomination this title belonged is not known,
and many of the articles could easily be used as Sunday school
tracts.
     The tract or pamphlet may even be a better designation for
this title. The first three issues are paged separately, and number
four begins with page seventy-three. Knap himself used the word
"pamphlet."
     A list of agents in the first issue included towns in New
York, Connecticut, and Vermont. Circulation may have been limited
to these places. When Knap moved from Pittsford, he promised to
continue the work, but nothing was forthcoming.
     The contents are entirely moralistic and polemic articles.
The only really lengthy one is a serialized essay discussing the

Book of Revelation.   The printing was poor, and only five issues
appeared.

49.   CHRISTIAN MESSENGER

Title: The Christian Messenger, Devoted to Doctrine, Religion and
         Morality
Place: Philadelphia   Dates: August 7, 1819-July 21, 1821
Editor: Jonathan Gardner (August 7-September 4, 1819); Adam
          Waldie (September 11-October 30, 1819); Abner Kneeland
          (November 6, 1819-July 21, 1821)
Printer: Adam Waldie (September 11, 1819-   )
Type: Religious - Non-denominational
Frequency: Weekly   Price: Not given
Size: 10 1/2 x 7 1/2   Length: 4 pp.
Availability: APS reel 82

Remarks: Adam Waldie started printing the Quarterly Theological
Review, another Philadelphia magazine, in January 1819, and this
may have inspired him to help found and print another magazine.
This earlier magazine was edited by a Presbyterian, and the men
who served as editors of The Christian Messenger were also of this
persuasion.
        The earlier magazine was a scholarly book review which
tended to be neutral in its doctrinal pronouncements.   The Christian
Messenger, while claiming to be non-denominational, had a Presbyterian slant, and it was for popular consumption.   Extracts from
books and magazines were accompanied by letters and answers to
questions which readers supposedly sent to the editor.
        The printing of this magazine was only fair, and its three-
column, four page format was that of a news sheet.   There was
some early popularity since the first five issues were reprinted as
three issues of a second edition.   But the magazine was like many
other similar ones and closed after two years.

50.   CHRISTIAN MIRROR

Title: Christian Mirror
Place: Charleston, S.C.   Dates: January 22-April 16, 1814
Editor: Not given
Publisher: Andrew P. Gready
Type: Religious - Presbyterian
Frequency: Weekly   Price: 37 1/2 ¢ per month
Size: 10 1/2 x 6 1/2   Length: 16 pp.
Availability: APS reel 82

Remarks: The title page and other possible front matter are missing

from the file in APS, and publication information is scarce. The
magazine is one of the very few from Charleston's early period to
have survived.
     The issues contain several moralistic essays; biography;
some poetry, history, and anecdotes. The later issues feature
summarized sermons which were published from notes taken on the
spot. The tone is rather fundamentalist, and could as easily be
Baptist as Presbyterian.
     The magazine appeared on Saturdays. This was done in the
hope that readers would add each week's issue to the reading permitted on Sunday. Nothing very lively brightened the pages, and
the magazine was too much like many other similar publications and
lacked the supported to last more than thirteen issues.

51. CHRISTIAN MONITOR

Title: The Christian Monitor; A Religious Periodical Work
Place: Boston   Dates: February 1806-1811
Editor: A Society for Promoting Christian Knowledge, Piety, and
         Charity
Publisher: Munroe & Francis (1810-1811)
Type: Religious - Unitarian (?)
Frequency: Irregular   Price: 37¢ an issue
Size: 6 5/8 x 3 7/8   Length: 14-180 pp.
Availability: APS reels 7, 82
Reference: Lewis, p. 134
Superseded by: The Society's Religious Tracts

Remarks: The issuing society is identified as The Christian Monitor Society. Aaron Bancroft addressed this group at times; and
from his own leanings, the magazine may have had a Unitarian slant.
     Each issue was limited to one topic; and since each volume
differed in the number of issues, it does not really fit the definition
of a magazine. This was its intention, however, and its pages are
of interest.
     Number thirteen, the first in 1810, contains "advice from
Farmer Trueman to his daughter Mary intended for the use of do-
mestics." The introduction, signed by Mr. Hanway, claims that
the work was "for the use and improvement of the youth of the
lower classes." This article is one type of children's material
published in magazines not solely intended for children.
     Despite an evident break from strict Congregational teaching,
the tone of The Christian Monitor still adheres to the long tradition
of strict and narrow Calvinism.

52. CHRISTIAN MONITOR

Title: Christian Monitor

Place: Hallowell, Me.   Dates: January/March 1814-October/
       December 1818
Editor: Not given
Printer and Publisher: Not given
Type: Religious - Presbyterian
Frequency: Irregular   Price: Not given
Size: 8 1/4 x 4 3/4   Length: 32 pp., 16 pp. in 1818
Availability: APS reel 83

Remarks: Quotations were made from many sources, but most
came from the Missionary Herald, The Advisor, and The National
Intelligencer. Material about many denominations other than Presbyterian appeared including groups like the Lutherans and the Church
of the United Brethren. The religious news is largely devoted to
the reports of Bible and other societies.
       The numbering of the later volumes is unusual and is listed
here to clarify possible confusion
                vol. 5, no. 1 - Jan./Feb. 1818
                vol. 5, no. 2 - March/April 1818
                vol. 5, no. 3 - May/June 1818
                vol. 6, no. 4 - July/Aug. 1818
                vol. 6, no. 5 - September 1818
                vol. 7, no. 6 - Oct./Nov./Dec. 1818
       The income from this periodical was to be used to educate
men for the ministry. Circulation seems to have been limited to
the New England states and was never large.

53. CHRISTIAN MONITOR

Title: The Christian Monitor
Place: Richmond, Va.
Dates: July 8, 1815-August 30, 1817. Not issued: June 29-
       September 14, 1816
Editor: John Holt Rice
Printer and Publisher: Philip DuVal, publisher, (July 8-December
       2, 1815); Arthur G. Brooker & Co., printer, (July 8-Decem-
       ber 2, 1815). Both functions by DuVal and Burke (December
       9, 1815-June 8, 1816); Ritchie, Trueheary, & DuVal (June
       15-June 29, 1816); John Warrock (September 14, 1816-August
       30, 1817)
Type: Religious - Presbyterian
Frequency: Weekly; later, bi-weekly   Price: $2.00
Size: ca. 8 x 5   Length: 8 pp., then 16 pp.
Availability: APS reel 596. Copy examined at the Union Theological
       Seminary Library, New York.
Superseded by: The Literary and Evangelical Magazine (1818-1828)

Remarks: John Holt Rice was asked to direct the Literary and
Evangelical Magazine (q.v.) which began in 1818. His editorial
activities with The Christian Monitor gave him good background for
this new assignment.

The Christian Monitor's principal purpose was to serve as a news source for Presbyterian congregations. Missionary activity, Bible societies, ordinations, and various annual meetings comprise the bulk of the pages. Both foreign and domestic news is included, and besides Presbyterian news, sectarian matter from the Episcopalians, Baptists, and The Society of Friends is included.

One article reports the recommendation to introduce the Bible into schools in Virginia. Holt supported this. Sermons are extracted, the Lancastrian teaching method is outlined, and some secular books, like Byron's Giaour, are reviewed.

The magazine became increasingly eclectic, the reviews shorter, and the material more and more denominational. Perhaps some indication of financial trouble is the constant shift in printer and publisher. Theatrical news from Washington and Baltimore was added to attract new subscriptions, but to no avail.

54. CHRISTIAN MONITOR

Title: Christian Monitor and Religious Intelligencer
Place: New York   Dates: June 20, 1812-August 28, 1813
Editor: Francis D. Allen
Printer: Abraham Paul and William Thomas
Type: Religious - Presbyterian
Frequency: Weekly   Price: $3.00
Size: 7 1/2 x 4 1/2   Length: 16 pp.
Availability: APS reel 83 (through June 26, 1813 only)

Remarks: Albaugh's bibliography identifies this as a Presbyterian magazine, probably from some internal evidence. The periodical expressed one point of view, and apparently this was the doctrine of the Presbyterian Church. Drinking, dancing, novel reading, and all manner of entertainment were considered the works of the Devil and were to be avoided.

The magazine's features included: Christianity, Reflections, various miscellaneous essays, To Youth, Select Sentences, Religious Intelligence, Poetry, and Obituaries. These features or divisions varied greatly from issue to issue; however, they give a general idea of what was included. To fill space when needed, an abstract of a sermon was inserted where space demanded.

Although fairly well printed and edited, trouble arose from inability to collect subscriptions, and since its appeal was limited to one sect, paid subscriptions were too few to support the publication.

55. CHRISTIAN REGISTER

Title: The Christian Register and Moral Theological Review
Place: New York   Dates: July 1816-July 1817

Editor: Thomas Y. How
Printer and Publisher: T. & J. Swords
Type: Religious - Episcopal
Frequency: Semi-annual   Price: $1.25 per issue
Size: 8 1/4 x 5   Length: 244-56 pp.
Availability: APS reel 88

Remarks: Thomas How was, according to the title page, the assistant rector of Trinity Church in New York. He thus was able
to speak from an important pulpit and to command a large audience
for the magazine.
      The religious reviews, the sermons, and the news are items
expected in a denominational magazine. Also found are economics,
travel, literature, science, and biography. The issues average two
biographies, several brief articles on a variety of subjects and at
least twenty-five reviews of a wide range of books. These are
long, sometimes borrowed, and in their tone seem to represent an
attempt to emulate the North American Review.
      Several hints indicate the intention to continue the magazine
past July 1817. For example, a list of Episcopal clergy was to be
printed "in our next number, " but this issue never appeared.
      Although the magazine has a theological viewpoint, it is
primarily a literary review. Its appearance added to the growing
list of magazines which appeared after the War of 1812 to satisfy
the demand for serious, American produced, literary material.

56. CHRISTIAN VISITANT

Title: Christian Visitant
Place: Albany   Dates: June 3, 1815-May 25, 1816
Editor: By a Layman. Possibly: Solomon Southwick
Printer and Publisher: Henry C. Southwick
Type: Religious - Non-denominational
Frequency: Weekly   Price: 28 shillings (!)
Size: 11 x 8 3/4   Length: 8 pp.
Motto: Nocturna Versate Manu, Versate Diurna.
Availability: APS reel 89

Remarks: Attached to the film copy of this magazine is a "Valedictory, " dated May 31, 1816, and reprinted from the Albany Register. It is here that the statement is made that the editor of the
paper edited the magazine, Christian Visitant. In this "Valedictory"
Southwick says he had been attacked for his connection with both a
religious magazine and a political newspaper and that he had been
forced to relinquish the Christian Visitant for this reason. He makes
an excellent point when he says:

            We have yet to learn, however, that there is any precept
            or dictum of our holy religion, which forbids a man to
            possess his own political opinions, and to maintain them
            with zeal and energy.[1]

The religious material he produced in his magazine was rather ordinary. News, essays, biography, obituaries, poetry, prayers, and the like form the bulk. Much was eclectic and many denominations are mentioned in coverage. College graduations, like those at Middlebury and William, are reported.

Notes: 1. "Valedictory," Christian Visitant, APS reel 89, follows
       p. 416.

57. CHRISTIAN'S MAGAZINE

Title: The Christian's Magazine: Designed to Promote the Knowl-
        edge and Influence of Evangelical Truth and Order
        Issue title: The Christian's Magazine, on a New Plan
Place: New York   Dates: December 6, 1806-December 1811
Editor: John Mitchell Mason
Publisher: Williams and Whiting (through April ? 1811); Samuel
        Whiting and Co. (May 1811); Whiting and Watson (June-
        December 1811).
Printer: J. Seymour
Type: Religious - Presbyterian
Frequency: Varies   Price: $3.00
Size: 8 5/8 x 4 3/4   Length: up to 136 pp.
Availability: APS reels 11, 90
Reference: Lewis, pp. 136-7

Remarks: Many issues open with a biography of a minister or church-
related individual. This is followed by several articles, religious intelligence, obituaries, book reviews, accounts of Bible and tract societies, and lists of proposed publications.
        The teaching articles are polemic and use many mnemonics,
diagrams, outlines, precise summaries, and parallels. The style of
some material indicates a desire to write for children. Certainly
there is variety in the pages and some real attempts for interest
within the bounds of conventional religious teaching.
        Improvements in the physical appearance resulted when a
volume was printed "at Earl Stanhope's new invented press." The
printing was of comparatively high quality, the issue length varied,
and there were no illustrations.
        Whiting and Watson operated a religious bookstore. The end
of the last issue includes thirty-four pages of book-seller advertise-
ments--a rather loud dying gasp.

58. CHRISTIAN'S MONITOR

Title: The Christian's Weekly Monitor; or, Sabbath Morning Repast
        (December 1814-March 1817); The Christian's Monitor (March
        1817-May 1818)

Original sub-title dropped after intermittent use in a few issues.

Place: Sangerfield, N.Y.   Dates: December 27, 1814-May 1818
Editor: Not given
Publisher: Joseph Tenny
Type: Religious - Presbyterian (?)
Frequency: Weekly   Price: $2.00
Size: 9 x 4 3/4   Length: 12 pp., later 8 pp.
Availability: APS reel 90
References: Brigham, p. 735
History: Merged into: Civil and Religious Intelligencer

Remarks: The file on film contains a manuscript note which claims the magazine began in September 1814 although no issues prior to December were found. The magazine was published separately until 1816 when Civil and Religious Intelligencer started; a gap in publication occurs from September 1817 until April 1818 by which time Civil and Religious Intelligencer had disappeared, and the May 1818 issue was apparently separate.

During the years 1816 and 1817, The Christian's Monitor may be called a supplement to Civil and Religious Intelligencer since paging was separate, and the first was inserted in the center of the second. After May 1818, The Christian's Monitor seems to have ceased although scattered and indefinite references indicate it may have existed until October 1819 or as late as 1830.

The magazine appears as a rather grubby and poorly printed item. Most material was rather sanctimonious and moralistic, and the most frequent subject was drinking and its evils.

59. CHURCHMAN'S MAGAZINE

Title: The Churchman's Monthly Magazine; or, Treasury of Divine and Useful Knowledge (January 1804-December 1805); The Churchman's Magazine (January 1806-March 1827)
Place: New York (May/June 1808-November/December 1811); Elizabethtown, N.J. (January 1813-June 1815)
Dates: v. 1-8 (January 1804-November/December 1811); ns v. 1-3 (January/February 1813-May/June 1815); s3v. 1-5 (January 1821-March 1827). Suspended: 1812; 1816-20; 1824
Editor: John Henry Hobart (May/June 1808-November/December 1811); John C. Rudd (January/December 1813-May/June 1815)
Publisher: T. and J. Swords (May/June 1808-November/December 1811)
Printer: Lewis Deare (January/December 1813-May/June 1815)
Type: Religious - Episcopal
Frequency: Bi-monthly   Price: $1.50
Size: 8 1/4 x 4 5/8   Length: 40-80 pp.
Quotation: The Church of the Living God, The Pillar and Ground of the Truth. Timothy iii, v5
Availability: APS reels 12, 91

Reference: Lewis, pp. 139-40
Superseded by: Episcopal Watchman

Remarks: Each series continued the same basic pattern: biography;
sermons; commentary on the Bible, doctrine, and ritual; letters;
accounts of missionary activity; Bible and tract societies; and a
variety of anecdotal and miscellaneous articles.
     The article, "On the Poetry of the Bible,"[1] clearly speaks
about the literary value of this verse and refrains from labored
scholarship. Many issues printed a transcription of a famous tomb-
stone, e.g. that of Samuel Seabury, Bishop of Connecticut and Rhode
Island.[2].
     One continuing theme concerns a comparison of the doctrines
of the Protestant Episcopal Church with the controversy between
Calvinists and Arminians. This, and other teaching material provided in The Churchman's Magazine's pages, probably supplied
sermons and Sunday school material through most of the magazine's
intermittent twenty-three year life.

Notes: 1.   The Churchman's Magazine, vii (March/April 1810) 155 f.
           2.   Ibid., viii (January/February 1811), 59.

60.   CIVIL AND RELIGIOUS INTELLIGENCER

Title: Civil and Religious Intelligencer (November 18, 1816-August
         28, 1817); Civil and Religious Intelligencer, or The Gleaner
         and Monitor (September 4? 1817-1819); Intelligencer, Civil
         and Religious (1819-1825); Sangerfield Intelligencer and Madi-
         son and Oneida Counties Gleaner (1825-1835)
Place: Sangerfield, N.Y.   Dates: November 18, 1816-1835
Editor and Publisher: Joseph Tenny (November 18, 1816-   )
Type: Religious - Presbyterian (?)
Frequency: Weekly   Price: ca. $2.00
Size: 10 x 5   Length: 4 pp.
Availability: APS reel 90
Reference: Brigham, p. 735

Remarks: At one period, this title seems to have been issued as a
part of The Christian's Monitor (q.v.), and since this may have been
a Presbyterian paper, the Civil and Religious Intelligencer probably
had the same viewpoint.
     This four-page insert summarized events and trends but did
not contain much current news. The fact that news was printed does
not affect its magazine appearance, nor does it detract from its
regular magazine features--essays, serialized features including
some fiction, and the like.
     Most of the material was of a broad general nature, and
when religious material appeared it was not always doctrinaire or
denominational. Only scattered issues of this paper are noted in
bibliographies, and a more detailed study seems impossible.

61. COBBETT'S AMERICAN POLITICAL REGISTER

Title: Cobbett's American Political Register
Place: New York   Dates: January 6, 1816-January 10, 1818
Editor: William Cobbett
Publisher: Henry Cobbett and G. S. Oldfield (January 6-September
    17, 1816); Henry Cobbett (May 1817-January 10, 1818)
Printer: Van Windle & Wiley (January 6-September 17, 1816);
    Henry Cobbett (May 1817-January 1818)
Type: News
Frequency: Bi-weekly   Price: Not given
Size: 9 1/2 x 5 3/4   Length: 18 pp.
Availability: APS reel 92
Re
Remarks: William Cobbett was British, and published Cobbett's
Political Register in England. When forced to leave England, he
came to America, added "American" to his title, and produced
parts of three volumes of his paper.
    Volume one (English volume 30) was published from May 21-
September 24, 1816, and covers events from January 6-June 29 of
that year. Volumes two and three (English volumes 33 and 34)
cover May 15, 1817-January 10, 1818. Cobbett hoped to fill the
gap and issue volumes 31 and 32. No evidence that this was done
was found.
    In a way this was an English magazine since it was written
and supervised by a British subject; but it was issued in America
and covers subjects of American interest in depth. In the issue of
August 28, 1817 Cobbett questions the representative nature of the
House of Commons and suggests reforms to assure more nearly
equal weight for population groups in England. Cobbett clearly suggests similar changes were needed in America, and this was in
mid-1817.

62. COHEN'S GAZETTE

Title: Cohen's Gazette and Lottery Register
Place: Baltimore, Md.   Dates: May 2, 1814-September 1, 1830
Editor: Joseph (?) I. Cohen
Publisher: Joseph Robinson
Type: Lottery
Frequency: Irregular   Price: $2.00; 1815- $3.00
Size: 11 x 8 1/4   Length: 4 pp.; 1815- 2 pp.
Motto: Hoc signo fortuna.
Availability: APS reel 92

Remarks: Cohen ran a lottery office and offered this sheet free to
customers who purchased ten tickets a year. Apparently he had a
group of "customers" large enough to support the magazine.
    The first issue contained about 150 Baltimore price currents

followed by five columns listing various day's drawings in the Washington Monument Lottery. These lotteries paid well--at times returning $20,000 for a $14.00 ticket. When one lottery was over, a new one would be announced, and the announcements were frequently florid and filled with a great variety of display types.

The size of the issues was frequently changed to accommodate added material, and issue numbering is somewhat different. Volume one, for example, has forty issues.

After 1817, price currents and bank rates re-appear and are a regular feature at least through 1819. The lottery information continues to supply an apparently large appetite for this form of gambling.

63. COLLEGIAN

Title: The Collegian; or, American Students Magazine
Place: New York   Dates: January-February 1819
Editor, Printer, Publisher: Not given
Type: Collegiate
Frequency: Monthly   Price: Not given
Size: 8 x 5   Length: 24 pp.
Motto: Disclosing the bright key of the mind.
Availability: APS reel 94

Remarks: The covers and any title page are lacking from the issues examined, and no indication or editorship could be found. He states, however, that the magazine is intended for college students and was to look for material written by students because:

> Whatever illiberal Europeans may assert, we are confident there is no dearth of talent in the western hemisphere: and we hope to render The Collegian not only entertaining and instructive, but worthy the attentive perusal of classical readers.[1]

The first issue contained several lengthy book reviews, and the essays and poetry seem to have been done by students. The second issue contains two biographies, some essays of literary criticism, a short piece on patriotism, a literary miscellany of paragraphs containing odd bits of information and original poetry.

All items are anonymous, but a few have Columbia College at the end. If there were a college or university connection in New York, this may have been the one.

Notes: 1. The Collegian, I (January 1819), 2.

64. COLUMBIA MAGAZINE

Title: The Columbia Magazine. Designed to Promote Evangelical
        Knowledge and Morality. To Oppose the Prevailing Licen-
        tiousness of Manners, Particularly the Violation of the Sab-
        bath, Intemperance, and Profanity; and to Diffuse Missionary
        and Religious Intelligence
Place: Hudson, N.Y.   Dates: September 1814-August 1815
Editor: Conducted by several friends of religion
Printer and Publisher: Ashbel Stoddard
Type: Religious - Presbyterian
Frequency: Monthly   Price: $1.50
Size: 8 3/4 x 5 1/4   Length: 32 pp.
Quotation: Prove all things ... hold fast that which is good.
Availability: APS reel 94

Remarks: The sub-title both in what it says and the language used
describes the pages of this rather secondary magazine. Borrowed
material, printing which was only fair, and a prosaic style typify
the issues.
     As the title states, the three worst sins in America were the
lack of Sunday church attendance, drinking, and swearing; and these
three failings occupy most of the editors' attention. As indicated
above, this may have been a Presbyterian magazine, but it could
easily have been produced by any one of a number of denominations.
     Only one volume appeared. The city of Hudson had poor
luck with magazines, and The Columbia Magazine, lacking material
that didn't exist elsewhere, failed to gather the support needed to
survive.

65. COLUMBIAN TELESCOPE

Title: Columbian Telescope and Literary Compiler: Being a Mis-
        cellaneous Repository of Literary Productions
Place: Alexandria, D.C.   Dates: June 16, 1819-May 20, 1820
Editor: By a Trio. Geoffrey Whimsical, Solomon Studiosus, Peter
        Quiz
Printer and Publisher: Samuel H. Davis
Type: Literary newspaper
Frequency: Weekly   Price: $3.00
Size: 10 x 6   Length: 4 pp.
Availability: Not in APS. Microfilm obtained from the Historical
        Society of Pennsylvania.
Reference: Brigham, p. 1108

Remarks: Samuel H. Davis is listed as printer and publisher, but
he probably was at least one of the editors as well. Who the other
members of the trio may have been remains a mystery; the issues
seem to contain no clues.

The three-column, four-page format and the size of this publication both give it some of the aspects of a newspaper. In contents, the editors included news summaries and marriage and death notices, all of which were newspaper features.

However, the heterogeneous nature of the other contents indicates this to be a magazine, or at least a literary newspaper. An unusual feature was a Masonic calendar published in each issue. This magazine was little different from many other similar publications and was not distinguished by any noteworthy contributions to literature.

66. COMET

Title: The Comet
Place: Boston	Dates: October 19, 1811-January 11, 1812
Editor: Walter Wildfire, pseud.
Printer and Publisher: Joseph Tinker Buckingham
Type: Literary miscellany
Frequency: Weekly
Price: 12 1/2¢ per issue or $2.00 for 26 issues
Size: 7 3/4 x 4 1/2	Length: 12 pp.
Cover Design: Wood-cut 1 x 1 1/2 of a comet
Quotation:				His course he bends
			Thro' the calm firmament; but whether up or down
			By centrick, or eccentrick, hard to tell.
					(Milton)
Availability: APS reel 97

Remarks: The opening statement reveals several superstitions about comets, including the idea that a comet would produce a deluge or set the world on fire. However, the statement also outlines the proposed contents as including: literary, critical, and moral essays; biographical sketches of eminent characters; anecdotes, aphorisms, and maxims; and information about the Boston state, including notices of new plays; some poetry, and announcements of new books.

The theatrical information occupies a lot of space and contributes yet another magazine which was concerned with this aspect of Boston life.

Material on Russia reflects the diplomatic contact opening up with this nation, but was not original. It, like other parts of the magazine, was quoted from a variety of sources.

Buckingham's connection with this magazine may have given him the experience necessary to make his later editorial and publishing adventures more of a success.

67. CONGREGATIONALIST AND HERALD OF GOSPEL LIBERTY

Title: Recorder (1816); Boston Recorder (January 7, 1817-December

4, 1824); many other changes partially indicated in ULS until title became Congregationlist and Herald of Gospel Liberty (February 27, 1930-March 29, 1934).

Place: Boston   Dates: January 3, 1816-March 29, 1934
Publisher: Nathaniel Willis (January 3-January 24, 1816); Ezra
     Lincoln (January 31-April 3, 1816); David J. Burr (April 10-
     June 12, 1816); Nathaniel Willis (June 19, 1816-   )
Printer: Ezra Lincoln (April 10-April 24, 1816); Nathaniel Willis
     (May 1, 1816-   )
Type: Religious - Non-denominational
Frequency: Weekly   Price: $3.00
Size: 20 x 13   Length: 4 pp.
Availability: APS reels 97-8, 539-46

History: On February 27, 1930, the Congregationlist merged into a publication called Herald of Gospel Liberty which was the descendant of The Christian Herald (q.v.) and not the publication previously known from 1808 to 1817 as the Herald of Gospel Liberty (q.v.) which was bibliographically a separate publication. The new Congregationlist and Herald of Gospel Liberty was superseded by Advance.

Remarks: As indicated above, some confusion exists between The Congregationlist and Herald of Gospel Liberty and two publications with titles beginning with "Herald." The notes here and with the entries for Herald of Gospel Liberty and The Christian Herald attempt to clarify this problem.
     At the outset, the Congregationlist stated it was to be a newspaper, and its four-page, five-column format give this appearance. This may have been done to avoid postal regulations against magazines which were in flux at the time. Much of its contents were those of a general newspaper, and included political news, weekly Boston news, Congressional reporting, marriages, deaths, agricultural reports, and advertisements. This was maintained throughout the decade.
     Much of the news was non-denominational religious reporting, and this slowly became more and more important. The first two names it used sounded like newspapers, and not until after 1824 did it take on a denominational complexion and a magazine format.

68. CONNECTICUT EVANGELICAL MAGAZINE

Title: Connecticut Evangelical Magazine and Religious Intelligencer
Place: Hartford, Conn.   Dates: July 1800-December 1815
Editor: Nathan Williams, John Smalley, and others.   No changes
     are noted.
Publisher and Printer: Peter B. Gleason (through 1815).   Oliver D.
     Cooke was a member of Peter B. Gleason and Co., (1813-
     1814).
Type: Religious

Frequency: Monthly   Price: 12 1/2¢ per issue
Size: 8 x 4 3/4   Length: 40 pp.
Availability: APS reels 14, 127-9
Reference: Lewis, pp. 148-9
Superseded by: Religious Intelligencer
R
Remarks: This was probably the second American magazine devoted
to missionary purposes.[1] Essays, expositions of the Bible, informa-
tion on missions, and a series devoted to explaining denominational
positions were among the contents. Some of the latter dealt with
the Roman Catholic Church and even non-Christian beliefs, e.g.
Mahometan (!)
       Perhaps the most important series in the whole magazine is
"An Historical View of the First Planters of New England";[2] over
two hundred pages in twenty issues briefly cover the early settlements, with emphasis on Puritan settlements, early governors, and
"some of the principal divines." This may have been one of the
longer historical essays to appear in an American magazine up to
1815.

Notes: 1. Mott, op. cit., p. 133.
        2. Connecticut Evangelical Magazine, IV-VI (October 1811-
        May 1813), passim.

69. CORRECTOR

Title: The Corrector; or, Independent American
Place: New York   Dates: July 1815-no month 1817
Editor, Printer, and Publisher: Not given
Type: Miscellany - Humor
Frequency: Irregular   Price: Not given
Size: 8 3/4 x 5   Length: 48 pp.
Motto: Respect Your Country, if you would be respected by the
        world.
Availability: Not in APS. Copies consulted at The American Anti-
        quarian Society and Yale.

Remarks: The editor claimed he wrote for his own pleasure, and
not for profit; and so his publication may have been distributed
without charge. He also claimed The Corrector would appear when
he felt like producing a copy when he had time to do so. With this
irregularity, The Corrector could properly be considered a pamphlet
series, but since it was a numbered series and intended to continue,
it is considered a magazine.
       The contents are mainly essays written with satirical, and at
times caustic, wit about contemporary literature and publication.
The Analectic's original material was referred as "at once affected,
puerile, and pendantic--full of laboured ease, and mighty pettiness."[1]
The major attack is on the "Naval Chronicle" which gives many false

impressions and ideas. On the other hand, the American Magazine, which began in June 1815, was effusively praised. 2

The second number of The Corrector contains an eight-page article reviewing the impact of The American Magazine, The Analectic Magazine, The Christian Visitant, The Friend, and Webster's Almanack. For all of these both good and bad are said, and for all the author feels free to speak his mind clearly and frankly.

In the reviewing and in the comments on manners and morals of the day, the editor of The Corrector asserts himself to be "independent" and he carries this idea out since he takes no sides but his own in any comment he may choose to make.

Notes: 1. The Corrector, no. 1 (July 1815), 33.
        2. Ibid., p. 37.

70. COUNTRY COURRIER

Title: The Country Courrier
Place: New York   Dates: June 3, 1816-March 24, 1817
Editor: Barent Gardenier (June 3, 1816-February 17, 1817); Theodore Dwight (February 20-March 24, 1817)
Printer and Publisher: Barent Gardenier (June 3-July 1, 1816); Abraham Vosburgh (July 4, 1816-January 23, 1817); Barent Gardenier (January 27-February 17, 1817); Theodore Dwight (February 20-March 24, 1817)
Type: Miscellany - General
Frequency: Bi-weekly   Price: $5.00
Size: 8 x 5 1/4   Length: 16 pp.
Availability: APS reel 100
Superseded: The Examiner

Remarks: Barent Gardenier also published the New York Courrier, a newspaper; and none of his publications had very long lives. Some local and general news summaries are always included in his papers, but The Country Courrier is more of a magazine than a newspaper.

Gardenier begins this periodical with a series of satire and humor detailing the adventures of one Signior Flibbertigibbet--a man who is amazed and bothered by American politics and manages to say so.

A heavy emphasis on serialized fiction and poetry characterize the pages; and these are supported by marine news, helpful interpretations of congressional bills, articles on "natural history," the Bank of the United States, and many topical articles. An article attacking the slave trade appeared on June 17, 1816. Gardenier had the basis of a good, general magazine, but failed to draw support in New York City for his ideas.

71.   CRICKET

Title: The Cricket; or, Whispers from a Voice in a Corner
         number three called: The Cricket, or Parapetic Student
         Other variations are minor.
Place: Geneva, N.Y.; Vernon, N.Y.; Lake Dunmore, Vt.; Potosi,
         Mo.
Dates: Nine numbered issues from 1808-1818
Editor: Henry Rowe Schoolcraft
Printer and Publisher: None.   A manuscript magazine
Type: Miscellany - Literary
Frequency: Irregular
Availability: Not in APS or ULS.   Photostats obtained from The
         Manuscript Division, The Library of Congress

Remarks: Schoolcraft was sixteen when this magazine started, and
he apparently intended it for a literary society, The Hamilton Union
Society, which is described in number two.

> It is proposed to make this simple word the nucleus of
> some remarks of an irregular ... character, & written
> from time to time when it is convenient to be read by a
> few friends the same way.[1]

The full titles, numbering, and places where these numbers
appeared is outlined by Kinietz.[2]   Numbers one through five are
two leaves; numbers six through nine are one leaf.   The format of
each issue varies slightly.   Some issues may have been misplaced,
the handwriting is often almost illegible, and the later the issue,
the less it contains.
      Schoolcraft's interest is reflected in a brief essay "An Indian
Family,"[3] and other articles border on the satirical.   The last few
issues apparently contained only notes of what Schoolcraft wanted to
include.
      In later years, Schoolcraft produced two other manuscript
magazines, The Muzziniegun or Literary Voyager and The Bow and
Arrow.[4]   This first magazine, although irregular, in manuscript
form, and of questionable importance, is included here primarily as
a curiosity.

Notes: 1.   The Cricket, leaf one.
         2.   Kinietz, op. cit., pp. 151-4.
         3.   The Cricket, leaf six.
         4.   Kinietz, loc. cit.

72.   CYNICK

Title: The Cynick
Place: Philadelphia   Dates: September 21-December 12, 1811

Editor: Growler Gruff, Esquire, aided by a confederation of Let-
        terd Dogs
Printer and Publisher: Not given
Type: Humor
Frequency: Weekly   Price: Not given
Size: 6 x 4   Length: 18 pp.
Availability: APS reel 100

Remarks: Small periodical publications like this one were numerous
in the early nineteenth century. They were used as sounding boards
for men whose ideas may have been rejected by the more "proper"
magazines; but these men wanted to be heard and often enough attempted a magazine or pamphlet series.
        Growler Gruff had a modern viewpoint by writing:

> No publication should be supressed which does not tend
> to degenerate virtue, corrupt the morals of the people, or
> defame the private characters of individuals, every other
> subject properly conducted, has a right to be placed before
> the world, and every free man will demand and enforce
> compliance ...[1]

Many theatrical articles hardly seem serious, but rather are
sarcastic slaps at what the editor held to be the bombastic, artificial, and shallow theatre of the day. A few names of actors and
theatres are used, but most seem to be pseudonyms--a device which
would help to avoid libel actions.
        Interestingly, most of the "essays" are in verse form. Many
are doggerel, and none is memorable as poetry.

Notes: 1. The Cynick, I (September 21, 1811), 3.

73. EMERALD

Title: Emerald
Place: Baltimore   Dates: November 3, 1810-March 2, 1811
Editor: Peter Pleasant, pseud.
Publisher: Benjamin Edes
Type: Humor
Frequency: Weekly   Price: $3.00
Size: 9 x 5 1/4   Length: 16 pp.
Quotation: With modest skill,
                To raise the virtues, animate the bliss,
                And sweeten all the toils of human life:
                This be the Emerald's dignity and praise.
Availability: APS reel 101

Remarks: Benjamin Edes was the son of a Boston printer of the
same name[1] who issued a Revolutionary newspaper known as an outspoken organ of anti-British opinion. The elder Edes died in 1803,

but the younger Benjamin may have remained in Botson long enough
to have seen issues of a magazine which eventually took the title The
Emerald. 2
              After moving to Baltimore, Benjamin Edes established a
printing business--probably to some degree influenced by his familial
background. The identity of "Peter Pleasant" remains uncertain, but
Edes' experience may have suggested the possibility of a magazine
to him, and humor and satire were not unfamiliar to him because
they played a part in his father's newspaper. Thus the suggestion
is made here that "Peter Pleasant" was Benjamin Edes--the second
of that name.
              Baltimore lacked a literary periodical in 1810, but Edes
hoped to fill the void by issuing a magazine aimed partially toward
"the ladies" to occupy "their leisure moments," and designed to include "moral essays," "historical sketches," and "many a well
seasoned joke." Edes' humor is expressed in his essay "A Petition
of the Genteel and Fashionable for the Repeal of the Ten Commandments."
              The Emerald continued for at least eighteen issues. Several
items promised they would continue, but none appeared.

Notes: 1.   DAB, VI, p. 17.
         2.   For details of this earlier magazine, see Lewis, pp.
         153-4.

74.   EMPORIUM OF ARTS AND SCIENCES

Title: The Emporium of the Arts and Sciences
Place: Philadelphia (May 1812-April 1813); Carlisle, Pa. (June
         1813-October 1814)
Dates: v. 1-2 (May 1812-April 1813); n.s. v. 1-3 (June 1813-
         October 1814)
Editor: John Redman Coxe (May 1812-April 1813); Thomas Cooper
         (June 1813-October 1814)
Publisher: Joseph Delaplaine (May 1812-April 1813); Kimber &
         Richardson (June 1813-October 1814)
Printer: William Brown (May 1812-April 1813); Alexander & Phillips
         (June 1813-October 1814)
Illustrations: One of the more profusely illustrated magazines from
         1810-1820.
Type: Scientific
Frequency: Monthly; n.s., bi-monthly   Price: $7.00
Size: 8 1/4 x 5 1/4   Length: From 80 to 200 pp.
Availability: APS reel 101
Indexed: Cargill
References: Polyanthas, n.s. II (June 1812), 72.
              Ibid., 3d ser., I (December 1812), 165-6.
              Port Folio, 3d ser., VII (June 1812), 569-72.
              Select Reviews, VII (June 1812), 535.

Cooper, Thomas, "Prospectus for the New Series,"
Port Folio, 4th ser., I (April 1813), 399-403.

Remarks: This magazine aimed to be a repository of "practical information in the various branches of scientific research."[1] Much of the material came from European sources since Coxe felt this the place where science was most advanced.

The lead article was a summary of a letter concerned with the value of scientific periodicals. Their worth was maintained chiefly on the basis of being a recent and constantly up-dated source of information for people at all levels--a source with utility for many abilities and disciplines.

The first volume included articles on: weights and measures used by the British and French, the manufacture of gun flints, wooden matches, spontaneous combustion, an engravers' table, and a list of patents. This latter feature continued throughout the whole run of the magazine.

At the end of volume two, a subscription list indicates over 1100 copies distributed to fourteen states. Philadelphia had the largest single group; 400 copies were sent to Charles Williams in Boston; and the Michigan Territory was represented with one copy sent to Aaron Greely. This was probably a strong list and certainly indicated the need for a scientific magazine.

The new series under Thomas Cooper changed the emphasis somewhat. The first issue offered a 155-page article on iron which was continued in the second issue. Other long articles on steel and the steam engine appeared; and mineralogy was covered with articles on copper, lead, and tin with emphasis on the ores, smelting, refining, and the various uses of the metals. These volumes amount to a text book on these subjects since they attempted to summarize current knowledge.

The new series intended to encourage domestic manufacturing by pointing out that Americans had depended on Britain for many articles which Americans now had both the skill and raw materials to produce themselves. This emphasis on a newly emerging national spirit apparently did not arouse support sufficient to permit the magazine to continue.

Notes: 1. Emporium of Arts and Sciences, I (May 1812), vi.

75. EVANGELICAL GUARDIAN

Title: The Evangelical Guardian and Review
Place: New York   Dates: May 1817-April 1819
Editor: An Association of Clergymen in New York
Publisher: J. Eastburn & Co.
Printer: Abraham Paul
Type: Religious - Presbyterian
Frequency: Monthly   Price: Not given
Size: 8 x 4 3/4   Length: 48 pp.

Quotation: Prove all things: Hold fast that which is good
                    To the Law and to the Testimony.
Availability: APS reels 102, 103

Remarks: In this title, the religious news was printed in a smaller
type and in two columns to the page. This material is thus easily
distinguished from the other contents. Most of this news was in
summary and dealt with Sunday schools and missionary activity.
     A hope was expressed to include engravings, but these did
not appear. The issues did include biography, which was usually
moralizing in nature; a series on prayer and one on baptism; and
usually one book review, often of a religious book or a sermon.
     Bible, tract, and missionary societies are heavily treated.
To fill out each issue, some scientific material appears; and there
are occasional bits of secular news.
     The Evangelical Guardian was rather ordinary, rather dull,
frequently straight-laced, and typical of the denominational, religious magazines in the period.

76. EVANGELICAL RECORD

Title: Evangelical Record and Western Review
Place: Lexington, Ky.   Dates: January 1812-December 1813
Editor: Thomas T. Skillman.   The Rev. John Page Campbell was
          named chief editor at the close of volume two, but no more
          issues appeared.
Printer: Thomas T. Skillman
Type: Religious - Presbyterian
Frequency: Monthly   Price: $2.00
Size: 16 3/4 x 6 1/2
Length: v. 1-- 32 pp.; v. 2 - 56 pp.
Availability: APS reels 129, 130
Superseded by: Presbyterian Advocate (?) An apparent ghost; see
          entry A90

Remarks: The main object of this religious magazine was "to give
only a short view of what hath been done within these last twenty
years to establish and extend the boundaries of the Mediator's kingdom."[1]
     Topics covered included, in the magazine's words: The Lon-
don and other Missionary Societies, Conversion of the Jews, British
and Foreign Bible Societies, Sabbath Day Schools, Religious Tract
Societies, and seminaries to train for the evangelical ministry. In
addition, the issues included book reviews, speeches, answers to
letters, and miscellaneous articles which, for example, drew moral
lessons from earthquakes.
     A church history, begun in issue two, was a thinly disguised
diatribe against Roman Catholics. Many items were drawn from
contemporary magazine and newspaper sources, and fill material of
an ephemeral nature appeared with increasing frequency.

The magazine is typical for the period both in its contents and in its failure to arouse support even by implying that the road to salvation would be made secure by payment for a year's subscription.

Notes: 1. Evangelical Record, I (January 1812), 6.

77. EVANGELICAL RECORDER

Title: Evangelical Recorder
Place: Auburn, N.Y.
Dates: January 31, 1818-September 8, 1821
Editor: Not given
Publisher: Dirck C. Lansing (January 31-September 5, 1818);
    Cornelius Davis (June 5, 1819-   )
Printer: T. M. Skinner (January 31-September 5, 1818); David
    Ramsey (June 5, 1819-   )
Type: Religious - Presbyterian
Frequency: Weekly   Price: $2.50
Size: 9 1/2 x 4 3/4   Length: 16 pp.
Availability: APS reel 103

Remarks: A gap on the film from volume one, number twenty-six (September 5, 1818) to volume two, number twenty-seven (June 5, 1820) has not been explained and is not mentioned in the magazine itself. It could be that the first volume only had twenty-six numbers; that there was a hiatus of eight months; and that issue numbering was continuous, thus opening volume two with number twenty-seven.

Material from the Massachusetts Peace Society and American Colonization Society reflect a growing concern in these areas. Articles on slavery detail its history in America, the Presbyterian Church's position, and various plans for abolition. Bible, missionary, and other societies are described; other denominational material is reported; and Sunday school activity among the Indians each have limited articles.

After 1820 the magazine was shifted to Utica, New York, apparently to seek a larger population group for subscribers.

78. EVANGELICAL REPOSITORY

Title: Evangelical Repository
Place: Philadelphia   Dates: January-December 1816
Editor and Publisher: Ebenezer Marlow Cummins
Printer: William Fry
Type: Religious - Non-denominational
Frequency: Monthly   Price: $3.00

Size: 12 x 7   Length: 16-24 pp.
Availability: APS reel 130

Remarks: Placing this magazine within one denomination or another seems impossible since its contents serve the purpose of advancing many viewpoints. The magazine has been claimed as Presbyterian,[1] but this is only one aspect of the contents.

The first issue opens with a "Biographical Memoir of the Messiah," a twenty-six page compilation of New Testament material. Other biographies are: Dr. Benjamin Rush, Rev. Samuel Davies, Patrick Henry, Isaac Newton, St. John, Alexander Hamilton, Rev. John Eliot, Sir William Jones, Fisher Ames, and Jonathan Edwards. It would be hard to select a more diverse group of men.

Other religious articles, many accounts of Bible and religious societies, and poetry fill out each issue. In April a Latin poem by "the apostolic Francis Xavier" appears. Denominational news includes Episcopalian, Presbyterian, Methodist, Baptist, and Congregational; and some items are not easily identified.

Notes.   1.   Albaugh, op. cit., p. 246.

79. EXAMINER

Title: Examiner: Containing Political Essays on the Most Important Events of the Time; Public Laws and Official Documents
Place: New York   Dates: October 25, 1813-May 27, 1816
Editor, Printer, Publisher: Barent Gardenier
Type: News
Frequency: Bi-monthly   Price: $3.00
Size: 9 1/4 x 5 1/2   Length: 16 pp.
Availability: APS reels 104, 105, 106
Indexed: Cargill

Remarks: Established in part to cover the War of 1812, the editor wrote that "the present war was unnecessarily commenced, and is, now at least, most unnecessarily continued."[1] The magazine gained quick support for its views and probably for its clear style and forceful opinions.

These opinions were in opposition to the war and to the government then in power, and Gardenier further felt that most military leaders were unqualified. Reports were given on investigations into the capture of Washington, but nothing was said about victories--especially the naval ones. In attacking the negative aspects of the war, the Examiner conveniently overlooked its own prejudice. Reprinted from the Columbian Centinel was a series called "The Road to Ruin" which gave one side of the picture concerning the effects of war.

The Examiner slanted everything not in agreement with the views of Gardenier. The administration, taxes, the public debt, and even the purchase of Thomas Jefferson's Library "for the use of Congress"--all were flayed with strong language.

Perhaps support for this vilification waned because the final volume deteriorated so that almost all its contents were borrowed. Articles, documents, New York legislative reports, and other routine items were published in the last few dull issues.

Notes: 1.   Examiner, I (October 25, 1813), 1.

80.   FARRIER'S MAGAZINE

Title: The Farrier's Magazine; or, The Archives of Veterinary
         Science; Containing the Anatomy, Physiology and Pathology
         of the Horse, and other Domestic Quadrupeds: Being an
         Outline of a Plan for Disseminating this Most Useful and
         Necessary Branch of Knowledge; Enabling the Gentlemen, the
         Farmer, the Grazier, & c. not medically educated, to be
         his own Farrier; whereby he may practice successfully on
         the Diseases of his own Animals, when placed in remote
         Situations in different parts of the United States, where no
         regular or scientific Aid can be procured. Compiled from
         the lectures and Practice of the Veterinary Colleges of Lon-
         don, France, Germany, Russia, and British India. With an
         Appendix Containing all the College Formulas
Place: Philadelphia   Dates: May 15-August 5, 1818
Editor: James Carver
Printer and Publisher: Not given
Illustrations: Several white-line wood-cuts, plus an engraving--all
         of animal diseases.
Type: Veterinary medicine
Frequency: Quarterly   Price: Not given
Size: 8 1/4 x 4 3/4   Length: 150 pp.
Availability: APS reel 106

Remarks: This title is a dated but not numbered series, and is, in some ways, only a group of pamphlets. Since it attempted some of the aspects of a magazine, and since it was probably America's first such publication to deal with veterinary medicine, it is included in this study.

The proposed topics were the anatomy and organs of animals; the diseases animals suffer; and cures and drugs to alleviate some of them. Forty-eight pages of introductory matter discuss the backgrounds of veterinary science and describe "The Character of a Veterinary Surgeon." He was qualified if he possessed youth, firmness, dexterity, acute sensation, sound judgment, and humanity.

From the rather lengthy title given above the idea behind the magazine becomes apparent. That such an ambitious task was undertaken is a credit to early American veterinary medicine, and an indication that the profession would some day be ready to support a literature.

81. FLORIAD

Title: Floriad
Place: Schenectady, N.Y.   Dates: May 24-December 6, 1811
Editor: Union College Literary Societies
Publisher: William S. Buell
Type: College magazine
Frequency: Semi-monthly   Price: $2.00
Size: 8 1/4 x 5   Length: 16 pp.
Availability: APS reel 106
                    .
Remarks: The Floriad seems to have been the second printed col-
lege literary magazine in America. The editors hoped to devote it
solely to literature, and to include original essays, poetry, biography,
and history.
        The first two issues contain a long poem, "Schenectady,"
signed by P. Camp. If this name is real, it is one of the few used
in the magazine. A long "oration on biography," for example, is
signed S. Bacus--certainly a pseudonym.
        One of the societies which helped produce this title was the
Themean Society, established in 1810. Perhaps its members acted
as editors. Many of the selections were written for classes by the
students and submitted to the magazine if the quality were high
enough.
        A few items were drawn from other "professional" magazines,
and religion was allowed to creep in on occasion. Some rather
amusing satire was included; a sample was "The Benefit of Slander"
in which the author attempts to show that "slander contributes greatly
to the increase of human happiness."[1]
        Although the general quality and tone of the Floriad did not
match the Harvard Lyceum, it was nonetheless a good early sample
of the college literary magazine.

Notes: 1. Floriad, I (October 11, 1811), 164-6.

82. FREEMASON'S MAGAZINE

Title: Freemason's Magazine and General Miscellany
Place: Philadelphia   Dates: April 1811-March 1812
Editor: George Richards
Publisher: Levis and Weaver
Illustrations: Each issue claimed a plate, and both volumes should
                have an engraved title page. Some are missing from file in
                APS. Interesting plates are those of Masonic symbols and
                printed forms.
Type: Miscellany - Freemasonry
Frequency: Monthly   Price: $6.00
Size: 8 1/4 x 5   Length: 80 pp.
Availability: APS reel 106

Remarks: About one-third of the pages in each issue covers various aspects of Freemasonry; the rest of the space is given over to the materials of a general miscellany. Regular features included a section called "The Temple of the Muses" which was poetry, original and selected. "The Ladies' Toilette" gathered general features presumed of interest to women; but the recipe and dress pattern were yet to come in women's magazines. The features here were generally moralistic and anecdotal materials. The last section was headed "General Miscellany" and into it George Richards threw a wide variety of items--apparently much of it gathered from other general magazines.

The history of the Masonic movement was treated at some length, and although a continuation was promised after March 1812, none seems to have appeared. The plates of Masonic symbols which accompanied the articles are of historic value and help to shed some light on the habits and ideas of this group.

Apparently no connection existed between this title and Buckingham's New England Galaxy and Masonic Magazine which appeared in 1817.

83.   FRIEND

Title: The Friend, A Periodical Work Devoted to Religion, Literature, and Useful Miscellany
Place: Albany   Dates: July 1815-June 1816
Editor: Not given
Printer and Publisher: Churchill and Abbey (July 1815-March 1816);
        D. & S. A. Abbey (April-May 1816)
Type: Miscellany - Literary
Frequency: Monthly   Price: $2.00
Size: 8 x 5   Length: 36 pp.
Motto: "The greatest blessing is a pleasant Friend."
Availability: APS reel 107
Reference: The Corrector, no. 1 (July 1815), 38.

Remarks: This magazine has some religious aspects and has been claimed as a Presbyterian magazine.[1] However, many magazines had religious aspects, but this did not mean these magazines were primarily religious in nature. And The Friend was not. As the title page says, The Friend served many purposes:

> ... containing original and selected essays on religious
> and literary subjects; biographical and historical sketches;
> reviews and notices of new publications; religious intelli-
> gence; accounts of new inventions, discoveries, and im-
> provements; and fragments in prose and poetry, grave
> humorous and sentimental.

Started in the same month as The American Magazine, the editor of The Friend pointedly attacks Spafford's editorial policy.

This connection, as well as announcement by The Corrector, leads
to the assumption there may have been interconnection among all
three. The Friend bears a high degree of similarity to modern
literary reviews and was much more skillfully produced than most
other contemporary magazines.

Notes: 1. Albaugh, op. cit., p. 249.

84. FRIEND OF PEACE

Title: Friend of Peace
Place: Boston   Dates: 1815-1827
Editor: Philo Pacificus (pseud. of Noah Worcester)
Printer: J. T. Buckingham (1815-1819); Hillard & Metcalf (1821-
        1827)
Type: Miscellany - Special
Frequency: Irregular   Price: Not given
Size: 10 x 6   Length: Varies
Motto: "Shall the Sword devour forever?"
Availability: APS reel 211

Remarks: This pacifist publication founded by Noah Worcester is
probably a series of pamphlets rather than a true magazine; but it
is covered here because it circulated like a magazine, and Worcester hoped it would achieve regular publication status.
        The issues are nearly always bound together as a book, and
later editions frequently contain Philo Pacificus' A Solemn Review
of the Custom of War; Showing That War is the Effect of Popular
Delusion, and Proposing a Remedy. This publication gave impetus
to the establishment of peace societies.
        An early such society was the Massachusetts Peace Society.
The annual reports of this society from 1816 to 1827 were included
in the issues of Friend of Peace. The first of these reports described other peace societies including the one in Cincinnati, Ohio
which issued an edition of Friend of Peace from 1817-1818.
        The first issue was a series of six letters from "Omar to
the President" which voice objections to war on historical and moral
grounds. The second issue was an outline of some possible arguments favoring war--all obviously weak. The third issue was called
"The Horrors of Napoleon's Campaign in Russia" and describes
battles and casualties.
        The sixth issue is devoted to a comparison of peace societies
with "other benevolent institutions." Those covered are societies
devoted to: humane purposes, the "suppression of intemperance,"
the "reformation of morals," medicine, charity, the Bible, and
missions.
        Other issues of this periodical are devoted to similar aspects
of the problem of local and universal peace.

85. GARDEN

Title: The Garden
Place: Bairdstown, Kentucky   Dates: March ? -July 11? 1810
Editor: Christopher Crabtree, Esq.   And Others
Publisher: William Dromgoogle
Type: Miscellany - Literary
Frequency: Bi-weekly (?)   Price: Not given
Size: 7 3/4 x 4 3/4   Length: 12 pp.
Quotation: So all agreed, through sweek diversitie,
           This Garden to adorne, with great varietie.
Availability: Not in APS. American Antiquarian Society has: v. 1,
           no. 8, July 11, 1810.

Remarks: The spelling of the town where this item appeared is
usually given as Bardstown, [1] and the form above may be either a
misprint or a variant.
           The Western Review, founded in 1819, has been called the
first literary magazine west of the Allegheny Mountains. [2] Not only
was The Garden from a more western town, but also it was established about nine years earlier than The Western Review.
           Only one twelve-page issue of The Garden was located, and
little can be deduced from this slim evidence. Both the editor and
publisher seem to have used pseudonyms and the real names of
these individuals were not discovered. The contents consisted of a
middle chapter of a serial work of fiction, some anecdotes and poetry. None was signed.
           How long The Garden continued is not known, nor is its exact
starting date. The magazine seems to have been established as a
literary journal--a rather unusual publishing venture for what was
then the frontier.

Notes: 1. Columbia Lippincott Gazetteer of the World, (New York:
          Columbia University Press, 1962), p. 166.
          2. Details are found in the annotation of The Western
          Review.

86. GENERAL REPOSITORY

Title: General Repository and Review
Place: Cambridge, Mass.   Dates: January 1812-October 1813
Editor: Andrews Norton (January 1812-April 1813); A Society of
          Gentlemen (July 1812-October 1813)
Publisher: William Hilliard
Printer: Hilliard and Metcalf
Type: Miscellany - Literary
Frequency: Quarterly   Price: Not given
Size: 8 3/4 x 5   Length: 228 pp.
Availability: APS reels 107, 108
Indexed: Poole, Cargill

References: Mott, I, pp. 277-8
              Karpinski, p. 583

History: Although this title did not actually supersede the Monthly
Anthology, it was closely related to other "Harvard" magazines; although it was not superseded by the North American Review, this
relationship again existed.
        The General Repository was to have been superseded by the
New England Magazine and Review (entry A44), but this title never
appeared.

Remarks: This was a Harvard magazine.   Andrews Norton, who also
wrote for the Monthly Anthology and the Literary Miscellany, drew
on other talents like Joseph Buckminster, Edward Everett, and John
Pickering.   The printing was excellent, and the clean, classicly
simple title page reflected the supreme confidence of these men.
        Four departments, Theology, Literature, Review, and Intel-
ligence each offered a part of the Harvard tone.   In theology the
editors favored a liberal interpretation of Christianity by saying that
the end of all religion is to make men better and that a man's specific religion is secondary to his additions to human progress.
        In literature, the General Repository offered long critical
articles, and did not hesitate to print material in Greek and Hebrew
on the assumption that readers could read both.   Interestingly, less
stress is made on a native American product than on a plea for an
interest in German culture.
        The "Intelligence" section frequently printed information about
other American colleges and universities.   Lists of foreign and
American publications as well as announcements of forthcoming books
and new editions provide some information on American publishing.
        The review section is perhaps the most important.   About
four reviews averaging seventeen to twenty pages appear and they
even cover some novels.   This was unusual in at least two ways:
First, a liberality toward fiction; and second, the length and importance of the reviews.   This latter factor came to be one of the
great traditions of the North American Review, and the groundwork
of American literary criticism, begun by the Monthly Anthology,
was continued and strengthened by the General Repository.
        The editor resisted the temptation of a long opening statement
to justify the magazine; he just began to issue it.   This confidence
was reflected in the pages of this magazine.   The excellence of the
material is continued in the long life of the North American Review
since the NAR derived its initial strength from the Cambridge magazine tradition.

87.   GENERAL SHIPPING

Title: General Shipping and Commercial List (February 21, 1815-
         September 10, 1816); New York Shipping and Commercial

List (September 13, 1816-September 8, 1820); other changes
through 1894
Place: New York   Dates: February 21, 1815-June 30, 1894
Editor: Not given
Printer and Publisher: Day and Turner (to September 7, 1819); C.
          Turner & Co. (September 10, 1819-April 28, 1820); other
          subsequent changes.
Type: Price-current
Frequency: Bi-weekly   Price: $4.00 in 1815; $5.00 from 1816
Size: 10 1/2 x 8 3/4   Length: 4 pp.
Availability: Not in APS.   Copy examined at the New York Public
          Library
Reference: Forsyth, pp. 45-53

Remarks: Several other price-currents (see entries A76-84) are
excluded from regular coverage; but this one, which is described
fully by David P. Forsyth, is included here as one of a type.
      Inspired by an English price list issued by Lloyd's, it began
on the inspired observation that the end of the war would bring increased commerce. The accuracy of this decision has resulted in
this list's being alive today after several mergers and changes in
format.
      Included were stock prices, rate of exchange, rates of in-
surance, lists of arrivals and departures of ships, and current
wholesale and retail prices of commodities for sale on the New York
market. Activities in fifteen or more United States ports are reported. About 450 prices are reported in each issue--prices which
give some insight into the changing economy in America.
      No literary or narrative material was included--other than
that needed to report economic events, and the publication is not to
be considered normally as a magazine.

88. GEOGRAPHICAL AND MILITARY MUSEUM

Title: Geographical and Military Museum
Place: Albany   Dates: February 28-June 6, 1814
Editor: Not given
Publisher: S. R. Brown
Type: News
Frequency: Weekly   Price: $3.00
Size: 10 1/2 x 8 1/2   Length: 8 pp.
Availability: APS reel 136
Reference: Brigham, p. 537

Remarks: Only a very few issues, numbers 5 and 8-13, are available on film; and no general statement of purpose was located. Presumably one main intention was to report the events of the War of
1812.
      Apparently another intention was to print a series of geo-
graphical descriptions of areas in the United States. This idea may

have been part of the growing feeling of nationalism based on the idea that citizens should know and appreciate their country. This series did not materialize--at least in the available issues.

Most of the military and naval accounts are in letters which are vague and sketchy, and contemporary material on the war is not of high quality or value.

Brief articles reported proposed buildings and "progress" in various parts of the country; anecdotal material and selected poetry, and some occasional essays fill the rest of the pages.

89.   GLOBE

Title: The Globe
Place: New York   Dates: January-June 1819
Editor: T. O'Connor
Printer: McDuffee & Farrand (January-May 1819); James Oram
         (June 1819, title page)
Type: News
Frequency: Monthly   Price: $3.00
Size: 8 1/2 x 5   Length: 64 pp.
Availability: APS reel 109

Remarks: The Irish who came to America maintained cohesiveness in at least two ways: most remained Catholic, and most maintained a fierce loyalty to ties with their homeland. Their religion helped to create The Shamrock, an early Catholic magazine edited for Irish interests, and their desire to maintain contact with relatives in Ireland gave rise to papers like The Globe.

This magazine supplies a monthly news summary about Ireland as well as giving other information felt to be of interest to Irish groups. The relations of the United States and Spain were outlined by using documents, and internal improvements were discussed in some detail. News of the Irish famine, ways to emigrate, and stories of famous Dublin residents gave readers a touch of home. Many of the marriages and deaths were reported from Ireland. Several agricultural items appear. The English are frequently assailed in a thinly veiled manner. The poetry was sentimental and pro-American.

The nationalistic feelings of the Irish group in America were a lesson to native Americans; and The Globe, as a special-interest magazine, may have added something, perhaps intangible, to the growing feeling of American nationalism.

90.   GOSPEL VISITANT

Title: The Gospel Visitant.   Being Principally Original Tracts on
         Moral and Religious Subjects: in which an Illustration of the
         Gospel of God our Saviour is Attempted by Arguments Drawn

from Scripture and Reason. The Whole Directed to the Promotion of Poetry and Morality

Place: Salem, Mass. (June-December 1811); Charlestown, Mass.
(March 1812-March 1818); Haverhill, Mass. (April-July 1818)

Dates: v. 1 (June 1811-March 1812); v. 2 (April 1817-January 1818);
v. 3 (April-July 1818). Suspended publication 1812-1817

Editor: Edward Turner and Hosea Ballou (June 1811-March 1818);
P. N. Green (April-July 1818). Superintended by: Thomas
Jones, Gloucester (Cape Ann), Mass.; Hosea Ballou, Ports-
mouth, N.H.; Abner Kneeland, Charlestown, Mass.; and
Howard Turner, Salem, Mass.

Printer: At the Register office, Salem, Mass. (June-September
1811); Ward and Coburn (December 1811); William S. and
Henry Spear (March 1812); Warwick Palfray, Jr. (April 1817-
January 1818); P. N. Green (April-July 1818)

Type: Religious - Universalist

Frequency: Quarterly - when published

Price: 25¢ per issue

Size: 8 3/4 x 5 1/4   Length: 64 pp.

Availability: APS reel 110

Remarks: An earlier magazine, The Berean, devoted to the Universalist viewpoint, did appear, but it was irregular. As its publishing history demonstrates, The Gospel Visitant also could not
maintain a regular schedule.

The Gospel Visitant was established because "The various
brethren of the conference have the liberty of proposing questions
upon any moral or divine subject. These questions are committed
to the members, to be by them, answered in writing."[1] Other
articles would also be included, but the answers to questions proposed by the members served as a launching pad for the evangelism
of the editors.

The majority of items are long discourses on theological issues. Communion, resurrection of the dead, the infallability of the
Pope, and others are discussed in rather dry terms and are slanted
to reflect the position of the Universalists.

The list of agents printed on the end papers of one issue indicate that circulation was limited to New England and New York.

Notes: 1.   The Gospel Visitant, I (June 1811), 1.

91.   HALCYON LUMINARY

Title: Halcyon Luminary and Theological Repository, a Monthly
Magazine Devoted to Religious and Polite Literature

Place: New York   Dates: January 1812-December 1813

Editor: Conducted by A Society of Gentlemen

Publisher: E. Riley

Printer: Samuel Woodworth

Type: Religious - New Jerusalem Church

Frequency: Monthly   Price: $3.00

Size: 8 x 4 1/2   Length: 48 pp.
Masthead: An open book held by an angel, surrounded by a glow,
       holding a scroll with motto.
Motto: In all our strictures placed we will be,
       As Halcyon brooding on a summer sea.
Availability: APS reel 112 (vol. 1, only). Vol. 2 consulted at
       Columbia.

Remarks: Small sects of Protestant Christianity began to appear in
increasing numbers in the early nineteenth century. Many of them
thought to promote their own special viewpoints through magazines,
and the Halcyon Luminary is such a publication.
       Samuel Woodworth may have been a member of this sect, but
the chances are rather that he accepted the job of publishing the
magazine as a business venture rather than a religious duty.
       The main purpose was to "promote" the tenets of one sect;
and, despite the title, precious little else appeared in the two
volumes which were issued.

92. HARVARD LYCEUM

Title: Harvard Lyceum
Place: Cambridge, Mass.   Dates: July 14, 1810-March 8, 1811
Editor: Edward Everett with Daird Damon, Nathaniel Langdon
       Frothingham, —— Fuller, Samuel Gilman[1]
Publisher: Hillard and Metcalf
Type: College magazine
Frequency: Semi-monthly   Price: $3.00
Size: 8 1/2 x 5   Length: 24 pp.
Quotation: And he is gone, and we are going all;
       Like flowers we wither, and like leaves we fall.
                                   (Crabbe)
Availability: APS reel 112
History: A proposed new series apparently did not appear. See
       entry A41

Remarks: Edward Everett, whose connections with Harvard included
teaching there and being its president, began this aspect of his long
and colorful life as chief editor of what claimed to be Harvard's
first undergraduate magazine.[2]
       The periodical was designed to cover all fields and depart-
ments of academic studies at Harvard, and included in the first
issues are articles on mathematics, botany, classical languages and
religion. Original essays, such as one which attempted to show that
Ben Jonson's "Drink to Me Only" was copied from the Greek Sophist
Philostratus, and poetry were also included.
       A few items are printed in Greek, Latin, or Hebrew--per-
haps to accommodate this magazine's special audience. The same
pattern of content was kept in each issue, and while a serious attempt to be original is evident, the magazine makes no outstanding

contributions to literary criticism.   The printing is excellent--in fact the appearance of this magazine makes it one of the few out-standing titles in a typographical sense to appear in the period from 1810 to 1820.

Everett was to work on magazines again--he was editor of the North American Review from 1820 to 1824.   Perhaps his early experience as a Harvard undergraduate helped to make this later editorship a contribution to the success of the NAR.

Notes: 1.   Joseph Allen, "Cambridge Sixty Years Ago," Boston Advocate (July 8, 1870).   The volume and page number are not shown in this newspaper clipping pasted inside the cover of the University of Michigan copy of the Harvard Lyceum.
             2.   This statement is made in the Harvard Lyceum, I (March 9, 1811) p. 431.   In a sense this statement is er-roneous.   Albert Matthews in the Harvard Graduate Magazine for June 1928 on page 445 makes note of: The Telltale, nos. 1-13 (September 9-November 1, 1721).   Ebenezer Turell, Harvard Class of 1721, wrote and issued in manuscript form this weekly or semi-weekly magazine in Cambridge, Mass. Not only is this a manuscript periodical, but also it may well be the first American student periodical, and it ante-dates the first American printed magazine by some twenty years. Extracts appeared in Publications of the Colonial Society of Massachusetts, XII (January 1908-December 1909), 220-7.

93.   HERALD OF GOSPEL LIBERTY

Title: Herald of Gospel Liberty
Place and Dates:
    Portsmouth, N.H. nos.   11-43   (September 1808-April 13, 1810)
    Portland, Me.   nos.   44-74   (April 17, 1810-June 1811)
    Philadelphia, Pa.   nos.   75-142 (July 5, 1811-January 1814)
    Portsmouth, N.H. nos. 143-181 (February 4, 1814-December 22, 1815)
    Boston, Mass.   VIII, no. 1-8   (August 1816-October 1817)
Editor and Publisher: Elias Smith; published in Portland, Me. by
    John P. Colcord (1810-1811)
Printer: Thomas G. Bangs (August 1816-October 1817)
Type: Religious - Christian denomination
Frequency: Bi-weekly   Price: $1.00
Size: 10 x 9   Length: 4 pp.
Availability: Not in APS for period 1810-1817.   See ULS.
Reference: Lewis, p. 168
    Brigham, p. 469
    Barrett, John Pressley.   The Centennial of Religious Journalism, 2d. ed. (Dayton, Ohio: Christian Pub-lishing Association, 1908), pp. 37-75.
    Historical Magazine, II (January 1858), 27-8.

History: Superseded in May 1818 by The Christian Herald (q. v.)
which lasted until 1835. This publication underwent several changes,
eventually assuming Herald of Gospel Liberty as its title in 1851.
This title merged with The Congregationlist in 1930 to become the
Congregationlist and Herald of Gospel Liberty (q. v.). In this study,
the first Herald of Gospel Liberty is considered to have lasted from
1808-1817; the Congregationlist and Herald of Gospel Liberty from
1816-1931; and the two are treated as bibliographically separate--
despite the entries in the Union List of Serials.

Remarks: Brief religious news, sermons, letters on religious subjects, brief moralistic anecdotes are the bulk of material. Designed
for Sunday reading, perhaps to supplement the Bible.
    The Herald has been referred to as a religious newspaper,
and indeed it had newspaper contents. Its purpose, however, was
larger than pure dissemination of the news. An attempt to promulgate a view of religious liberty which would be compatible with civil
liberty gave it an intellectual appeal which enabled it to survive.
The eventual merger with The Congregationlist enabled it it live
about 124 years, although bibliographically it lasted only nine years.
John Barrett's history of religious journalism, referred to above,
supports this contention.

94. HERALD OF LIFE AND IMMORTALITY

Title: The Herald of Life and Immortality
Place: Boston   Dates: January 1819-October 1820
Editor: Elias Smith
Printer and Publisher: Not given
Type: Religious - Universalist
Frequency: Quarterly   Price: Not given
Size: 7 x 4   Length: 36 pp.
Availability: APS reel 113

Remarks: This fairly short, small magazine was entirely devoted
to the teachings of the Universalists. Its pages offered explications
of the scriptures, essays on doctrinal position, and news of the
denomination's activities. The eight issues almost became a text
for those who followed this branch of Protestant Christianity.
    Elias Smith closed his magazine in October 1820 because he
felt that other magazines which devoted their pages to the Universalists eliminated the need for his own magazine. He referred his
readers to the Universalist Magazine, and this may have been a
unique act of charity among magazine editors. For a magazine
editor to admit that another publication was better than his own must
be some sort of milestone in editorial honesty. Nonetheless, the
two volumes of Smith's magazine are a yet another interesting piece

of early American church history.

95. HISTORICAL REGISTER

Title: Historical Register of the United States
Place: Washington, D.C. (vol. 1); Philadelphia (vol. 2-4)
Dates: No month 1812-1814/15. Vols. 1-2 cover from June 1812-
          January 1814; vols. 3-4 cover 1814
Editor: Thomas H. Palmer
Publisher: Thomas H. Palmer (vol. 1); G. Palmer (vols. 2-4)
Printer: G. Palmer, all vols.
Type: History
Frequency: 4 vols. in 2 years, not semi-annual
Price: Not given
Size: 8 1/2 x 5   Length: Up to 500 pp.
Availability: APS reels 113, 114
Indexed: Cargill

Remarks: The all-over purpose of this title was to present and to
preserve a collection of American state papers which could be used
to study American political history.
        Volume one began with the settlement of the English colonies,
and carried the story through the Constitution. The chapters are
brief but cogent; the documents generally abstracted, but pertinent.
The Congressional history covers through the first session of the
thirteenth Congress.
        Volume two has two basic points, the first of which sum-
marizes the War of 1812. The second contains about fifty documents
from both sides.
        Volume three returns to the pattern of the first by reviewing
and summarizing American political institutions with an emphasis on
the Constitution. The second session of the thirteenth Congress is
covered in depth.
        Volume four follows volume two by giving a summary of the
war and documents relating to both sides of the conflict.
        Some attempt to be arbitrary is evident, and the selection is
meant to include only the most important material. This title continues the traditions of The American Register and the American
Review of History and Politics with an attempt to provide carefully
selected source material as background for a study of American
Political institutions.

96. HIVE

Title: The Hive

Place: Lancaster, Pa.   Dates: May 19-December 11, 1810
Editor: Will Honeycomb
Publisher: Not given until July 24, 1810 when William Hamilton's
        name is added and remains throughout.
Printer: William Greer (May 19-July 24, 1810); William Hamilton
        (July 24-December 11, 1810)
Type: Miscellany - Literary
Frequency: Bi-weekly   Price: $2.00
Size: 8 3/4 x 5 1/4   Length: 8 pp.
Quotation: Our labor such, as when, from flow'r to flow'r
            The BEE, in newborn summer's shining hour.
            The toil-sought essence sips, on busy wings,
            And to the HIVE, her nect'rous treasure brings.
Availability: APS reel 114
Superseded: The Monthly Magazine (1808-1809); or possibly a pre-
        vious newspaper, The Hive, published in Lancaster[1]

Remarks: Although a previous magazine came from Lancaster, no
evidence in the magazine indicates an editorial connection between
the two. Who "Will Honeycomb" was is not known, but it could have
been William Hamilton, The Hive's publisher during most of its brief
life; or it may have been William Greer. A connection did exist between The Hive covered here and the earlier newspaper which was
published by Greer.
        The Hive's introduction calls this a new series, and perhaps
the writer meant to indicate The Monthly Magazine. This earlier
title contained news, especially political news;[2] but The Hive never
placed any emphasis on this aspect.
        The majority of the contents consisted of short anecdotes,
one-page literary essays, and poetry. No names ever appeared as
authors, and even pseudonyms are not used.
        The quality of the magazine's writing is not high. The Hive
appeared in a block-page format with only average printing. No
doubt, distributional problems and the lack of a public contributed
to this title's quick demise.

Notes: 1. Brigham, p. 867.
         2. Lewis, p. 208.

97. HIVE

Title: The Hive; or Repository of Literature
Place: Washington, D.C.   Dates: March 30-September 7, 1811
Editor: H. C. Lewis
Printer and Publisher: W. Cooper (March 30-June 15, 1811); H. C.
        Lewis (June 22-September 7, 1811).
Type: Humor
Frequency: Weekly   Price: $4.00
Size: 10 1/4 x 7 1/2   Length: 8 pp.
Motto: "To Raise the Genius and Mend the Heart."

<u>Availability</u>: Not in APS or ULS. Microfilm obtained from the
Library of Congress.
<u>References</u>: Gilmer, <u>Checklist</u>, p. 34
Shaw, no. 23019

<u>Remarks</u>: The Hive shall be a repository of literary amusement,
information, and instruction; original and selected, with
translations from various languages: --a cabinet, entirely destitute of political warfare, yet embracing all
useful intelligence, both foreign and domestic, where in
ladies and gentlemen, of talents, are politely invited to
deposit the effusions of their literary hours.[1]

Early in the magazine music was promised, but apparently
none appeared. In the June 15th issue, a geographical breakdown
of contemporary newspapers lists 158 as Republican, 157 as Federal,
and 50 as "neuter"--a rather unique political designation. All signed
articles use pseudonyms such as Coriander Grimbolt, Tim Rattle-
brain, and Will Spindleshank. The magazine also made some rather
strong statements against slavery.

"The Trifler," a series of humorous essays or short stories,
ran through most issues. Dedicated to the advantures of the Rattle-
brain family, the series claimed to be "Just as interesting and instructive as the adventures of Tom Jones," and it was quite satirical
and amusing.

<u>Notes</u>: 1. <u>The Hive</u>, I (March 30, 1811), 1.

98. HONEY BEE

<u>Title</u>: Honey Bee
<u>Place</u>: Philadelphia <u>Dates</u>: December 18? 1819-January 22, 1820
<u>Editor</u>: "Boston Bard" <u>pseud.</u> of R. S. Coffin
<u>Printer</u>: John H. Cunningham
<u>Type</u>: Miscellany - Literary
<u>Frequency</u>: Weekly <u>Price</u>: $2.00
<u>Size</u>: 13 1/2 x 8 <u>Length</u>: 4 pp.
<u>Masthead</u>: Title words divided by a beehive and an eagle, facing
lift, clutching a scroll inscribed: "The Eagle shall the Bee
Protest."
<u>Availability</u>: Not in APS. Copies of numbers 2-4, 6 consulted in
the Boston Public Library.

<u>Remarks</u>: Number three of this magazine was dated January 1,
1820; and thus two issues must have appeared in 1819 although only
number two was located. This issue contains brief articles and
comments on numerous literary subjects, and a few notices of contemporary authors. Number six for January 22, 1820 indicated
several intentions to continue publication; for example, items yet to
be published were announced. Also printed was a plea for readers

to pay subscription fees. No issues beyond number six were located. Interestingly, many of the articles beg for a more severe criticism of American literature. Praise, when it was not due, did not encourage the effort necessary to produce a truly great poet; and Coffin felt that harsher criticism had to exist before America could produce a literature comparable to Europe's.

99. HUNTINGDON LITERARY MUSEUM

Title: Huntingdon Literary Museum, and Monthly Miscellany
Place: Huntingdon, Pa.   Dates: January-December 1810
Editor: William R. Smith and Moses Canan
Printer: John McCahan
Type: Miscellany - Literary
Frequency: Monthly   Price: $3.00
Size: 7 3/4 x 4 1/4   Length: 48 pp.
Availability: APS reel 114

Remarks: The editors hoped to present original essays on many topics, history, literary criticism, poetry, and art. Also promised were descriptions, section by section, of the United States, and finally an analysis of the counties of Pennsylvania which would include "boundaries, population, soil, productions, and manufactures." This series was unfortunately not completed.
     Continuing their policy statement, the editors stated that:

> Any attempt to oppose, and put down prevailing vices, and absurdities, will always meet with the warmest approbation of the editors; at the same time, due regard must be preserved towards private character, and individual feeling.[1]

This statement expresses an attitude about social behavior typical in the period, but at the same time it implies a rather sophisticated view of an editor's social responsibility, and possibly a realization that freedom of the press involves self-imposed restraints.
     The major literary contribution of this magazine is a prose piece which runs through all twelve numbers: Matthew G. Lewis' Mistrust; or, Blanche and Osbright, A Feudal Romance. Lewis was an English author of the Gothic School who apparently based this work on Heinrich von Kleist's Die Familie Schroffenstein.[2] Thus the Huntingdon Literary Museum's contribution was neither American, nor really even British. But the magazine, in printing European literature, may have added to the growing impetus, need, and possibility for a native American literature.

Notes: 1. Huntingdon Literary Museum, I (January 1810), 2.
       2. Louis F. Peck, A Life of Matthew G. Lewis (Cambridge: Harvard University Press, 1961), p. 140.

100. IDIOT

Title: The Idiot; or, Invisible Rambler
Place: Boston   Dates: January 10, 1818-January 2, 1819
Editor: Samuel Simpleton
Publisher: Henry Trumbull
Printer: Nathaniel Coverly
Type: Miscellany - Humor
Frequency: Weekly   Price: $1.50
Size: ca. 10 x 6   Length: 4 pp.
Masthead: A vignette presumed to be the magazine's namesake.
Availability: Not in APS. Microfilm obtained from the American
        Antiquarian Society.
Reference: Brigham, p. 306.
Merged into: The Boston Kaleidoscope on January 9, 1819.

Remarks: Although several aspects of the newspaper were present,
The Idiot should be considered a magazine. Among the items
which were always straight forward were the notices of marriages
and deaths; and when "moral reflections" and poetry appeared, they
were generally serious and somewhat pious. Humor and anecdotes
are a small part of each issue.
        The bulk of the magazine was made up of a wide variety of
miscellaneous, human-interest, literary, descriptive, historical,
and scientific essays. These were usually informed, and they were
nearly always informative. Theatrical reviews appeared irregularly
and were supposedly written by an omniscient cat who wore glasses
and answered to "Puss."
        This magazine joined forces with The Kaleidoscope on Janu-
ary 9, 1819 to form a new title, The Boston Kaleidoscope.

101. INDEPENDENT BALANCE

Title: Independent Balance
Place: Philadelphia
Dates: March 20, 1817-December 22, 1832
Editor: Democritus, the Younger, a Lineal Descendent of the
        Laughing Philosopher; pseud. of George Hembold
Publisher: George Hembold
Type: Miscellany - Humor
Frequency: Weekly   Price: Average $5.00
Size: 17 3/4 x 15 1/4   Length: 4 pp.
Masthead: Vignette of a kneeling man shooting a pheasant.
Availability: Not in APS or ULS. Two issues examined at the
        American Antiquarian Society.
References: Brigham, p. 919
        Smyth, pp. 184-5

Remarks: This publication could be classified as a literary newspaper, and it indeed carried several columns of news in each issue. Advertisements, usually found only in the newspapers, were numerous. They were supposed to be limited to the first page, but at times spilled into the inner pages. The newspaper contents were average, and included reporting of political and international events. Where the Independent Balance differed was in its satire and humor. Much of this is in dialect, and presumably in letters to the editor:

> Ise reseeft your burdy ledter vat ye dit rite me, apout bekomming a riter for yure funnee baper, vat yu kalls de Pallanz, dough afder Ise hat lookt at one of dem for a long dime, I kuddent see anney ding in at dall like eider de bick order liddel skales dat ve haf kot in ower stoar.[1]

The dialect opened the way for some rather humerous misunderstandings, and the editor could reply as if speaking to a child-- itself an opportunity for sly digs at the established authorities in Philadelphia. Apparently Democritus kept out of serious trouble and attracted an audience strong enough to support his magazine for nearly fifteen years--a respectable accomplishment for the time.

Notes: 1.   Independent Balance, III (October 1, 1819), 2.

102.   INDEPENDENT MECHANIC

Title: Independent Mechanic
Place: New York   Dates: April 6, 1811-March 28, 1812
Editor: Joseph Harmer
Printer and Publisher: Joseph Harmer (April 6-July 27, 1811);
          Joseph Harmer and John M. Eliott (August 3-10, 1811);
          Joseph Harmer & Co. (August 17-December 28, 1811); George
          Asbridge (January 4-March 28, 1812)
Type: Miscellany - General
Frequency: Weekly   Price: $2.00
Size: Large quarto   Length: 4 pp.
Masthead: Title words divided by an upraised hand holding a short-
          handled sledge hammer.
Availability: Not in APS.   Microfilm obtained from the New York
          State Library.
Reference: Brigham, p. 652.

Remarks: Among the editor's purposes was "to furnish ... a weekly repoast calculated at once to please the fancy, improve the heart, and strengthen the mind."[1]   The "progress of the arts" was an emphasis; in one article alone several paragraphs each were devoted to a chain bridge, a mapping instrument, a patent boom, a domestic spinner, muskets, a steam engine, and weaving.
          Articles were abstracted from such sources as the National Intelligencer.   Other news--especially that of New York--was given

in brief paragraphs. About twenty appear in each issue, and they are followed by marriages and deaths. Advertisements (by the end of 1811 nearly a full page), poetry, anecdotes, and a few short stories complete the contents. This is an excellent example of the literary newspaper form. The news function is supported by a wide variety of articles and literature the total effect of which seems to have been educational. Although a mechanic's library was established in Portland, Maine in 1815, the movement for mechanic's education did not gain real impetus until a few years later. However, a periodical like the Independent Mechanic may have provided a helpful precedent.

Notes: 1. Independent Mechanic, I (April 6, 1811), 1.

103. INQUISITOR

Title: The Inquisitor
Place: Philadelphia
Dates: December 30, 1818-January 19, 1820
Editor: Not given
Publisher: James M'Minn
Illustrations: Small title-page vignette repeated in masthead starting
              with number two.
Type: Miscellany - Literary
Frequency: Weekly   Price: 37 1/2 ¢ per quarter
Size: 10 x 5   Length: 4 pp.
Motto: To raise the virtues, animate the bliss,
        And sweeten all the toils of human life.
Availability: APS reel 211

Remarks: The editor, whose name is not known, put himself forward as a guide to the inexperienced in literature. In his introductory essay, he said: "This work is principally designed for the inculcation of correct principles, the dissemination of useful knowledge among the rising generation." Perhaps the editor hoped for a children's audience.

The bulk of the first issue was "Sophia; or, The Dangerous Indiscretion, a Tale Founded on Facts." This rather moral tale set the tone for all the short fiction, informal essays, and miscellaneous articles. Starting on March 3, 1819, a column headed "The Inquisitor" began. This was to be a series of literary essays and this completed the basic pattern of the magazine: two pages of fiction and biography, two literary essays, poetry, fiction, marriages, and deaths--all standard and expected in the literary miscellany.

Toward the end of 1818, M'Minn claimed 300 subscriptions. Although this seems to have been average, The Inquisitor gave way to bigger and better magazines then being started and continued in Philadelphia.

104. INTELLECTUAL REGALE

Title: Intellectual Regale; or, Ladies' Tea Tray
Place: Philadelphia
Dates: November 19, 1814-December 30, 1815
Editor: Mrs. Mary Carr
Printer: Dennis Heartt (November 19, 1814-April 1, 1815); Mrs.
       Mary Carr (April 8-December 30, 1815)
Type: Woman's magazine
Frequency: Weekly   Price: $3.00 a year
Size: 8 x 5   Length: 16 pp.
Motto: Happy to Deceive the Time, not Waste It.
Availability: APS reel 115
Indexed: Cargill

Remarks: The direct association of a woman with this magazine
is one unusual feature; another is that the magazine was started as
one for women.
       The general pattern followed throughout included: short,
serialized fiction; moralistic paragraphs; anecdotes; marriages and
deaths; and news briefs. Some of the material had real charm
and wit:

>   Some females discoursing of the vices of a certain man,
> one of them observed that in the early part of her acquain-
> tance with him he was a respectable member of the baptist
> Society, and had been dipped. Another replied, it had not
> cleansed him much. No, said a girl of about sixteen years
> of age, he should have been put to soak over night!

No woman's features, as they developed later, appeared.
Recipes, plans, patterns, sewing suggestions, and the like were
probably not thought proper. Most material was literature of the
sort apparently thought proper for the delicate minds of women in
Philadelphia society.

Notes: 1. Intellectual Regale, I (December 10, 1814), 43.

105. JOURNAL OF BELLES LETTRES

Title: Journal of Belles Lettres
Place: Lexington, Ky.
Dates: November 20, 1819-February 26, 1820
Editor: ——— Mariano and ——— Everett
Publisher: Thomas Smith
Type: Miscellany - Literary
Frequency: Bi-monthly   Price: $4.00
Size: 8 x 5   Length: 16 pp.
Motto: Quod deceat, quod non, quo virtus, quo ferat error.

Availability: APS reel 116

Remarks: In the opening address, the editors expressed the idea that American literature needed "exertion" rather than "encouragement." This frequently found idea was further promulgated by Mariano and Everett in an effort to aid the rise of an indigenous literature.
The editors felt that native writing could be aided by printing a careful selection of European literature in translation. This idea of teaching by example led to an eclectic literary miscellany which offered material from literatures originally in French, German, Italian, and Scandanavian languages. Certainly this was an unusual idea, and it was a challenge for what was then the American frontier--even if it did have the support of nearby, newly-founded Transylvania College.
The editors quickly found that Lexington was not yet ready for so sophisticated an idea, and the magazine failed after three months.

106. JOURNAL OF FOREIGN MEDICAL SCIENCE

Title: The Eclectic Repertory, and Analytical Review, Medical and Philosophical (1810-1820); Journal of Foreign Medical Science and Literature (1821-1824)
Place: Philadelphia   Dates: October 1810-October 1824
Editor: A Society of Physicians
Publisher: The prospectus names Edward Earle; he did not publish the magazine. Anthony Finley (1810); Thomas Dobson (1811-1813); Thomas Dobson & Son (1814-1820)
Printer: Fry and Krammer (1810-1811); William Fry, (1812-1813); not given (1814-   )
Illustrations: Many issues contained plates most of which were either anatomical or of medical instruments and most reveal an interest in experimental medicine.
Type: Medical
Frequency: Quarterly   Price: $3.00
Size: 8 1/8 x 5   Length: 128 or more pp.
Availability: APS reels 116-7
Reference: "Proposal," Port Folio, 3d series, IV (October 1810), 280-4.
Merged into: American Medical Recorder

Remarks: The growing trend to publish journals specializing in material for the medical profession is well represented by this title. Eight to twelve articles per issue covered a very wide range of subjects, examples of which were: vaccination, pathology of body membranes, coagulation of the blood, women's disorders, contagion, and the experimental use of substances like opium and turpentine as drugs. Booklists and some reviews provided a partial record of contemporary medical publishing.

Some of the articles involve misconceptions such as the
nature and function of "oximuriatic" acid; and some of this apparently results from discussions based on faulty observations, not
empirical laboratory evidence.
Disciplines now considered beyond the normal scope of medicine are covered. Agriculture, meteorology, geography, and geology
are each given some space.
One unusual item, taken from the Edinburgh Medical and
Surgical Journal, is worthy of note:

> Two cases with Observations, demonstrative of the Powers
> of Nature to reunite parts which have been, by accident,
> totally separated from the Animal System. By William
> Balfour[1]

In these two cases, amputated fingers were replaced for nature to
heal. Unfortunately, few details are given, but both cases are reported as successes.
The consistent quality of the articles and a critical selection
policy resulted in an excellent magazine which attempted to inform
the medical profession and to provide some information on their
current interests.

Notes: 1. Journal of Foreign Medical Science, V (October 1815),
            417-30.

107. JOURNAL OF MUSICK

Title: Journal of Musick. Composed of Italian, French, and English
        Songs, Romances and Duetts, and of Overtures, Rondas, &c.
        for the Forte-Piano
Place: Baltimore   Dates: February 15, 1810-1811?
Editor and Publisher: Madame Le Pelletier
Printer: George Willig
Type: Music
Frequency: Bi-monthly (?)   Price: $12.00
Size: 12 3/4 x 9   Length: 6 pp.
Availability: APS reel 119
Reference: Wunderlich, pp. 57-9, 390-3

Remarks: Mott[1] believes that no true music magazine existed before 1825, and that the publications which were called magazines
were merely song books. Although he does not elaborate his reasons, they no doubt include the fact that these publications did not
include articles about music, but only the music itself.
This description applies to the Journal of Musick. Only two
"parts" were found, one of twelve numbers and the other of eleven.
Four pieces for piano, three Italian, eleven French, and fifteen
English songs make up the entire contents. No printing, other than
the words to some of the songs, appears; and no attempt appears to

have been made to provide any other material. Thus it may be fair
to say that this title was not a magazine but only a serially issued
song book.

Wunderlich's dissertation included an extensive analysis of
the contents, and his consideration of this as a magazine is the
justification for inclusion here.

Notes: 1. Mott, p. 172.

108. JOURNAL OF THE TIMES

Title: Journal of the Times
Place: Baltimore
Dates: September 12, 1818-March 6, 1819
Editor: Paul Allen
Publisher: Schaeffer and Maund
Type: News
Frequency: Weekly   Price: $4.00
Size: 9 1/2 x 5 3/4   Length: 16 pp.
Quotation: "Tros Tyriusque nullo discrimine habetur" Virgil
Availability: Not in APS. Copy consulted at the American Anti-
          quarian Society.
Reference: Brigham, p. 238
Superseded by: Morning Chronicle, see: Brigham, p. 243.

Remarks: Despite the title, this publication set out as a news magazine and in the introduction, it was proposed:

> to give a summary or an analysis of the passing events
> both foreign and domestic, accompanied by such observa-
> tions as the subject is calculated to inspire without ming-
> ling in the party politicks of the day ...[1]

Aside from reporting, a news magazine should preserve the details
of events, or as Allen said:

> It is proposed to make the contemplated Journal in some
> measure a record of our domestic concerns.[2]

Also to be included were biography, American literature notices,
book reviews, religious news, and poetry.

The first issue, aside from a brief news summary, started
a series on the history of Maryland "by a Gentleman of Baltimore";
printed biographies of Dr. Richard Watson, Lord Byron, Washington,
and The Duke of Wellington; and added some poetry. The biographies
tended to deal with one aspect of the man rather than his entire
career. Later in the magazine's life, Parisian fashions were reported.

Paul Allen soon found that news, especially local news which
he did not as a rule include, became cold by the end of a week since

it had appeared in newspapers.   Allen hoped to serve as a commentator on the passing scene, but he did not have the facilities or the staff to provide wide enough coverage for his ideas, and his magazine, as the current phrase put it, failed of support.

Notes: 1. Journal of the Times, I (September 12, 1818), 1.
        2. Ibid.

109. KENTUCKY MISSIONARY

Title: Kentucky Missionary and Theological Magazine
Place: Frankfort, Ky.   Dates: May 1, 1812-1814?
Editor: Starke Dupuy
Printer: Mrs. William Gerard
Type: Religious - Baptist
Frequency: Quarterly (?)   Price: $1.00
Size: 8 x 5   Length: 36 pp.
Availability: Not in APS or ULS.   Photostats of the only issue located were obtained from The Filson Club, Louisville, Ky.
Reference: Jillson, pp. 62-3
Superseded by: The Gospel Herald (A25).   No copy located.

Remarks: Only one issue of this magazine was discovered, and the contents are not of supreme importance.   Sixteen pages are devoted to an extracted sermon; and the rest to: missionary information from India, an article on Bible translations, and revivals in Virginia.   The contents seem not to have been concerned with Kentucky, but rather with the Baptists in general.
    This title was apparently superseded by The Gospel Herald, but no copies of this title were located.   Perhaps this dearth of copies can be attributed to early conditions in Kentucky, and it may indicate that only a small number of issues appeared.
    One fact of interest is that this magazine was printed by a woman.   Women printers had been known before, but they could not have been very numerous at any time.

110. LADIES' LITERARY CABINET

Title: The Ladies' Literary Cabinet, being a Miscellaneous Repository of Literary Productions, in Prose and Verse
Place: New York   Dates: May 15, 1819-December 14, 1822
Editor: Samuel Woodworth
Publisher: Woodworth and S. Heustis (May 15-November 27, 1819);
        Samuel Heustis (December 4, 1819-   )
Printer: C. S. Van Winkle (May 15-November 27, 1819); Broderick and Ritter (December 4, 1819-   )
Type: Woman's magazine

Frequency: Weekly   Price: $4.00
Size: 10 1/2 x 7 1/2   Length: 8 pp.
Motto: From grave to gay -- from lively to severe.
Availability: APS reel 121
Indexed: Cargill

Remarks: This magazine was one of several which were produced
with women in mind, and with the idea that they would be the primary readers. Serialized fiction, several original essays, and
biography of famous women were the mainstays. A rhyming dictionary ran through several issues, perhaps with the idea of helping
ladies find the right word for poetry they might write. Several
times lists of synonyms appeared. Two features, "The Ladies'
Toilet," and "The Housewife's Manual," are perhaps among the
earliest columns to include, on a regular basis, grooming and house-
hold tips. Music was promised, and one piece, "Believe Not Sweet
Maiden," was published on November 6, 1819.
    The basic character and contents of this magazine did not
change before 1820; and despite only three and a half years of life,
the magazine helped to establish firmly the idea of a magazine designed specifically for women.

111. LADIES MAGAZINE

Title: The Ladies' Magazine
Place: Savannah, Ga. Dates: February 13-August 7, 1819
Editor, Printer, and Publisher: Barton & Edes (February 13-May
        8, 1819); Russell & Edes (May 15-August 7, 1819)
Type: Woman's magazine
Frequency: Weekly   Price: $5.00
Size: 8 1/2 x 5 1/4   Length: 8 pp.
Motto: "Various - That the mind of desultory man, studious change,
        and pleas'd with novelty, may be indul'd"
                                        Couper
Availability: Not in APS. Copy consulted at Harvard University.

Remarks: The basic purpose William Baron and Richard Edes had
was to produce a magazine which would help women become better
mothers and housekeepers. The reception the magazine received
was not universally high:

        Messrs. Barton and Edes have issued the first number of
        "The Ladies Magazine," a Saturday paper, at Savannah
        (Geo.). Their motto is the same which has adorned our
        journal nearly twenty years, and the paper, in other re-
        spects, evinces a lamentable lack of invention.[1]

    One novel idea the editors did have was to try a four-page
addition to the magazine called Ladies' Advertiser. This supplement

was wrapped around the issue for July 3, 1819, and carries separate material and is, in some ways, actually a separate publication. These pages were to carry advertisements of interest to women. The ads would cost 50¢ for each sixteen lines with 25¢ charged for each subsequent use. One purpose was to increase circulation, but the idea was used with one issue only. A few ads were carried on the last page of issues after July 3, 1819.

Literary essays, usually signed with pseudonyms like Tom Queerfish and Polly Proportion, were the usual opening item. Some short fiction, a miscellany, announcements of marriages and deaths, and poetry were other items nearly always found.

Various editorial tricks were attempted, but the difficulty in obtaining material, rising costs, and the refusal of subscribers to pay all conspired to close this magazine which lasted through twenty-six issues.

Notes: 1.   Port Folio, series 5, VII (April 1819), 337.

112.   LADIES VISITOR

Title: Ladies' Visitor
Place: Marietta, Pa.   Dates: May 24, 1819-April 18, 1820
Editor: Not given
Publisher: William Peirce (!)
Type: Woman's magazine
Frequency: Monthly   Price: $1.00
Size: 8 x 5   Length: 16 pp.
Motto: Virtue our present peace ... our future prize.
Availability: APS reel 212

Remarks: Marietta, Pennsylvania was a small town in 1819, but William Peirce thought there were enough women in the town and surrounding areas to support a magazine designed to interest housewives and mothers. The first six pages of the issue examined are missing and so any possible statement of purpose was not located, but the contents and general appearance of the magazine were both typical for the period.

Serialized fiction, literary and moral essays, poetry, biography, obituaries of famous women were to be found in each issue. Much of this was original; however, nearly half was borrowed and not always with proper credit being given.

Very little material like fashions and homemakers advice appeared. Apparently the publisher felt that women's minds were delicate, and most of his material is of little consequence. The title lasted through thirteen issues and died with no notice.

113.   LADIES' WEEKLY MUSEUM

Title: Impartial Gazetteer, and Saturday Evening Post (May 17-
         September 13, 1788); New York Weekly Museum (September
         20, 1788-May 7, 1791); The Weekly Museum (May 14, 1791-
         August 10, 1805); New York Weekly Museum (August 17,
         1805-April 30, 1814); New York Weekly Museum; or Polite
         Repository of Amusement and Instruction (May 7, 1814-
         April 26, 1817); The Ladies' Weekly Museum; or, Polite
         Repository of Amusement and Instruction (May 7-October 25,
         1817)
Place: New York   Dates: May 17, 1788-October 25, 1817
Editors and Publishers: Harrison and Purdy (May 17, 1788-May 7,
         1791); John Harrison (May 14, 1791-February 8, 1806);
         Margaret Harrison (February 15, 1806-March 26, 1808);
         Charles Harrison (April 2, 1808-May 2, 1812); James Oram
         (May 9, 1812-October 25, 1817)
Printer: Only one listed.   Robert Magill, May 3, 1817
Type: Popular miscellany
Frequency: Weekly
Price: $1.50 (1810); $2.00 (1813); $3.00 (1815)
Size: Small to large 4⁰   Length: 4 pages
Motto: With sweetest flowers enriched, from various gardens
         cull'd with care[1]
Availability: APS reels 561-565
Indexed: , Cargill
Superseded by: Weekly Visitor, and Ladies' Museum (1817-1823)

Remarks: Nearly every issue had three columns and had the superficial appearance of a newspaper.   The volume and issue numbers
vary and are a nightmare of complexity.   Considering the changes
in editor and the factors which affected magazine publishing, The
Ladies' Weekly Museum had a long life of twenty-nine years.
      During most of its life, the printing was of poor quality;
and almost nothing like an illustration appeared.   The closest thing
was an occasional line-cut used in an advertisement or as a column-
head.   The advertisements were usually from local merchants, but
want ads and book announcements are also found.
      The motto describes the contents, especially after 1810.
Serialized fiction, poetry, brief announcements, advertisements, and
obituaries form the bulk.   A weekly retrospect summarized the news,
and during the War of 1812 this contained many interesting facts.
Editorials tended to be borrowed from newspapers, but not those
limited to the New York area.
      As the magazine grew older, more and more articles and
essays of a miscellaneous nature crept in.   Some of the humor was
genuinely funny, and some of the poetry had some style.   Not until
1817 did an emphasis for the ladies become a major part of the
magazine.
      The file on film is incomplete, and many of the issues show
hard wear.   From this alone it may be assumed that this was a

popular magazine in its day, but even good magazines had trouble
when circulation was small and when the subscribers failed to pay
for the issues they received. No reason is given for the demise of
this title; but James Oram changed his address five times in as
many years, and he may well have had financial troubles made more
difficult by a failing magazine. He finally transferred his interest
in the magazine to Alexander Ming who published a magazine as successor to this one.

Notes: 1. This motto was also used by The Casket.

114. LADY'S MISCELLANY

Title: Weekly Visitor, or Ladies' Miscellany, vols. 1-4 (October 9,
       1802-October 25, 1806); The Lady's Weekly Miscellany,
       vols. 5-11, no. 2 (November 1, 1806-May 5, 1810); The
       Lady's Miscellany, or the Weekly Visitor for the Use and
       Amusement of Both Sexes, vols. 11, nos. 3-15, no. 26
       (May 12, 1810-October 17, 1812)
Place: New York   Dates: October 9, 1802-October 17, 1812
Printer: McCarty and White (December 2, 1809-October 20, 1810);
         Samuel White (October 27, 1810-October 17, 1812)
Illustrations: Numerous, small wood-cuts of flowers, urns, and
       the like decorate the issues as column heads.
Type: Miscellany - Popular
Frequency: Weekly   Price: $1.50-$3.00
Size: 8 3/8 x 5 1/8   Length: 16 pp.
Masthead: Small oval of a woman's face centered in title.
Availability: APS reels 20-1, 212-3
Indexed: First in title series indexed by Cargill.
Reference: Lewis, pp. 175-6

Remarks: The major contents include: serialized fiction, some
news from abroad, anecdotes, marriage and death notices, geographical articles, biography--especially of women--a "variety,"
and the inevitable poetry.
       Women's fashions occupy several articles, although no plates
exist. Music appeared fairly regularly and seems to have had an
Irish emphasis. Advertisements were carried and generally con-
centrated on the commonplace--except possibly a series advertising
slave children for sale.
       At the magazine's close, the editor's plea was not lack of
money, but rather lack of time to concentrate on his paper. A
rather unusual statement in this period of subscription default.

115. LATTER DAY LUMINARY

Title: The Latter Day Luminary

Place: Philadelphia Dates: February 1818-December 1825
Editor: By a Committee of the Baptist Board of Foreign Missions
 for the United States
Publisher: Anderson and Meehan
Type: Religious - Baptist
Frequency: Five times a year Price: Not given
Size: 8 x 4 3/4 Length: 64 pp.
Availability: APS reel 122

Remarks: One prominent aspect of this magazine is like many other contemporary publications--it was almost entirely anonymous. Perhaps the publisher is identified so that subscriptions could be sent in. The primary purpose of the magazine was to report missionary activity. These were to be missions, both in the United States and scattered over the world, which were connected with the Baptist Board of Foreign Missions. The Board may have felt that some publicity about their missionary activity would attract the funds necessary to continue. Also included in each issue were accounts of Bible and tract societies and items about Sunday school associations. The news of missions took the form of letters from these people and these letters serve as another repository of information about this activity.
 Book reviews, poetry, hymns, and news of ordinations and deaths fill out each issue.

116. LAYMAN'S MAGAZINE

Title: Layman's Magazine
Place: Martinsburgh, Va. Dates: November 16, 1815-November
 7, 1816
Editor: Not given
Printer: John Alburtis
Type: Religious - Episcopal
Frequency: Weekly Price: $2.00
Size: 8 1/4 x 4 1/2 Length: 8 pp.
Motto: Thou shalt love the Lord thy God with all thy heart, with
 all thy soul, and with all thy mind--and thy neighbor as
 thyself.
Availability: APS reel 123

Remarks: Short moralistic fiction, brief sermon-like essays, poetry, and some news--these are the basic contents. News of other Episcopal churches, especially in Connecticut and Pennsylvania, is also included.
 Some seasonal material pertaining to church and calendar dates explains the Episcopalian viewpoint in clear, elementary language. This style may mean the magazine was designed for Sunday school purposes. One such item is curiously placed: a hymn for the Third Sunday in Advent was not published until January 25 in 1816--over a month late!

Many church-related societies and activities are reported and several well-chosen articles are borrowed from other magazines, both religious and secular.

No mention is made of reasons for stopping publication, but money and small circulation are probably at least factors.

117. LITERARY AND EVANGELICAL MAGAZINE

Title: The Virginia Evangelical and Literary Magazine (January 1818-December 1820); The Evangelical and Literary Magazine, and Missionary Chronicle (January-December 1821); The Evangelical and Literary Magazine (January 1822-December 1823); The Literary and Evangelical Magazine (January 1824-December 1828)
Place: Richmond, Va.   Dates: January 1818-December 1828
Editor: John Holt Rice
Printer: William W. Gray
Type: Religious - Presbyterian
Frequency: Monthly   Price: Not given
Size: 8 x 4 1/2   Length: 48 pp.
Motto: Because of the House of the Lord our God, I will Seek thy good.
Availability: APS reel 124
Superseded: The Christian Monitor (1815-1817)

Remarks: Both the editor and the printer of this magazine probably changed, but not until after 1820. While the scope of the magazine was altered somewhat in its later life, in its early years its title matched its purpose. The magazine was for Virginia, and it was evangelical in its contents and attitude. Later emphasis on literature was not evident in the first few years.

Started frankly to promote the course of Presbyterianism, the magazine also hoped to promote internal improvements in other areas. Agriculture, inland navigation, roads, and schools were among the topics the editors hoped to cover. Cover them or not, Rice's concept of "internal improvements" was an innovation which led to many areas of reform.

Other articles deal with such topics as: family life, Divinity, classical education, and Lord Byron. Basically a religious magazine, it hoped to cover many areas of national life and actually succeeded to a degree.

118. LITERARY AND MUSICAL MAGAZINE

Title: Ladies' Literary Museum; or, Weekly Repository (July 5, 1817-March 28, 1818); Ladies' Literary Museum (April 4-July 13, 1818); Lady's and Gentleman's Weekly Museum, and

Philadelphia Reporter (July 27-September 30, 1818); Lady's
and Gentleman's Weekly Literary Museum and Musical Maga-
zine (January 1-March 1, 1819); Literary and Musical Maga-
zine (March 8, 1819-July 1820)
Place: Philadelphia   Dates: July 5, 1817-July 1820
Editor, Printer, Publisher: Henry C. Lewis. W. H. P. Tuckfield
    named as owner on June 28, 1819, but not thereafter.
Illustrations: Unsigned vignettes used on title pages and in some
    mastheads.
Type: Miscellany - Literary. From 1819, music
Frequency: Weekly   Price: $1.00
Size: 10 x 7 1/4   Length: 4-8 pp.
Motto: Requiring with various taste, things widely different from
    each other.
Availability: APS reel 213
Reference: Wunderlich, pp. 63-69; 397-402

Remarks: As may be seen from the title changes, this magazine
had a varied career by changing its contents and purpose in a
marked way. This change by Henry Lewis was not only original
and clever, but also it may have been the first time an American
magazine so drastically altered its whole format in an apparent attempt to stay alive by offering an appeal to a different audience.
    The first volumes offered light, serialized fiction; anecdotes;
Sunday reading, marriages, deaths, and poetry. Women's features
as they were later known did not appear; but the reading is of the
sort then thought proper for the tender, feminine mind. The
"benevolent societies" which women started and supported were
discussed, and some scattered advertisements for women were included. A theatrical column was promised but did not appear with
regularity.
    Various title changes, designed to attract more readers, were
not successful. The magazine temporarily suspended in October 1818
and resumed the following January with a new face--music.
    In the final year the magazine was largely musical: articles
on musical subjects, announcements of concerts, ads for music
books, criticism, and always the score for a song. The poetry and
a few odds and ends found in each issue fill in the pages.
    Despite the change, Lewis had troubles with money. He tried
to sell out, changed to four pages, eventually became a monthly, and
finally had to cease publication.

119.   LITERARY AND PHILOSOPHICAL REPERTORY

Title: The Literary and Philosophical Repertory: Embracing Dis-
    coveries and Improvements in the Physical Sciences; the
    Liberal and Fine Arts; Essays Moral and Religious; Occa-
    sional Notices and Reviews of New Publications; and Articles
    of Miscellaneous Intelligence
Place: Middlebury, Vt.   Dates: April 1812-May 1817

Editor: Edited by A Number of Gentlemen
Publisher: J. Swift
Printer: T. C. Strong
Type: College magazine (?)
Frequency: Six times a vol., irregular   Price: Not given
Size: 8 1/4 x 4 3/4   Length: 88 pp. avg.
Availability: APS reel 126
Indexed: Cargill

Remarks: The periodicity of this magazine is quite irregular, and is indicated in this list.

Vol. I, no. 1: April 1812
         no. 2: November/December 1812
         no. 3: March 1813
         no. 4: May/June/August 1813
         no. 5: October/November/December 1813; January 1814
         no. 6: March/April 1814
Vol. II, no. 1: July/August 1814
         no. 2: September/October/November/December 1814; January 1815
         no. 3: February/March/April 1815
         no. 4: June/July/August 1815
         no. 5: January/February/March 1816
         no. 6: July/August/September/October/November/ December 1816; January/April/May 1817

This odd irregularity may be explained if this is a collegiate magazine which it may have been. The promise of the title was at least attempted, and the first issue included reviews, a missionary sermon, an article on biography, a letter from France, and articles on porcelain and grapes. The series of letters from France continued in all issues and described many aspects of life in Paris and much of the city itself. Some attempts at satire, such as "On the Folly of Book-learning" added humor to otherwise rather interesting pages. If this was a college magazine it was certainly different from other such early magazines in both its contents and its relatively long life.

120. LITERARY CADET

Title: Literary Cadet
Place: Cincinnati, Ohio   Dates: November 22, 1819-April 27, 1820
Editor: Joseph Buchanan
Printer: Looker, Reynolds & Co.
Type: Miscellany - Literary
Frequency: Weekly   Price: $1.00
Size: ca. 8 x 5   Length: 4 pp.

Availability: Not in APS or ULS. Film of 1819 borrowed from the
          Ohio Historical Society Library
Merged with: Western Spy after 1820

Remarks: This magazine may have been the earliest periodical in
the Miami Valley[1] but it was not the earliest magazine to appear in
Ohio. Although it was small, its four-page, three column format
gave it the appearance of a newspaper.
     Occasional biography, a few book reviews, and miscellaneous
essays opened each issue. Running throughout 1819 a series on
banks discussed the presumed benefits and evils of these institutions--
especially those operated by the states. An article discussing a
brain operation, several items on the colonization of slaves, and
summaries of national events also appeared.
     Buchanan attempted to be neutral in politics, and religion is
barely mentioned. Advertisements were accepted for common items
and to announce various medical services. Up to twelve lines
cost $1.00 for three issues with 25¢ charged for additional in-
sertions.

Notes: 1. Lawrence Mendenhall, "Early Literature of the Miami
          Valley," Midland Monthly, VIII (August 1897), 146.

121. LITERARY MISCELLANY

Title: Literary Miscellany; or, Monthly Review, a Periodical Work
Place: New York   Dates: May-August 1811
Editor: Charles N. Baldwin
Publisher: Riley and Adams
Illustrations: "An elegant engraving" was to have been printed with
          "The Hermit. A Tale" in June 1811. Engraving is not in
          the film copy. Three other plates are also missing.
Type: Miscellany - Literary
Frequency: Monthly   Price: Not given
Size: 5 1/2 x 3 1/4   Length: 68 pp.
Availability: Cargill

Remarks: This magazine was simply another unsuccessful attempt
to provide a literary magazine for an audience in New York. No
first-rate magazine covering this field was published at this time
in New York, and apparently the audience did not exist--especially
for a second-rate periodical.
     A serialized "tale" began in the first issue. Baldwin must
have had a publishing conscience because when, after four numbers,
it became apparent that the Literary Miscellany was about to fail,
he issued a supplement completing "Netley Abbey: A Gothic Tale."
     The other noteworthy feature was the republication of "Na-
tional Prejudice; or the Reviewers Reviewed." This article chas-
tized the contemporary British view of American publishing which

held that American literature was simply non-existent. Americans
had a right to defend themselves, and that they did so with some
vehemence is another indicator of growing feeling of literary nationalism.

122. LITERARY REGISTER

Title: Literary Register
Place: Philadelphia   Dates: July 25, 1813-December 17, 1814
Editor: George Booth
Printer and Publisher: John B. Austin
Type: Miscellany - Literary
Frequency: Weekly   Price: $4.00
Size: 12 x 10   Length: 8 pp.
Masthead: Small vignette between two title words
Availability: Not in APS. Microfilm obtained from the Historical
        Society of Pennsylvania.

Remarks: The announced intention was to accept literary items,
but to avoid "political or religious discussions; ... party censure,
bitter invective, or personal abuse..."[1]
        The pattern included a literary essay or two; biography--
generally in serial form; anecdotes; a thoughtful or serious essay;
marriages and deaths; and poetry. Fiction was generally serialized,
and reviews were produced by "The Desultory Observer."
        Attempts to attract the ladies included recipes and a column
of odd definitions and facts. "The Ladies' Toilet" discussed attitudes and behavior on subjects like gambling.
        Booth claimed that religious controversy was out, but occa-
sional religious columns appeared, such as "Thoughts on Deism" in
which members of the sect were called "blackheads."[2]
        No mention is made of the War of 1812, and this lack of in-
formation may, in itself, be considered an opinion.
        The magazine was intended merely as an entertaining, not
necessarily funny, miscellany. Generally it succeeded.

Notes: 1. Literary Register, I (July 31, 1813), 9.
        2. Ibid., I (February 17, 1814), 226.

123. LITERARY VISITOR

Title: Literary Visitor
Place: Wilkesbarre, Pa.   Dates: July 15, 1813-September 29, 1815
Editor: Not given
Publisher: Steuben Butler
Type: Literary newspaper
Frequency: Weekly   Price: $2.00

Size: 9 x 5 1/2   Length: 8 pp.
Availability: Not in APS. File consulted at Trinity College, Hart-
          ford, Conn.

Remarks: The editor proposed "... it would be an object ... to
diffuse knowledge ... and ... to prepare, tho' not a mental banquet,
yet an intellectual refreshment." He went on that "this paper may
justly be styled a miscellany--for it will be devoted to every department of knowledge ..." Biography, wit and humor, poetry, and essays on all subjects promised to be "free from the asperity of personal abusage."[1]
          The biography came as promised, but it was unoriginal.
Travel articles frequently appeared in the early issues, but they
were borrowed. Other items were as varied as they were numerous.
          The title is called a newspaper since this feature appeared
with number three and continued by summarizing national and local
news with no attempt at editorial comment. Marriages and deaths
appeared.
          Statistical material and treaties from the War of 1812 were
printed, but no direct attempt was made to report its events in
detail. The magazine was undistinguished and could not gain support enough to survive.

Notes: 1. Literary Visitor, I (July 15, 1813), 2.

124. LITERARY VISITOR

Title: The Literary Visitor; or, Entertaining Miscellany Comprising
          Meritorius Selections and Original Productions in Prose and
          Verse
Place: Baltimore   Dates: nos. 1-6, no months 1812-1813
Editor: Not given
Publisher: Edward J. Coale
Type: Miscellany - Literary
Frequency: Bi-monthly (?)   Price: Not given
Size: 5 3/4 x 3 1/4   Length: 80-110 pp.
Availability: Not in APS or ULS.   Copy consulted at the Houghton
          Library, Harvard University.

Remarks: Six issues with no months appeared over a two year
span. According to a note on the card in the Houghton Library
card catalog at Harvard, "Nos. 1-3 were advertised in the Baltimore & Georgetown newspapers on November 23, 1812; January 12
& March 11, 1813, respectively ..." Thus this could have started
late in 1812.
          Each issue differs from every other. The first is entirely
one biography; and the second, seven articles on varied topics such
as shubbery, Lord Bacon, and periodical literature.
          Partly eclectic and partly original, an attempt was made to
follow the title's promise. The wide variety leads to some interest-

and to the unusual. Volume two includes "On Gymnastics" by the
Countess De Genks. Gymnastics was a somewhat different term
from that known today since it included track, riding, swimming,
archery, shooting, military exercises, billiards, shuttlecock and
dancing.[1]
    This title may have been omitted from other magazine bib-
liographies since it is very much like a pamphlet series; but since
the unknown editor considered it to be a magazine it is included
here. It certainly was more entertaining than literary, but should
be recognized as a part of Baltimore's literary history.

Notes: 1.   The Literary Visitor, II (1813), pp. 122-140.

125. A MAGAZINE

Title: A Magazine
Place: Baltimore   Dates: no. 1, September 24, 1810
Editor: Will Whimsical (Pseud. of George Lemmon?)
Publisher: George Lemmon
Printer: Not shown
Illustrations: None in the single issue seen
Type: Miscellany - General
Frequency: Only one issue discovered
Price: If under 20 pp., 11 pence; 20-30 pp. "a Quarter of a Dollar"
Size: 6 x 3 1/2   Length: 12 pp.
Availability: Not in APS or ULS. Microfilm obtained from The
        Library Company of Philadelphia.

Remarks: The single issue seen contains a prospectus, an essay
attacking the Pope, a book review, and two poems. Only eleven of
the twelve pages contain material, and the pages are small. A
Magazine would have been excluded from consideration except that
the editor announced his intention to appear as a magazine should:

> The Golden Age of wisdom and virtue should not be suf-
> fered to sink into oblivion for want of an historian ... I
> intend to paint our pure country as it rises bright and
> beautiful on the eye. It excells in every thing, and there-
> fore in the course of my numbers no topic shall be left
> entirely untouched.[1]

    The topic which was touched was religion, and in an essay
entitled Popery,[2] the editor says the United States "have not been
protected from its poison," and that "an able and artful body of its
supporters" had come to Baltimore. These were "the remnants of
that pernicious set of men the Jesuits." The editor then states
with candor that "To expose the errors and danger of this supersti-
tion, is one object of this Magazine." This may have been the only
purpose; and if so, Catholic Baltimore was not the place to try.
George Lemmon's publication apparently lasted but one issue.

Notes: 1. A Magazine, no. 1 (September 24, 1810), 3.
       2. Ibid., pp. 6-7.

126. MASSACHUSETTS AGRICULTURAL REPOSITORY

Title: Massachusetts Agricultural Repository and Journal
       Caption title: Massachusetts Agricultural Journal
Place: Boston   Dates: November 1813-April 1832
Editor and Publisher: Massachusetts Society for Promoting Agri-
       culture
Printer: Russell, Cutter, and Co. (November 1813); Hilliard and
       Metcalf (May 1814); A. Belcher (January 1815); Ezra B.
       Tileston (June 1815); Tileston and Weld (January and June
       1816); Tileston and Parmenter (January 1817); Wells and
       Lilly (July 1817-June 1823)
Illustrations: Scattered plates of farm animals, crops, and equip-
       ment.
Type: Agricultural
Frequency: Semi-annual (irregular)
Price: $1.00 per year; $5.00 for life
Size: 8 3/4 x 5   Length: 70-100 pp.
Availability: APS reel 214
Superseded: Massachusetts Society for Promoting Agriculture:
       Papers

Remarks: The society mentioned above decided to make its Papers
more wide-spread and changed the nature of this publication to that
of a magazine. The major purpose was to include agricultural inventions and experiments, especially those dealing with soils, cross-
breeding, new crops, and crop rotation. These articles were generally papers presented at meetings of the society.
       Some of the illustrations are schematic drawings of inventions
and others are botanical drawings which show things like a newly
developed strain or a fungus growth.
       There was an interest in crop improvement since the United
States was forced in 1812 to develop its own produce, and a growing
population demanded more food from farmers who needed to be
taught. This purpose was performed by this magazine until it was
replaced by more popularly written journals.

127. MASSACHUSETTS BAPTIST MISSIONARY MAGAZINE

Title: The Massachusetts Baptist Missionary Magazine
Place: Boston   Dates: September 1803-December 1816
Editor: Thomas Baldwin
Publisher: Massachusetts Baptist Convention. Known as: Massa-
       chusetts Baptist Missionary Society (1803-1807); Baptist

Missionary Society of Massachusetts (1808-16)
Printer: Manning and Loring. Vol. 3 also by Lincoln & Edmonds.
Type: Religious - Baptist
Frequency: Semi-annual (September 1803-September 1805); then
    quarterly. I, nos. 1-12 (September 1803-January 1808);
    II, nos. 1-12 (March 1808-December 1810); III, nos. 1-12
    (March 1811-December 1813); IV, nos. 1-12 (March 1814-
    December 1816)
Price: 12 1/2¢ per issue
Size: 8 1/2 x 4 5/8   Length: 32 pp.
Quotation: Ye shall be witnesses unto me, both in Jerusalem, and
    in all Judea, and in Samaria, and unto the uttermost.
Availability: APS reels 25, 216
Indexed: Baptist Missionary Magazine has an index volume covering
    the years 1803-1883 which include this title.
References: Lewis, pp. 189-90
Superseded by: American Baptist Magazine and Missionary Intelli-
    gencer; later: Baptist Missionary Magazine

Remarks: Sermons and "dissertations" on theological subjects, Biblical criticism, biography, and poetry add to a great weight of missionary information. Ordinations, articles concerned with Biblical
and tract societies, and some book reviews all provide a basis for
promulgating the Baptist viewpoint.
    The missionary matters concentrate on India, and generally
they take the form of letters and journals from men working in that
country. A very real concern for the underprivileged spills over to
the United States and results in recounting the activities of domestic
reform groups.

128. MASSACHUSETTS WATCHMAN

Title: The Massachusetts Watchman and Periodical Journal
Place: Palmer, Mass.   Dates: June 1809-May 1810
Editor and Publisher: Ezekiel Terry
Type: Miscellany - General
Frequency: Monthly   Price: 62 1/2¢ per vol.
Size: 8 1/4 x 4 3/4   Length: 12 pp.
Quotation: How pleasant's a well furnish'd page! -
    Cordial repast for every age.
Availability: APS reels 26, 216
Reference: Lewis, p. 193

Remarks: On the verso of the title page, Terry said, "nothing inconsistent with the purest virtue shall ever darken these pages."[1]
In number eleven, less than a year later, he published "The Squire
and the Farmer's Daughter."[2] This ribald story, which plays on
the confusion between "lass" and "ass" while the squire, in trying
to get the one to bed, winds up with the other, is worthy of another
age and rather surprising for a magazine of this period.

Other articles deal with a wild variety of matters from duels
to witchcraft. Many of these are written in a humorous way--even
the obituaries may well be merely parodies.
The type is frequently old-fashioned and often simply old.
The printing is not of very high quality and the magazine probably
never had a wide circulation.

Notes: 1. The Massachusetts Watchman, I (June 1809), title page
verso.
2. Ibid., I (April 1810), 128-31.

129. MEDICAL AND SURGICAL REGISTER

Title: The Medical and Surgical Register: Consisting Chiefly of
Cases in the New York Hospital
Place: New York   Dates: no months: 1818-1820
Editor: John Watts, Valentine Mott, Alexander Hodgdon Stevens
Publisher: Collins and Co.
Printer: J. & J. Harper
Illustrations: Volume one contains four anatomical drawings.
Type: Medicine
Frequency: Bi-annual   Price: Not given
Size: 8 x 4 1/2   Length: 150 pp.
Availability: APS reel 216

Remarks: Only two parts of this title actually appeared, and they
might be called the two sections of a medical text the authors of
which were Watts, Mott, and Stevens. These three men wrote
nearly all the material and based it on their own clinical experience.
Like other medical publications of the time, these two issues
were collections of case studies. The preface claims that this was
the first time it had been done, which is doubtful; but the two issues
do serve to gather work by three noted doctors and to clarify medical symptoms which could be rare to the average practitioner.
Frequently, the treatments used and the drugs prescribed may
seem strange, but this was a period lacking in adequate laboratory
knowledge, and instrumentation was largely an underdeveloped field.
The pages do have considerable value for the medical historian.

130. MEDICAL REPOSITORY

Title: The Medical Repository and Review of American Publications
on Medicine, Surgery, and the Auxiliary Branches of Philos-
ophy
Place: New York   Dates: July 26, 1797-1824
Editor: Samuel Latham Mitchell and Edward Miller (1789-1812); S.
L. Mitchell, Felix Pascalis, and Samuel Akerly (1813-1818);

S. L. Mitchell and Felix Pascalis (1819-1820)
Publishers: Collins and Perkins (1808-1812); John Forbes (1813-
    1814); T. and J. Swords (1815-1817); C. S. VanWinkle (1818);
    William A. Mercein (1819-1820)
Illustrations: About half the plates published from 1810-1820 were
    non-medical in nature including rare animals and even maps.
    Other smaller illustrations, printed as part of the text, ap-
    peared occasionally.
Type: Medical
Frequency: Quarterly   Price: Not given
Size: 8 x 5   Length: ca. 100 pp.
Availability: APS reels 132-3
Reference: Lewis, pp. 197-9

Remarks: In 1813, the title page reads: "The Medical Repository,
Comprehending Original Essays and Intelligence Relative to Medicine, Chemistry, Natural History, Agriculture, Geography, and the
Arts; and a Review of American Publications on Medicine, and the
Auxiliary Branches of Science." This rather boastful and mildly
inaccurate phrase summarizes what America's first medical periodical attempted. Each quarterly issue ran about one hundred pages
and offered a half-dozen or so articles on topics which the editors
thought would hold an audience. The illustrations were sparse and
generally poor; but considering the lack of adequate technique, the
attempt to illustrate such material was a striking innovation.
    Formal medical education was rare in the early nineteenth
century, and this periodical was designed to serve as a text-book
and as a sort of vicarious experience. The case study method was
the basis of what was published. A second important feature was
the book review--long enough to serve in lieu of the book itself
when this was not available to the practitioner. Nearly all the
cases were reports of successful treatment, and many dealt with
the rare and exotic ailments rather than the common and humdrum.
The treatment of venereal and pulmonary diseases, women's disorders, and the medical uses of mercury and urine are examples
of frequently discussed topics.
    This was an experimental period in medicine, and the specu-
lations of some very great minds are to be found in the pages of
this magazine.

131. METHODIST REVIEW

Title: The Methodist Magazine (1818-1828). Several changes until
    finally becoming The Methodist Review
Place: New York   Dates: January 1818-May/June 1931
Editor: Joshua Soule and Thomas Mason (through 1820)
Publisher: J. Soule and T. Mason (January 1818-   )
Printer: John C. Totten (January 1818-   )
Illustrations: Volumes one and two, 1818-1819, each has a fron-
    tispiece.

Type: Religious - Methodist
Frequency: Montly   Price: Not given
Size: 10 1/4 x 6 1/4   Length: 40 pp.
Availability: APS reel 135
Indexed: Poole
Reference: Mott, I, pp. 299-301

Remarks: Despite several name changes and mergers, this magazine eventually lasted over a century. A separate index covering
through 1881 was published in 1884.
    From 1810-1820, seven of the sections covered such standard
items: divinity, biography, explication of the Scriptures, religious
and missionary news, obituaries, poetry, and miscellaneous. Two
other sections added "The Attributes of God displayed in the works
of Creation and Providence," and "The Grace of God Manifested."
    This was a doctrinal, polemic publication and the promised
sections appeared with regularity. The miscellaneous section reported on dozens of religious societies, reviewed books, gave extracts of sermons, and contained the only variety in the magazine.
The rest appeared with monotony in a drab format, but managed to
live over 112 years.

132. MILITARY MONITOR

Title: Military Monitor and American Register
Place: New York   Dates: August 17, 1812-April 2, 1814
Editor: Thomas O'Connor and S. Wall (August 17-November 23,
         1812); Thomas O'Connor (December 14, 1812-April 2, 1814)
Printer and/or Publisher: Joseph Desnoues (August 17-September
         7, 1812); John Hardcastle and Peter Van Pelt (September 14-
         October 5, 1814); Joseph Desnoues (October 12, 1812-April
         2, 1814)
Illustrations: Aside from scattered decorations, one plate showing
         an Indian attack.
Type: News
Frequency: Weekly   Price: $3.00
Size: 10 1/2 x 8 1/2   Length: 8 pp.
Motto: The Public Good our End.
Availability: Not listed in ULS. APS reel 136
Indexed: Cargill
Reference: Brigham, p. 665

Remarks: Containing a Correct Record of the Events of the War
             Between the United States of America and their terri-
             tories, and the United Kingdom of Great Britain and
             Ireland, and the Dependencies Thereof.

    This title-page statement explains the purpose and contents
of the Military Monitor which includes the events of the war, state

papers, proceedings of Congress, political and economic essays, foreign and domestic news, lists of prizes taken from the enemy, military information, and other similar items. The Military Monitor expressed a strong nationlistic view from the outset. Early issues had a brief history of the United States from the days of Columbus through the Revolution, and the history, while basically accurate, was biased. Frequently, articles were continued from issue to issue without any explanation of continuation.

One interesting item appeared on July 5, 1813: The Constitution and Washington's Farewell Address, accompanied a proposal to publish by subscription a history of the Revolution. The issue amounted to an early form of the anniversary number of a magazine.

133. MIRROR OF TASTE

Title: The Mirror of Taste and Dramatic Censor
Place: Philadelphia   Dates: January 1810-December 1811
Editor: Stephen Cullen Carpenter
Publisher: Bradford and Inskeep (1810); Thomas Barton Zantzinger
        and Co. (1811)
Printer: Smith and M'Kenzie (January-June 1810); J. Maxwell
        (July-December 1810); Fry and Krammerer (1811)
Illustrations: A promise to illustrate each issue may have been
        kept, but only eight plates were found. Most of the dis-
        covered plates and those promised were of actors.
Type: Theatre
Frequency: Monthly   Price: $8.00
Size: 8 1/4 x 4 3/4   Length: Up to 144 pp.
Availability: APS reel 218
Indexed: Cargill

Remarks: Of the magazines which appeared in the period 1810-1820, this was no doubt the most important, if for no reason other than it lasted more than one theatrical season.

Biographies of actors, a serialized history of the stage, and commentaries on classical and contemporary drama are the major contents. The Mirror reflected the Philadelphia theatre by listing major performances and actors, and by publishing many reviews. Other American and European theatrical centers are given some attention.

Carpenter had previous editorial experience on other magazines,[1] and could see the value of a periodical devoted to this subject. If the magazine were good, it could help "to inculcate a just and sober taste" which might help to create a theatrical audience which in turn would increase the demand for good theatre and provide a market for his publication.

Several entire plays were included with the magazine, and Carpenter hoped to illustrate every issue. As time passed, the later issues were mainly historical, biographical, and review articles.

Although the journal of the Philadelphia stage continued, other cities were dropped. Carpenter does not state reasons for discontinuing The Mirror, but the reason probably was the lack of an interest sufficiently strong to sustain a publication like this one.

Notes: 1. Mott, I, pp. 260-1.

134. MISSIONARY HERALD

Title: The Panoplist; or, The Christian's Armory (July 1805-May
        1808): The Panoplist and Missionary Magazine United (June
        1808-December 1817); The Panoplist, and Missionary Herald
        (January 1818-December 1820); The Missionary Herald (Janu-
        ary 1821-1827); The Missionary Herald, Containing the Pro-
        ceedings of the American Board of Commissioners for
        Foreign Missions (1828-March 1934); Missionary Herald at
        Home and Abroad (April 1934-March 1951)
Place: Boston   Dates: July 1805-March 1951
Editor: An Association of Friends to Evangelical Truth.   Jedidiah
         Morse (1805-1810); Jeremiah Evarts (1810-   )
Printer: Samuel T. Armstrong (in period)
Type: Religious - Congregational
Frequency: Monthly   Price: $2.75
Size: 11 x 6 1/4   Length: 48 pp.
Availability: APS reels 139-41
Reference: Lewis, pp. 230-33
            Mott, I, pp. 262-5

History: Outlined above under "Title." Two other publications with the first title listed above existed in the mid-nineteenth century, but no connection between them and this has been shown. See ULS under Panoplist ...

Remarks: Started by Jedidiah Morse, The Panoplist (as it was then known) was ten years old when the North American Review appeared, and it outlived the NAR by more than a decade. Such strength in a magazine is almost unique, and much of it came from its first two editors. Jedidiah Morse is well remembered for his geographies and other writings, and he lent this skill to the early years of his magazine.
        The reins were passed in 1810 to Jeremiah Evarts who served as editor for more than a decade. Evarts was a founder of the American Board of Commissioners for Foreign Missions, and printed the first annual report of the American Bible Society in August 1817. He felt the purpose of a religious magazine was to spread Christian doctrine--in his case orthodox Congregationalism --but he was too intelligent to limit his pages to this area alone.
        Evarts' style was simple; however, he had the ability to see through problems and to relate individual concerns to many areas of knowledge. His articles, and those by contributors, discussed

secular, social, and even political problems without imposing rigid
doctrinal arguments on their proposed solutions.
    Biography was emphasized, book reviews appeared, religious
and literary news and announcements were published as space allowed, and numerous articles were published dealing with the education of children as a "necessary and just" occupation.
    A social problem such as the death penalty came under
Evarts' eye when he wrote "On the Execution of Criminals."[2] In
this article some fairly sound arguments, expressed in rather
modern terms, are offered in opposition to this punishment.
    Despite a doctrinal slant, the Missionary Herald was given
a firm foundation by two wise and able editors. The push they
supplied gave enough momentum to the magazine to enable it to live
to the respectable age of 146.

Notes: 1. W. Randall Waterman, "Jedidiah Morse," Dictionary of
            American Biography, (New York: Charles Scribner's 1928-
            37), XIII, p. 245.
        2. Ibid., XV (January 1819), pp. 19-22.

135. MONTHLY ANTHOLOGY

Title: The Monthly Anthology, and Boston Review. Containing
        Sketches and Reports of Philosophy, Religion, History, Arts,
        and Manners
Place: Boston   Dates: November 1803-June 1811
Editor: Edited by a Society of Gentlemen who were members of the
           Anthology Club. From December 1807 to June 1811, William
           Smith Shaw and James Savage
Printer: T. B. Wait and Co. (1810-June 1811)
Type: Miscellany - Literary
Frequency: Monthly   Price: 37 1/2¢ per issue
Size: 8 1/2 x 5   Length: 72 pp.
Motto: Omnes undique flosculos carpam atque delibem.
Availability: APS reels 30-2, 43-4
Indexed: Cargill
References: Lewis, pp. 205-7
             Mott, pp. 253-9
             Anthology Society. Journal of the Proceedings of the
                 Society.... Boston: The Boston Athaenaeum, 1910.
Superseded by: General Repository and Review

Remarks: The book on the Anthology Society, mentioned above, contains a complete bibliographic description of each issue, a list of
contributors, a list of all books mentioned, and many other details
about this early Boston literary magazine.
    The seventy-two page issues contained no illustrations after
1809, and they would have seemed out of character anyway.
    Each issue was divided into two parts: the section devoted
to a wide variety of articles ranging from the art of book reviewing

to suggestions on dealing with the bite of mad dogs, and the review
section.   This section contained reviews or announcements of 258 titles
in the life of the magazine, [1] and results in an interesting list of
what the editors considered best.   December 1810 included Isaiah
Thomas' History of Printing in America and the tenth edition of M.
L. Weems' Life of George Washington as well as a brief mention
of the Panoplist, a contemporary magazine.
      A brief series describing early books in America was early
evidence of a growing nationlistic feeling.   This series was later
echoed in the Baltimore Repertory and in William Tudor's series
in the first volumes of the North American Review.
      Little is generally remembered about The Monthly Anthology
today, and this is unfortunate.   In Philadelphia, the Port Folio
stood at the end of that city's long literary life; in Boston, The
Monthly Anthology stood at the beginning of New England's intellectual and literary importance.   The Monthly Anthology also opened
two paths for the periodical to follow: "one religious but liberal,
the other literary and critical." [2]   The first found an immediate
spokesman in Andrews Norton and his General Depository and Review (q.v.) which was quickly followed by Noah Worcester's Christian Disciple (q.v.).   The second path began a landmark difficult
to overlook in American letters, the North American Review (q.v.).

Notes: 1. Anthology Society. Journal of the Proceedings of the
        Society ... (Boston: The Boston Athenaeum, 1910), pp.
        261-93.
        2. Herbert B. Sparks, The Life and Writings of Jared
        Sparks (Boston: Houghton Mifflin, 1893), II, 223-4.

136. MONTHLY MAGAZINE

Title: The Monthly Magazine and Literary Journal
Place: Winchester, Va.   Dates: May 1812-April 1813
Editor, Printer, and Publisher: John Heiskell
Illustrations: Several, usually with a war theme.
Type: Miscellany - General
Frequency: Monthly   Price: $4.00
Size: 8 1/2 x 5 1/2   Length: 64 pp.
Availability: APS reel 145

Remarks: The prospectus repeated Montesquieu's adage that durable,
free governments find their strength in the wisdom and virtue of the
governed.   Heiskell added that "the surest barrier to the distribution of our free government, is to keep the people virtuous and sufficiently enlightened to know and appreciate their own rights." [1]
Heiskell felt that the best way to do this, lacking a national system
of education, was through magazines.
      Heiskell compared his magazine to the Port Folio and claimed
as much material at a lower cost.   True or not, he borrowed from

Dennie's pages as well as from the Freemason's Magazine and The Mirror of Taste in his first issue. This issue contained material on Valley Forge, an article giving traits of American character, an obituary of Captain Lewis, a "retrospect" for 1811, a brief biography of Fisher Ames, a number of short, miscellaneous articles, several pages of anecdotes, and four pages of poetry.

Although The Monthly Magazine had a potentially wide appeal, Heiskell was unable to collect for his subscriptions and could not continue the magazine more than one year. One reason for the failure may have been the degree of copying from other magazines most of which were also available in Virginia.

Notes: 1. The Monthly Magazine, I (May 1812), 1.

137. MONTHLY RECORDER

Title: The Monthly Recorder
Place: New York   Dates: April-August 1813
Editor: Not given
Publisher: D. Longworth
Illustrations: Four portraits
Type: Miscellany - Literary
Frequency: Monthly   Price: Not given
Size: 8 x 4 1/2   Length: 75 pp avg.
Availability: APS reel 146

Remarks: The available file is incomplete and lacks a title page. The introduction, which may have outlined the magazine's purpose, is also missing. However, the pattern of this title is much the same as most other similar journals. One exception is the inclusion of illustrations, at least four of which were found.

The contents include: biography, letters from a traveller in Europe, poetry, reviews, announcements of coming publications, material on the fine arts, a record of the New York stage, and domestic and national news. This last item included the War of 1812.

Two unusual items can be mentioned. In June 1813 an article on "Asiatic Literature" dealt mainly with Persian material--an interest surely almost unique in this period. Also somewhat different was a translation of a French article which questioned the idea that Negroes were inferior. The article pointed to intellectual and biological equality and plainly was opposed to racial inferiority.

The magazine's interests were wide and showed no apparent bias. Its life of five months was not unusual.

138. MONTHLY VISITANT

Title: The Monthly Visitant; or, Something Old

Place: Alexandria, Va.   Dates: July-December 1816
Editor: Not given
Printer: S. Snowden
Type: Religious - Non-denominational
Frequency: Monthly   Price: Not given
Size: 8 x 4 1/2   Length: 40 pp.
Motto: No man, having drunk old wine, straightway desireth new;
       for he saith, the old is better.
Availability: APS reel 146

Remarks: The major contents of this short-lived magazine are
quite ordinary and follow an expected pattern. Comments on communion, the grave, and other aspects of a Christian's life form
the basic sections. Anecdotes, letters, extracted sermons, society
announcements, and news of religious activity are used when necessary and in amounts needed to fill out the pages.
     Perhaps the editor's idea in his motto about "old wine" re-
fers to his penchant for copying material from other sources and
keeping original material to a minimum. The magazine was eclectic without being selective, and although the sources of his articles
are seldom identified, in all probability most were available to his
potential subscribers who decided not to pay for the same material
twice and thus refused to support a poorly edited journal.

139. MORALIST

Title: Moralist
Place: New York   Dates: May 27-November 7, 1814
Editor and Printer: Garrit C. Tunison and Thomas Snowdon
Type: Miscellany - General
Frequency: Irregular   Price: Not given
Size: 5 3/4 x 3 1/4   Length: 12 pp.
Availability: APS reel 146

Remarks: Since the Moralist was dated and numbered it could be
counted a magazine, but it probably was something more like a
series of pamphlets brought out either to satisfy the editors or to
serve as a tract for a religious group. The printing was poor and
suffered from frequent lapses of spelling, punctuation, broken type,
and the like.
     The contents can perhaps only be called miscellaneous es-
says. Each issue was one essay, and all are somewhat allegorical,
first-person tales with a moral point generally connected with behavior, and the evils of drink and laziness. Some are amusing and
all are highly imaginative.
     The magazine seems not to have had a connection with any
particular group, and no attempt was made to print any of the
regular magazine features.

140. NANTUCKET WEEKLY MAGAZINE

Title: Nantucket Weekly Magazine: Literary and Commercial
Place: Nantucket, Mass.
Dates: June 28, 1817-January 3, 1818
Editor and Publisher: A. G. Tannatt
Type: Literary newspaper
Frequency: Weekly   Price: $2.00
Size: 11 1/2 x 9 1/2   Length: 4 pp.
Availability: Not in APS or ULS. Copy consulted at the Boston
       Public Library.
Reference: Brigham, p. 369

Remarks: Twenty-seven issues of this magazine appeared, and A.
G. Tannatt hoped it would be a newspaper as well. He felt that
not enough support could be found for a purely literary publication
or for one which would only report the passing tide.
       The first issue contained a literary column, a letter from
Benjamin Franklin to Mrs. Bache, an editorial, local news, a
marine list, advertisements, poetry, and anecdotes. News was
not gathered, and Tannatt printed only what came to him. Nantucket was a busy port, at times reporting twenty-odd arrivals or
departures a day.
       From the advertisements much can be learned about Nantuc-
ket in 1817. Auctions are reported, as are marriages and deaths.
Public apathy for such a magazine apparently was high since this
was Tannatt's main reason for closing the magazine.

141. NATIONAL MUSEUM

Title: National Museum and Weekly Gazette of Discoveries, Natural
       Science, and the Arts
Place: Baltimore
Dates: November 13, 1813-November 12, 1814
Editor and Publisher: Camill M. Mann
Printer: George Dobbin and Thomas Murphy (November 13-Decem-
       ber 4, 1813); Joseph Robinson (December 11, 1813-January
       1, 1814)
Type: Literary newspaper
Frequency: Weekly   Price: $5.00
Size: 14 x 11 1/4   Length: 8 pp.
Availability: APS reel 149 (incomplete)
Reference: Brigham, p. 224

Remarks: The best file, at the University of Pennsylvania, lacks
issues number 2, 5 and 6; and most other files are even more
broken. Perhaps the War of 1812 interfered with a solid start for
the magazine.
       The original title was to have been The Museum and Weekly

Gazette, but the ambitious prospectus promised much for the magazine. The hope was to produce a general miscellany written for the
average man including material on all subjects.
     The first issue contained two literary essays, news summa-
ries, short notices, Baltimore news, and poetry. Biography soon
appeared, as did pleas for money to support the magazine. The
promised scientific and artistic material appeared, and almost no
mention is made of the war.
     Although high in hopes, the magazine was short of promise,
and another magazine attempt faltered and fell almost as soon as it
began.

142. NATIONAL REGISTER

Title: The National Register, a Weekly Paper, Containing a series
        of the important public documents, and the Proceedings of
        Congress; Statistical Tables, Reports and Essays, Original
        and Selected, upon Agriculture, Manufactures, Commerce,
        and Finance; Science, Literature and the Arts; and Biographi-
        cal Sketches; with Summary Statements of the Current News
        and Political Events
Place: Washington, D.C.
Dates: March 2, 1816-February 5, 1820
Editor and/or Publisher: Joel K. Mead (March 2, 1816-July 18,
        1818); James Cochran (July 25-October 31, 1818); Jonathan
        Elliot (May 15, 1819-October 7, 1820). Intervening issues
        printed without names.
Printer: Lawrence & Wilson (July 25-February 5, 1820?)
Type: News
Frequency: Weekly   Price: $5.00
Size: 10 x 6   Length: 16 pp.
Availability: Not in APS.   Copy consulted at the American Antiquar-
        ian Society.
Indexed: Cargill

Remarks: The various shifts in editorship, publisher, and printer
are not clear from the issues examined. For some reason this
publication has not been listed in some bibliographies even though
the eight volumes contain over 4,000 closely packed, two-column
pages.
     Almost half of each issue consists of reprinted documents of
a wide variety--national local and foreign. A large amount of correspondence from and to American officials has been reproduced,
usually with no comment.
     In keeping with the sub-title, many issues contain an assort-
ment of essays on a wide variety of topics which appear in a ran-
dom pattern.
     The prospectus was reprinted in the first issue, and it gives
the sub-title as "Spirit of the Public Journals, Foreign and Domestic." Although this was not used, it gives the clue to the source of

most material--it was selected from many other contemporary magazines and newspapers.   Although most, if not all, the material was available elsewhere, The National Register is indeed a storehouse of contemporary documentary material.

143. NEW ENGLAND GALAXY

Title: New England Galaxy and Masonic Magazine
Place: Boston   Dates: October 10. 1817-March 29, 1839
Editor: Joseph T. Buckingham, and Samuel L. Knapp (who served
    to the summer of 1818)
Printer and Publisher: Samuel T. Buckingham
Type: Miscellany - General
Frequency: Weekly   Price: $3.00
Size: 19 x 12   Length: 4 pp.
Motto: "To raise esteem, we must benefit others; to promote love,
    we must please them."
Availability: APS reel 150
Reference: Brigham, p. 323
               Buckingham, Joseph T.   Personal Memoirs and Recol-
                   lection of Editorial Life. 2 vols.   Boston: Ticknor,
                   Reed, and Fields, 1852. I, 73-256.
Superseded: Polyanthas
Superseded by: New England Galaxy and United States Literary
          Advertiser

Remarks: The memoirs of Buckingham contain a long section on this magazine in which many contributors are identified, the first subscriber's name reported, and other details given.
    The periodical's purpose was first as a general literary miscellany. An emphasis was to be placed on books, history, biography, new inventions, and other scientific material. All of this was a disguise for Buckingham's second purpose--to expose what he felt was sham and hypocrisy in any area of public life which came to his attention. It must be he did this with some success since people obviously read his magazine.
    Buckingham was also an experienced journalist. He had been associated with a number of magazines by the time he started the New England Galaxy, and he could judge what the public expected in a magazine. Theatrical notices, Congressional reporting, marriages, advertisements, lottery drawings, poetry, and anecdotes are but some of the miscellaneous items with which he filled the pages. Buckingham gave his readers what they wanted and added what they didn't expect--the satirical attacks which sometimes approach the exposé. The Boston public apparently enjoyed these articles despite what the purists must have said about the magazine and its editor.

144. NEW ENGLAND JOURNAL OF MEDICINE

Title: New England Journal of Medicine and Surgery, and Collateral
 Branches of Science
Place: Boston   Dates: January 1812-December 1826
Editor: Conducted by a "number of physicians"; probably: John
 C. Warren, John Gorham, and James Jackson.
Publisher: T. B. Wait and Co. (1812); Bradford and Reed (1813-
 1816); Wells and Lilly (1817-1819)
Printer: Nathaniel Willis (1813); Joshua Belcher (1814); Ezra B.
 Tileston (1815); Tileston and Parmenter (1816)
Illustrations: Anatomical, physiological and architectural engravings
 scattered irregularly throughout.
Type: Medical
Frequency: Quarterly   Price: $2.00
Size: 8 x 5   Length: 100 pp.
Availability: APS reels 153-55
Indexed: Vols. 1-15 indexed in vol. 25 (1853) of Boston Medical
 and Surgical Journal, now: New England Journal of Medicine

History: 1. New England Journal of Medicine and Surgery ...
 Boston. v. 1-15 (January 1812-December 1826)
        Superseded by:
        2. New England Medical Review and Journal. Boston.
           v. 1 (January-October 1827)
        United with:
        3. Boston Medical Intelligencer. Boston. v. 1-5, no.
           39 (April 29, 1823-February 12, 1828)
        to form:
        4. Boston Medical and Surgical Journal. Boston. v. 1-
           197, no. 33 (February 19, 1828-February 16, 1928)
        reverted to:
        5. New England Journal of Medicine. Boston. Volume
           numbering continues to the present.

Remarks: The chronology of magazines in Appendix B lists this
magazine as having a continuous publishing history since 1812.
While this is perhaps not strictly true, the claim for this continuous history is partly based on the indexing listed above. This indexing indicates that the editors of the Boston Medical and Surgical
Journal which is now published as the New England Journal of
Medicine considered the early title a part of a continuum; and if
they make this decision, the same conclusion may be drawn at
present.
    The range of articles covered a surprisingly wide number of
topics. In the first few issues are found: syphilis, heart diseases,
diabetes mellitus, children's diseases, hydrophobia, amputations,
gun-shot wounds, "electro-chemical" research and blood letting.
Drugs discussed included mercury, urine, and lead. Aside from
these, historical, meterological, and book-review articles appear.
The pattern is continued throughout, and although most articles discuss only successful treatment, most are based on experimental

clinical medicine rather than the results of laboratory-proven meth-
ods--a technique not available at this time.
   The prices of various drugs on the London market are
printed,[1] probably on the assumption that such items were not
available domestically. Some of the treatments used are strange,
even to non-medically trained ears. For example, epilepsy was
reportedly cured by taking the superacetate of lead in doses of
three grains night and morning for five days, starting three days
before the full moon and repeating for five lunar periods. After
each dose a tablespoon of olive oil was to be swallowed.[2]
   The techniques, drugs, and treatments should be examined
by contemporary standards; and the quality of the magazine by
similar journals available at the time. On this basis, and despite
a high rate of borrowing in early issues, the magazine maintained
a consistently high level. Later in the first decade, more and more
original and domestic articles were used, and the magazine quickly
became one of the best early American medical journals.

Notes: 1. New England Journal of Medicine, V (October 1816),
          413-5.
       2. Ibid., VI (October 1817), 407.

145. NEW ENGLAND LITERARY HERALD

Title: The New England Literary Herald
Place: Boston   Dates: September 1809-January 1810
Publisher: Ferrand, Mallory, and Co.
Printer: Samuel T. Armstrong
Type: Publisher's catalog
Frequency: 2 issues only   Price: Free
Size: 8 1/8 x 4 5/8   Length: 20, then 16 pp.
Availability: APS reels 34, 218
Reference: Lewis, p. 218

Remarks: Publishers frequently listed books at the end of magazines or other books, but did not frequently issue well printed
brochures like this one. The second issue, and the last, contained
sixteen pages which listed twenty-seven items in press, two dozen
books available, gave some details about four periodicals, and long,
wordy announcements about forthcoming materials.
   This magazine is a sort of pre-publisher's weekly or catalog.
Both the publisher and the printer listed above were very active in
the period, and one reason for their success may be that they were
inventive enough to create this early advertising device.

146. NEW ENGLAND MISSIONARY INTELLIGENCER

Title: The New England Missionary Intelligencer, and General

Repository; for the Promotion of Useful Knowledge and Evangelical Doctrine

Place: Concord, N.H.   Dates: January-October 1819
Editor: Conducted by a Society of Gentlemen Connected with the New Market Wesleyan Academy.
Printer: Hill & Moore
Type: Religious - Methodist
Frequency: Quarterly   Price: Not given
Size: 6 1/2 x 4 1/2   Length: 84 pp.
Availability: APS reel 157

Remarks: This quarterly, religious magazine presents some problems. The Library of Congress card states that three issues existed, but the film in the American Periodicals Series shows no breaks or separate title pages. The first appearance may not have been in July 1819 since an experimental number of differing size and type style seems to have been issued:

> In consequence of a dissatisfaction at the size and manner of the first number of the Magazine expressed by some of its patrons, the size has been altered from duodecimo to octavo, a different type has been adapted, and the present is calculated for the first number of the series. This arrangement has caused a delay of three months in the appearance of this work; it will not proceed regularly, and appear successively in July, October, January, and April. [1]

Biography, sermons, descriptions of missions, from books on religious topics, religious news, and poetry form the basic contents. The religious discussions were from the Methodist viewpoint.

Notes: 1. Quoted in Otis G. Hammond, Bibliography of the Newspapers and Periodicals of Concord, New Hampshire (Concord: Ira C. Evans, 1902), p. 19.

147. NEW ENGLAND MISSIONARY MAGAZINE

Title: New England Missionary Magazine, for Promoting Useful Knowledge and Evangelical Doctrine
Place: Concord, N.H.   Dates: Nos. 1-4, 1816 (no months)
Editor: Martin Ruter
Printer: Isaac and W. R. Hill
Type: Religious - Methodist
Frequency: Quarterly (?)   Price: Not given
Size: 6 3/4 x 4 1/4   Length: 36 pp.
Motto: And ye shall know the Truth, and the Truth shall make you free.
Availability: APS reel 157

Remarks: The magazine opens with a flattering biographical sketch of John Wesley which sets the tone for all the material and all the issues. Other biographies were included in other issues; and these were Methodist people, articles, and doctrine. The issues were evangelical, polemic, and dogmatic. The main purpose was as an aid to missionaries, both as a teaching tool and as a means of raising money. The publication was not well conceived or well produced. Most material was gathered from other sources, and these were magazines already available in New Hampshire.

148. NEW JERUSALEM CHURCH REPOSITORY

Title: New Jerusalem Church Repository
Place: Philadelphia   Dates: January 1817-October 1818
Editor: The American Society for the Dissemination of the Doctrines
        of the New Jerusalem Church
Printer: Lydia R. Bailey
Illustrations: Frontispiece showing the New Jerusalem Temple in
        Philadelphia
Type: Religious - New Jerusalem Church
Frequency: Quarterly   Price: $2.00
Size: 8 x 5   Length: 64 pp.
Availability: APS reel 157

Remarks: This is the second magazine of the 1810-1820 period which advocated the teachings of Emanuel Swedenborg. The first was the Halcyon Luminary.
        The magazine was a repository of information about this sect and its teaching, doctrine, practice, and ceremonial. The literature of the sect was reviewed, and special attention was paid to Swedenborg's works which were extracted with explications of his ideas.
        Only one volume of eight quarterly issues appeared. Perhaps support was not found despite this congregation's ability to build its own church in Philadelphia. The issues do contain a basic outline of this group's teaching and have value for the religious historian.

149. NEW YORK CITY HALL RECORDER

Title: The New York City Hall Recorder. Title page of volume one
        has: The City Hall Recorder
Place: New York   Dates: January 1816-January 1822
Editor: Daniel Rogers
Publisher: Abraham Vosburgh (January-December 1817)
Printer: Charles N. Baldwin (January-December 1816); Clayton and
        Kingsland (January 1817-December 1819)
Type: Law
Frequency: Monthly   Price: Not given

Size: 9 x 5 1/2   Length: 12-24 pp.
Motto: Lex potentior armis.
Availability: APS reel 211

Remarks: The Union List of Serials gives the opening date as 1817,
but the first issue appeared in January 1816. The monthly issues
for a year were gathered and bound with an introduction in annual
volumes.
    The title page for each year carries a sub-title which reads:

> Containing Reports, of the Most Interesting Trials and
> Decisions Which Have Arisen in Various Courts of Judi-
> cature, for the Trial of Jury Cases in the Hall, during
> the Year, Particularly in the Court of Sessions.

    The purpose was not only to report New York legal events
but also to make these clear for the general public. Each case is
treated in paragraphs giving background, principles, court conduct,
general evidence, testimony, and decisions. Insight into social
values and legal interpretation is plentiful here although an expert
would be needed to interpret some cases correctly.
    Two indexes give a personal name and subject approach. If
the lawyer wanted cases dealing with affidavit, evidence, manslaugh-
ter, or slaves, a consultation here would possibly lead to several.
    Although limited to New York courts, the issues comprise a
fairly comprehensive case summary of trial law for seven years.

150. NEW YORK JUDICIAL REPOSITORY

Title: New York
Dates: September 1818-February/March 1819
Editor: D. Bacon
Publisher: Gould & Banks, New York; W. Gould, Albany
Printer: William Grotton
Type: Law
Frequency: Monthly   Price: Not given
Size: 8 1/2 x 5   Length: Up to 100 pp.
Motto: Quid sit pulchrum, quid turpe, quid utile, quid non.
Availability: Not in APS or ULS. Original in the Library of the
          Association of the Bar of the City of New York. Photo-
          offset copy in the University of Michigan Law School.
Reference: Shaw, item #45074
          LC 108:117

Remarks: Apparently only a few copies of this title were produced
since only a very few libraries report copies. The issues are un-
even in length, and in fact decrease with each issue to a low of
about twenty-four pages. The printing quality seems good, and
some attempt was made to achieve editorial uniformity.
    The magazine was to report New York General Sessions

involving cases of libel, assault, larceny, fraud, and other major
infractions. Very few cases of criminal law are reported in other
journals and this magazine may be unique in this feature.
The reports were not stenographic but were detailed summaries of trial proceedings, cogently stating the meat of testimony.
The issues serve as a case book of early New York State criminal
law and court decisions.

151. NEW YORK LITERARY JOURNAL

Title: The Belles-Lettres Repository, and Monthly Magazine (May
        1819-April 1820); The New York Literary Journal and Belles-
        Lettres Repository (May 1820-April 1821)
Place: New York   Dates: May 1819-April 1821
Editor: Not given
Publisher: A. T. Goodrich & Co. (May 1819-   )
Printer: G. L. Birch & Co. (May-July 1819); C. S. Van Winkle
        (August 1819-   )
Type: Miscellany - General
Frequency: Bi-weekly for two issues; then, monthly
Price: $5.00
Size: 8 1/4 x 5   Length: 40 pp. for two; then, 80 pp.
Indexed: Cargill

Remarks: Some slight variations in the above title occur from
issue to issue, but they do not interfere with identification.
       The editor intended to include current book reviews of do-
mestic and foreign publications; "views of society, manners, and
morals"; biographies; articles on fine arts, inventions and travel;
and other miscellaneous material.
       Two issues appeared in the first month, but the title changed
to a monthly almost immediately. The editors claimed the magazine
was cheaper than any other periodical published in the United States,
but the five dollar tab for a subscription denies this.
       Much of the material was drawn from outside sources, about
half being British. Although the selection was good and the editing
excellent, lack or originality in a market like New York forced the
magazine to cease after two years.

152. NEW YORK MAGAZINE

Title: The New York Magazine, and General Repository of Useful
        Knowledge
Place: New York   Dates: May 1-July 1814
Editor: James Hardie
Printer and Publisher: James Oram
Type: Miscellany - General

Frequency: Monthly   Price: $4.50
Size: 7 3/4 x 4 1/2   Length: 64 pp.
Availability: APS reel 162

Remarks: Literature, education, peace, morality, and religion were
announced as the major topics. Other things covered at times were
agriculture, manufactures, and mechanical inventions. These latter
three appear regularly, although the details are brief and the material borrowed from other sources.

The first issue contained an essay grandly called: "A Brief
Sketch of the Origin and Progress of These Periodical Works Commonly Called Magazines; with a Short Biographical Account of their
Projector Mr. Edward Cave." The article contains nothing of importance not available elsewhere, but is an early article on the
subject.

The magazine contains no material outstanding in importance,
style or originality. Probably begun to take advantage of a growing
trend, it was unable to catch on despite having a well known and
quite competent printer, James Oram.

153. NEW YORK MEDICAL AND PHILOSOPHICAL JOURNAL

Title: New York Medical and Philosophical Journal and Review
Place: New York   Dates: 1809-1811
Editor: J. Augustine Smith and Benjamin DeWitt
Printer: T. and J. Swords
Illustrations: Four plates were included in volume three: one illus-
        trating an abdominal operation, one of a throat obstruction,
        and two much-copied plates of "electrochemical apparatus."
Type: Medical
Frequency: Semi-annual   Price: 75¢ per issue
Size: 8 1/4 x 4 5/8   Length: 160 pp.
Availability: APS reels 34, 162
Indexed: Cargill
Reference: Lewis, p. 222

Remarks: Four illustrations add some interest to the rather wide
variety of material included in this magazine. Articles in chemistry,
optics, and the physiology of animals, among other non-medical subjects, mingle freely with material on diabetes and "midwifery."

Mortality statistics form the basis of investigations to deduce
major medical problems; and while they may have failed in that,
they do provide some insights into medical history and even contemporary social problems.

T. and J. Swords were printers for the faculty of Columbia
University, but this connection did not provide a long life to this
magazine. Only six issues appeared, and while each was around
160 pages long, the title is of secondary importance.

154. NEW YORK MEDICAL MAGAZINE

Title: The New York Medical Magazine
Place: New York   Dates: January 1814-January 1815
Editor: Valentine Mott and Henry U. Onderdonk
Printer: N. Van Riper
Type: Medical
Frequency: Annual   Price: Not given
Size: 9 x 5 1/2   Length: 180 pp.
Availability: APS reel 164

Remarks: Although an annual publication, this should be considered
a magazine since this was the intention of the editors. Mott was
Professor of the College of Physicians and Surgeons in New York;
Onderdonk was a member of the Royal College of Surgeons in London. This teamwork demonstrated the possibility of international
cooperation on intellectual efforts despite a war.
    The two issues both had the same pattern--book reviews,
case reports, discussions of autopsies, and "intelligence." The
first issue's first review was of a book on weather and climate.
Eight other reviews followed. Some were of society publications,
and some over twenty pages. The writing was clear, and the style
generally devoid of the usual nineteenth century convoluted syntax.
    Perhaps other responsibilities took Mott's time, and perhaps
the war interfered with communications; under whatever circum-
stances the magazine lasted only through two issues.

155. NILES' WEEKLY REGISTER

Title: The Weekly Register (September 1811-August 1814); Niles'
        Weekly Register (September 1814-August 1837); Niles' National
        Register (September 1837-September 1849)
Place: Baltimore   Dates: September 1811-September 1849
Editor: Hezekiah Niles (September 1811-August 1836)
Printer and Publisher: Published by the editor at The Franklin
        Press
Type: News magazine
Frequency: Weekly   Price: $5.00
Size: 9 3/4 x 6   Length: 16 pp.
Motto: The Past - The Present - For the Future.
Availability: APS reels 167-73
Indexed: Cargill
          Poole
          Niles Weekly Register. General Index to the First Twelve
          Volumes, or First Series of Niles Weekly Register.
          Being a Period of Six Years: from September 1811 to
          September 1817. (Baltimore: The Franklin Press, 1818)
References: Mott, pp. 268-270
          Luxon, Norval Neil. Niles' Weekly Register; News

Magazine of the Nineteenth Century (Baton Rouge:
Louisiana State University Press, 1947)

Remarks: The title page description continues: "Containing Political,
Historical, Geographical, Scientific, Astronomical, Statistical, and
Biographical, Documents, Essays, and Facts; together with notices
of the Arts and Manufactures, and a Record of the Events of the
Times." This phrase gives an accurate feeling of the contents as
the motto quoted above gives of the purpose of this magazine. The
most scholarly study of the magazine is Luxon's book cited above,
and none of this work need be repeated here. However, some brief
comments are necessary to point to one of the truly important magazines in the decade 1810-1820.

Perhaps one of the greatest difficulties in any consideration of
early nineteenth century American periodicals involves making the
decision between a newspaper and a magazine. Niles' Weekly Register was both. For the first time, Niles conceived the idea of
preserving the news and of publishing background material simul-
taneously with both sides of important issues. Politically, news
organs in this period were generally partisan, biased, and often
vituperative. Niles promised in the prospectus to "be open to all
parties, temper, moderation and dignity being preserved."[1] Niles
followed this dictum quite well, despite his Anglo-phobia, and frequently devoted equal space to factual material about opposite political views.

The War of 1812 was well covered; much material appears on
the growing slavery issue, and many added features were used to
fill, but not to pad, each week's sixteen pages.

The single most important innovation made by Niles was his
concept of preservation of news for the future. He wanted to put
down the facts, people, and issues so the future could better understand the period when he lived. His success resulted in America's
first news magazine of any importance the pages of which have lasting
value.

Notes: 1. Niles' Weekly Register, I (September 7, 1811), 2.

156. NORTH AMERICAN REVIEW

Title: North American Review and Miscellaneous Journal (May 1815-
April 1821); North American Review (August 1821-Winter
1939/40)
Place: Boston (May 1815-1878)
Dates: May 1815-Winter 1939/40
Editor: William Tudor (May 1815-March 1817); Jared Sparks with
Willard Phillips and others (May 1817-1818); Edward Tyrrel
Channing with Richard Henry Dana and others (1818-1819);
Richard Henry Dana (1819-1820)
Publisher: Wells and Lilly (1815-1816); Cummings and Hilliard
(1817-1830)

Printer: Hilliard and Metcalf (1815-   )
Owner: William Tudor (1815-1816); North American Review Club
        (1817-1820)
Illustrations: None
Type: Literary review
Frequency: Bi-monthly (May 1815-September 1818); Quarterly
        (December 1818-   )
Price: $4.00
Size: 8 1/2 x 5   Length: 144-232 pp.
Availability: APS reels 167-173
Indexed: Cargill
        North American Review. General Index ... 1815 ...
            Boston: Gray & Bowen, 1829.
        _____. Index ... 1815-1877. By William Cushing.
            Cambridge: J. Wilson and Son, 1878.
References:
Adams, Herbert Baxter, "The 'North American Review,'" in his
    The Life and Writings of Jared Sparks. Boston: Houghton,
    Mifflin, 1893. Vol. I, pp. 98-102.
Clark, Harry Hayden. "Literary Criticism in the North American
    Review, 1815-1835," Transactions of the Wisconsin Academy
    of Sciences, Arts, and Letters, XXXII (1940), 299-350.
Farrior, John Edward. "A Study of the North American Review:
    The First Twenty Years," Unpublished Ph.D. dissertation,
    University of North Carolina, 1954.
Hudson, Laura Thermo. "The North American Review and Atlantic
    Monthly: Their Places in the History of American Literature."
    Unpublished Master's dissertation, John B. Stetson University,
    1927.
Mott, Frank Luther. "The North American Review," in his A
    History of American Magazines. 2d printing. Cambridge:
    Harvard University Press, 1957. Vol. II, pp. 219-261.
Paine, Gregory. "Cooperaand The North American Review,"
    Studies in Philology, XXVIII (October 1931), 799-809.
Shrell, Darwin. "Nationalism and Aesthetics in the North Ameri-
    can Review, 1815-1850," in Waldo McNeir and Leo B. Levy
    (eds.) Studies in American Literature. Baton Rouge: Louisi-
    ana State University Press, 1960, pp. 11-21.
Streeter, Robert E. "Critical Thought in the North American Re-
    view, 1815-1865." Unpublished Ph.D. dissertation, North-
    western University, 1943.
Tassin, Algernon de Vivier. "The Making of the Boston Tradition,"
    in his The Magazine in America. New York: Dodd, Mead and
    Company, 1916, pp. 28-41.
Tudor, William. Miscellanies. Boston: Wells and Lilly, 1821.

Remarks: No direct ancestor of the North American Review existed,
but the NAR did have precedents and a tradition behind it. The
foremost of these was the Monthly Anthology (q.v.) which had been
started and conducted by members of Boston's Anthology Society.
Many of the members of this literary group, especially the NAR's
first editor, William Tudor, brought their skills with them.
        The intermediate state between the Monthly Anthology's death

in June 1811 and the NAR's founding in mid-1815 is more hazy.   In
January 1812 the General Repository and Review (q.v.) (sometimes
referred to as the Cambridge Repository) continued the Boston-Cam-
bridge-Harvard concept of a magazine featuring a heavy emphasis on
literary reviews.   This second important Cambridge magazine lasted
through October 1813.   At this point, The New England Magazine,
which never actually appeared, was proposed.   Since the publisher
of the Polyanthas and the editors of the General Repository and Review were to fulfill these responsibilities on the new magazine, both
these latter titles ceased publication.   Tudor was opposed to the new
magazine, and the members of the Anthology Society, acceding to
Tudor's wishes, held off until Tudor's return from England when
planning for the NAR began.

The first issue opened with an article of "Books Relating to
America," a feature which continued at least through July 1817.
Other items were letters, brief literary and critical articles, poe-
try, a meterological journal, literary "intelligence," and obituaries.
"Virtually all of this first number and a good three-fourths of the
first four volumes were written by the editor himself."[1]

Tudor turned the review over to the North American Review
Club in 1817, and Jared Sparks became editor.   The most important
event for American literature in this second editorship was the
anonymous appearance of Bryant's "Thanatopsis" in September of
1817.   By publishing this landmark of American poetry, the NAR
became a spokesman for American literary nationalism.

Edward Channing became editor in December 1818 and altered
the policy in two important ways: first, he omitted news, general
essays, and other less scholarly items; and, second, he made the
magazine a quarterly.   By so doing, the NAR achieved the rank of
a pure literary review--the first really important magazine in
America to have this purpose.

Tudor tried to realize three ideas in his concept of a magazine.   He aimed for usefulness.   He hoped to achieve a balance in
American criticism among the political, social, and literary areas
in which American books were appearing.   And he intended to promote a feeling for literary nationalism.

Tudor was fortunate in three ways, and all three combined to
insure the success of the NAR.   Such a review was needed; and
after America's second war of independence, the need was promoted
by a demand for an indigenous American literary review.   Second,
Tudor had the right place to start such a magazine.   Cambridge and
Boston had Harvard, and both provided an instant audience.   And,
third, the Anthology Society, along with allied groups like the men
associated with the Boston Athenaeum, provided a long series of
capable, well-trained intellectuals who could keep the NAR on a
sound footing until it had the chance of obtaining wide-spread attention.

The signal that the NAR had achieved recognition came from
England, a country which previously scorned American products.   In
October, 1829, the British periodical, Colburn's New Monthly said
of the NAR:

No literary performance of the Americans has done so

much to wipe away the reproach of imbecility, supposed to be deserved by their intellectual character and efforts, as the North American Review. It is really an excellent periodical, and we have more than once referred to its pages for reflections more just, and views and opinions more striking, than were afforded, of the same subjects, by the colossal reviews of our own island.[2]

In the 1870's, the NAR moved to New York where it changed its character but lasted until the end of 1939. During most of its early years it was somewhat pontifical, often prudish, and at times ponderous. But the NAR did become the voice of Boston and, to a large extent, the arbiter of nineteenth century American literature. During its life it became the single most important American magazine dealing with American letters; and for the period covered by its 148 volumes it has remained one of America's long-lived and important magazines.

Notes: 1. Mott, op. cit., II, 222-3.
          2. Quoted in: William B. Cairns. "British Criticisms of American Writings, 1815-1833." Wisconsin University. Studies in Language and Literature, no. xiv (April 1922), 281-82.

157. NORTH CAROLINA MAGAZINE

Title: North Carolina Magazine; Political, Historical, and Miscellaneous
Place: None given   Dates: August 1813
Editor, Printer, Publisher: None given
Type: Miscellany - General
Frequency: To be monthly (?)   Price: Not given
Size: 7 x 4   Length: 32 pp.
Availability: APS reel 400

Remarks: The printing quality of this magazine, or at least the only issue seen, is very poor; and at first glance appears to be from the eighteenth century, or even earlier.
    The August 1813 issue contains some brief articles about the Navy, among which is one comparing the costs of a 76-gun and a 44-gun frigate. The smaller is priced at $202,110 and the larger at $330,000. A biography of Decatur was borrowed from The Analectic, and several brief articles on agriculture were probably gathered from some other source.
    The concept of this magazine seems to have been to provide a miscellany with wide popular appeal, but this one known issue, probably experimental, failed to elicit the support needed to continue.

158. OBSERVER

Title: The Observer
Place: New York   Dates: October 14, 1810-April 21, 1811
Printer and Publisher: Elliot and Crissy
Type: Literary newspaper
Frequency: Weekly   Price: $2.00; later $4.00
Size: 9 1/2 x 7 1/2   Length: 4 pp.; later 8 pp.
Masthead: Between title words, cut of a human eye.
Availability: APS reel 218

Remarks: A self-description of the magazine continues by claiming
to include: "The Foreign and Domestic News of the Week, arranged
in such a manner as to give a connected history of the passing
events of the times ... Moral and religious Essays ... original and
didactic Pieces in Prose and Verse ... Valuable Improvements and
Discoveries in Arts, Sciences, and Manufactures--A list of the
names of all the Marriages and Deaths which occur in New York--
Advertisements of new Books, or any articles connected with literature."
    These claims were never quite carried out although much of
this did appear. The average issue offered: an essay, usually
published serially; several brief literary essays, poetry, news,
marriages, and deaths. The paper was issued on Sunday--a rather
unusual idea for the time. The intention to publish two Sunday editions was announced but never fulfilled.
    On February 3, 1811, the paper doubled its length and price.
Advertisements were accepted, news increased, and items like stock
prices and ship arrivals were added. These changes may have been
made to increase circulation, but only about two more months remained in the paper's life. Its literary content, while extensive,
remained undistinguished, and the paper's importance was its contribution to the growing impetus in magazine publishing.

159. OLIO

Title: The Olio, A Literary and Miscellaneous Paper
Place: New York   Dates: January 27, 1813-February 5, 1814
Editor, Printer, Publisher: Samuel Marks
Type: Miscellany - General
Frequency: Weekly   Price: $2.00
Size: 7 3/4 x 6 1/4   Length: 8 pp.
Motto: Miscens utile Dulci.
Availability: APS reel 219
Indexed: Cargill
Reference: Brigham, p. 674

Remarks: The title-page statement continues:

Containing, Biographical Sketches of the most eminent
Naval and Military Characters in the United States; Extracts from History, Travels, Geography, and Novels;
Poetry, Anecdotes, Bon-Mots, Etc. Etc. Together with a
brief Account of the Passing Events of the Day.

The Olio, according to Marks, would be run on principles "of
religion, morality, public and private virtue, rational and innocent
amusement."[1] Marks also hoped to devote most material to women,
and this title can be considered an "undiscovered" woman's magazine.
Basically the contents were short fiction, biography, small
tidbits of non-essential information, marriages, deaths, and poetry.
Slowly, news was added; and some of this was for the New York
area. Fiction was usually the lead article, and this was always a
serialized novel.
The magazine soon became a light literary miscellany and
could not survive among so many other similar magazines.

Notes: 1.   Olio, I (January 27, 1813), I.

160.   OLLA PODRIDA

Title: Olla Podrida: Being the Delectable Musings of the Trio
Place: Providence, R.I.   Dates: July-August 1816
Editor: Euphronius Philolagas
Printer: Miller & Hutchens
Type: Miscellany - Humor
Frequency: Monthly   Price: Not given
Size: 6 3/4 x 4 1/4   Length: 16 pp.
Availability: Not in APS.   Copies consulted at Harvard University
           and The New York Historical Society.

Remarks: The copy of number one in Harvard has only eight pages,
and no printer or place is indicated.   The New York Historical Society copy seems complete, but says it was revised, corrected, and
reprinted.   Thus it may not be a first printing.
Like so many similar periodical publications in the early
nineteenth century, Olla Podrida may be only a series of pamphlets
prepared and issued by one man.   The introductory pages mention
a literary club but no hints are given about the exact nature of this
group.   A third number was promised; no evidence of one was located.
The short essays are brief and informal.   Like the essays in
verse, they criticize contemporary "sacred cows," especially those
involving social conventions limiting one's friends and associations
within a community.   Narrow-minded ideas in religion and politics
are attacked as hypocritical.   There is little of real literary merit
and nothing like a book review or a serious discussion among the
thirty-two pages of this title.

161. OMNIUM GATHERUM

Title: Omnium Gatherum, a Monthly Magazine Recording Authentick
        Accounts of the Most Remarkable Productions, Events, and
        Occurrences, in Providence, Nature, and Art
Place: Boston   Dates: November 1808-October 1810
Printer and Publisher: Timothy Kennard
Illustrations: Four plates appeared in 1810: the first, facsimile
        signatures of the first four presidents; the third, Lord Timo-
        thy Dexter. The plates were intended to support the highly
        miscellaneous nature of the contents.
Type: Miscellany - General
Frequency: Monthly   Price: Not given
Size: 11 3/8 x 7   Length: 48 pp.
Availability: APS reels 36, 219
Reference: Lewis, p. 227

Remarks: "Potpourri" might be a better word than "miscellany" to
describe this magazine. The attempt to include something for every-
one made the magazine such a hodgepodge that no one continued support long enough to give the magazine a solid financial footing.
        A series for children called "The Juvenile Traveller," a note
about and selections from Eliot's Indian Bible, a history of the mer-
maid, and a list of newspapers and periodicals were typical. The
latter gave twenty-five names, all but one living at the time of the
list, April 1810.

162. PARTERRE

Title: The Parterre, A Weekly Magazine
Place: Philadelphia   Dates: June 15, 1816-June 28, 1817
Editor: Conducted by a Trio. (Cora and Charles Chandler[1])
Printer: Probasco and Justice
Illustrations: Volume one has a masthead vignette of a figure seated
        in a garden.
Type: Miscellany - General
Frequency: Weekly   Price: $3.00
Size: 8 1/2 x 5   Length: 8 pp.
Quotation: A blooming garden
            Adorned with flowers of every rainbow hue,
            And fragrant odour.
Availability: APS reel 184

Remarks: The first volume includes a list of subscribers with 336
names--a fairly long list for the time. Nearly all were Southern
except two from Burlington, Vermont.

        This work is principally designed for the inculcation of
        correct principles, and the dissemination of useful knowledge

among the rising generation, and those whose situation and pursuits preclude the possibility of their applying to the many different sources from whence intelligence is acquired. [2]

The editors' promise of a general miscellany was well carried out since dozens of subjects are covered even if only in a paragraph. As the magazine grew older, the articles grew longer, and many were continued from month to month. News was not covered. No children's features were labeled as such, but much of the contents' was written at a child's level, and children may have been meant by the phrase "the rising generation." Also, the concluding message printed in 1817 says one of the editors left Philadelphia and neither of the other two had reached twenty. The Parterre may thus have been intended as a children's magazine, and it was certainly produced in part by young people who had begun the magazine when they were about seventeen.

Notes: 1. Smyth, op. cit., p. 193.
       2. The Parterre, I (June 15, 1816), 2.

163. PELISSIER'S COLUMBIAN MELODIES

Title: Pelissier's Columbian Melodies
Place: Philadelphia   Dates: January-December 1812
Editor: Victor Pelissier
Publisher: G. Willig (January-June 1812); J. Taws (July-December 1812)
Type: Music
Frequency: Monthly   Price: $6.00
Size: 11 3/4 x 8 3/4   Length: 10 pp.
Availability: Not in APS or ULS. Copy consulted in The Library of Congress.
Reference: Wunderlich; pp. 60-1, 394-96.

Remarks: Many of the musical publications in the early nineteenth century were issued periodically, but they were tune books and not magazines. Since this title was a numbered and dated series which seemed to have an intention to continue indefinitely, it may be considered a magazine even though no material other than music appeared.
      Each ten-page issue was entirely engraved music--except for a title page which had a copyright notice on the verso. The issues averaged four songs, and these are analyzed in some detail by Wunderlich.
      Both Willig and Taws had connections with the Musical Magazine (A50). That any city could have two musical magazines, even for a short period at this time, may indicate a growing interest in the piano. Perhaps at least some elements of society were acquiring both the wealth and the leisure time necessary to practice and enjoy this instrument.

164. PHILADELPHIA MAGAZINE

Title: The Philadelphia Magazine (January 14-February 14, 1818);
The Philadelphia Magazine, or Weekly Repository of Polite
Literature (February 21-August 8, 1818); The Philadelphia
Magazine, and Weekly Repertory (August 15-November 7, 1818)
Place: Philadelphia   Dates: January 14-November 7, 1818
Editor: Joseph R. Chandler
Printer and Publisher: George Goodman (January 14-August 8,
1818); Dennis Heartt (August 15-November 7, 1818)
Type: Miscellany - Literary
Frequency: Weekly   Price: $4.00
Size: 10 3/4 x 8   Length: 8 pp.
Motto: either: "The mean pleasures, the end virtue."
or: "Born to no Master, of no Sect are we."
Availability: APS reel 186

Remarks: Dennis Heartt was one of the busiest printers in Philadelphia, and his product was of high quality. The printing of The
Philadelphia Magazine improved when Heartt took over in the summer
of 1818, but his ministrations were not enough to save an otherwise
mediocre magazine.
Articles on geography, general history, and biography generally opened each issue. Short stories, serialized fiction, romantic stories, essays and poetry all added to the literary aspects of
the pages. Some local news, marriages, and deaths frequently appeared. A few theatrical articles and occasional notices of books
were added when needed. Both The Quarterly Theological Review
and The Academician were reviewed in the November 7, 1818 issue.
This title added little if anything which was not already
available in Philadelphia magazines and newspapers. Competition
was increasing, and enough other magazines of better quality existed
to drive this one from the Philadelphia market.

165. PHILADELPHIA MEDICAL MUSEUM

Title: The Philadelphia Medical Museum
Place: Philadelphia   Dates: September 17, 1804-1811
Editor: John Redman Coxe
Printer and Publisher: J. and A. Y. Humphreys
Illustrations: The first six volumes contain eleven plates. See
Lewis, p. 328 for details of these. The volume for 1810-
1811 contained four plates: three portraits and a medical
device.
Type: Medical
Frequency: Quarterly   Price: $2.00
Size: 8 1/2 x 4 5/8   Length: About 60 pp.
Availability: APS reels 38, 186
Reference: Lewis; p. 238

Remarks: John Redman Coxe was one of the founders of the Philadelphia College of Pharmacy, supported the idea of vaccination, and
owned one of the country's largest private libraries--some 1,500
volumes.[1] He was also a contemporary of Benjamin Rush, and his
editorial policy featured the work of Rush, especially articles and
speculations on yellow fever. These articles are a landmark in
American medical investigation.
      A number of articles on children's diseases, which were sel-
dom discussed in other magazines, appeared in 1810. Many of the
other items deal with the rare and unusual and thus follow the pattern of other early American medical magazines.
      In 1810, the magazine divided into two parts. The second of
these, the Medical and Philosophical Register, has been cited as a
separate title but is simply a department of the whole magazine. It
was divided into two sections, "Empiricism" and a biography. "Empiricism" was an eclectic miscellany whose first two articles in
1810 were devoted to medical quacks, and other topics such as
an eye operation. The biography section presented the lives of
three doctors in four issues: Thomas Sydenham, William Harvey,
and Richard Mead.
      America's second medical periodical lived only five years,
but it did presage the importance of Philadelphia as a medical
center, an importance still true.

Notes: 1. Ebert, op. cit., p. 248.

166. PHILADELPHIA REPERTORY

Title: Philadelphia Repertory
Place: Philadelphia   Dates: May 5, 1810-May 16, 1812
Editor, Printer, and Publisher: Dennis Heartt. Sometimes signs
            as: Obadiah Oded.
Type: Miscellany - Literary
Frequency: Weekly   Price: $4.00
Size: 10 1/2 x 8 1/2   Length: 8 pp.
Quotation: Variety's the very spice of life,
            That gives it all its flavor. (Cowper)
Availability: APS reel 186
Indexed: Cargill
Superseded by: The Bureau

Remarks: At the beginning, Dennis Heartt desired "to present the
public with a paper in which Domestic Intelligence should be considered of primary importance."[1] Also added were: useful arts,
improvements in agriculture and manufactures, a summary of the
legislative action, foreign news, biography, scientific and "entertaining" subjects, poetry, "merriment and wit and humor," marriages, deaths, and some fashions. Most of these promised features
did not appear at all, and many issues contained only a few of them.
      At least one engraving was promised but probably never

appeared. The biography ran the gamut from David Rittenhouse and William Penn to John Milton. Many other articles such as one on "Mahomet" contained a flair for popular magazine editing. Heartt wanted to promote native American literature:

> to adorn the columns of our paper (with original contributions); without this aid, our most strenuous endeavors will prove abortive, and the Reportory by ceasing to exist will return to the oblivion from whence with no small exertion it was drawn. [2]

To oblivion it did return--one of many such short-lived magazines.

Notes: 1. Philadelphia Repertory, I (May 5, 1810), 1.
2. Ibid., II (March 21, 1812), 352.

167. PHILANTHROPIST

Title: The Philanthropist
Place: Mt. Pleasant, Ohio   Dates: August 29, 1817-May 15, 1822
Editor: Charles Osborn
Printer and Publisher: Not stated
Type: Literary newspaper
Frequency: Weekly   Price: $3.00
Size: 12 x 10   Length: 8 pp.
Availability: APS reel 187
Reference: Brigham; p. 811

Remarks: For the first few years of its existence, much of The Philanthropist's contents were abolitionist and pacifist. An example of the first is blunt and outspoken:

> We are not guiltless of the blood and wrongs of these murdered and enslaved men. Whilst slavery exists in this land, it is the solemn duty of every good man, constantly and steadily to press for its abolition. [1]

Such phrases as "this Hellish traffic in human blood" and "the violated rights of man" are strong and leave no doubt as to the position taken by this magazine.

The subscriber lists indicate circulation limited to Ohio, Pennsylvania, North Carolina, Delaware, and Maryland. Some of these were strong slave states, and it is interesting to speculate on the influence Charles Osborn may have had on the slave owners.

The other contents were typical of the newspaper, each eight-page issue containing serialized articles and essays, news summaries, speeches, and the like. The magazine's major importance is its abolitionist viewpoint and articles.

Notes: 1. The Philanthropist, I (December 19, 1817), 113.

168.   PIONEER

Title: The Pioneer, Consisting of Essays Literary, Moral and
         Theological
Place: Pittsburgh   Dates: February 28-October 8, 1812
Editor: David Graham
Publisher: S. Engles and Co.
Type: Miscellany - General
Frequency: Irregular   Price: Not given
Size: 8 1/2 x 4 3/4   Length: 24 pp.
Motto: Fossor Castrensis Ago.
Availability: APS reel 189

Remarks: The first issue of The Pioneer produced an essay "On
the Origin and Progress of Periodical Essay Writing" which praised
this genre of essay as having "variety of topic, brevity of execution,
unity of design, dramatic effect, and classical expression."[1]   The
magazine essay was being recognized as a literary force, and this
particular essay no doubt was designed to elicit contributions.
         The issues contained material on reading, the classics, edu-
cation, and other similar topics.   Although Albaugh[2] claims this as
a Presbyterian magazine, it was not primarily religious in content
even if the religious material did take a Presbyterian viewpoint.
         A later issue contained "On the Origin and Progress of
Written Language," an essay which briefly outlined the pictographic,
hieroglyphic, "marks for sound," and alphabetic stages of writing.[3]
This and other similar material indicates that Graham hoped to
produce an interesting general magazine which would attract a
general audience.   He unfortunately was unable to last long enough
to attract a stable audience in an area still highly rural.

Notes: 1.   The Pioneer, no. 1 (February 28, 1812), 7.
         2.   Albaugh, op. cit., p. 57.
         3.   The Pioneer, no. 7 (October 8, 1812), 189-200.

169.   PLOUGH BOY

Title: The Plough Boy
Place: Albany, N.Y.   Dates: June 5, 1819-June 17, 1823
Editor: Henry Homespun, Jr. pseud. of Solomon Southwick
Printer: John O. Cole
Type: Agricultural
Frequency: Weekly   Price: $3.00
Size: 11 1/4 x 9   Length: 8 pp.
Quotation: He that observeth the wind shall not sow; and he that
         regardeth the clouds shall not reap; but he that tillith his
         land shall have plenty.
Masthead: Small vignette of a farm
Availability: APS reel 190

Reference: Brigham, p. 539
Later: Plough Boy and Journal of the Board of Agriculture

Remarks: Although this magazine was not the first devoted to agriculture, it may well have set the pace for later farm periodicals
since much of the material had some practical value. The chief
aim was to discuss the areas of political and domestic economy,
but to remain politically neutral.
A weekly news summary and obituaries gave some of the
features of a newspaper, but this was mainly a farm magazine. An
emphasis was placed on the need for internal improvements, especially new roads and canals as transportation routes for farm
produce. Stage coach schedules, current prices, and land sales
were regular features.
Early attempts at scientific investigation for farms were detailed and the attempt of the Department of Agriculture to distribute
seed, free of charge, was reported. The farmer was becoming
more important to the American economy, and The Plough Boy
hoped to help him produce more and better crops and to provide a
growing America with the food needed for an expanding population.

170. POLYANTHOS

Title: The Polyanthos; A Monthly Magazine, Consisting of Original
         Performances and Selections from Works of Merit
Place: Boston
Dates: v. 1-5 (December 1805-July 1807); nsv. 1-2 (February-
         September 1812); series 3 v. 1-4 (October 1812-September
         1814)
Editor and Publisher: Joseph Tinker Buckingham
Illustrations: Nearly every issue in the latter two series contained
         one engraving, and sometimes two. David Edwin and J. R.
         Smith did the major portion, but many are unsigned.
Type: Miscellany - Literary
Frequency: Monthly   Price: From October 1812: $5.00
Size: 6 1/4 x 3 1/2   Length: 72 pp.
Quotation: We shall never envy the honors which wit and learning
         obtain in any other cause, if we can be numbered among
         the writers who have given ARDOR to virtue and confidence
         to truth.   Dr. Johnson
Availability: APS reel 191-2
Indexed: Cargill
Reference: Lewis, pp. 245-6
Superseded by: The New England Galaxy and Masonic Magazine
         (1817-1839)

Remarks: Joseph T. Buckingham worked much of his publishing
life on or for magazines; and, in his words:

         My first attempt to amuse, instruct, and edify the
         public, was publication of The Polyanthos ...[1]

Every volume was to have an engraved title page and an engraved portrait. Buckingham lists the subjects and engravers of some of these portraits,[2] but some of the engravings listed do not appear in the volumes examined, some of the engravers named apparently did not actually work for the magazine, and some engravings appear which Buckingham did not list.

Each issue had a biography which usually accompanied the portrait, and Buckingham wrote twelve of these. Eight were by other men.[3]

A miscellaneous collection of other biographical notices, drama reviews, history, criticism, and somewhat romantic fiction filled the pages each month. The biography frequently dealt with a naval hero, and a chronology of the War of 1812 appeared in March 1813.[4]

Buckingham had an eye on a wide audience and tried to capture one by including an occasional Mirror of Fashion, Lectures on Natural Philosophy, the Moral Censor, brief scientific notes on discoveries and inventions, Letters on Mythology, a Monthly Dramatic Review, music, and the inevitable Miscellany. At least eighteen pieces of music appeared from 1812 to 1814.

As the magazine grew older, it grew more hurried and careless. Perhaps Buckingham had other interests, and in fact he did announce that:

> The publisher of this work having undertaken the publication of another literary monthly publication, entitled the New England Magazine, the present series of the Polyanthos will terminate with the next number. The New England Magazine will be conducted by the editors of the Cambridge Repository, (which work will also be discontinued) and will be sent to all the present subscribers of the Polyanthos, unless directions are previously given to the contrary. The first number will appear about the first of October.[5]

The New England Magazine (entry A44) never did appear, apparently because William Tudor opposed the idea. The magazine Cambridge Repository referred to by Buckingham probably was the General Repository and Review, published in Cambridge. This magazine had already ceased in October 1813--fully a month prior to Buckingham's announcement. Interestingly, the editors of the General Repository themselves said that their magazine would be followed by The New England Magazine, which of course did not happen. The editors, mainly members of the Anthology Club, did not, in fact, again work on a magazine until the appearance of the North American Review in 1815.

Buckingham probably discontinued The Polyanthos in an effort to win the publication rights to whatever new magazine the Anthology Club would sponsor. In this venture Buckingham was unsuccessful.

Notes: 1. Joseph T. Buckingham. Personal Memoirs and Recollections of Editorial Life (Boston: Tinker, Reed and Fields, 1852), pp. 53-4.

2. Ibid., p. 55.
3. Ibid., p. 56.
4. The Polyanthos, new series, I (March 1813), 333-4.
5. Ibid., third series, LV (August 1814), 272.

171. PORT FOLIO

Title: The Port Folio, A Monthly Magazine (Minor variations occur
throughout the magazine's history)
Place: Philadelphia   Dates: January 3, 1801-December 1827
Editor: "Oliver Oldschool, Esq." (pseud. of Joseph Dennie) (Janu-
ary 3, 1801-January 1812); Nicholas Biddle (1812-1814);
Charles Caldwell (1814-1816); John Elihu Hall (1816-1827).
Also, as possible associates of the editors after Dennie,
were: Paul Allen, Thomas Cooper, and Judge Workman.
Publisher: Bradford and Inskeep (1810-June 1815); Thos. Desilver
(July-December 1815); Harrison Hall (January-February 1816);
John E. Hall (March 1816-   )
London: John Souter (February 1817-December 1818);
John Miller (January 1819-   )
The cover of series 3, IV (August 1810) lists eleven
additional American publishers, but these were local dis-
tributors.
Printers: Smith and Maxwell (until June 1810); James T. Maxwell
(July 1810-   )
Illustrations: The Port Folio was the most profusely illustrated
American magazine up to 1820. Many of the important en-
gravers contributed portraits, scenery, scientific diagrams
and prints, reproductions of paintings, and a host of other
items. Among the important engravers' names are David
Edwin, Cornelius Tiebout, William Leney, Benjamin Tanner,
John Boyd, William Kneass, William Strickland, Cephas
Childs, and the firm of Charles Goodman and Robert Piggot.
Type: General miscellany
Frequency: Monthly   Price: $6.00
Size: 8 x 4 1/2   Length: 80-90 pp.
Quotation: Various; that the mind
Of desultory man, studious of change,
And pleased with novelty, may be indulged.   (Cowper)
Availability: APS reels 220-26
Indexed: Cargill,
Poole
References:
Caldwell, Charles. Autobiography of Charles Caldwell, M.D.
Philadelphia: Lippincott and Grambo, 1855. Chapter XI, pp.
321-348.
Ellis, Harold Milton. Joseph Dennie and His Circle: A Study in
American Literature from 1792-1812. (University of Texas,
"Studies in English," no. 3) Austin, Texas: The University
of Texas, 1915.

Lewis, op. cit., pp. 247-50.
Mott, Frank Luther. "The Port Folio," in his A History of Ameri-
    can Magazines. 2d printing. Cambridge: Harvard University
    Press, 1939. Vol. I, pp. 223-46.
Oberholtzer, Ellis Paxton. "The Port Folio," in his The Literary
    History of Philadelphia. Philadelphia: George W. Jacobs,
    1906. pp. 168-188.
Queenan, John T. "The Port Folio: A Study of the History and
    Significance of an Early American Magazine." Unpublished
    Ph.D. dissertation, University of Pennsylvania, 1954.
Randall, Randolph C. "Authors of the Port Folio Revealed by the
    Hall Files," American Literature, XI (January 1940), 379-416.
Smyth, Albert Henry. "The Nineteenth Century: The Port Folio,"
    in his The Philadelphia Magazines and Their Contributors,
    1741-1850. Philadelphia: Robert M. Lindsay, 1892. pp. 86-
    151.

Remarks: In many respects, the Port Folio remains a landmark in
American publishing as one of the more important early magazines.
Harold Ellis, whose book is listed above, covers well the early
period of this magazine and describes in detail Joseph Dennie's con-
tribution to the Port Folio and other areas of American literature.
When Dennie began, an early issue said:

> The words, Port Folio, from the French Porte Feuille,
> are not to be found in Johnson's Dictionary, but they are
> currently employed, in pure English, to signify a portable
> repository for fugitive papers, which is the exact defini-
> tion of this miscellany.[1]

The papers may have been "fugitive," but they were pure
Dennie, and very strongly reflected his own opinions. His early
support came from the professional and literary classes of Philadelphia; and, to some degree, in other cities. The circulation
never climbed above 3,000,[2] and only slowly rose from 1,750 in
1803 to about 2,500 in 1816.[3] Part of this may be attributed to
Dennie's Federalist politics which led him to be anti-nationalistic
and which adversely affected the magazine's popularity, although
not its literary merit which was very high during its first decade.
    How does the Port Folio reflect America's growing feeling
of nationalism after Dennie's departure? His immediate successor
was Nicholas Biddle whose main interest was art. Although the
magazine began a very worth-while series of engravings duplicating
famous painting masterpieces, "nationalism" is hardly mentioned.
The War of 1812 is given scant attention, only one important article
appearing before June 1813;[4] and that, part of a series resumed
only sporadically. American themes are given some attention, however, with an emphasis on American naval biography, many engravings of scenery, and a contest for the best naval song. But
these do not constitute an editorial opinion favoring nationalism, and
Biddle published no American fiction at all in his tenure as editor--
a fact which leads to the conclusion that he did not particularly support literary nationalism.

Charles Caldwell became editor in 1814, but did not substantially improve the magazine's format or content. He said:

> ... the Port Folio soon became much more popular than
> it was when I took charge of it, or than it had ever been
> previously; and by the end of the first six months from
> the commencement of my editorship, its catalogue of sub-
> scribers had increased five and twenty per cent. [5]

These figures can be doubted if only by comparison with
another claim Caldwell made. He said that reports of the war would
soon appear in the magazine, [6] but only one appeared, and it came
in September 1814.

Caldwell did much more for American literature than either
of his two predecessors. Long articles on this typic began to appear in July 1814, and the authors, who have generally been identified, [7] strongly advocate American nationalism in literature. The
controversy over "Inchquin's Letters," for example, is one frequently
seen.

In its last decade, the Port Folio almost became a one-
family magazine: John Elihu Hall succeeded Caldwell as editor;
Harrison Hall was the Publisher at one point; and the other two
Hall brothers, James and Thomas Mifflin, made numerous contributions. [9] The political slant became neutral, and John E. Hall's
anglophilism peeks through on occasion.

After Dennie's death, more than the Port Folio changed. In
1812, the New England Journal of Medicine appeared; and in 1818 the
American Journal of Science began. These two magazines quickly
achieved distinction, and the editors of the Port Folio had to realize
that it was not the only important periodical in America. Add to
this the eminence the North American Review quickly established as
a literary journal, and the first national competition among magazines appears. America was no longer a country where locally
produced magazines could monopolize a local intelligentsia; a publishing battleground had developed where well-produced magazines
had to compete on more of a national scale for a share of a more
wide-spread intellectual audience which had a broad diversification
of interests, education, training, and ability. That the Port Folio
failed to do this led to its suffocation.

Notes: 1. Quoted in: John T. Queenan, The Port Folio: A
Study of the History and Significance of an Early American
Magazine (Ph.D. dissertation, University of Pennsylvania,
1954), p. 2.
           2. Ibid., p. 14.
           3. "Biography--For the Port Folio," The Port Folio,
5th series, II (October 1816), pp. 273-7.
           4. Port Folio, 4th series, I (January 1813), pp. 86 ff.
           5. Charles Caldwell, Autobiography of Charles Caldwell,
M.D. (Philadelphia: Lippincott and Grambo, 1895), p. 323.
           6. Ibid., pp. 323-4, 327. See also: Mott, p. 240.
           7. Randolph C. Randall, "Authors of the Port Folio

Revealed by the Hall Files," American Literature, XI (January 1940), pp. 379-416.
    8. Port Folio, 5th series, III (June 1817), 530.
    9. Randall, op. cit., passim.

172. PORTICO

Title: The Portico, a Repository of Sciences and Literature
Place: Baltimore   Dates: January 1816-April/June 1818
Editor: Conducted by Two Men of Padua. Tobias Watkins and
        Stephen Simpson (January 1816-June 1817); Tobias Watkins
        (July 1817-April/June 1818)
Publisher: Neale Wille and Cole (January-December 1816); E. J.
        Coale (January 1817-April/June 1818)
Printer: B. Edes (January-December 1817)
Illustrations: Each volume has an engraved title-page, and some
        few other illustrations are included.
Type: Miscellany - General
Frequency: Monthly through June 1817; July-December 1817; two
        double issues and two single issues; January-June 1818: two
        triple issues.
Price: Not given
Size: 9 x 5   Length: 80-90 pp.
Availability: APS reels 192, 193
Indexed: Cargill
Reference: Mott, pp. 293-6

Remarks: The intention at the start was to have four sections in
the magazine: first, a miscellany to include letters, essays, and
biography; second, "The Review" which would be original and selected criticism; third, "The Chronicle," a sort of calendar of
national events without political bias; and, fourth, "The Repository,"
a section of poetry. "The Chronicle" never appeared and was replaced by a section devoted to arts and sciences. In this section,
mathematical puzzles made an appearance in late 1816.
        The first issue began with a series devoted to the educational
and literary level of America. Tobias Watkins' purpose seems to
have been to encourage and support the development of an indigenous
American literature. Although Watkins borrowed much material, his
selection was good, and excellence of literature was his aim.
        As time went by, Watkins' interests developed outside his
magazine, and he was eventually to enter government service. At
this time, he surrendered the magazine having no time to continue
as editor and not having been able to find a successor.

173. QUARTERLY CHRISTIAN SPECTATOR

Title: The Christian Spectator (1819-1828); The Quarterly Christian
        Spectator (1829-1838)

Place: New Haven, Conn.   Dates: January 1819-November 1838
Editor: An Association of Gentlemen
Publisher: Howe & Spaulding (through 1820)
Printer: S. Converse (January 1819-   )
Type: Religious - Presbyterian and Congregational
Frequency: Monthly (1819-   )   Price: Not given
Size: 9 x 5 1/4   Length: About 60 pp.
Availability: APS reel 194
Indexed: Poole (as: Christian Spectator)

Remarks: Two denominations cooperated on this journal, perhaps
in the hope that support from both would keep it alive. The editors,
in their opening statement, expressed the feeling that too many magazines, especially religious ones, had been produced. They also felt
that a magazine with a broader base could survive.
     The contents were quite typical: religious communications,
book reviews, literary and religious news, notices of new books,
obituaries, and miscellaneous essays. The first item, at least
until 1820, was usually a biography. Many societies were described, especially those dealing with religious areas. One of the
more important sections was the book review since many of the
more important publications of the day were noted here.
     The quarterly nature of the magazine helped to prevent
saturation, and the relatively short issues avoided too much dupli-
cation. But the contents were dull and conventional. No attempt
apparently was made to relieve the pages with engravings.

174. QUARTERLY THEOLOGICAL MAGAZINE

Title: The Quarterly Theological Magazine, and Religious Repository
Place: Burlington, N.J. (1813); Philadelphia (1814)
Dates: January 1813-October 1814
Editor: Charles H. Wharton (1813); James Abercrombie (1814)
Publisher: Samuel Allinson (1813); Moses Thomas (1814)
Printer: D. Fenton (1813); James Maxwell (1814)
Type: Religious - Episcopal
Frequency: Quarterly   Price: $5.00
Size: 8 1/4 x 4 7/8   Length: 225 pp.
Availability: Not in APS. Microfilm obtained from the Union
         Theological Seminary Library, New York.
References: The Literary Visitor, II (1813), 91-100.
             Port Folio, series 4, I (March 1813), 314-6.
             Ibid., series 4, IV (July 1814), 117-8.

Remarks: The life of an eminent Christian, a homily, unpublished
sermons, essays, selections from European periodicals, literary
and philosophical intelligence, and poetry--these form the basic contents. Some mention is made of engravings which were planned,
but none appeared.
     The magazine may have tried quarterly publication since so

few monthly magazines achieved success, but quarterly publication
was no more successful.
    The book reviews average twelve pages and are not limited to
religious topics. The religious news included notices, foreign and
domestic, which were arranged by the publisher. Thirteen religious
societies are described in the first issue. Much of these two sections are of high quality, were aimed at a literary audience, and
have been lost to scholars since they have not been indexed.

175. QUARTERLY THEOLOGICAL REVIEW

Title: Quarterly Theological Review
Place: Philadelphia   Dates: January 1818-October 1819
Editor: Ezra Styles Ely
Publisher: Anthony Finley (1818); "Published for the author, no.
        200 Spruce Street" (1819)
Printer: William Fry (1818); Adam Waldie (1819)
Type: Review
Frequency: Quarterly   Price: Not given
Size: 8 3/4 x 5   Length: 98-152 pp.
Quotation: Whosoever transgresseth, and obideth not in the doctrine
        of Christ, hath not God; he that obideth in the doctrine of
        Christ, he hath both the Father and the Son.
Availability: Not in APS. Copy consulted at the Union Theological
        Seminary Library, New York.

Remarks: The major value of this magazine is as a book review.
The religious viewpoint is secondary, and other matter of comparatively little value.
    The first issue contains fifteen articles reviewing twenty
books, and announcements of fourteen others. The second issue
contains twelve articles again reviewing twenty books. These are
inter-denominational covering Protestant, Catholic, and even Jewish
books. One example is an article which compares "A Defense of
Modern Calvanism" with "Remarks on the Refutation of Calvanism."[1]
Thirty-seven pages compare and contrast these two books and their
arguments to produce not only a book review but also a pro-and-
con essay of some merit which maintained a neutral opinion.
    Other intellectual efforts such as a review of Benjamin
West's painting "Christ Healing in the Temple" give the magazine
some elements of wider scope in criticism, but nearly every page
deals with books and literature. In a way this may have been New
York's answer to Boston's North American Review.

Notes: 1. Quarterly Theological Review, I (July 1818), 317-54.

176. RAMBLER'S MAGAZINE

Title: The Rambler's Magazine and New York Theatrical Register
        for the Season 1809-1810
Place: New York   Dates: October? 1809-January? 1810
Publisher: David Longworth
Type: Theatrical
Frequency: Intended to be bi-weekly   Price: Not given
Size: 5 1/2 x 3 1/4   Length: 72 pp.
Availability: APS reel 43
Indexed: Cargill
Reference: Lewis, pp. 254-6
           Mott, p. 166

Remarks: Although it is not dated, internal evidence indicates that
the final issue of this title appeared in January 1810, just as the
decade, covered in this study began. In his study of the earlier
decade, Benjamin Lewis includes a long annotation for this title in
which the spirited quality of the magazine is mentioned. Certainly
"The Perambulator" series offered witty and sane comments on
theatrical matters; but also of considerable value to theatre history
is the "Theatrical Register." One issue contained thirteen pages
which listed plays and gave a brief comment on each. A knowledge
of theatrical taste can give added depth to a cultural interpretation
of a period, and herein may be found one of the values of The
Rambler's Magazine.
        The death of Tom Paine was noted here as it was in a
myriad of other magazines and newspapers. The last issue also
contains a brief biography of Mozart and other interesting miscellanies.

177. RED BOOK

Title: Red Book
Place: Baltimore   Dates: October 23, 1819-March 1820
Editor: Pantagruel and Sidrophel, pseuds.
Publisher: Joseph Robinson
Type: Miscellany - Humor
Frequency: Irregular   Price: Not given
Size: 6 3/4 x 3 1/4   Length: 26-40 pp.
Availability: Not in APS. Copy consulted at Yale University.

Remarks: This humorous magazine had a few rather caustic comments made about it by contemporaries. One contains a colorful
pun:

        The "Red Book" published in Baltimore, as our old friend
        the Inveterate Punster would say, is not read at all.[1]

The essays were apparently original and contain some genu-
ine funny passages. Perhaps the remark in the Independent Balance
was in jest for the Red Book did have some good material and was
a relief from the average, humdrum magazine.

> This little work comes before the publick eye the careless
> offspring of chance, unsupported by patronage and unadorned
> by the tinsel of name of fashion. [2]

The intention was to provide satire on human vanity, and
people have always enjoyed laughing at others, but not at themselves. The editors felt it would be read by those seeking a good
barb about their neighbors. Perhaps the editors had librarians in
mind when they promised the magazine would appear at irregular
intervals, in varying sizes, and at differing prices. Only seven issues appeared, and these were approximately bi-weekly.

Notes: 1. The Independent Balance, III (October 1, 1819), 4.
         2. "Advertisement," Red Book, I (1819), ix.

178. RELIGIOUS ENQUIRER

Title: The Religious Enquirer
Place: Cooperstown, N.Y.   Dates: October 1811 / /?
Editor: Ambrose Clark (?)
Printer: J. H. and H. Prentiss
Type: Religious - Universalist
Frequency: One issue only   Price: Not given
Size: 7 3/4 x 5 1/4   Length: 30 pp.
Availability: APS reel 197

Remarks: Two previous magazines of this religious persuasion had
been started in Massachusetts - Berean and The Gospel Visitant.
Why Cooperstown, in remote Otsego County, New York was chosen
for still another such magazine remains a mystery.
    The title page statement continues:

> Being principally original tracts on theoretical and practi-
> cal religion, in prose and verse; and, also, answers to
> such questions as are presented in writing to the Western
> Universalist Conference respecting their faith, or any
> particular passages of scripture.

    The Gospel Visitant also tried the same method of gathering
material and with only slightly more success.

> We do not expect that our work will stand the test of the
> scrutinizing eye of the connoisseur, but that is the least
> of our concern; if it has a tendency to induce the people
> to read the scriptures, and practice virtue, it will an-
> swer the desires and wishes of the Publishers. [1]

The first part of the statement proved accurate, at least insofar as only one issue appeared; the success of the latter part of the statement will never be known, but it might well be assumed that the publishers were doomed to disappointment.

Notes: 1. The Religious Examiner, no. 1 (October 1811), 5.

179. RELIGIOUS INFORMER

Title: Religious Informer (1819-1821); Religious Informer and Free-
        Will Baptist Register (1822-1825)
Place: Andover, N.H. Dates: July 20, 1819-December 1825
Editor and Publisher: Ebenezer Chase
Type: Religious - Baptist
Frequency: Bi-weekly (July 20-December 25, 1819); then monthly
Price: 75¢ through November 1819; then 50¢
Size: 8 1/2 x 5 1/2   Length: 8 pp.
Quotation: Behold, I bring you good tidings of great joy, which
        shall be unto all people.
Availability: APS reel 197

Remarks: The purpose of this magazine was clearly stated in an announcement printed in September 1819:

> It is designed to give a general statement of the reports of the several quarterly and yearly meetings of the Free-will Baptist Society in New Hampshire, Vermont, and the district of Maine; and such religious information as can be obtained that will be thought refreshing to the friends of Zion.[1]

These reports, along with obituaries, meditations, and poetry, form the major elements of the magazine.

The title page included in the film copy is apparently not the original one since the imprint reads "Enfield; Collected for Binding, 1827." The sub-title begins: "Being a selection of Numbers from a Periodical Work, Bearing the Above Title..." The Magazine, according to the announcement quoted above, was originally issued in Andover, New Hampshire, and this place has been used in this study as the original home of the periodical.

Notes: 1. The Christian Herald, I (September 1819), 28.

180. RELIGIOUS INSTRUCTOR

Title: Religious Instructor; Designed to Promote Useful Knowledge,
        Sound Morality, and Vital Piety

Place: Carlisle, Penn.   Dates: September 1810-August 1811
Editor: Under the Supervision of Several Ministers of the Presby-
terian Church.
Publisher: Archibald Loudon
Type: Religious - Presbyterian
Frequency: Monthly   Price: Not given
Size: 8 1/4 x 8 1/4   Length: 40 pp.
Availability: APS reel 168

Remarks: Carlisle, Pennsylvania was an unlikely place to find support for a magazine, and indeed the support apparently lasted only
a year. Carlisle's location just west of Harrisburg places it in the
way toward Pittsburgh and the West. Perhaps the ministers felt
that missionary zeal would provide the necessary income.
    The introduction promised original matter, but frankly stated
that the magazine intended to republish "such productions as shall
appear best calculated to promote useful knowledge, sound morality,
and vital piety."[1]
    Biography, and characteristics of the Christian religion,
moralistic essays, news of Bible societies, commentaries on scripture, and some miscellaneous material comprise the basic contents
of each issue. Nearly none was original, and even the New Year's
address was lifted wholesale from the Connecticut Evangelical Magazine.
    The missionary zeal of the period may have prompted the
magazine, but religious fervor was not high enough in Carlisle to
provide the needed support to carry the magazine longer than one
year.

Notes: 1. Religious Instructor, I (September 1810), iii.

181. RELIGIOUS INTELLIGENCER

Title: The Religious Intelligencer
Place: New Haven, Conn.   Dates: June 1, 1816-October 7, 1837
Editor and Publisher: Nathan Whiting (June 1, 1816-   )
Type: Religious - Non-denominational
Frequency: Weekly   Price: $3.00
Size: 11 x 7   Length: 16 pp.
Motto: Behold I Bring You Good Tidings of Great Joy.
Availability: APS reels 198, 199
Superseded: Connecticut Evangelical Magazine (1800-1815)

Remarks: This magazine seems to have had good financial backing
since it lasted despite the lack of support afforded to similar publications. The primary purpose was to detail missionary activities
at home and abroad, and no special favoritism was made toward
any particular denomination. Many people might have been willing
to support this type of magazine and the work it represented rather
than one of the more narrowly conceived magazines.

Many of the articles deal with India, and one of the few illustrations depicts a suttee. Other articles tend to point out the cultural differences, but they do not always do so in a derogatory fashion. Often the tone is one which says that missionaries should add to a foreign culture rather than raising it from a presumed depth of heathenism.

Much of the rest of the magazine's articles discuss Bible societies and other groups which had a religious purpose, and here, also, no distinction as to denomination was made.

182. RELIGIOUS MAGAZINE

Title: Religious Magazine
Place: Portland, Vt.
Dates: v. 1 (January 1811-October 1812)
        v. 2 (August 1820-September 22, 1822)
Editor: John Buzzell
Printer: John P. Colcard (January, April 1811); J. M'Kown (July, October 1811; January, April 1812); Arthur Shirley (July, October 1812)
Type: Religious - Freewill Baptist
Frequency: Quarterly   Price: Not given
Size: 7 x 4 1/4   Length: 36 pp.
Availability: APS reel 202

Remarks: The title page statement, after the word "magazine," continues:

> Containing a Short History of the Church of Christ, Gathered at New-Durham, N.H. in the year 1780; and now Spreading its various branches in almost every direction through the States of New Hampshire, Vermont, the District of Maine, and in Many Other parts of America. Also a Particular Account of Late Reformations and Revivals of Religion.

While somewhat verbose, the words describe the contents and purpose of this series.

And a series of pamphlets this may well have been, merely using "magazine" in the sense of a storehouse of information. About half of each issue was devoted to the history; about half, to the reformations. The format and wording of the title pages vary slightly with each issue, but the intent remains the same.

In 1820, operations shifted to Kennebunk, Maine, where printing was resumed with "An Account of the United Churches of Christ Commonly Called Freewill Baptists." The circulation of the issues, to judge from the list of agents, was limited to Vermont, New Hampshire, and Maine. Perhaps insufficient new material caused the magazine to wither away.

183.   RELIGIOUS MUSEUM

Title: The Religious Museum
Place: Northumberland, Penn.
Dates: July 15, 1818-July 21, 1819
Editor: F. N. Smith
Publisher: Henry Frick
Type: Religious - Non-denominational
Frequency: Weekly   Price: $2.00
Size: 12 1/2 x 9 3/4   Length: 4 pp.
Motto: Do good in thy good pleasure unto Zion.
Availability: APS reel 203

Remarks: Henry Frick, who published a newspaper called the
Miltonian, lived in Miltown, Pennsylvania which is a short distance
from Northumberland.   Certainly it must have been unusual to have
a magazine published in one town and printed in another.
The basic purpose F. N. Smith had was to spread religious
knowledge through biography, church history, reporting the state of
world-wide religion, religious revivals, missionary activity, explication of scripture, accounts of Bible societies, and news of Sabbath
school activities.   These are the basic elements repeated in nearly
all contemporary religious journals.
        Some attention is paid to the education of children, poetry
was used on the last page, and slavery is condemned in several
columns which outline the official position taken by several church
groups.   The last issue contained a long letter setting forth the
value and purposes of the American Colonization Society.

184.   RHODE ISLAND LITERARY REPOSITORY

Title: Rhode Island Literary Repository, a Literary Magazine
Place: Providence, R.I.   Dates: April 1814-March 1815
Editor: Isaac Bailey
Publisher: Robinson and Howland
Printer: H. Mann and Co.
Illustrations: Two, both portraits
Type: Miscellany - Literary
Frequency: Monthly   Price: Not given
Size: 8 x 4 1/2   Length: 56 pp.
Motto: New to the eye and shifting every hour.
Availability: APS reel 204
Indexed: Cargill

Remarks: The title page claimed the magazine would contain: "Biographical Sketches, Reviews, Dissertations, Literary Researches,
Poetry, Anecdotes, &c."   Actually the issues did contain the biography and poetry, but the remainder of each issue was made up of
four or five miscellaneous essays with no specific pattern or

predictable subject continuity. Only two of the biographies were accompanied by plates, and these were William Henry Allen and Enos
Hitchcock.
     The editor attributed his failure to the War of 1812 saying
that it prevented distribution. He also mentioned the lack of Rhode
Island magazines. Perhaps he felt competition would stimulate
interest. Certainly he felt that people depended on out-of-state publications, and he probably had Massachusetts in mind.
     Original literature and scientific material was promised for
the future, but there was no future after March 1815.

185. ROBINSON'S MAGAZINE

Title: Robinson's Magazine, A Weekly Repository of Original Papers;
        and Selections from the English Magazines
Place: Baltimore   Dates: July 18, 1818-June 26, 1819
Editor, Printer, and Publisher: Joseph Robinson
Type: Miscellany - Literary
Frequency: Weekly   Price: $4.00
Size: 8 x 5   Length: 16 pp.
Availability: APS reels 204, 205

Remarks: At the start of this magazine, the title varied to the
extent that the words "weekly" and "the" were not included. Also
at the start, the material was entirely from British sources.
     Both the British nature of the articles and the wording of the
title varied intermittently until finally the title was as given above,
and the articles and poetry were always British.
     Many of the items were travel articles and letters describing
foreign lands. Biography and light fiction also appear. These were
generally the more popular items, and Robinson's idea may have
been to attract a less intellectual audience than that which read
other Baltimore magazines.
     A lessening of tension between England and America may have
been one reason for starting such an eclectic miscellany. A growing
desire to produce and patronize magazines with more of an American
basis may have been one reason Robinson's Magazine lasted only
about one year.

186. RURAL MAGAZINE

Title: The Rural Magazine and Farmer's Monthly Museum, Devoted
        to History, Biography, Agriculture, Manufacture, Miscellany,
        Poetry, and Foreign and Domestic Intelligence
Place: Hartford, Conn.   Dates: February-July 1819
Editor: Samuel Putnam Waldo
Publisher: J. & W. Russell

Printer: Roberts and Burr
Illustrations: Portraits and landscapes promised; one appeared
Type: Agriculture
Frequency: Monthly   Price: $3.00
Size: 9 x 5 1/2   Length: 40 pp.
Availability: APS reel 205

Remarks: Although the title promised all sorts of information, the introduction claimed the emphasis would be placed on agriculture. Throughout the issues, the farming information was entirely a rehash of material available elsewhere; and not only was it unoriginal, but it also dealt almost entirely with events rather than practical information.
　　The first issue began with a brief history of Connecticut and continued with a biography of General David Humphrey who lived in that state. The farming events announced were to be held in Connecticut, and the contents point to this being designed for a Connecticut audience.
　　Promised portraits failed to appear, except for one of President Monroe; the magazine was relatively expensive; and the contents uninspired. Probably the competition of The Plough Boy played no small part in forcing Samuel Waldo's journal to cease publication.

187. RURAL VISITER (!)

Title: The Rural Visiter; a Literary and Miscellaneous Gazette
Place: Burlington, N.J.   Dates: July 30, 1810-July 22, 1811
Editor and Publisher: David Allinson (July 30, 1810-February 11, 1811); Allinson & Co. (February 11-July 22, 1811)
Type: Literary newspaper
Frequency: Weekly   Price: $2.62 (!) per year
Size: Small quarto
Length: 4 pp. through October 6, 1810; every second week was 8 pp. starting October 13, 1810; all issues 8 pp. starting February 4, 1811; on May 6, 1811 all issues reverted to 4 pp.
Motto: Homo Sum; humani nihil a me alienum puto.
Availability: Not in APS. Microfilm, with no size indicated, obtained from The American Antiquarian Society.
Reference: Brigham, p. 494

Remarks: This magazine attempted to include material for as many interests as possible and to place it all in a small space. One of a series of miscellaneous essays opened each issue, and for a time "Memoirs of Socrates" brought the reader brief translations and commentaries intended as an introduction to the classics.
　　Poetry, the usual "intelligence," some local news, and advertisements made up the bulk of the remainder. Frequently, as many as two pages of ads appeared making The Rural Visiter a

storehouse of information on contemporary products and professional
services which were then offered in this way.
    Bible society reporting lent a religious flavor, and some book
reviews and essays remove this from the class of the usual newspaper. The literary contents are of ephemeral value, but the magazine provides added evidence of the growing trend to produce more
magazines for a growing audience in America.

188. SATIRIST

Title: The Satirist (January 16-April 11, 1812); The Boston Satirist
        (April 20-May 9, 1812)
Place: Boston   Dates: January 16-May 9, 1812
Editor: Lodowick Lash'em, pseud.
Publisher: James L. Edwards
Type: Miscellany - Humor
Frequency: Weekly - irregular   Price: $3.00
Size: 16 3/4 x 10 1/4   Length: 4 pp.
Masthead: Title words divided by an upraised arm holding a lash
           over a cowering dog.
Quotation: Yes--while I live, no rich or noble knave
            Shall walk this world in credit to his grave,
            To virtue only, and her friends, a friend,
            The world beside may murmur or command.
Availability: APS reel 205
Reference: Brigham, p. 345

Remarks: Our main object ... will be to lash vice and folly, in
          what soever shape it may be found ... To attack in the
          abstract, without touching persons, may be safe fighting
          indeed, but it is fighting with shadows ... There are
          some who
                "Safe from the bar, the pulpit, and the throne,
                 Are touch'd and sham'd by ridicule alone."[1]

    With this aim in mind, The Satirist poked fun at local politics
and society. The men in the Massachusetts State House were a
major target, the arrows being speeches, in their styles and techniques, which discussed completely unimportant topics.
    Letters to the editor were probably written by the editor
himself, serving as the lead-in to some satirical attack. Many of
the comments contain difficult contemporary allusions, and some
seem to be libelous. They may have led to the death of the magazine.

Notes: 1. The Satirist, no. 1 (January 16, 1812), 1.

189. SATURDAY MAGAZINE

Title: The Philadelphia Register, and National Recorder (January-
        June 1819); The National Recorder (July 1819-June 1821);
        The Saturday Magazine (July 1821-June 1822)
Place: Philadelphia   Dates: January 2, 1819-June 29, 1822
Editor: Eliakim Littell
Publisher: Littell and Henry
Printer: Clark and Raser
Type: Miscellany - General
Frequency: Weekly   Price: $5.00
Size: 9 x 5   Length: 32 pp.
Availability: APS reel 237
Reference: Mott, I, pp. 306-7
Superseded by: Museum of Foreign Literature and Science
        Later: Museum of Foreign Literature, Science, and Art
        Superseded by: The Eclectic Magazine

Remarks: Internal improvements came in for attention with material
on the proposed Pennsylvania canal which appeared on January 7,
1819. The avowed purpose continued to be the advancement of internal improvements and a contribution to literature in the United
States. Many items were eclectic, and most show life, society, and
culture in America. As 1819 went on, intellectual news, poetry,
foreign and domestic news summaries, descriptions of inventions,
and some agricultural news were added.
        In July 1821 this magazine changed its name to the one used
here. It is possible that The Saturday Evening Post was started in
competition. The Saturday Magazine changed its name in 1822, but
continued long after in a variety of guises.
        The early emphasis on internal improvements probably gave
this magazine the impetus it needed to survive. Men were interested
in an expanding America, and they were interested in magazines
which prompted American nationalism.

190. SCIENTIFIC JOURNAL

Title: The Scientific Journal, Containing Disquisitions in Natural
        Philosophy, Chemistry, and the Arts, with an Extensive
        Mathematical Correspondence
            Issue title: The Monthly Scientific Journal
Place: New York (February-August 1818); Perth Amboy, N.J. (July
        1819-January 1820)
Editor: W. Marrat
Publisher: W. Marrat (February-August 1818)
Printer: Joseph T. Murden (July 1819-January 1820)
Type: Science, mathematics
Frequency: Monthly, then quarterly   Price: 25¢
Size: 8 1/4 x 5   Length: 24 pp., later 8 pp.

Availability: APS reels 146, 239
Suspended: September 1818-June 1819

Remarks: The American Periodicals Series reel 146 contains issues one through six from the New York Historical Society, and
they are cited as The Monthly Scientific Journal. The APS reel
239 contains issues one through ten from Yale University, and they
are cited as The Scientific Journal. The entry used here is from
the longer run.
    The pages were open to every branch of science, the essays
were extremely short, sometimes less than one hundred words. The
first issue devoted half its length to Mathematics. Other articles
were popular in style and contents dealing with such topics as
"damp" in houses and the antiquity of clock making. Later issues
devoted more and more space to mathematics, especially to problems.
    There is a publishing hiatus from August 1818 to July 1819.
August 1818 was issue seven; July 1819, number eight. At this
point printing shifted to Perth Amboy, New Jersey. Issue nine is
dated October 1819 and contains sixteen pages. A Roman numeral
"X" appears in the upper right-hand corner of page 185. A note
on the top of the preceding page indicates that page 184 was the
last page of number nine, and that number ten would appear on
January 1, 1820. The Roman numeral is the only indication that
the following eight pages constitute a new number. This sequence
of pages has no separate title page, the half-title has been omitted,
and no running title appears. Apparently this was the last issue.
The item is not listed in the Karpinski bibliography of mathematical
publications in the United States.

191. SCOURGE

Title: The Scourge
Place: Baltimore   Dates: May 26-November 24, 1810
Editor: Titus Tickler, Esq. & Co., pseud.
Printer and Publisher: Samuel Magill
Type: Literary newspaper
Frequency: Weekly   Price: 12¢, or $4.00 per year
Size: Large quarto   Length: 4 pp.
Motto: Be Just - Fear Not.
Availability: Not in APS or ULS. Microfilm obtained from The
         Maryland Historical Society.
Reference: Brigham, p. 248

Remarks: The first issue of this title was not located, and whatever the editor may have said about his purpose remains unknown.
However, much of the effort was spent in pointing to the failings of
man in general. Opportunities were given to "correspondents" to
express their ire at practically any social practice; and letters appear, pro and con, on gambling, drinking, boxing, trespassing, and

other activities. Not always moralistic, these are frequently satirical and often quite funny.   Several times a brief note appears to remind readers of an anniversary, a coming event, the availability of domestic products, and other items considered of importance. The slavery material is scarce, but when it appears, it is outspokenly against the practice.

There are newspaper features: deaths, marriages, ship news, and local news summaries.   The format was that of a newspaper. However, the material beyond the scope of news is more important, and this title should be considered a magazine.

192. SCOURGE

Title: The Scourge
Place: Boston   Dates: August 10-December 28, 1811
Editor: Tim Touchstone, pseud. of Merrill Butler
Publisher: Merrill Butler (?) (Possibly: James L. Edwards)
Type: Miscellany - Humor
Frequency: Weekly   Price: 10¢, or $1.50 for 26 issues
Size: 10 1/2 x 8   Length: 4 pp.
Masthead: Public Justice scourging Vice and Scurality
Motto: Weak men demand our pity--bad men deserve our stripes.
Availability: APS reel 239
Reference: Brigham, p. 346

Remarks: This magazine, like many other contemporaries, depended on satire which bordered on libel:

> Democracy opens a wide field for Satire; yet the Editor of the Scourge feels it will be a Herculean task to touch her sensibilities so to the quick as to make her either blush with shame, or retract her errors.   The attempt however, shall be made. --The gauntlet of defense has been thrown at us;--we take it up and declare that we shall neither ASK, RECEIVE, NOR GIVE QUARTER.[1]

This was an anti-Democratic (i.e. Republican) statement, and one dart was aimed toward the Navy:

> Who that ever heard the thunder, and witnessed the awful spectacle of one of our mighty men-of-war gun boats, at that interesting and sublime moment, when day was departing, and gold and purple streaked the west! but must confess that the following lines are truly descriptive:--
>   "Niddle noddle" goes the boat,
>   "Bang!" goes the gun;
>   "Quack!" goes the frightened bird,
>   And down goes the sun![2]

Little was sacred to Butler, and "Touchstone's Biographical

Dictionary" took apparently effective swipes at anyone. The Scourge
was forced to depart after sixteen issues.

Notes: 1. The Scourge, no. 1 (August 10, 1811), 1.
        2. Ibid., p. 2.

193. SELECT REVIEWS

Title: Select Reviews, and Spirit of the Foreign Magazines (January
        1809-June 1811); Select Reviews of Literature and Spirit of
        Foreign Magazines (July 1811-December 1812)
Place: Philadelphia   Dates: January 1809-December 1812
Editor: Samuel Ewing[1]
Publisher: Edward Earle (1810); John F. Watson (1811-1812)
Printer: Enos Bronson (1810); Thomas T. Stiles (1811-1812)
Illustrations: Some volumes have engraved title pages, and the four
        volumes in the period have eight scattered plates. Nearly
        all are portraits, and possibly more were intended.
Type: Miscellany - Literary
Frequency: Monthly   Price: $5.00
Size: 8 x 4 1/2   Length: 72 pp.
Motto: The wheat from all these publications should, from time to
        time, be winnowed, and the chaff thrown away.
Availability: APS reels 44, 239-40
Indexed: Cargill
Reference: Lewis, p. 266
Superseded by: Analectic Magazine

Remarks: Enos Bronson conducted much of the operations until
July 1811 and printed Select Reviews on his Lorenze Press. At
this time John F. Watson purchased the magazine and ran it from
July 1811 until December 1812. At this point Moses Thomas
purchased Select Reviews and began a new series called the Analectic Magazine which continued the history, despite two name changes,
until 1820.

    Long reviews, eclectic articles, poetry, literary intelligence,
and a miscellany are the sections which form the bulk of the material. The reviews, which came first, were generally original to
the magazine; but the articles from foreign magazines, which formed
the second major section, were naturally gathered from outside
sources. The selection was done with a Philadelphia intellectual
audience in mind.

    In May 1811, a long omnibus review covering several pam-
phlets dealing with the Lancastrian System of education appeared.
The opinion was favorable, and one purpose may have been to serve
as a substitute for the pamphlets themselves since long quotations
were a part of the review.

    One interesting note about the contents is that not one mention
of the War of 1812 was made. This attitude toward the war, and

indeed it must have been an attitude, reveals at least two things about the era: the war itself was a localized thing which could be ignored in areas separated from conflict; and, for those who disagreed with the purpose of the conflict the way was easy to remain aloof.

America was still dependent on English models for magazines, but Select Reviews makes an attempt and a beginning toward a break by providing American criticism of literature. The great literary magazines were to come later, but this one is an early example of a trend which was gathering momentum.

Notes: 1. Lewis, op. cit., p. 266. See also Polyanthos, 3d
        series, I (February 1813), 277.

194. SHAMROCK

Title: The Shamrock; or, Hibernian Chronicle (December 15, 1810-
        June 5, 1813); The Shamrock (June 12, 1813-August 16, 1817)
Place: New York
Dates: December 15, 1810-August 16, 1817. Suspended: June 5,
        1813-June 18, 1814; January 28-September 2, 1815; August
        17-December 2, 1816
Editor: Edward Gillespy
Publisher: Edward Gillespy (December 15, 1810-June 5, 1813);
        Edward Gillespy and Thomas O'Connor (June 25, 1814-January
        28, 1815); Thomas O'Connor (September 7, 1815-August 17,
        1816 and January 4-August 16, 1817)
Printer: George Largin and Thomas Thompson (December 15, 1810-
        September 12, 1812); William Peluse and _____ Gould (Septem-
        ber 12-November 14, 1812); The Shamrock Press (November
        14, 1812-June 5, 1813); Nicholas VanRiper (June 25, 1814-
        January 1, 1815); Henry Clayton and Daniel Fanshaw (July
        20-August 3, 1816) and January 4-January 16, 1817); Peter
        VanPelt and Benjamin Riley (January 25-August 16, 1817)
Type: Religious - Catholic
Frequency: Weekly   Price: $3.00
Size: 18 1/4 x 11 3/4 (until January 18, 1814); then 10 3/4 x
        8 1/2
Length: 4 pp. (until January 18, 1814); then 8 pp.
Masthead: American eagle holding a shield and carrying the harp
        of Ireland
Motto: Fostered under thy wing, we die in thy defense.
Availability: Not in APS. The Library of Congress has the best
        file; copy examined at The New York Historical Society.
Reference: Brigham, p. 690

Remarks: This was not the first American periodical publication
with a slant for Catholic interests, but the Journal des Dames (A6)
was meant for children. The Shamrock may well be the first adult
Catholic periodical published in the United States.

The magazine was actually intended for an Irish audience, but the contents are not those of a present-day diocesan newspaper. In the first years, The Shamrock looked like other newspapers and reported only a few items in a manner of defense of the Catholic position. Regular advertising was always carried; and local news, marriages, and deaths were generally to be found.

In 1814 the size changed and stories with a viewpoint began. More and more the news was of Catholic interests. Since both the literary content and the news were frequently slanted, this magazine became a publication for a special interest group. The Shamrock retained this complexion until its death.

Perhaps one other special aspect of this title should be noted. Most Irish in America at the time were immigrants, and The Shamrock made a point to print news of Ireland--especially marriages and deaths--in order to fill the void of information from home. This may have been a reason why The Shamrock had such a relatively long life despite its on-again-off-again publishing record.

195. SOMETHING

Title: Something
Place: Boston   Dates: November 18, 1809-May 12, 1810
Editor: Nemo Nobody, Esq., pseud. of James Fennell
Publisher: Ferrand, Mallory and Co.
Type: Miscellany - Humor
Frequency: Weekly   Price: $3.00 (1809); $4.00 (1810)
Size: 10 x 6 1/4   Length: 16 pp.
Motto: "Tis Something - Nothing"
Availability: APS reels 44, 671
Indexed: Cargill
Reference: Lewis, pp. 267-8

Remarks: Referring to the motto above, one is tempted to add: "pity 'tis, 'tis true." The twenty-six issues of Something do not quite succeed in being as witty as Fennell liked to think they were. The letters to the editors frequently were based on weak puns, and the religious essays were dull and labored. In a comment on "Rouge or Paint," Fennel wrote:

> Although we seriously believe that young ladies of Boston
> are at present the least deviatory from strict and steady
> principles of any in the United States, we cannot but ob-
> serve with regret, a practice which if not already fashion-
> able, threatens to become so, that of giving unnatural
> colours to the cheeks.[1]

Fennell also deemed himself a judge of morality:

> ... the attachment which young females exhibit to novel
> reading must originate in the weakness of their minds,

resulting from a deficiency in their education;... A young girl accustomed or addicted to novel reading, opens wider the two great avenues to seduction and susceptibility.[2]

The old-fashioned syntax is understandable, but the opinions do not seem those of a witty or urbane man, but rather those of a conventional, if not conservative, one. Something may not have succeeded as a humor magazine, but it did add to the trend of diversification in magazines published by offering something beyond the review and the sermon.

Notes: 1. Something, no. 9 (January 13, 1810), 136.
       2. Ibid., no. 2 (May 12, 1810), 403-4.

196. SOUTHERN EVANGELICAL INTELLIGENCER

Title: The Southern Evangelical Intelligencer
Place: Charleston, S.C.
Dates: March 27, 1819-December 29, 1821?
Editor: Not given
Printer: W. C. Young
Type: Religious - Non-denominational
Frequency: Weekly   Price: $4.00
Size: 8 1/2 x 7   Length: 8 pp.
Motto: And Many Shall Run To and Fro, and Knowledge Shall be Increased.
Availability: Not in APS. Microfilm through 1820 obtained from The New York Historical Society.
Reference: Brigham, p. 1043

Remarks: The purposes were three: to report local and foreign news, to lessen religious prejudice, and to summarize legislative action on local and national levels. The news was rather ordinary and not a major part of the magazine. The legislative articles were frequently long and frequently transcribed whole speeches. The religious aspects of the magazine were more important, more fully covered, and nondenominational in nature.
     Missionary activity in many countries was reported, and the first issue contains a list of British missionary societies, each described in a paragraph. The domestic activities and missionary work of several American denominations are reported in neutral tones, and the editor took pains to avoid taking sides in any dispute.
     The closing date above is the date of the last issue examined for this study. However, the United States Catholic Miscellany for January 7, 1824 contains a reference indicating that this magazine was still being published in that year,[1] and William Hoole lists the magazine as continuing as late as 1826.[2]

Notes: 1. Guy Adams Cardwell, Charleston Periodicals, 1795-1860 ... (Ph.D. dissertation, University of North Carolina, 1936), p. 302.

2. William Stanley Hoole, Checklist and Finding List of Charleston Periodicals, 1732-1864 (Durham, N.C.: Duke University Press, 1936), p. 23.

197. SPIRIT OF THE FORUM

Title: Spirit of the Forum, and Hudson Remarker
Place: Hudson, N.Y.   Dates: April 16, 1817//
Editor: Conducted by An Association of Gentlemen
Printer: Mr. Corss
Type: Miscellany - General
Frequency: One issue only   Price: Not given
Size: 9 x 5   Length: 16 pp.
Motto: Et prodesse volunt, et delectare.
Availability: APS reel 240

Remarks: Members of the Association of Gentlemen are not identified, but they may have also been The Forum of the City of Hudson since the avowed purpose of this publication was to support the activities of this group and report them to the citizens of Hudson. Also included as a purpose was to report and summarize the "affairs" of Hudson.
"The Editors do not intend to publish this paper with periodical regularity... If they can prepare a number once in two weeks, they will."[1] Apparently they carried out their intention since only one number appeared. The contents were two informal essays, a report of the first meeting of the Forum, and some poetry.

Notes: 1. Spirit of the Forum, no. 1 (April 16, 1817), 3.

198. SPIRITUAL MAGAZINE

Title: Spiritual Magazine; or, Gospel Treasury
Place: Freetown, Mass.   Dates: January 1813-May 1814
Editor: George S. White
Printer and Publisher: Not given
Type: Religious - Lutheran
Frequency: Quarterly   Price: Not given
Size: 8 x 5   Length: 40 pp.
Availability: APS reel 240

Remarks: Only two issues of this title appeared. The first stated that the magazine would be devoted to an attack on Hopkinsianism.
The material is frequently signed with a pseudonym like Augustus Toplady, and generally attacks what are called "false doctrines." The first issue includes articles about the Protestants of Scotland, brief testaments and doctrinal statements, extracts from

Calvin and Luther, a short essay credited to Thomas Paine, and a poem. The second issue borrowed its material, but credit is not given to the sources. The magazine is called Lutheran since the largest share of the material takes this viewpoint. However, the magazine may well have only been the distillation of one man's thought rather than the opinion of a group.

199. STAR OF FREEDOM

Title: The Star of Freedom. Literary, Political, and Agricultural
Place: Newtown, Penn.   Dates: May 21, 1817-March 25, 1818
Editor: Asher Miner
Printer: Simeon Siegfried
Type: Literary newspaper
Frequency: Weekly   Price: $2.00
Size: ca. 12 x 10   Length: 8 pp.
Quotation: Pledged to no Party's arbitrary sway -
          I follow Truth where'er it leads the way.
Availability: Not in APS. Microfilm obtained from The American
          Antiquarian Society.
Reference: Brigham, p. 883

Remarks: The American Antiquarian Society has a broadside prospectus of this paper dated January 10, 1817 which contains an article dated April 24, 1817. The first issue seen was dated May 28, 1817 and it is numbered as the second one. Thus the opening date of May 21, 1817 is a speculation.

Biography was nearly always on the opening page; and box advertisements were printed on the last page, and sometimes filled nearly two pages. These sold for $1.00 per "square" with 35¢ charged for each subsequent use.

Serialized fiction, marriages, deaths, a weekly "retrospect," and poetry are regular items. At times, congressional debate is reported, societies are described, and inventions announced.

Neutrality was maintained in politics and religion, not by avoiding topics, but by printing material expressing as many views as possible. The miscellaneous nature of the magazine may also be seen in the titles of four essays contained in the issue of October 15, 1817: "Description of the Church of St. Peter in Rome," "Extirpation of Garlic," "The Ladies Friend--Beauty," and "The Shakers." A curiosity is the opening of a speech by one Thomas Knott, an English Quaker, who said: "Unaccustomed as I am to speak in a public assembly..."[1]

In many ways The Star of Freedom was a newspaper, but its other contents reveal a great deal about contemporary society and culture; and the pages carry enough material outside the scope of a newspaper for the title to be considered as a magazine.

Notes: 1. Star of Freedom, I (June 4, 1817), 18.

200. STRANGER

Title: Stranger, A Literary Paper
Place: Albany, N.Y.   Dates: July 3, 1813-June 25, 1814
Editor: John Cook
Printer: E. and E. Hosford
Type: Miscellany - Literary
Frequency: Weekly for two issues, then semi-monthly
Price: $2.50
Size: 8 x 5   Length: 8 pp. for two issues, then 16 pp.
Motto: Therefore as a Stranger, bid it Welcome.
Availability: Not in APS. Copy consulted at The University of
          Michigan
Indexed: Cargill

Remarks: New publications from America and foreign sources
were listed in each issue, and many of these include brief annotations. Selected poetry was usually from the English "greats."
Several articles are credited to eighteenth English sources.
     Aside from the poetry and reviews, the contents include a
wide variety of essays, generally of three types: biography, literature, and history. Some are serious, some are humorous, and
most are informative and rather interesting. A meterological
journal records various readings for most weeks, but no direct
forecasts are attempted. News does not appear as a regular feature; and the magazine, despite its being the only such publication
in Albany at the time, lasted only one year.

201. SUNDAY SCHOOL REPOSITORY

Title: The Sunday School Repository
Place: New York   Dates: October 1816-February 1819
Editor, Printer, and Publisher: Not given
Type: Religious - Non-denominational
Frequency: Bi-monthly   Price: $1.50
Size: 6 1/4 x 3 3/4   Length: 40 pp.
Availability: APS reel 333
Reference: Congregationalist, III (January 1, 1818), 3.

Remarks: The reference cited above does not imply that this was
a Congregationalist publication; rather, internal evidence indicates
it was non-denominational. The files are very incomplete suggesting
that issues were well used when they circulated.
     The purpose was to publish information about Sabbath schools
of which the magazine says there were 5,000 in operation serving
half a million people. New schools were announced, plans of instruction were given, the effect of the schools was discussed, and
reviews of appropriate books were intended.
     The New York Sunday School Union Society's annual report

was extracted, and other similar societies were described. Several anecdotes about Sunday schools were included as were somewhat moralistic biographies of young people.

Although some material was written at a rather young level, and some seems to have been designed for children, the magazine probably was intended to have a wide audience of which children were to form but a part.

202. THEOLOGICAL REPERTORY

Title: The Washington Theological Repertory (August 1819-December 1828); The Theological Repertory (January 1829-December 1830)
Place: Washington City   Dates: August 1819-December 1830
Editor: By Clergymen of the Protestant Episcopal Church
Printer: Davis and Force
Type: Religious - Episcopal
Frequency: Monthly   Price: Not given
Size: 8 x 5   Length: 32 pp.
Motto: Let us hold fast the profession of our faith without wavering.
Availability: APS reel 241

Remarks: This magazine was divided primarily into three sections: articles dealing with theology, reviews of books on religious topics, and religious news. The basic purpose of the magazine was to explain the structure of the Protestant Episcopal Church, to describe the rites and ceremonial used in its services, and to explicate the doctrine presumably preached in the pulpits of the church.

The magazine was slow to start. Much of the material in the first issues was eclectic; but the arrangement, tone, and general subject matter of the essays follows closely the outlined intention.

The magazine changed its name for its last few years and perhaps tried to expand its subscription list. This was but one of several excellent Episcopalian magazines and undoubtedly it tried to overreach itself when an interest was on the wane and the market was flooded with material.

203.   THEOPHILANTHROPIST

Title: Theophilanthropist; Containing Critical, Moral Theological and Literary Essays in Monthly Numbers
Place: New York   Dates: January-September 1810
Editor: By A Society
Publisher: H. Hart
Illustrations: Only one woodcut, and several small cuts.
Type: Religious - Deist
Frequency: Monthly   Price: Not given

Size: 8 1/4 x 4 3/4   Length: 40 pp.
Availability: APS reel 333

Remarks: The Deists, who preferred reason over revelation, had
earlier produced Temple of Reason, [1] perhaps the first magazine
devoted to this viewpoint. No direct connection between the two
magazines seems to have existed.
    Biography, critical reviews, material on agriculture, manu-
factures, discoveries, and inventions were all to be considered; but
top priority was awarded to articles which would "correct false
opinions, promote the progress of reason, and increase the sum of
human happiness. "[2]
    Articles on several sects of Christianity appear, but perhaps
one of the more interesting series concerns the "Morality of Moho-
metanism. " In this extracts from the Koran are arranged by subject.

    A knowledge of the Mohometan system, may be deemed
    as important, as tending to blunt that rancorous preju-
    dice, which bigotry engenders in the mind of ignorance
    against those of different religious persuasions. [3]

This series, with commentaries, ran for over sixty pages and
provides an interesting attempt to understand a different people.

Notes: 1. Lewis, op. cit., pp. 271-2.
        2. Theophilanthropist, title page, 1810.
        3. Ibid., (September 1810), p. 383.

204. TICKLER

Title: The Tickler
Place: Philadelphia
Dates: September 16, 1807-November 17, 1813
Editor: Toby Scratch'em (possibly: George Helmbold)
Publisher: George Helmbold (September 16, 1807-July 21, 1812);
        Henry K. Helmbold (July 28, 1812-November 17, 1813)
Type: Miscellany - Humor
Frequency: Weekly   Price: $4.00
Size: 18 x 11 1/4   Length: 4 pp.
Masthead: Between the title words a woodcut of a raised hand
        holding a four-tailed whip, and to the right a cowering dog.
Availability: APS reel 45 through 1809. 1810-1813 obtained on
        microfilm from The American Antiquarian Society.
Reference: Lewis, pp. 280-1

Remarks: George Helmbold was "Junior" until his father died in
1808. What the relationship was between George and Henry is not
known.
    Henry Helmbold operated the paper with moderate success

placing some emphasis on independent political satire.   Barbs were
cast at both major parties, and this was done in the letters column
where Helmbold took apparent delight in writing himself letters
which he answered with some relish.

Theatre announcements, news of the War of 1812, the words
of songs, and brief miscellaneous articles and essays occupy most
of the four pages.   Advertisements began to appear with number
thirty-seven, and they continued to appear in varying quantity from
then on--always on the front page.   The format was standard--
small blocks of space set in three columns which were relieved at
times by small woodcut decorations.   Local merchants, book sellers,
and patent medicines appear most frequently.

At least one "Extra" appeared on October 30, 1811.   This
was not a national emergency but was an answer to criticism of
Toby.   It caused a flurry of excitement and may also have been a
rather clever publicity trick.

Helmbold went off to war in 1813.[1]   Although The Tickler
ceased, Helmbold revived the idea with the Independent Balance
when he returned, and his humorous editing thus carried on during
most of the decade.

Notes: 1. Mott, op. cit., I, p. 171.

205. TRANGRAM

Title: The Trangram; or, Fashionable Trifler
Place: Philadelphia
Dates: August 10, 1809-February 1, 1810
Editor: Christopher Crag, Esq., his Grandmother, and Uncle.
         (Two of these were: Mordecai Manuel Noah and Alexander
         F. Coxe)
Publisher: George E. Blake
Printer: T. and G. Palmer
Type: Miscellany - Humor
Frequency: Irregular   Price: Not given
Size: 5 5/8 x 3 1/2   Length: 20 pp.
Availability: Not in APS or ULS. A film of the three known issues
         was obtained from The Historical Society of Pennsylvania.
Reference: Smyth, pp. 181-3
            Seilhamer, p. 274

Remarks: A trangram is an "odd or intricate contrivance of some
kind, a knick-knack, a puzzle."[1] The magazine was intended to be
one of satire and indeed did call men like Andrew Hamilton and
Joseph Dennie to task.[2] Dennie was called "Oliver Crank" a name
which no doubt bothered him somewhat.

There were apparently three editors, Mordecai Manual Noah,
Alexander F. Coxe, and a third whose name is now known.[3] The
examined copy has four pages of manuscript notes added after the
title page written by one William Duane and dated January 27, 1874.

Seilhamer says Duane was an editor, but this must have been an
error.   The contents were ironic and informal essays which may
have little merit but their allusions must have been met with roars
of laughter or anger--depending upon the reader.   The introductory
essay parodied Macbeth and set the tone of the magazine's intent:

> How now, ye cunning, sharp and secret wags,
>   What is't ye do?
> A deed with double name.

Why no more than three issues appeared remains a mystery.
Perhaps Noah and Coxe tired of their publishing adventure, and perhaps they were in trouble for libel--a common enough problem
among early journalists.   However, The Trangram added something
to the growing list of early American humor magazines.

Notes: 1.   The Oxford English Dictionary (Oxford: Clarendon
              Press, 1933), XI, p. 249.
          2.   Smyth, op. cit., p. 183.
          3.   Seilhamer, op. cit., p. 274.

206. TRUE BRITON

Title: The True Briton
Place: Boston   Dates: June 9-December 8, 1819
Editor, Printer, and Publisher: J. Jackson
Type: Miscellany - Special
Frequency: Weekly   Price: One shilling
Size: 8 x 5   Length: 8 pp.
Motto: Union gives firmness and solidity to the humblest aids.
Availability: Not in APS.   Microfilm obtained from The University
          of Illinois.

Remarks: Anglophilism was never unusual in America, and there
had been editors like Joseph Dennie who were always outspokenly
pro-British.   Nonetheless, this magazine is a bit surprising especially after America's second war for independence had been suc-
cessfully brought to a conclusion.
          The editor, J. Jackson, was loudly pro-British; he advocated
monarchy, a parliament, British taxes, the use of British money,
and the English educational system.   He seemed to realize that
Britain's strength lay in a strong but friendly America, but he only
grudgingly admitted it.
          Despite Jackson's admiration of things British and his arti-
cles favoring an English economy as well as other aspects of
English life, he was forced to publish his magazine in the United
States because English law did not permit the statements he wanted
to make.   That is the great paradox of this magazine; and it is the

paradox of American publishing to allow a magazine which advocated something different from the government which permitted its publication. Perhaps this alone is Jackson's contribution to the history of magazine publishing in America.

207. UNIVERSALIST MAGAZINE

Title: The Universalist Magazine, Devoted to Doctrine, Religion, and Morality
Place: Boston   Dates: July 3, 1819-December 28, 1878
Editor: Hosea Ballou
Printer: Henry Bowen
Type: Religious - Universalist
Frequency: Weekly   Price: $2.50
Size: 12 x 9   Length: 4 pp.
Quotation: Fear not: for behold I bring you tidings of great joy, which shall be unto All people.
Availability: APS reel 243
History: Published through June 28, 1828 with the title above.
         Later: Trumpet and Universalist Magazine; Trumpet and Christian Freeman; Trumpet and Freeman; and eventually Universalist Leader

Remarks: Hosea Ballou had earlier chosen the doctrine of universal salvation as opposed to the more selective Calvinistic doctrine with which he had been raised. To this magazine he brought years of practice in the ministry, his self-education, and his ability as a clear thinker.
         Under three headings, Doctrine, Religion, and Morality, Ballou advocated the Universalist Viewpoint; but he also accepted and printed articles from other persuasions. His reason for this obviously was that it gave him the opportunity to answer these statements and thus to reinforce his own teaching.
         Some eclectic material, sermons, announcements of marriages and deaths, a long-standing squabble with the Boston Kaleidoscope, and a column of questions and answers make up a generally interesting and better than average religious magazine.

208.   UTICA CHRISTIAN MAGAZINE

Title: The Utica Christian Magazine, Designed to Prompt the Spirit of Research, and Diffuse Religious Information
Place: Utica, N.Y.   Dates: July 1813-June 1816
Editor: Committee of Congregational and Presbyterian Clergymen
Publisher: Cornelius Davis
Printer: Merrell and Camp
Type: Religious - Non-denominational

Frequency: Monthly   Price: Not given
Size: 8 1/4 x 5   Length: 40 pp.
Availability: APS reel 244

Remarks: Although Albaugh's bibliography lists this as a Presbyterian magazine, and although much of the material was pro-Hopkins
and Congregational, the magazine probably was intended as non-, or
at least inter-, denominational. Almost the entire first year was
selected from the Connecticut Evangelical Magazine, the Massachusetts Baptist Missionary Magazine, and the Missionary Herald.
Only a few articles were original, and for those selected, no credit
was given.

The contents were quite varied, and aside from cutting sectarian lines, including literature, history and biography were all
typical of the format of the magazines of the time. Support must
have waned since the last three issues were bi-monthly and showed
signs of less skillful editing. The magazine may have been used as
a teaching tool, but local support was not to be found even by
combining congregations of different denominations.

209. VERMONT BAPTIST MISSIONARY MAGAZINE

Title: The Vermont Baptist Missionary Magazine
Place: Rutland, Vt.   Dates: January 1811-April 1812
Editors: Obed Warren, Isaac Sawyer, Henry Green, William Har-
          rington, Sylvanus Haynes, Clark Kendrick, Samuel Rowley
Printer: W. Fay
Type: Religious - Baptist
Frequency: Quarterly   Price: 12 1/2¢
Size: 7 3/4 x 4 1/4   Length: 32 pp.
Availability: APS reel 246

Remarks: Sermons and religious poetry, reports of religious revivals, extracts from sermons, shorter pieces with polemic mes-
sages, and extracts from other religious and secular magazines
form the bulk of this title.

The Vermont Baptist Association decided to publish a magazine to promulgate their viewpoint and to serve as an evangelical
organ for Christianity. The seven men named above comprised the
committee appointed to plan and produce such a magazine. One
point of contention concerned the position of Freewill Baptists.
This group was roundly criticized in the pages of each issue.

The committee tried to begin at the beginning by telling in
brief fashion the history of Christianity from the time of creation
which was placed some 6,000 years previously. Pleas were made
for both money and material for the magazine. Both went unan-
swered. Much of the material became reports of missionary activity.

Although this magazine's purpose was perhaps worthwhile,
the autonomous nature of Baptist congregations doomed the

experiment to failure. Without wide support, which was impossible
at the time, the magazine was soon to disappear.

210. VILLAGE MUSEUM

Title: The Village Museum
Place: York, Penn. Dates: August 1819-July 1823
Editor: Conducted by an Association of Young Men
Publisher: Peter Hardt
Printer: Gemmill Lewis
Type: Miscellany - Literary
Frequency: Monthly   Price: $1.00
Size: ca. 8 x 5   Length: 16 pp.
Motto: Along the cool sequester'd vale of life,
        We keep the noiseless tenor of our way.
Availability: Not in APS. Microfilm obtained from The Historical
        Society of Pennsylvania.

Remarks: Whoever the Association of Young Men may have been
is unknown. Equally unknown is why they started this magazine in
York, Pennsylvania. The publisher, Peter Hardt, also issued a
newspaper, the York Recorder, and he may have had considerable
responsibility for selecting the contents.
        The intention was to produce a neutral and independent
literary miscellany. The essays were largely original; and the
magazine's poetry, agricultural information, and selected essays
were added to announcements of marriages and deaths and several
generally entertaining columns.
        During 1819 the magazine was small and designed to be read
for fun and leisure. No attempt to be partisan toward any one view
in politics or religion can be found. Surprisingly, the magazine
lasted for three years--slightly longer than the average life a magazine could expect in this period.

211. VILLAGER

Title: The Villager, A Literary Paper
Place: Greenwich Village, N.Y.   Dates: April-June 1819
Editor: Not given
Printer: Priod and Dunning
Type: Literary newspaper
Frequency: Bi-monthly   Price: Not given
Size: 8 x 4 3/4   Length: 16 pp.
Availability: APS reel 246
Indexed: Cargill

Remarks: Greenwich Village has changed somewhat from the time when this magazine first appeared, and certainly the contents of this journal are different from what is now found in magazines issued in this section of New York City.   The basic purpose of this publication, expressed in contemporary syntax, was to spread morality and promote manners.   Book reviews, selected essays on "moral" subjects, poetry, literary announcements, and short informal essays such as one discussing the origins of All Fool's Day make up the basic contents, and this array of material does not differentiate this magazine from others in the period.

The magazine may be considered a literary newspaper since national news, local summaries, marriages and deaths, and a few notices all appear in the magazine's two column, sixteen page format.

In May and June 1819 a series called The Lay Preacher appeared, but the essays were not by Dennie.   The editors may have called on Dennie's name to give this impression, but the association did not help the magazine to survive.

212. VISITOR

Title: The Visitor
Place: Richmond, Va.
Dates: February 11, 1809-August 18, 1810
Editor: Not given
Publisher: Lynch and Southgate
Type: Miscellany - Literature
Frequency: Bi-weekly (February 11, 1808-January 27, 1810);
        Weekly (February 10-August 18, 1810)
Price: $2.00 (v. 1); $3.00 (v. 2)
Size: 9 3/8 x 7 1/2
Length: 8 pp. (to February 10, 1810); 4 pp. (February 17, 1810
        to end)
Motto: A sober guest, whose philanthropic views are to instruct,
        or harmlessly amuse.
Availability: APS reels 46, 246
Reference: Lewis, p. 287

Remarks: News was printed, and it consisted of a summary of intelligence, marriages, deaths, and some notices of coming events; but this was a minor part of the magazine.   Essays, brief but well written, appeared on literature, science, criticism, agriculture, education, and biography.   Poetry was at all times presented with typographical tricks such as printing a poem in a pyramid.   Short stories and serialized fiction became more frequent.   The news feature was slowly shortened and at times even dropped.

Music was promised, and the promise was carried out.   In 1810, "The Unquenchable Flame," "The Canary Bird," and "Cotillions" were printed with hand-set type rather than being engraved. The music was a simple melody.

Most of the contents were borrowed from other sources, and frequently shortened to suit the space available. No reason was offered for the magazine's disappearance.

213. WAR

Title: The War
Place: New York
Dates: June 27, 1812-September 6, 1814; February 24, 1817
Editor: Thomas O'Connor; Samuel Woodworth (issue of 1817)
Printer and Publisher: Samuel Woodworth (June 27, 1812-September 6, 1814); Charles N. Baldwin (issue of 1817)
Type: News
Frequency: Weekly   Price: $2.00
Size: 11 1/2 x 9   Length: 4 pp.
Motto: Let the Rallying Word, Through all the Day, Be "Liberty or Death."
Availability: Not in APS. Copy consulted in The Clement's Library, The University of Michigan.

Remarks: The title page statement continues by describing The War as "A Faithful Record of the Transactions of the War Between the United States of America and their Territories, and the United Kingdom of Great Britain ..." The magazine opens with a brief background summary of events up to June 1812, and deals summarily with the American Revolution:

> The Americans, whose breasts beat high with a love of liberty, took the field, and, by perseverance and bravery, overthrew the collosean forces of England, whose proud king was thus obligated to relinquish all claim of sovereignty to the thirteen United States of America.[1]

The War of 1812 is treated somewhat more fully with hundreds of details of day-to-day events. Government documents, official communications, letters to and from field commanders, the President or the Secretary of the Navy, Congressional debates, speeches, and hundreds of other items detailed in parallel with a chronology of the events of the War.
Although the War of 1812 officially ended on December 24, 1814 with the Treaty of Ghent, communication problems prevented the word from reaching the United States. The Battle of New Orleans is discussed in The War as "the battle of MacPrardie's Plantation," and several other post-treaty events are given in some detail. The last of these was the capture of the Brig Penquin on March 23, 1815--an event which The War apparently considers the final event of the War of 1812.[2]
Although several other magazines reported the events of this war, The War carries the most details and remains a valuable

source of documents and description. Certainly, it is the most
complete magazine source, and all others pale by comparison.

Notes: 1.   The War, I (June 27, 1812), 1.
         2.   Ibid., III (February 24, 1817), 67.

214. WATCHMAN-EXAMINER

Title: Christian Watchman (May 29-November 20, 1819); Christian
        Watchman & Baptist Register (December 4, 1819-May 11,
        1848); Later: Watchman and Reflector; and on May 8, 1919,
        the union of twenty-three Baptist papers became: Watchman-
        Examiner
Place: Boston   Dates: May 29, 1819-May 11, 1848
Editor: Not given
Printer: True and Weston
Type: Religious - Baptist
Frequency: Weekly   Price: $2.00
Size: 11 3/4 x 9 1/2   Length: 4 pp.
Availability: APS reel 246

Remarks: This magazine is listed as Watchman-Examiner although
it did not assume that name for over 100 years. The connection
between the Christian Watchman and the later title is somewhat
tenuous, and for this reason an ending date of 1848 has been used.
Some connection did, however, exist among this long series of titles.
     At the outset this magazine contained mainly morally-toned
essays on numerous subjects. Religious liberty was advocated--with
the limitation that it be for those who adhere to certain, well-defined
beliefs. Religious news, accounts of revivals, extracted sermons,
national news, announcements of marriages and deaths, and some
eclectic articles make up the other pages.
     Despite the autonomous nature of the Baptist congregations,
enough regional New England support was found to keep this paper
alive. And a paper it indeed became, assuming the functions of a
religious newspaper in later years. The later history of this magazine covers the development of the Baptist movement throughout the
nineteenth century and a file of this title is of great value to the
religious historian.

215. WEEKLY RECORDER

Title: The Weekly Recorder, a Newspaper Conveying Important
        Intelligence and Other Useful Matter Under the Three General
        Heads of Theology, Literature, and National Affairs
Place: Chillicothe, Ohio
Dates: July 5, 1814-October 6, 1821//?

Editor, Printer, and Publisher: John Andrews
Type: Literary newspaper
Frequency: Weekly
Price: $2.00 (1814-1815); $3.00 (1816-   )
Size: 11 1/2 x 9 1/4   Length: 8 pp.
Quotation: Righteousness exalteth a nation: but sin is a reproach
          to any people.
Availability: APS reels, 248, 249, 250
Reference: Brigham, p. 788
History: Later became: Presbyterian Banner

Remarks: This could easily be called a religious paper, and it was
non-denominational in its first few years, publishing material relating
to Presbyterians, Baptists, Methodists, and occasionally Catholics.
The major items were: religious news, moralistic columns, a
column covering arts and sciences, publication notices, a geography
column, new inventions, national and local news, and advertisements.
The religious news often concerned Bible societies, their
meetings and activities. These columns contain names, statistics,
and details of the activities which were local and difficult to identify
and locate in other sources. Articles on education and teaching
methods were common. The other features, like the geographical
articles, all combine to give the publication more than an average
interest.
     Some naval news appears, but details and names almost never
are given. The peace was announced on February 23, 1815--and the
article appeared on page five! An unusual feature of this announcement is what appears to be an embryonic headline--the one word
PEACE centered in the column. No extensive details are given--
merely the announcement that the War had ended.
     John Andrews' illness was announced on October 6, 1821.
Also mentioned was the need for repairs in the printing shop. Both
factors were to cause a delay in the appearance of the first number
of volume eight. Apparently, it is still delayed.

216. WEEKLY VISITOR

Title: The Weekly Visitor
Place: New York   Dates: May 12, 1810-May 25, 1811
Editor, Printer, and Publisher: Alexander C. Morton
Type: Miscellany - Literary
Frequency: Weekly   Price: $2.00
Size: 8 1/4 x 5   Length: 16 pp.
Masthead: A Winged female blowing a trumpet
Availability: APS reel 251

Remarks: The Weekly Visitor is not particularly an unusual publication for the period. Like dozens of other similar papers it published a very great variety of short, at times, humorous, paragraphs
dealing with hundreds of miscellaneous topics. In fact, the

heterogeneous nature of its pages may have prevented enough really wide-spread interest to support the title.

Some brief poetry was used to fill the back page, a few theoretical columns appear, and at least one tale was serialized by the episode--History of Rinaldo Rinaldini--which ran through twenty numbers. While not distinguished, the Weekly Visitor may have added some weight to the growing tradition of American magazines many of which followed the pattern duplicated by this literary miscellany.

217. WEEKLY VISITOR, AND LADIES' MUSEUM

Title: The Weekly Visitor, and Ladies' Museum
Place: New York
Dates: v. 1-4 November 1, 1817-October 30, 1819; n.s. v. 5
         May 4-October 12, 1822
Editor, Printer, Publisher: Alexander Ming
Type: Women's magazine
Frequency: Weekly   Price: $4.00
Size: ca. 12 x 10   Length: 16 pp.
Motto: To wake the soul by tender strokes of Art,
         To raise the genius, and to mind the heart.
Availability: Not in APS. Microfilm obtained from the American
         Antiquarian Society.
Reference: Brigham, p. 705
Superseded: Ladies' Weekly Museum; or, Polite Repository (1788-
         1817)

Remarks: The Ladies' Weekly Museum had been started in 1788 by John Harrison whose family continued the publication after his death about 1806. Finally, in 1812 the magazine was transferred to James Oram. Prior to 1817, Oram's magazine had different titles and a different purpose, but in 1817 he gave it its last title and made it a woman's magazine. In late 1817, Oram transferred the title to Alexander Ming who altered the publication again and changed the title to the one used here: The Weekly Visitor, and Ladies' Museum. Despite no break in dating, the numbering started over and no mention was made that the titles were connected. They are, therefore, considered as separate publications.

        The magazine was not unusual except that it seemed aimed at women, and even this had been done before. Fiction, biography, literary essays, poetry, news, drama, fashions, anecdotes, marriages and deaths make up the items to be found in each issue. The sermons were moralizing as were the fiction and essays. Much of the contents was garnered from outside sources, and no real attempt to produce original material for women was made except for brief descriptions of fashions.

        Alexander Ming's illness caused the first series to cease in 1819. The second, started in 1822, may have been printed by Alexander Ming, Junior; but it was unable to recapture the subscriptions

enjoyed in the previous years.   By this time, however, the idea of
a woman's magazine had been firmly planted; eventual success for
the idea was yet to come.

218.   WESTERN CHRISTIAN MONITOR

Title: The Western Christian Monitor
Place: Chillicothe, Ohio   Dates: January-December 1816
Editor: William Beauchamp
Printer: J. Bailhache
Type: Religious - Methodist
Frequency: Monthly   Price: $2.00
Size: 7 1/2 x 4 3/4   Length: 48 pp.
Availability: APS reel 252

Remarks: Sermons, meditations, and letters are the three main
elements of this polemic, tract-like magazine which may have been
used as a Sunday school paper.
      One wonderful chance for moralizing exists in a series of
"Letters from the Dead to the Living," but nothing much of life
after death is learned in these humorless essays. Simple, "easy-
to-understand" language is used to explain the basic doctrines of
the Methodist faith, and each issue ends with selected poetry.
      The essays cover many other topics which have some morally
related value such as the evil of too much sleep. Some biographical
value may exist in the lists of church members carried in each
issue.
      Much of the magazine is rather close to the standard pattern,
and little original or valuable work is to be found. At the end of
one year, the magazine ceased publication with no explanation and
no expressed regrets.

219. WESTERN GLEANER

Title: The Western Gleaner, or Repository for Arts, Sciences and
        Literature
Place: Pittsburgh   Dates: December 1813-September 1814
Editor: Not given
Publisher: Cramer, Spear and Eichbaum, Franklin Mead (three co-
        publishers ?)
Printer: Robert Ferguson
Type: Miscellany - General
Frequency: Monthly   Price: Not given
Size: 8 1/4 x 4 3/4   Length: 72 pp.
Motto: Utile Dulci.
Availability: APS reel 253

Remarks: At this time, Pittsburgh was indeed on the Western
frontier. Publishing was slowly making its way from the major
centers, but local support was difficult to find.
    Agriculture, science, letters from abroad, book reviews,
and miscellaneous essays were all aimed at providing recreational
reading. An interesting feature is the appearance of translations
from French, German, Italian and Spanish. Very few magazines
attempted to be so cosmopolitan.
    The publisher hoped to provide a true miscellany with care-
fully selected articles on as many topics as possible which would
provide valuable information for as many groups as possible. Most
material was borrowed, and no local news was printed. Only the
Pioneer preceded this magazine in Pittsburgh, and the next attempt
was not to come until after 1820.

220. WESTERN MONITOR

Title: The Western Monitor and Religious Journal, A Newspaper,
        Containing a Variety of Useful and Important Theological In-
        formation, Together with Biography, Obituary, Poetry and
        Anecdotes
Place: Knoxville, Tenn.   Dates: July 31, 1818-May 12, 1820
Editor: F. S. Heiskell
Printer and Publisher: F. S. Heiskell and H. Brown
Type: Literary newspaper
Frequency: Bi-weekly   Price: $1.50
Size: 9 1/4 x 5 1/4   Length: 16 pp.
Motto: Peace o're the world, her olive wand extends,
        And white rob'd innocence from heaven descends.
Availability: Not in APS. Microfilm obtained from The Library of
        Congress.

Remarks: Although the title page uses "newspaper" this was a magazine. The major purpose Heiskell had was to make selections from
as many theological publications as he could with the idea of quality
and the hope of attracting subscribers from many sects.
    The typical issue contained accounts of four or five societies,
generally religious in nature; extracts from one or more books;
news of religious activity, usually in the Southern States; and several
general religious articles. The general tone was frequently optimistic since missionary activity was reported as increasing and secular
education as improving.
    The magazine was issued on Friday in the hope that it would
be used as Sabbath reading, and many of the articles were suitable
as Sunday school material. Only occasionally was secular news included, and then it seemed to be used only as a filler.

221. WESTERN NEW YORK BAPTIST MAGAZINE

Title: The Vehicle; or, Madison and Cayuga Christian Magazine
        (May 1814-November 1816); The Western New York Baptist
        Magazine (February 1817-November 1825)
Place: Morrisville, N.Y.   Dates: May 1814-November 1825
Editors: Hamilton Baptist Missionary Society (Elders John Lawton,
        John Peck, Daniel Hascall)
Printer: John B. Johnson
Type: Religious - Baptist
Frequency: Irregular   Price: Not stated
Size: 7 x 4   Length: 48 pp.
Availability: APS reel 252
History: Merged into: New York Baptist Register
        Later: Examiner

Remarks: The publication of this magazine was approximately
quarterly through 1819, although the quarters were not well defined.
The first two issues were anonymous since control was not obtained by the Hamilton Society until 1814.
        Much of the magazine's contents were typical: news, es-
pecially of missions and missionaries; brief, moralistic articles
and anecdotes; news of religious revivals; articles with a polemic
viewpoint; and other material on matters like conversion. Baptist
societies are named and reported, and there is some material concerned with doctrinal belief.
        Perhaps the magazine was intended not only to convert but
also to be used as a Sunday school tract. Some of the articles are
arranged like teaching lessons with questions and answers. Central
New York State had a heavy concentration of Baptist congregations,
and this may have led to the long history of this magazine.

222. WESTERN REVIEW

Title: The Western Review and Miscellaneous Magazine, A Monthly
        Publication Devoted to Literature and Science
Place: Lexington, Ky.   Dates: August 1819-July 1821
Editor and Publisher: William Gibbs Hunt
Type: Miscellany - General
Frequency: Monthly   Price: Not given
Size: 10 x 6   Length: 64 pp.
Availability: APS reel 253
Indexed: Poole
        Cargill
Reference: Mott, I, pp. 311-2

Remarks: The area around Lexington, Kentucky produced a number
of magazines in the first years of the nineteenth century, and most
tend to imitate English models. The Western Review tried to look

like the North American Review. It contained three major but un-
equal sections: reviews, which occupied over half of each issue, a
miscellany, and poetry.
    At least two reviews appeared in each issue before 1820, and
each was long and involved, often quoting long passages. The miscellaneous articles tended to be biography, natural science, history,
and education. Indian antiquities were covered in a long series by
John D. Clifford; and the series included several accounts of battles
with various Indian tribes, especially in the period when Kentucky
was being settled.
    This was not the first literary magazine west of the Allegheny
Mountains; this honor belongs to The Garden about which little is
known. Although not the first, it was certainly one of the best in
this area during the decade from 1810 to 1820.

223. WHIM

Title: The Whim
Place: Philadelphia   Dates: May 14-July 16, 1814
Editor: James Fennell
Printer: John Bioren
Type: Theatrical
Frequency: Weekly   Price: 20¢
Size: 8 1/2 x 5   Length: 24 pp.
Availability: APS reel 362

Remarks: A manuscript note in the Historical Society of Pennsylvania's copy calls this a theatrical paper and one which was "ephemeral." A good word. Perhaps it was intended for the amusement
of theatre people rather than to carry theatrical information--a thing
it did not do.
    The Whim was distributed at the Falstaff, a watering place
in Philadelphia used constantly by actors. Fennell, himself a noted
stage personality, may have had some connection with the Falstaff,
and he had previously tried another unsuccessful weekly paper, Theatrical Garden, before coming to America from England.[1]
    Included are a smattering of amusing articles and poetry. A
theatrical speech or two was quoted, and an analysis was made of
Anthony's funeral oration and of Jaques in "As You Like It." Other
articles dealt with such non-theatrical items as education, reading,
speaking, national pride, and manners.
    In July, Fennell admitted that he didn't have enough "powder
to fire his cannon." His cannon's sound became weaker and weaker
with each issue, and finally failed to fire at all.

Notes: 1. DAB, VI, p. 321.

PART III

APPENDIX

APPENDIX A

EXCLUSIONS

Excluded from major consideration in this study are ninety-two publications which are divided into the eight groups briefly discussed below. Each exclusion has a brief bibliographical description, such notes as will further identify the title, and some brief reason for individual exclusion. Most of the reasons are fairly specific, but some decisions have been subjective. The eight groups were formed on the basis of some common feature, but in some cases placement in one group or another has been arbitrary.

This appendix is meant to be representative, and no claim for comprehensiveness is made. Other magazines may have been announced; other newspapers may have had magazine features; and additional publications may have been cited as magazines or may have had "magazine" as a word in the title.

Of the publications in this appendix, the foreign-language and children's titles were certainly magazines. No question exists with these except that the lists may be incomplete. Problems are presented by the other titles. When is a magazine not a magazine? How many periodical publications existed at one time but have now been lost or destroyed? This appendix attempts to make the history of magazine publishing from 1810 to 1820 more complete by briefly describing known titles in addition to those covered in the main body of the study, and at the same time to mention titles about which some doubt or confusion exists.

Foreign Language Magazines

Seven titles--six French and one German--are covered. The French-language magazines are frequently cited, and information on

four of them is summarized by Smauel Marino in his study of the
French-refugee press.[1] Bibliothéque Portative (entry A2) is listed
by Isaiah Thomas in his History of Printing in America.[2] This
title may well never have existed, or may have been mis-cited by
Thomas, since no copy was located nor was a listing found elsewhere.
The German-language press in America traditionally begins on
May 6, 1732 when Benjamin Franklin issued the first German-American newspaper, Philadelphische Zeitung. Details of this and about
five thousand other German-American newspapers and periodicals
issued through 1935 are given by Karl Arndt's bibliography.[3] Since
these titles are well covered in this publication, the decision was
made not to repeat the listings here. The one sample German-
language magazine in this appendix is Evangelisches Magazin (entry
A3).

No magazines in languages other than German or French
were located for the period 1810-1820.

Children's Magazines

At least thirteen periodicals conceived for children existed
at one time or another in the second decade of the nineteenth
century. Only one, The Guardian and Monitor (entry A8), lived as
long as ten years--actually a rather extensive time for this period.

Since work has been done on children's periodicals, the
decision was made to exclude these titles. Much of the material
in them was ephemeral, and most were polemic in nature. One
title, Juvenile Mirror (entry A11), could be considered a special
problem since it has been cited, apparently incorrectly, by Henry
Barnard[4] and others as Juvenile Monitor. No copies of such a
title were located.

Such non-magazine publications as The Young Misses Magazine (entry A68) could have been entered with this group, as could
have been the many magazines which had some features for children.
The non-magazines are, however, treated as such; and magazines
with children's features are generally covered in the main body of
this study.

No Copy Located

This group covers fifteen titles that are mentioned by some authority, are included in a check-list, or which have appeared in bibliographies. In most cases no indication of a file was found. One exception is the Southern Intelligencer (entry A32). A broken set of this is located in the library of the Southern Baptist Theological Seminary, Louisville, Kentucky; but this set includes no numbers prior to January 5, 1822. Since no copies for the period covered by this study were located, it was decided to exclude this title. Details of the run are given with the entry in this appendix.

Prospectus Only

Twelve announced titles are included in this group. Most of these citations were found in contemporary magazines, but some have been referred to in other ways. In no case was a file discovered, and in no case was any indication found that a file had ever existed.

Non-Magazines

This group of twenty-one titles includes items cited as magazines or which have the word "magazine" in their titles. Investigation of each revealed that none really is a magazine in the sense used in this study. In four of these titles, "magazine" means a storehouse of information, and not a periodical publication.

Newspapers Called Magazines

The seven publications in this group have been considered magazines by someone at some time. Usually each had the appearance of a magazine at some point in its life, and all were examined at least in part as possible inclusions. In each case it was decided that the main purpose of the publication, especially in the period 1810-1820, was to disseminate news. Six of these titles are listed by Clarence Brigham[5] who gives sufficient bibliographic information and often an annotation.

Price-Currents, Public Sale Reports
and Shipping Lists

Periodical publications whose contents included commercial,
business, and shipping news have been called price-currents, public
sale reports, and shipping lists. The basic study of these business
papers is David P. Forsyth's The Business Press in America, 1750-
1865 published by Chilton Books in 1964. At least ten of these
existed at one time or another from 1810 to 1820. Nine of these
have been excluded from regular coverage because they fall outside
the definition of a magazine as used in this study. The tenth,
General Shipping and Commercial List, is regularly annotated in the
main body of this study. This is by far the most important of this
group of publications and may be taken as a typical example. This
title was first discovered at the New York Public Library where a
microfilm of the entire set is available.

The three classes of publications are very close in their
scope, and the titles are almost self-explanatory. Aside from the
wholesale and retail prices of a wide variety of goods, the papers
included insurance rates, lottery announcements, exchange rates,
arrivals and departures of ships, and the like.

All four major publishing centers in the period had at least
one of these publications. While they began to appear before 1810,
the decade 1810-1820 saw their real growth, and they laid the foundations for the business press of today.

Miscellaneous

The three American editions of English magazines were excluded on the ground that they were really English and not American
in origin.

Four titles were found to be ghosts. A brief explanation is
given with each entry for this decision. Proving that a certain title
never appeared is often difficult. It is hoped that the proof offered
here will be considered sufficient.

The one final exclusion, Friend of Peace (entry A92) is
merely a variant edition of a title in the main body of this study

and is included here since it is given a separate place in the Union
List of Serials.

Other arrangements of these "excluded" titles are possible.
The title Monitor (entry A14) is placed as a children's magazine,
but it could easily be included with the group for which no copy
was located. The Juvenile Monitor (see entry A11) is discussed
under its probable real name as a children's magazine and not as
a ghost. These are but two of the possible re-arrangements, but
the titles were placed in these eight groups since they seemed to
fall naturally into these categories and not because the categories
are mutually exclusive.

The thirty-four starred (*) items are also included in the
chronology and the register of printers, publishers, editors and engravers. This has been done since some evidence of the existence
of each of these magazine titles can be produced.

Some numbered references are made in the annotations which
will be found in the footnote section, not at the bottom of the pages.
To avoid confusion and to simplify the appendix many citations are
made at the end of an annotation to an author's last name with page
numbers only. In each case, the full information is given in the
list of works found at the end of this study.

An appendix of exclusions might be questioned as being un-
necessary. The answer is simple. One purpose of this study is to
gather information on all known American magazines which existed
in the decade 1810-1820. To keep the number of items treated at
length within reasonable bounds, titles covered in other magazine
studies were placed in this appendix. Another purpose is to clarify
bibliographic mysteries and to list many items which may have been
cited as magazines or which are supposed to have existed. As
many of these items as I have found have been listed here. In the
course of searching for the titles to include in the basic list covered
by the main body of this study, many problems were discovered. I
hope that this appendix serves to solve most of them.

CLASSIFIED LIST OF EXCLUSIONS

Foreign Language Magazines

A1 *L'Abeille Américaine (1815-1818)
A2 *Bibliothèque Portative (1810?)
A3 *Evangelisches Magazin (1811-1817)
A4 *L'Hémisphère (1809-1811)
A5 *Journal de Musique (1809-1810?)
A6 *Journal des Dames (1810)
A7 *Le Médiateur (1814)

Children's Magazines

A8   *The Guardian and Monitor (1819-1828)
A9   *Juvenile Gazette (1819-1820)
A10 *The Juvenile Magazine (1811-1813)
A11 *The Juvenile Mirror (1810?-1813)
A12 *The Juvenile Port-Folio (1812-1816)
A13 *Juvenile Repository (1811)
A14 *Monitor (1815?)
A15 *The Monthly Preceptor (1815)
A16 *The Parlour Companion (1817-1819)
A17 *The Sunday Visitant (1818-1819)
A18 *The Weekly Monitor (1817)
A19 *Youth's Cabinet (1815)
A20 *Youth's Repository of Christian Knowledge (1813)

No Copy Located

A21 Annual Law Register of the United States (1819?-1822)
A22 *Carr's Musical Miscellany (1813?)
A23 *The Evening Spy (1813?)
A24 *Focus and Weekly Messenger (1813?)
A25 *The Gospel Herald (1813-1814)
A26 *Literary Reporter (1810?)
A27 *The Lounger (between June 1812? and April 1817?)
A28 *Luncheon (1815?-1816?)
A29 *Lynchburg Evangelical Magazine (1810?)
A30 *Museum (1810?)
A31 *Porcupine (1813?)
A32 *Southern Intelligencer (1819-1822?)
A33 *Swallow (1817?)
A34 *The Union Magazine (1818?)
A35 *Wanderer, A Literary Magazine (1816?)

Prospectus Only

A36   Academical Herald and Journal of Education (1812?)
A37   Broken Harp (1815?)
A38   The Christian Traveller (1819?)
A39   The Chronicle (1814?)
A40   Churchman's Recorder and Family Expositor (August 1814?)
A41   The Harvard Lyceum; new series (1814?)
A42   Hemisphere Journal (1810?)
A43   The Massachusetts Garden (1810?)
A44   New England Magazine and Review (1814?)
A45   United States Quarterly Review (1817?)
A46   The Weekly Musical Visitor (1819?)
A47   Western Magazine and Monthly Miscellany (1817?)

Non-Magazines

A48   Annals of Congress (1789-1824)
A49   The Clerk's Magazine (1812)
A50   The Congressional Reporter (1811-1813)
A51   The Farmers, Mechanics, & Servants' Magazine (1812)
A52   The Ladies' and Gentlemen's Diary (1819-1821)
A53   Louisiana Merchant's and Planter's Almanac (1817-1842)
A54   Militia Reporter (1810)
A55   The Mirror of Literature (1815?-1825?)
A56   The Musical Magazine (1792-1810?)
A57   The New American Clerk's Magazine (1811)
A58   Pamphleteer (1819-1820?)
A59   Philadelphia Literary Weekly Advertiser (1819)
A60   The Round Table (1819-1820?)
A61   Salmagundi (1819-1820)
A62   Sketch Book (1819-1820)
A63   The Stand (1819-1820)
A64   Thomas's Massachusetts, Connecticut, Rhode Island, New
         Hampshire, and Vermont Almanack (1782-1819?)
A65   The Truth (1819)
A66   Watchman (1819)
A67   The Weekly Monitor (1810)
A68   The Young Misses' Magazine (1818)

Newspapers Called Magazines

A69   American (1819-1820)
A70   Christian Observer (1813-1823)
A71   Connecticut Courrier (1813-1826?)
A72   The Corrector and American Weekly Review (1814-1815)
A73   Farmer's Watch Tower (1812-1813)
A74   New Hampshire Journal (1793-1810)
A75   True American (1798-1818)

Price-Currents, Public Sale Reports, and Shipping Lists

A76   Baltimore Price Current (1803-1830)

A77 Boston Weekly Report (1819-1828)
A78 Daily Items (1815-1816?)
A79 Grotjan's Philadelphia Public Sale Report (1812-1827)
A80 Hope's Philadelphia Price Current (1804-1813)
A81 New York Price-Current (1796-1817?)
A82 New York Public Sale Report (1814-1816?)
A83 Scott's Philadelphia Price Current (1813)
A84 United States' Shipping and Prices Current (1810-1812?)

Miscellaneous

American Editions of English Magazines
A85 Christian Observer (1802-1866)
A86 The Journal of Science and the Arts (1816-1818)
A87 The Quarterly Review (1809-   )

Ghosts
A88 Chapman's Journal (1813-1837)
A89 Evangelical Magazine (1810- ?)
A90 Presbyterian Advocate (1814?)
A91 Weekly Visitor; or, Ladies' Miscellany (New York, 1817)

Variant Edition
A92 Friend of Peace (Cincinnati, 1817-1818)

EXCLUSIONS

FOREIGN LANGUAGE MAGAZINES

A1   *L'Abeille Américaine, Journal Historique, Politique et
      Littéraire. (Philadelphia. April 15, 1815-July 9, 1818).
      Edited by Jean-Simon Chaudron. Published by Andrew J.
      Blocquerst, 130 South Fifth Street, Philadelphia. Issued
      weekly.
      Excluded as a French language magazine.
      See: Marino, pp. 97-116.
      Port Folio, 4th series, V (May 1815), 477-8.

A2   *Bibliothèque Portative. (Boston. 1810?)
      Issued by Buckingham, True, and Titcomb. Monthly.
      No files were located, and no reference other than that
      in Thomas was found. This is possibly a miscitation for
      some other publication, and may not have been a magazine
      at all.
      Excluded as a possible French language magazine.
      See: Thomas, II, p. 292.

A3   *Evangelisches Magazin; Unter der Aufsicht der Deutsch
      Evangelisch-Lutherischen Synode. (Philadelphia.
      October 1811-1817).
      Edited by the Rev. Justus Heinrich Christian Helmuth.
      Printed by Conrad Zentler. Quarterly, 1811-1814; annual,
      1815-1817.
      Excluded as a German language magazine.
      See: Arndt, p. 556.
      APS reel 104.

A4   *L'Hémisphère, Journal Français: Contenant des Variétés
      Littéraires et Politique, Dédié aux Americains, Amateurs
      de la Langue Français. (Philadelphia. October 7, 1809-
      September 28, 1811).
      Edited and published by Jean Jacques Negrin. Printed by
      William C. Keen, 181 South Fifth Street, Philadelphia.
      Excluded as a French language magazine.
      See: Marino, pp. 142-160.
      APS reels 19, 113.

A5   *Journal de Musique. (Baltimore. 1809-1810?).
      This title may have been published by Madam Le Pelletier,
      and was intended to have at least twenty-four numbers since
      its price was advertised at twelve dollars for this number of
      issues.

Despite the title, this publication was a numbered series of sheet music issued at irregular intervals and probably not a magazine. Known issues are entirely music with words and headings in French. Excluded as a possible French language magazine.
See: Marino, p. 162.
Shaw, #20472.

A6 *Journal des Dames; ou, Les Souvenirs d'un Viellard. (New York. January-December 1810).
Edited by Guillaume Hyde de Neuville. Benjamin Chaigneau's name appears on the title pages from January to March, and is replaced from April to December by Francis Durand. Durand had two addresses, 131 William Street and 6 Carlille (!) Street.
Printed by Joseph Desnoues and assisted by the children of the Economical School, 56 Chapel Street. Monthly.
Excluded as a French language magazine.
See: Marino, pp. 163-172.
APS reel 115.

A7 *Le Médiateur, Journal Politique et Littéraire. (New York. April 2-July 16, 1814. Philadelphia. July 23-August 8, 1814).
Edited by C. A. F. Levavasseur. Printed by Joseph Desnoues, 7 Murray Street, New York; and by Andrew J. Blocquerst, 130 South Fifth Street, Philadelphia. Weekly.
Excluded as a French language magazine.
See: Marino, pp. 184-191.
APS reel 132.

CHILDREN'S MAGAZINES

A8 *The Guardian and Monitor; a Monthly Publication Devoted to the Moral Improvement of the Rising Generation. (New Haven. January 1819-December 1828).
Edited by E. B. Coleman. Published by Nathan Whiting at the Office of the Religious Intelligencer. Monthly.
Published as The Guardian; or, Youth's Religious Instructor for the period 1819-1821.
Excluded as a children's magazine.
See: APS reels 111, 112.

A9 *Juvenile Gazette. (Providence, R.I. November 1819-January 1820).
May have been edited by Origen Bachelor and/or William H. Smith. Printed by J. Jones and Company at the office of the Providence Patriot. J. Jones and Company consisted of Josiah Jones, Bennett H. Wheeler, and Barzillai Cranston.
Excluded as a children's magazine.
See: APS reel 121.

A10   *The Juvenile Magazine, Consisting of Religious, Moral, and
       Entertaining Pieces in Prose and Verse; Original and
       Selected, Designed Principally for the Religious Improve-
       ment, Moral Instruction, and Literary Aid of Youth; and
       Particularly Calculated for the Schools.   (Philadelphia.
       May 1811-August 1813).
       Edited by Arthur Donaldson, 88 Front Street.   Printer not
shown.   Four issues dated May 1 and June 1, 1811; July 1
and August 1, 1813.   A small quarto which doubles in length
from thirty-six to seventy-two pages in 1813.
       Excluded as a children's magazine.
       See: APS reel 121.

A11   *The Juvenile Mirror, and Teacher's Manual; Comprising a
       Course of Rudimentary Instruction Intended as an Auxiliary
       in the Hands of Parents and Preceptors, and to Open the
       Tender Minds of Youth to an Acquaintance with Life,
       Morals, and Science.   (New York.   1810?-1812?).
       Edited by Albert Picket and John W. Picket.   Printed by
Smith and Forman, 195 and 213 Greenwich Street.
       Juvenile Mirror; or, Educational Magazine is the title of
the only available issue (Vol. I, no. 4, March 1812); but a
title page for volume one is attached and carries the title used
in the entry above.
       A letter reproduced on the inside cover of this issue is
from Timothy Alden of Newark, New Jersey.   It expresses
appreciation for numbers one and two of the Juvenile Mirror.
The letter is dated January 21, 1811.   If this is a mis-print
for "1812" the magazine is possibly a bi-monthly which began
in September 1811; or it may have been a quarterly which began in June 1811.   If this January 21, 1811 date is correct,
the magazine must have started in 1810.   Of course, the
letter could be a publicity gimmick, in which case some confusion still exists.
       Several citations are found to the Juvenile Monitor, or
Educational Magazine.   Barnard[6], Betty Lyon,[7] Mott,[8] and
Shaw[9] all use this title, and each seems to have repeated an
error originally made by Barnard.   No such periodical was
located.   This title may be a ghost--an incorrect citation for
The Juvenile Mirror.   Lyon erroneously states that Sereno
Watson[10] uses "Monitor," whereas he actually uses the title
Juvenile Mirror.   Since Watson's article is the earliest mention of this title, and since this title corresponds with the
title of the film copy of the magazine, it is assumed that
Watson is correct, and the others are not.
       Thus: Juvenile Monitor, or Educational Magazine probably
never existed.   Juvenile Mirror; or, Educational Magazine is
the issue title of the only discovered copy.   But the full title;
and, in the last analysis, the probable intended title is The
Juvenile Mirror, and Teacher's Manual.   Not three magazines;
only one.
       Excluded as a children's magazine.
       See: APS reel 121.

A12   *The Juvenile Port-Folio, and Literary Miscellany; Devoted to
          the Instruction and Amusement of Youth.   (Philadelphia.
          October 17, 1812-December 7, 1816).
          Edited and published by Thomas G. Condie, Jr., 22
      Carter's Alley.   Printed by John Bioren, 88 Chestnut Street.
      A weekly quarto.
          Condie was about fourteen when this magazine was first
      issued, but the publication was one of the best of its kind.
          Superseded by The Parlour Companion (A16).
          See: APS reel 121.

A13   *Juvenile Repository. (Boston. July 1811- ?).
          Editor, printer, and publisher are not given in the single
      issue available on microfilm.   The issue is thirty-six pages
      long, and a quarto.
          Excluded as a children's magazine.
          See: APS reel 121.

A14   *Monitor. (Utica, New York. no month, 1815- ?).
          The only references known to this title are made in the
      Youth's Cabinet, and statements about Monitor are generally
      critical in nature, claiming that the Monitor was started as
      competition for the Youth's Cabinet.   If so, Monitor may have
      been published in Utica, and probably in New York State--if
      it really existed.
          Another possibility is that Monitor is a shortened form of
      a real title, and that the proper connection has not yet been
      made.
          Excluded as a possible children's magazine.
          See: APS reel 333 (Youth's Cabinet).

A15   *The Monthly Preceptor; or, Universal Repository of Knowl-
          edge, Instruction, and Amusement.   (Colchester, Conn.
          March 1815- ?).
          Editor's name is not given, but he may have been the
      owner of the printing firm, T. M. Skinner, and Co.
          A small quarto which may have been monthly, but probably
      was intended as a quarterly.   First issue has seventy-two
      pages.
          Illustrated with two plates, one colored.
          Excluded as a children's magazine.
          See: Collections of The American Antiquarian Society.

A16   *The Parlour Companion. (Philadelphia. January 4, 1817-
          August 21, 1819).
          Edited by Thomas G. Condie, Jr., 22 Carter's Alley.
      Printed by John Bioren, 88 Chestnut Street.
          The second magazine issued by Condie who was about
      nineteen at this time.
          Superseded The Juvenile Port-Folio (A12).
          Excluded as a children's magazine.
          See: APS reel 219.

A17 *The Sunday Visitant; or, Weekly Repository of Christian
        Knowledge. (Charleston, S.C. January 3, 1818-Decem-
        ber 25, 1819).
        Edited by Andrew Fowler. Volume one for 1818 was
     printed in Georgetown, S.C. "At the Office of the Winyaw
     Intelligencer" by Eleazer Waterman. Volume two for 1819
     was printed by T. B. Stephens, first at 266 E. Bay Street
     through March 13, 1819; and later at 8 Tradd Street.
     Stephens operated in Charleston, S.C.
        This weekly cost between $2.50 and $3.00, was four pages
     long, and, according to Cardwell, was "the first juvenile re-
     ligious periodical published in Charleston."
        The major emphasis was on the teaching and ritual of the
     Protestant Episcopal Church.
        Excluded as a children's magazine.
        See: Cardwell, pp. 340-1.
             Shaw, #45826.
             APS reel 240.

A18 *The Weekly Monitor, Entertaining and Instructive, Designed
        to be Interesting to All, but Particularly Intended As a
        Guide to Youth in the Way of Morality and Religion.
        (Boston. June 4-September 20, 1817).
        Edited and published by Robert Farnham and Thomas
     Bager, Jr., 4 Suffolk Building, Congress Street, Boston.
     A weekly, a large quarto, and polemic in nature.
        Excluded as a children's magazine.
        See: APS reel 248.

A19 *Youth's Cabinet. (Utica, N.Y. March 31-April 21, 1815?).
        Editor, printer, and publisher are not given in the issues
     on film. A weekly quarto which spent some time in each of
     the four issues quarreling with another possible magazine, the
     Monitor (A14).
        Excluded as a children's magazine.
        See: APS reel 333.

A20 *Youth's Repository of Christian Knowledge. (New Haven
        March-September 1813).
        Edited by Henry Whitlock. Published by Oliver Steele.
     A monthly of varying length which was polemic in content.
        Excluded as a children's magazine.
        See: APS reel 333.

NO COPY LOCATED

A21 Annual Law Register of the United States. (Burlington, N.J.
        v. 3-4, 1821-1822//).
        Edited by William Griffith. The Union List and the Li-
     brary of Congress card both say that volumes one and two
     were never published. Had they been, dating may have started
     in 1819.
        Excluded as having no copy for 1810-1820.

A22 *Carr's Musical Miscellany in Occasional Numbers. (Baltimore. 1813?).
The following entry was found in the Shaw bibliography:[11]

> Carr's musical miscellany in occasional numbers.
> Title page, prospectus and no. 1 "Tell me Soldier."
> Baltimore, J. Carr, 1813. (American Clipper, May
> 1936, No. 195).

A copy of the May 1936 American Clipper was located in
the Sterling Memorial Library at Yale University, but this
issue contains no mention of Carr's Musical Miscellany.[12]
Excluded as having no copy for 1810-1820.
See: Shaw, #28081.

A23 *The Evening Spy. (Charleston, S.C. 1813? possibly 1816?).
Edited by William Henry Timrod.
According to Hoole, this magazine contained much of the
poetry written by Timrod. Hoole cites three references to
this magazine, but no evidence of a file was found.
Excluded as having no copy for 1810-1820.
See: Hoole, pp. 21-2.

A24 *Focus and Weekly Messenger. (Philadelphia. 1813?).
The only reference to this title was found in the essay by
Seilhamer. He gives only the information cited above, and no
other listings checked revealed a title which this could have been.
Excluded as having no copy for 1810-1820.
See: Seilhamer, p. 274.

A25 *The Gospel Herald. (Frankfort, Ky. August 1813-1814).
Edited by Silas M. Noel who was an active Baptist
preacher in Franklin and Scott Counties, and President of
the Board of Trustees of Georgetown College. The printer
and publisher are not known. Quarterly.
Superseded: Kentucky Missionary and Theological Magazine (q.v.).
Exlcuded as having no copy for 1810-1820.
See: Jillson, p. 63.

A26 *Literary Reporter. (Philadelphia. 1810?).
Supposed to have been printed by David Hogan. No other
information is given by Thomas, and no references were
found in any other source.
Excluded as having no copy for 1810-1820.
See: Thomas, II, p. 293.

A27 *The Lounger. (Hudson, N.Y. Sometime between June 1812
and April 1817?).
A magazine of this title may have appeared in Hudson,
N.Y., and may have been edited by Caleb N. Bement. If it
superseded The Casket (q.v.) and appeared chronologically
before Spirit of the Forum (q.v.), it was published sometime
between June 1812 and April 1817.

In the latter magazine may be found this statement:
'(Bement was) the publisher of a small periodical yclep'd
"The Casket." To this succeeded "the Lounger," a child al-
most without a father, which lived upon this "mundane
sphere" about the space of six months, and died without a
struggle or a groan --"unwept--unsung."'
No other mention of this title was discovered, and no
file was located.
Excluded as having no copy for 1810-1820.
See: Spirit of the Forum, no. 1 (April 16, 1817), 1.

A28 *Luncheon. (Philadelphia. July 1815-January 1816).
Edited by Lewis P. Franks. Printer and publisher not
given. At least four references are made to this title, but
no other information was found, and no trace of a file was
located.
Excluded as having no copy for 1810-1820.
See: Mott, I, pp. 171, 795.
     Shaw, 1815, p. 165, entry #35147.
     Seilhamer, p. 247.
     Smyth, p. 184.

A29 *Lynchburg Evangelical Magazine. (Lynchburg, Va. 1810- ?).
Edited by William W. Gray. Printer and publisher are
not known. No other information was found in other sources,
and no trace of a file was located.
Excluded as having no copy for 1810-1820.
See: Gilmer, Checklist, p. 38.

A30 *Museum. (Nashville, Tenn. 1810- ?).
Editor given as T. G. Bradford. Printer and Publisher
not known. Monthly. Only one citation, and no evidence of
a file.
Excluded as having no copy for 1810-1820.
See: Kerr, passim.

A31 *Porcupine. (Philadelphia. 1813- ?).
The only reference found to this title was found in the
essay by Seilhamer. He gives only the information cited
above, and no other listings checked revealed a title which
this could have been.
Excluded as having no copy for 1810-1820.
See: Seilhamer, p. 274.

A32 *Southern Intelligencer. (Charleston, S.C. 1819-1822).
The editor, printer, and publisher for this period of this
title's life are not known. Only one incomplete file has been
located in the James P. Boyce Centennial Library at The
Southern Baptist Theological Seminary.[13] This file is:
     IV, nos. 1-38, 40-52 (January 5-September 21, October
     5-December 28, 1822).
     V, nos. 1-5, 7-13 (January 4-February 1, February 15-
     March 29, 1823).

No other issues were located, and no other information
was found in other sources.
Excluded as having no copy for 1810-1820.

A33   *Swallow. (Pittsburgh, Penn. 1817- ?).
Editor of this may have been Henry Eddy.   The printer
and publisher are not known.   The best reference to this
title is in Brigham.
Excluded as having no copy for 1810-1820.
See: Brigham, p. 967.

A34   *The Union Magazine. (Arlington, Vt. 1818- ?).
The publisher of this title may have been E. Gilman
Storer.   No other names connected with this title are known.
McCorison refers to the Hill article cited below which says:

On the discontinuance of the (American) Register,
Mr. (E. Gilman) Storer published for a year, at
Arlington, a religious periodical called "The Union
Magazine," but not meeting with sufficient encourage-
ment its publication was stopped, and he with his press
moved to Sunday Hill, N.Y.

Excluded as having no copy for 1810-1820.
See: McCorison, #2050.
Hiland Hall, "Country Items," The Vermont Histori-
cal Gazetter, I (1867), 252.

A35   *Wanderer, A Literary Magazine. (Baltimore. 1816?).
Printed and published weekly at $4.00 per year by Richard
J. Matchette, at the corner of South Gay and Water Streets.
The reference given below does not include other informa-
tion, and no locations were found.   No file was located.
Excluded as having no copy for 1810-1820.
See: Silver, Baltimore, p. 54.

PROSPECTUS ONLY

A36   Academical Herald and Journal of Education. (York, Penn.
1812- ?).
The announced editor was S. Bacon.   A prospectus was
listed by Barnard, but neither the prospectus nor any other
information was found.
Excluded as having only a prospectus.
See: Barnard, p. 944.

A37   Broken Harp. (Philadelphia. May 1815- ?).
Two references in the Port Folio are cited below.   In one
of them, the Broken Harp is announced as a magazine; in the
other, as a book.   The title is included here since it was, at
least once, proposed.
In the first announcement, the Port Folio stated:

"Miscellanies dedicated exclusively to the muse of song, however in this, are not uncommon in other countries," and went
on to say: "That the present is a period auspicious for the
establishment of such a work, we cannot for a moment permit
ourselves to doubt." At the end of the announcement a paragraph was added which said, in part: "Since the foregoing was
in type, Mr. Knight has relinquished his intention of con-
ducting a periodical work ..."
Other than the editor's name, the first announcement contained no important bibliographic information.
The second announcement is an extensive review of:

Knight, H. C. The Broken Harp. Philadelphia: John
Conrad & Co., 1815.

This was a book of poems, 180 pages in length, and
costing 75 ¢. Naturally, no mention is made that this was
ever intended as a magazine.
Thus a magazine of this title was at one time considered
and even announced, but the title was never issued as a magazine.
Excluded as having only a prospectus.
See: Port Folio, 4th series, V, (May 1815), 473-4.
_____, 5th series, I (January 1816), 59-73.

A38   The Christian Traveller. (Baltimore, Md. 1819?).
Announced in the prospectus cited below. The editors
were to be "An Association of Gentlemen," and the printer,
John D. Toy. Weekly, at $3.00 per year.
This title was to supersede The Christian Messenger, and
its purpose was to benefit sabbath and free schools. A rather
high 800 subscribers were expected before publication would
start. No other references were found, and no trace of a file
was found.
Excluded as having only a prospectus.
See: "Prospectus," The Christian Messenger, IV (May 1,
1819), 402-4.

A39   The Chronicle; or, An Annual View of History, Politics, and
Literature, Foreign and Domestic. (Philadelphia. 1814?)
This title was announced as an attempt to continue Charles
Brockden Brown's American Register. It was to be edited by
John E. Hall, and published by Moses Thomas, both of Phila-
delphia. The magazine was to be quarterly, despite the title;
contain about 250 pages an issue; and cost $6.00 a year. No
title of this name seems to have appeared, although the se-
quence of coverage after the American Register did include the
American Review of History and Politics and the Historical
Register of the United States. These titles were independent
of one another and are covered elsewhere in this study.
Excluded as having only a prospectus.
See: Port Folio, 3d series, VIII (October 1812), 406-8.
The Bureau, I (September 12, 1812), 199-200.

A40   Churchman's Recorder, and Family Expositor.   (Baltimore,
          Md. August? 1819?- ?).
          Announced as a monthly of thirty-two pages at cost $2.00
       a year, and to be published by Joseph Robinson, corner of
       Market and Belvidere Streets.
          The magazine was to be aimed at members of the Protes-
       tant Episcopal Church, especially in the Diocese of Maryland;
       and was to include material which would "advance the interests
       of religion." It was to be like the Christian Observer, having
       original material, biography, sermons and "discourses," re-
       views, essays, news, poetry, some political matter, and a
       miscellany.
          An attempt to locate a file through The General Theologi-
       cal Seminary Library in New York City revealed that the
       chances are that the magazine was never published. [14]
          Excluded as having only a prospectus.
          See: "Prospectus," The Christian Journal, and Literary
                 Register, III (July 1819), 223-4.

A41   The Harvard Lyceum, new series.   (Cambridge, Mass., and
          Boston. 1814?).
          The editors of this magazine were to have been the class
       of 1814 at Harvard University. The publishers were announced
       as Hilliard's Bookstore in Cambridge, and Cummings & Hilliard
       in Boston. The title was to be semi-weekly and would cost
       $3.00 a year. A proposal was made to issue the first number
       on the first Saturday in July 1814. The prospectus dated
       April 25, 1814 was printed in the Columbian Centinal for
       April 30 and May 28, 1814. The contents were announced as:
       general subjects of literature and science, classical studies,
       Greek and Latin poetry, criticisms of ancient and contemporary
       works, some poetry in English, and a "Miscellany."
          Excluded as having only a prospectus.
          See: Albert Matthews, "A Projected Harvard Magazine,"
                 Harvard Graduate Magazine, XXXVII (June 1929),
                 445-7.

A42   Hemisphere Journal.   (Philadelphia. December 12, 1810- ?).
          The editor was announced as Jean Jacques Negrin, and
       the publisher as William C. Keen, 131 South Fifth Street,
       Philadelphia. The cost of the weekly folio was to be $3.00
       a year, and it probably was designed as an English-language
       version of L'Hémisphère (A4). In the latter magazine, the
       statement "we published the first number of a Gazette in Folio
       entitled The Hemisphere Journal" appeared on Wednesday,
       December 12, 1810. No other references to this title have
       been found, and no file was located.
          Excluded as having only a prospectus.
          See: Marino, p. 161.
                 L'Hémisphère, II (December 22, 1810), 39-40.

A43   The Massachusetts Garden, and the Patriot's Common-Place
          Book. (Boston. 1810?).

The editor was announced as Thomas Wallcut. No publisher is given in the prospectus. A version of this prospectus was published in Omnium Gatherum, and a broadside copy
is in the American Antiquarian Society. This was to be
either quarterly or monthly. No price given. It was to
cover: natural sciences, agriculture, inventions, chemistry,
and medicine. It was aimed not for the scholarly, but "to
serve the learned societies and the publick." To use some
of the expressions in the prospectus, the reader would find
typographical descriptions, the progress of manufactures,
machines of new invention, historical accounts of institutions,
analysis of various mineral waters, medical reports, and
descriptions of trees, shrubs, plants, and flowers. No trace
of a file was found.
    Excluded as having only a prospectus.
    See: Omnium Gatherum, I (March 1810), 220-5.

A44 New England Magazine and Review. (Boston? 1814?).
    Andrews Norton was announced as the editor in the
Polyanthos, and Mott says that Willard Phillips and others
in the Anthology Society were to be connected with this new
magazine. Joseph T. Buckingham, Winter Street, Boston,
was to be the publisher. In fact he dropped the Polyanthos
to make room for this new title. Mott says that Harvard's
President Kirkland and Professor Channing originated the
idea, but that it was opposed by William Tudor, later the
first editor of the North American Review. The New England
Magazine was thought of as a successor to the Monthly Anthology. There is little doubt that the New England Magazine
never went past the planning stage.
    Excluded as having only a prospectus.
    See: Mott, II, p. 220.
    Polyanthos, 3d series, III (August 1814), 272.

A45 United States Quarterly Review and Literary Journal. (Place?
    1817?).
    James Eastburn was announced as the publisher of this
title. No sign of this magazine was found in other lists or
card catalogs. This may have been a proposed magazine the
title of which was later changed, but no connection can be
made with any other periodicals. The idea was probably
dropped before plans went beyond the talking stage.
    Excluded as having only a prospectus.
    See: Port Folio, 5th series, III (June 1817), 433.

A46 The Weekly Musical Visitor. (Philadelphia? 1819?).
    An announcement appeared in the Literary and Musical
Magazine on March 8 and 15, 1819 which detailed the proposal
by H. C. Lewis to publish a subscription periodical devoted
to music. It was to appear weekly in two pages, and would
cost $1.50 per quarter. The address of the publisher was
given as 272 Market Street. No trace of a file has been
located.

Excluded as having only a prospectus.
See: Wunderlich, p. 403.
Literary and Musical Magazine, III (March 15, 1819),
        170.

A47   Western Magazine and Monthly Miscellany.   (Canandaigua,
        N.Y.   1817?).
        J. D. Benis (!) was announced as the editor of this maga-
      zine which was to contain literary history of the day; book
      reviews; articles from foreign sources; reports of progress in
      science, agriculture, and manufacturing; geographic articles;
      travel; religion; politics and politcal development from a neu-
      tral view; literary essays; and poetry.   No trace of a file was
      located.
        Excluded as having only a prospectus.
        See: Port Folio, 5th series, II (December 1816), 531.

NON-MAGAZINES

A48   Annals of Congress.   (Washington, D.C.   1789-1824).
        Although cited by Gilmer as a magazine, this title is not
      a periodical.   The main entry in the Library of Congress card
      catalog is:

            U.S. Congress.
              The debates and proceedings in the Congress of the
            United States ... First to Eighteenth Congress, first
            session ... March 3, 1789-May 27, 1824.
              Half-title: Annals of the Congress of the United
            States.

        This publication was continued in the Register of Debates
      and has been continued in other series since that time.
        Excluded as a non-magazine.
        See: Gilmer, Checklist, p. 20.

A49   The Clerk's Magazine: Containing the Most Useful and Neces-
            sary Forms of Writing...   (Albany, N.Y.:   Webster's and
            Skinner's, 1812).
        This is the fourth edition of a book which first appeared in
      1800 (?), and the fifth edition of which appeared in 1815.   Des-
      pite the word "magazine" in the title, this is not a magazine,
      but a dated book.
        The historical sense of the word "magazine" as a store-
      house of information probably is meant here.
        Excluded as a non-magazine.
        See: The American Antiquarian Society card catalog.

A50   The Congressional Reporter.   (Concord, N.H.   November 1811-
            March 1813).
        The First publisher listed on the title page of the volumes
      examined is I. & W. R. Hill.   The sub-title reads: "Containing

a list of members of the twelfth Congress, the President's
message, the public documents, and the debates on all interesting questions agitated during the session, commencing on
the first Monday of November, 1811."
   The publication is divided into two volumes, the first, of
forty numbers from November 1811 to June 1812; and the
second, of seventeen numbers from December 1812 to March
1813.
   Despite this format of dated numbers, the American
Antiquarian Society considers this publication to be a dated
book and not a magazine. This decision was probably made
since the title was issued as a whole and not in a periodical
series.
        Excluded as a non-magazine.
        See: Shaw, #25142.
        The American Antiquarian Society card catalog.

A51   The Farmers Mechanics & Servants' Magazine.   (New York.
        1812).
   The author of this item is Marie Le Prince de Beaumont.
It was published by Whiting and Watson, and printed by Paul
and Thomas. It appeared in a two Volume format. The sub-
title reads: "For the benefit of the widows and orphans'
societies of the City of New York." Despite the word "magazine" in the title, this is not a magazine, but a dated book.
   The historical sense of the word "magazine" as a storehouse of information probably is meant here.
   The title will be found in the Library of Congress Catalog
of Printed Cards under: Le Prince de Beaumont.
        Excluded as a non-magazine.
        See: Shaw, #25847.
        The American Antiquarian Society card catalog.

A52   The Ladies' and Gentlemen's Diary; or, United States Almanac
        and Repository of Science and Amusement.   (New York.
        1819-1821).
   The editor of this was M. Nash, and the issues were
printed by J. Seymour "for the Company of Booksellers and
Stationers." Three issues appeared, and one was announced
to cover 1823 and would have been dated 1822. No trace of
this last was found.
   This publication is really an almanac, and each issue
follows the pattern of being dated one year while intended for
use the following year. The title page contains an additional
description which says: "Intended for an Annual Magazine,
Including a variety of Matter, Chiefly Original, on Subjects
of General Utility, in the Arts, Sciences, Agriculture, Manufacture, etc., etc."
   The historical sense of the word "magazine" as a storehouse of information probably is meant here.
   "Lady's and Gentleman's Diary" had been used as a sub-
title of the New England Almanac which appeared from 1763
to 1881. In the decade of this study, the editor of this

publication was the pseudonymous Isaac Bickerstaff. The
above title may have been started in competition.
    The references cited below, except Drake, list this title
as a magazine, or a periodical. The Drake numbers are
given to show that this item is to be considered bibliographically
an almanac, and not as a magazine. The title is also excluded on the basis of being an annual publication.
    Excluded as a non-magazine.
    See: Bolton, p. 324, #2602.
          Karpinski, p. 589.
          Shaw, #48449.
          Smith, p. 281.
          Drake, v. I, p. 645, #6555; p. 648, #6584; p. 652,
              #6625.

A53 Louisiana Merchant's and Planter's Almanac. (New Orleans,
         La. 1817-1842).
     This publication has four volumes and twenty-six num-
bered issues. A man named Spofford was the editor, but
neither the printer nor the publisher were given in the sources
examined.
     This title is covered here since it has been cited in at
least two places as a magazine. Drake lists the publication
properly as an almanac.
     Excluded as a non-magazine.
     See: Bolton, p. 341.
           Gilmer, Checklist, p. 38.
           Drake, v. I, p. 187, #1898.

A54 Militia Reporter. (Boston. 1810).
     The editor is not given, but the printer was Timothy
Kennard, 78 State Street, Boston. This small quarto contained courts martial proceedings which occurred from 1805
to 1810, and which were "taken from authentic documents for
the information of the officers of the militia." Four trials
were included. The transcripts provide insight into the
military trial of the period and can be used as special documents. The publication is not, however, a magazine. The
decision to include this in the American Periodicals Series
may have been made on the title, but there is only one
"issue," and no mention is made that there were to be additional numbers.
     Excluded as a non-magazine.
     See: APS reel 137.

A55 The Mirror of Literature, Amusement, and Instruction.
         (Boston. 1815?-1825?).
     The editor of this is not given, but the publisher was
Perkins, Wait & Co., Boston. Volume six notes that it was
issued by the "Press of the North American Review."
     The title continues after the word "Instruction" to say:
"Containing Original Essays, Historical Narratives, Biographical Memoirs, Manners & Criticism, Sketches, Tales of

Humor, Anecdotes, Gems of Wit, Sentiment, Poetry, &c."
Each volume has a half-title page which reads: "The New
Monthly Magazine." The historical sense of the word "maga-
zine" as a storehouse of information probably is meant here.
The Boston Public Library has volumes five, six, and
ten--the last dated 1825. On this basis the Union List of
Serials speculates that the title may have begun in 1815.

In volume five, for example, number 25 consists of
twelve, four-sheet gatherings; and all are dated 1823. The
last group of gatherings in the volume is called Number 30.
No indication is made that these are monthly issues. In
volume six, the numbers are 31 to 36; but all are again
dated 1823. In the two volumes, there are twelve issues,
but none is dated with a month. Also, many of these numbered parts end at some inconvenient place such as the middle of a sentence or of an article. The indication here is
that these were fascicles of a multi-volume publication not
intended as a periodical.

If two volumes were issued in a year, publication would
have started in 1821; and thus, even if this may be considered
a magazine, it began to publish after the period covered by
this study.

Sabin notes a "Prospectus and Specimins of the new periodical publication to be entitled the Mirror and Repository of
Amusement ... published by Lazarus Beach. New York,
1815. 8vo, pp. 16." It may be that the title listed by Sabin
and the title in this entry were really the same, but this
would be speculation since no copy of this prospectus nor of
the title were found. Also, the listed publishers are different.

Since no dated copies for the period under consideration
were found, and since this publication seems to be a book
published in numbered parts, it has been omitted from complete coverage.
        Excluded as a non-magazine.
        See: Sabin, #66077.
             APS reel 138.

A56   The Musical Magazine: Being the Third Part of the Art of
        Singing; Containing a Variety of Anthems and Favorite
        Pieces. (Cheshire, Conn. 1792-1810?).
      Andrew Law is given as the editor, and William Law as
the publisher. Numbers one through six were dated October
8, 1792 through November 17, 1801; and later editions were
issued through at least 1810. Wunderlich's coverage of this
publication includes the statement: "The Musical Magazine
was little more than a series of tune books. Both the
frequency of publication and the manner in which the individual
numbers were issued tend to nullify, or at least to minimize,
many of the features characteristic of a periodical."
        Excluded as a non-magazine.
        See: Wunderlich, pp. 331-46.

A57 The New American Clerk's Magazine, and a Complete Prac-
        tical Conveyancer... (Staunton, Va. 1811).
        The title page says: "By a Gentleman of the Bar." This
     was Jacob D. Dietrick.
        This title is the third edition of a book which first ap-
     peared in 1806, and certainly as late as 1814. Some aspects
     of an almanac were included, but this is certainly not a maga-
     zine despite the use of the word "magazine" in the title. The
     historical sense of the word "magazine" as a storehouse of
     information probably is meant here.
        A possible ancestor of this title may have been:

              Freeman, Samuel. A Valuable Assistant to Every
                 Man; or, the American Clerk's Magazine. Boston:
                 I. Thomas and E. T. Andrews, 1794.

        This was the first edition of a work whose fourth edition
     appeared in 1800. Evans' bibliography gives further details.
        Excluded as a non-magazine.
        See: The American Antiquarian Society card catalog.

A58 Pamphleteer. (Richmond, Va. 1819-1820).
        From the Franklin Press, W. W. Gray, printer. An
     annual publication, and a series of pamphlets which have no
     connection.
        The American Antiquarian Society has numbers one and
     two.
        Excluded as a non-magazine.
        See: The American Antiquarian Society card catalog.

A59 Philadelphia Literary Weekly Advertiser. (Philadelphia.
        1819).
        This phrase was not applied to a separate magazine pub-
     lication in the decade 1810-1820.
        This is the title, of a page of book sellers'
     advertisements which appeared on the last page of three is-
     sues of Literary and Musical Magazine (q.v.) when it was
     known as Ladies' Literary Museum. These issues are from
     June 29 to July 13, 1818.
        Excluded as a non-magazine.
        See: Dated issues of Literary and Musical Magazine.

A60 The Round Table. (Hartford, Conn. 1819-1820).
        The publisher of this series was the Knights of the Round
     Table, and the editor is given as George Bickerstaffe--per-
     haps the pseudonym of William L. Stone.
        The three numbers of this title are dated from August
     23, 1810 to March 1, 1820. They were little more than
     pamphlets containing informal essays written by the members
     of a literary society. The numbers are irregular in sequence.
        Excluded as a non-magazine.
        See: The Connecticut Historical Society, Hartford, Conn.

A61 Salmagundi, 2d Series. (Philadelphia and New York. May
      30, 1819-September 2, 1820).
      The editor is given as Launcelot Langstaff, Esq. This
      was the pen name of James Kirk Pauling who was associated
      with Washington Irving and the earlier Salmagundi. The
      printer was J. Maxwell, and the publishers were M. Thomas,
      Johnson's Head, 108 Chestnut, between Third and Fourth
      Streets, Philadelphia; and J. Haley and C. Thomas, 55 Maiden
      Lane, New York.
      This title was issued as a book of dated parts, and not
      as a magazine. To include this title, or the Sketch Book
      (A62), would open the way to the inclusion of all books which
      appeared in dated or numbered parts, and thus to include
      many items which were not magazines in purpose or content.
      Excluded as a non-magazine.

A62 The Sketch Book of Geoffrey Crayon. (New York. 1819-1820).
      Geoffrey Crayon was the pen name of Washington Irving,
      used in issuing this particular publication. The Sketch Book
      was issued in parts sent from England to his American pub-
      lisher. Parts one through five, which were paged continu-
      ously, were dated 1819; and parts six and seven were dated
      1820.
      The first American publisher was C. S. Van Winkle in
      New York.
      This title was issued as a book of dated parts, and not
      as a magazine. To include this title, or Salmagundi (A61),
      would open the way to the inclusion of all books which ap-
      peared in dated or numbered parts, and thus to include many
      items which were not magazines in purpose or content.
      Excluded as a non-magazine.
      See: Williams, Life, pp. 173, 426.

A63 The Stand. (Hartford, Conn. 1819-1820).
      The editors of this series were "A Society of Young Men"
      called the Invincibles. The printer and publisher of this title
      are not known.
      Issue one has three colored engravings which show fashions
      of the times.
      The Hartford group, Knights of the Round Table, editors
      of The Round Table (A60), were satirically addressed as the
      Knights of the Square Table. Other intellectual bickering may
      be found throughout The Stand.
      The seven numbers examined were irregularly dated from
      December 18, 1819 through August 14, 1820. These items
      were really pamphlets, and were not the issues of a magazine.
      Excluded as a non-magazine.
      See: The Connecticut Historical Society, Hartford, Conn.

A64 Thomas's Massachusetts, Connecticut, Rhode Island, New
      Hampshire, and Vermont Almanac, with an Ephemeris.
      (Worcester, Mass. 1782-1819).

The twenty-nine issues of this title were continued as:
Isaiah Thomas, Junior's Town and Country Almanack; or,
Complete Farmer's Calendar. This title lasted from 1811 to
1819, and was issued in nine numbers.
This publication was certainly an almanac, and not a
magazine. It is mentioned here since it has been cited at
least once as a magazine.
Excluded as a non-magazine.
See: Bolton, #4498.
      Davis, #3311, and passim.
      Shaw, #20441, and passim.

A65   The Truth. (New Haven. September-October 1819).
            Edited by J. Ironside (pseud?), but the printer and pub-
       lisher are not given.
            Although two sixteen-page, numbered, and dated monthly
       issues in a regular sequence appeared, the purpose of The
       Truth was to be a series of personal essays rather like The
       Sketch Book (A62).
            Social conventions which were thought to be shams, politi-
       cal actions which were felt to be hypocritical, and publications
       which were seen as pompus, like The Round Table (A60) were
       satirically attacked.
            Excluded as a non-magazine.
            See: APS reel 242.

A66   Watchman. (New Haven. 1819).
            The author, printer, and publisher of this title are not
       known.
            The twenty-four pages of this pamphlet are devoted to
       answering attacks made in other New Haven pamphlets against
       the Protestant Episcopal Church. A long review of The
       Christian Journal, and Literary Register (q.v.) praises the
       magazine.
            Although another number of the title was promised, none
       seems to have appeared.
            Excluded as a non-magazine.
            See: APS reel 246.

A67   The Weekly Monitor; A Series of Essays on Moral and Religious
            Subjects. (Philadelphia. 1810).
            The author of this title is given as "A Layman." The
       publisher was Brannan & Marford; and the printer was James
       Maxwell.
            Forty-one numbered essays make up this book which takes
       its title from a series of articles published prior to 1810 in
       the Charleston Courrier, a newspaper. Although numbered
       separately, they were here published as an anthology and can-
       not be considered a periodical.
            Excluded as a non-magazine.
            See: The Boston Public Library card catalog.

A68 The Young Misses' Magazine. (New York. 1818).
     The author of this item is Marie Le Prince de Beaumont.
     It was published by Samuel Campbell and appeared in a two
     volume format.
     Despite the word "magazine" in the title, this is not a
     magazine, but a dated book. The historical sense of the word
     "magazine" as a storehouse of information probably is meant
     here.
     The title will be found in the Library of Congress Catalog
     of Printed Cards under: Le Prince de Beaumont.
     Excluded as a non-magazine.
     See: Shaw, #44562.
     The American Antiquarian Society card catalog.

NEWSPAPERS CALLED MAGAZINES

A69 American. (New York. March 3, 1819-March 1, 1820).
     This title was conducted by "An Association of Young
     Men" which included the possible editor, Richard R. Morris.
     It was printed by J. Seymour, 49 John Street. This item
     was certainly a newspaper, although some of the contents
     were literary in nature. The paper became a daily on
     March 1, 1820. The contents included: speeches, news of
     the courts, extracts from American and English papers which
     gave summaries of the news, an occasional poem, public
     lectures, bank and exchange lists, and government documents
     at all levels. The emphasis and major purpose was that of
     a newspaper and not of a magazine.
     Excluded as a newspaper.
     See: Brigham, p. 607.

A70 Christian Observer. (Philadelphia. September 4, 1813-
     August 16, 1823.
     The first editor of this title was John Welwood Scott.
     At one time it was issued by Ezra Styles Ely as the Phila-
     delphian. The title was also published in Richmond, Va.;
     and Louisville, Ky. The earliest issues were called the
     Religious Remembrancer, and the publication supersedes the
     Southern Religious Telegraph, a newspaper. The emphasis
     was on Presbyterian matters, and the editorial slant fre-
     quently took this viewpoint. In the period under consideration
     this was a four-page weekly newspaper, and not a magazine
     in content or scope.
     Excluded as a newspaper.
     See: Mott, I, p. 137.
     Historical Magazine, I (October 1857), 316.

A71 Connecticut Courrier. (Bridgeport, Conn. November 10,
     1813?-March 15, 1816?).
     The publisher of this title was Nathaniel L. Skinner.
     The item was considered for inclusion because there was

some literary content, but examination of the issues at the
Connecticut State Library shows that the major emphasis and
scope are those of a newspaper.
   Excluded as a newspaper.
   See: Brigham, p. 11.

A72 The Corrector, and American Weekly Review. (Philadelphia.
      1814-1815).
      The editor of this title was the pseudonymous Cadwallader
Crabtree. The printer and publisher are not known. The
American Antiquarian Society has the issue for September 16,
1814; and The Library Company of Philadelphia has: "Address
of the Carriers of the Corrector and American Weekly Review
to their Patrons on the Commencement of the 1815." Examination of these two items reveals that the purpose and content of
this title were those of a newspaper.
   Excluded as a newspaper.
   See: Brigham, p. 898.

A73 Farmer's Watch-Tower. (Urbana, Ohio. July 1, 1812-
      August 11, 1813).
      From the commencement of this title until February 24,
1813, the publishers were Moses B. Corwin and William
Blackburn. From February 24, 1813 until the close, they
were Corwin and Allen M. Poff. The American Antiquarian
Society has three issues of this title, and examination of these
reveal that this title was a newspaper with some of the features
of a magazine.
   Excluded as a newspaper.
   See: Brigham, p. 816.

A74 New Hampshire Journal; or, Farmer's Weekly Museum.
      (Walpole, N.H. April 11, 1793-October 15, 1810).
      Since the editor at one time was Joseph Dennie, this title
was considered for inclusion. However, the purpose, scope,
and content of the issues were those of a newspaper and not
those of a magazine--despite the appearance of some periodical
features such as the Lay Preacher Essays.
   Excluded as a newspaper.
   See: Brigham, p. 486.

A75 True American. (Philadelphia. July 2, 1798-March 7, 1818).
      This was a true daily newspaper and it is mentioned here
since it had literary content throughout its entire life. The
Dessert to the True American was a literary supplement to
the True American which was issued from July 14, 1798 to
August 19, 1799. This part of the paper superseded The
Philadelphia Minerva, and lent a magazine air to the publica-
tion. The purpose, scope, and contents--especially in the
period covered in this study--were not those of a magazine.
   Excluded as a newspaper.
   See: Brigham, pp. 955-6.

PRICE-CURRENTS, PUBLIC SALE REPORTS
AND SHIPPING LISTS

A76   Baltimore Price Current.   (Baltimore.   February 14, 1803-
      December 25, 1830).
      Joseph Escavaille established this paper and published it
      at least as late as 1820.
      During the period from 1810 to 1820, it was printed by
      James A. Hunter and/or Joseph Robinson.
      Prices, insurance premiums, stock prices, rates of ex-
      change, and other commercial and marine news make up the
      contents.
         Excluded as a price-current.
         See: Brigham, p. 247.
              Forsyth, pp. 41-3, 342.

A77   Boston Weekly Report.   (Boston.   May 1, 1819-May 1828).
      Established by Peter Pane Francis DeGrand and probably
      printed by Elisha Bellamy.
      This paper served as both a public sale report and as a
      price-current for the Boston market.
         Excluded as a price-current.
         See: Brigham, p. 349-50.
              Forsyth, p. 56, 343.

A78   Daily Items.   (New York.   November 1, 1815-March 1, 1816//?).
      Alexander Ming was the publisher of this title the Saturday
      issue of which was supplied by Ming's New York Price-Current.
      According to Forsyth, this was "the first daily paper
      devoted wholly to business and commerce in the United
      States."   The contents were devoted to commercial, business,
      and shipping news.
         Excluded as a price-current.
         See: Brigham, p. 626.
              Forsyth, pp. 38-40, 342.

A79   Grotjan's Philadelphia Public Sale Report.   (Philadelphia.
      May 11, 1812-1827).
      Peter A. Grotjan established and published this paper.
      In 1819 Stephan Blatchford became Grotjan's partner.
      The printers associated with this title were: Samuel
      Merritt, Adam Waldie, and Jasper Harding.
      Aside from the price-current features, this paper issued
      information on auction and stock sales.   It was imitated in
      New York by the New York Sale Report.
         Excluded as a price-current.
         See: Brigham, p. 917.
              Frosyth, pp. 56-7, 342.

A80   Hope's Philadelphia Price Current.   (Philadelphia.   October
      25, 1804-December 28, 1813).
      Thomas Hope established the paper, and early issues were
      printed by John W. Scott; the later ones by S. Merritt.

Many other financial problems were topped by the theft of Hope's subscription list by Scott who started Scott's Philadelphia Price-Current. The resulting competition killed both papers.
Excluded as a price-current.
See: Brigham, pp. 918-9.
    Forsyth, pp. 29-32, 342.

A81   New York Price-Current. (New York. January 1796-December 31, 1817//?).
James Oram, Alexander Ming, and Samuel Dickinson are the three most important names connected with this title. Several name changes are outlined by Brigham, and the title entry here is that used by Brigham.
From 1815 to 1816 New York Price-Current was the Saturday issue of Daily Items.
Forsyth identifies the first issue as December 19, 1795.
Excluded as a price-current.
See: Brigham, pp. 680-1.
    Forsyth, pp. 33-40, 342.

A82   New York Public Sale Report. (New York. January 1814-December 30, 1816//?).
Published by Nathaniel T. Eldredge. In December 1816, John Wood joined the firm eventually taking complete charge. New York Public Sale Report was superseded by Wood's New York Sale Report and Price Current, a separate publication. No separate entry is made for this item since only two issues, both in 1820, are listed by Brigham.
This publication served the same purpose in New York as did Grotjan's Philadelphia Public Sale Report in Philadelphia.
Excluded as a price-current.
See: Brigham, pp. 683, 706.
    Forsyth, pp. 57, 342.

A83   Scott's Philadelphia Price Current. (Philadelphia. May 31-November 22, 1813//?).
John W. Scott established and issued this paper--apparently for only twenty-six issues.
Scott had stolen Thomas Hope's subscription list and used it to compete with Hope's Philadelphia Price Current. Competition killed both papers.
Excluded as a price-current.
See: Brigham, p. 951.
    Forsyth, pp. 29-32, 342.

A84   United States' Shipping List and Prices Current. (New York. November? 1810-November 20, 1812//?).
Published at the Tontine Coffee House by Jonathan Elliott. Issued bi-weekly, it contained cargo lists, lists of ships arriving and leaving, and a price-current. Also included was information on the arrival and departure of mail bags. The

paper was discontinued with the general decline of shipping
in 1812.
        Excluded as a price-current.
        See: Brigham, p. 697.
             Forsyth, pp. 46-7, 342.

MISCELLANEOUS

American Editions of English Magazines

A85   Christian Observer. (Boston, New York. 1802-1866).
       "Conducted by Members of the Established Church."
       This phrase stood for the Church of England. The magazine
       was issued simultaneously in Boston and New York until 1816.
       The Boston publisher was William Wells and T. B. Wait; the
       New York publisher was Whiting and Watson, 96 Broadway.
       After 1816, it was issued only in Boston and by David Hale--
       at least through 1819. Examination of the film reveals that
       this was an American edition of an English magazine. Only
       the title page differed in that American firm names were
       used in the imprint. The remainder of the pages are the
       same as the edition with the English imprint.
              Excluded as an English magazine.
              See: APS reels 83-86.

A86   The Journal of Science and the Arts. (New York. February
       1816-May 1818).
       Although issued by James Eastburn, Literary Rooms,
       Corner of Pine Street and Broadway; and printed by Abraham
       Paul of New York City; this title was a direct reprint of the
       English magazine The Quarterly Journal of Science and the
       Arts edited under the direction of the Royal Institution of
       Great Britain. There were no changes in contents or arrange-
       ment.
              Excluded as an English magazine.
              See: The file located in The New York Academy of Medi-
                   cine Library.
              APS reel 120.

A87   The Quarterly Review. (New York. 1810-   ).
       Printed in the decade from 1810 to 1820 by David and
       George Bruce, this title was the American printing of a
       wholly English magazine. There were no changes in the
       contents.
              Excluded as an English magazine.
              See: Shaw, #21166.

Ghosts

A88   Chapman's Journal. (Philadelphia. 1813-1837).
       The above title is listed in the Union List of Serials as

having had fourteen volumes published in the period listed in
the entry. The only file listed is reported in the Philadelphia
College of Pharmacy and Science Library. This entry is
incorrect.[15]
    The title really is The Philadelphia Journal of the Medical
and Physical Sciences. This magazine was edited by N.
Chapman, and the above entry may have come from this name.
The first volume was published in 1820 by M. Carey and Son,
Chestnut Street, Philadelphia; and the magazine had fourteen
volumes, two a year, from 1820 until 1827.
    Excluded as a ghost.

A89 Evangelical Magazine. (Hartford, Conn. 1810- ?).
    This title is mentioned in Kerr's thesis, but no magazine
of this title was published in Connecticut or by Peter B.
Gleason.[16] The title probably was meant to be the Connecticut
Evangelical Magazine and Religious Intelligencer. This title
is discussed in its proper place in this study.
    Excluded as a ghost.

A90 Presbyterian Advocate. (Lexington, Ky. 1814?).
    At least two secondary sources mention a magazine of
this title and date. The title is not included in any of the
magazine bibliographies checked for this study.
    In the sources cited below, Presbyterian Advocate super-
seded Evangelical Record and Western Review (q. v.); and
The Almoner (q. v.) was a separate publication. The real
link existed between the second and third of these titles.
    Thomas Skillman, the editor and publisher of the two
known magazines, was supposed to have been the editor of
Presbyterian Advocate. Other than the sources given below,
no other references connecting the two were found.
    A check of the collections at The Filson Club, and at
the Presbyterian Theological Seminary, both in Louisville,
Kentucky, revealed no other trace of this title, and both
librarians feel that the title never existed.[17]
    Excluded as a ghost.
    See: James Miller, p. 85.
        Perrin, p. 62.

A91 Weekly Visitor; or, Ladies' Miscellany. (New York. May
      10-October 25, 1817).
    The entry for this title in the Union List of Serials says
that this title had twenty-five numbers, and the entry gives
the dates shown above. In the holdings listed below the entry,
Yale University is shown as having numbers 1-36, 38-52.
This inconsistency led to an investigation which reveals the
title to be a ghost. No magazine of this title was published
in the year 1817.[18]
    There was a magazine of this name, but it was published
in four volumes from October 9, 1802 to October 25, 1806.
This title is the first in a series covered in this study under:
The Lady's Miscellany; or, The Weekly Visitor, its last, and

consequently, its bibliographic title. The sequence of numbers listed as being at Yale are the numbers of the first
volume of the earliest title in this series. (Yale also has
parts of the second volume which are not shown in this entry,
namely: numbers 53-104, December 7, 1803-September 20,
1804).
The dates in the entry above belong to twenty-five of the
twenty-six issues of Ladies' Weekly Museum; or, Polite Repository of Amusement and Instruction which were issued from
May 3 to October 25, 1817. The latter title is a completely
separate publication and is covered under this title in this
study.
Thus, there was a title as shown above, but it was published at a time other than that indicated; and it is bibliographically known by another name.
The holdings shown in the Union List are an incomplete
record of Yale's file of this earlier title; and the dates belong
to a magazine of a completely different origin and name.
Excluded as a ghost.

Variant Edition

A92   Friend of Peace. (Cincinnati. 1817-1818).
        This title is given a separate place in the Union List of
Serials. The only library shown as having a file is the library now known as The Cincinnati Historical Society. This
entry represents a book which includes four of the numbers
of Noah Worcester's Friend of Peace published in Boston
from 1815 to 1827.19 Photostats of the title page and of the
first page of text in the Cincinnati edition show it to be the
same as the Boston publication.
        Excluded as a variant edition.

NOTES TO APPENDIX A

1. Samuel Joseph Marino, The French Refugee Newspapers and
        Periodicals in the United States, 1789-1825 (Ph.D. dis-
        sertation, University of Michigan, 1962).

2. Isaiah Thomas, History of Printing in America (2d ed. Al-
        bany: Joel Munsell, 1874), II, 292.

3. Karl J. R. Arndt and May Olson, German-American News-
        papers and Periodicals, 1732-1955, Deutsche Pressefor-
        schung, Bd. 3 (Heidelberg: Quelle & Meyer, 1961), 578;
        passim.

4. Henry Barnard, "Educational Periodicals and Reports,"
        American Journal of Education, XXXII (1892), 942.

5. Clarence Saunders Brigham, History and Bibliography of American Newspapers, 1690-1820 (Worcester: American Antiquarian Society, 1947), I-II, passim.

6. Henry Barnard, loc. cit.

7. Betty Longenecker Lyon, A History of Children's Secular Magazines Published in the United States from 1789-1899 (Ph.D. dissertation, Johns Hopkins, 1942), pp. 39-43.

8. Frank Luther Mott, A History of American Magazines, 1741-1850 (Cambridge, Mass.: Harvard University Press, 1939), pp. 148, 794.

9. Ralph Robert Shaw, American Bibliography; A Preliminary Checklist, 1811 (New York: Scarecrow Press, 1962), p. 124.

10. Sereno Watson, "The American Journal of Education," The New Englander, XXIV (July 1865), 514.

11. Ralph Robert Shaw, American Bibliography; A Preliminary Checklist, 1813 (New York: Scarecrow Press, 1962), p. 52.

12. Information obtained in correspondence with Miss Marjorie Wynne and Mr. John A. Braswell, Yale University Library.

13. Information obtained in correspondence with Mr. Leo T. Crismon, Librarian, Southern Baptist Theological Seminary.

14. Information obtained in correspondence with Mr. Hugh H. Tidwell, Assistant to the Librarian, The Union Theological Seminary Library.

15. Information obtained in correspondence with Mrs. Theodora Jackson, Acting Librarian, Philadelphia College of Pharmacy and Science.

16. Information obtained in a conversation with Mr. Thompson R. Harlow, Librarian, Connecticut Historical Society.

17. Information obtained in correspondence with Mrs. Dorothy Thomas Cullen, Curator and Librarian, The Filson Club, Louisville, Kentucky.

18. Information obtained in correspondence with Mr. John A. Braswell, Yale University Library.

19. Information obtained in correspondence with Mrs. Andrew N. Jergens, Jr., Acting Librarian, The Cincinnati Historical Society.

APPENDIX B

CHRONOLOGICAL LIST

The number of magazines published in any one year, the length of time each lasted, as well as the variety and scope of each year's production results in part from a chronological arrangement of the titles covered by this study. All titles which appeared before January 1, 1810 are placed in two groups; all others are arranged by the year of first publication.

The sub-arrangement is by month, with titles having no specific date within the month listed first and titles for which no specific month within the year is known coming last of all. In all cases the brief entry contains only minimum information. Full titles, editors, subsequent places of publication, and the like are detailed in the main annotations.

Also on this list are the thirty-four starred (*) titles which are excluded from full coverage but which are found in Appendix A.

The total number of magazines listed here, 257, is the total number presumed to have existed sometime in the decade from 1810 to 1820.

LIST OF MAGAZINES

Before 1800

May 17, 1788   The Ladies' Weekly Museum; or, Polite Repository of Amusement and Instruction. (New York). October 25, 1817.

July 26, 1797   Medical Repository. (New York). 1824.

1800 - December 31, 1809

July 1800	Connecticut Evangelical Magazine and Religious Intelligencer. (Hartford). December 1815.
January 3, 1801	Port Folio. (Philadelphia). December 1827.
January 5, 1802	The Balance and State Journal. (Albany). December 24, 1811.
April 1802	The Berean. (Boston). no month 1810.
October 9, 1802	The Lady's Miscellany; or, The Weekly Visitor. (New York). October 17, 1812.
September 1803	The Massachusetts Baptist Missionary Magazine. (Boston). December 1816.
November 1803	The Monthly Anthology. (Boston). June 1811.
January 1804	The Churchman's Magazine. (New York). March 1827.
September 17, 1804	The Philadelphia Medical Museum. (Philadelphia). April 1811.
June 1805	Missionary Herald at Home and Abroad. (Boston). March 1951.
December 1805	Polyanthos. (Boston). September 1814.
February 1806	The Christian Monitor. (Boston). no month 1811.
December 6, 1806	The Christian's Magazine. (New York). December 1811.
September 16, 1807	Tickler. (Philadelphia). November 17, 1813.
no month 1807	The American Register. (Philadelphia). no month 1810.
January 1808	The American Law Journal. (Philadelphia). December 1817.
September 1, 1808	Herald of Gospel Liberty. (Portsmouth, N.H.). October 1817.
October 22, 1808	The Boston Mirror. (Boston). July 21, 1810.
no month 1808	The Analyst; or, Mathematical Museum. (Philadelphia). no month 1814.

January 1809	The Advisor. (Middlebury, Vt.). December 1815.
January 1809	Select Reviews. (Philadelphia). December 1812.
February 11, 1809	The Visitor. (Richmond, Va.). August 18, 1810.
June 1809	The Massachusetts Watchman. (Palmer, Mass.). May 1810.
August? 1809	The New York Medical and Philosophical Journal and Review. (New York). no month 1811.
August 10, 1809	Trangram. (Philadelphia). February 1, 1810.
September 1809	The New England Literary Herald. (Boston). January 1810.
October? 1809	The Rambler's Magazine. (New York). January? 1810.
October 7, 1809	*L'Hémisphère. (Philadelphia). September 28, 1811.
November 1809	Omnium Gatherum. (Boston). October 1810.
November 18, 1809	Something. (Boston). May 12, 1810.
no month 1809	The Cricket; or, Whispers from a Voice in a Corner. (Hamilton Village, N.Y., etc.). no month 1818.
no month 1809	*Journal de Musique. (Baltimore). 1810?

1810

January	American Mineralogical Journal. (New York). January 1814.
January	Huntingdon Literary Museum. (Huntingdon, Penn.). December 1810.
January	*Journal des Dames. (New York). December 1810.
January	The Mirror of Taste and Dramatic Censor. (Philadelphia). December 1811.

January	Theophilanthropist. (New York). September 1810.
February 15	Journal of Musick. (Philadelphia). 1811?
March?	Garden. (Bardstown, Ky.). March? 1810.
May 5	Philadelphia Repertory. (Philadelphia). May 16, 1812.
May 12	Weekly Visitor. (New York). May 25, 1811.
May 19	Hive. (Lancaster, Penn.). December 11, 1810.
May 26	Scourge. (Baltimore). November 24, 1810.
July	American Medical and Philosophical Register. (New York). April 1814.
July	Archives of Useful Knowledge. (Philadelphia). April 1813.
July 4	Agricultural Museum. (Georgetown, D.C.). May 1812.
July 14	Harvard Lyceum. (Cambridge, Mass.). March 9, 1811.
July 30	Rural Visiter (!). (Burlington, N.J.). July 22, 1811.
September	Religious Instructor. (Carlisle, Penn.). August 1811.
September 24	A Magazine. (Baltimore). September 24, 1810?
October	Journal of Foreign Medical Science and Literature. (Philadelphia). October 1824.
October 14	Observer. (New York). April 21, 1811.
November 3	Emerald. (Baltimore). March 2, 1811.
December 15	The Shamrock. (New York). August 16, 1817.
no month	*Bibliothèque Portative. (Boston). 1810?
no month	*Juvenile Mirror. (New York). March 1812?
no month	*Literary Reporter. (Philadelphia). 1810?

no month   *Lynchburg Evangelical Magazine. (Lynch-
                  burg, Va.). 1810?

no month   *Museum. (Nashville, Tenn.). 1810?

1811

January   American Review of History and Politics.
                  (Philadelphia). October 1812.

January   Baltimore Repertory. (Baltimore). June
                  1811.

January   Religious Magazine. (Portland, Vt.).
                  September 22, 1822.

January   The Vermont Baptist Missionary Magazine.
                  (Rutland, Vt.). April 1812.

January/March   Baltimore Medical and Philosophical Lyceum.
                  (Baltimore). October/December 1811.

January 5   Cabinet. (Boston). March 23, 1811.

March 30   Hive; or, Repository of Literature. (Wash-
                  ington, D.C.). September 7, 1811.

April   Freemason's Magazine. (Philadelphia).
                  March 1812.

April 6   Independent Mechanic (New York). March
                  28, 1812.

May   Literary Miscellany. (New York). August
                  1811.

May 1   *The Juvenile Magazine. (Philadelphia).
                  August 1, 1813?

May 24   Floridad. (Schenectady). December 6, 1811.

June   Gospel Visitant. (Charlestown, Mass.).
                  July 1818.

July   *Juvenile Repository. (Boston). July 1811.

August 10   Scourge. (Boston). December 28, 1811.

September 7   Niles' Weekly Register. (Baltimore).
                  September 19, 1849.

September 21   Cynick. (Philadelphia). December 12, 1811.

October   *Evangelisches Magazin. (Philadelphia). 1817.

October   Religious Enquirer. (Cooperstown, N.Y.).
                  October 1811?

October 19   The Comet. (Boston). January 11, 1811.

November 27   Beacon. (Philadelphia). December 11, 1811.

December 7   Casket. (Hudson, N.Y.). May 30, 1812.

1812

January   Evangelical Record and Western Review.
                  Lexington, Ky.). December 1813.

January   General Repository and Review. (Cambridge,
                  Mass.). October 1813.

January   Halcyon Luminary and Theological Repository.
                  (New York). December 1813.

January   New England Journal of Medicine. (Boston,
                  Mass.). still published.

January   Pelissier's Columbian Melodies. (Philadel-
                  phia). December 1812.

January 16   Satirist. (Boston, Mass.). May 9, 1812.

February 28   The Pioneer. (Pittsburgh). October 8, 1812.

March 28   The Bureau. (Philadelphia). November 14,
                  1812.

April   Literary and Philosophical Repertory.
                  (Middlebury, Vt.). May 1817.

May   The Emporium of Arts and Sciences. (Phila-
                  delphia). October 1814.

May   Monthly Magazine and Literary Journal.
                  (Winchester, Va.). April 1813.

May 1   Kentucky Missionary and Theological Maga-
                  zine. (Frankfort, Ky.). 1814?

June 20   Christian Monitor and Religious Intelligencer.
                  (New York). August 28, 1813.

June 27   The War. (New York). February 24, 1817.

June?   *The Lounger. (Hudson, N.Y.). April 1817?

August 17   Military Monitor and American Register.
                 (New York). April 2, 1814).

October 17   *The Juvenile Port Folio. (Philadelphia).
                 December 7, 1816.

no month   Historical Register of the United States.
                 (Washington, D.C.). 1814/15.

no month   The Literary Visitor. (Baltimore). no month
                 1813.

1813

January   The Analectic Magazine. (Philadelphia).
                 December 29, 1821.

January   The Quarterly Theological Magazine. (Bur-
                 lington, N.J.). April 1814.

January   Spiritual Magazine; or, Gospel Treasury.
                 (Freetown, Mass.). May 1814.

January 27   The Olio. (New York). February 5, 1814.

March   Carolina Law Repository. (Raleigh, N.C.).
                 September 1816.

March   *Youth's Repository of Christian Knowledge.
                 (New Haven). September 1813.

April   The Monthly Recorder. (New York). August
                 1813.

May   The Christian Disciple. (Boston). November/
                 December 1823.

July   The Utica Christian Magazine. (Utica, N.Y.).
                 June 1816.

July 3   Stranger. (Albany). June 25, 1814.

July 15   Literary Visitor. (Wilkesbarre, Penn.).
                 September 29, 1815.

July 25   Literary Register. (Philadelphia). December
                 17, 1814.

August   *The Gospel Herald. (Frankfort, Ky.). no
                                month 1814?

August   North Carolina Magazine. (n.p.). August
                                1813//?

September 25   American Weekly Messenger. (Philadelphia).
                                September 17, 1814.

October 25   Examiner. (New York). May 27, 1816.

November   Massachusetts Agricultural Repository and
                                Journal. (Boston). April 1832.

November 13   National Museum and Weekly Gazette of Dis-
                                coveries. (Baltimore). November 12,
                                1814.

December   The Western Gleaner. (Pittsburgh). Septem-
                                ber 1814.

no month   *Carr's Musical Miscellany. (Baltimore). no
                                month 1813.

no month   *The Evening Spy. (Charleston, S.C.). no
                                month 1813 (possibly 1816?).

no month   *Focus and Weekly Messenger. (Philadelphia).
                                no month 1813.

no month   *Porcupine. (Philadelphia). no month 1813.

1814

January   The New York Medical Magazine. (New York).
                                January 1815.

January/March   Christian Monitor. (Hallowell, Maine).
                                October/December 1818.

January 1   The Boston Spectator. (Boston). February
                                25, 1815.

January 22   Christian Mirror. (Charleston, S.C.). April
                                16, 1814.

February 12   Atheneum. (New Haven). August 6, 1814.

February 28   Geographical and Military Museum. (Albany).
                                June 6, 1814.

April	The Almoner. (Lexington, Ky.). May 1815.
April	Rhode Island Literary Repository. (Providence, R.I.). March 1815.
April 2	*Le Médiateur. (Philadelphia). August 8, 1814.
May	The Western New York Baptist Magazine. (Hamilton, N.Y.). November 1825.
May 1	The New York Magazine. (New York). July 1814.
May 2	Cohen's Gazette and Lottery Register. (Baltimore). September 1, 1830.
May 14	The Whim. (Philadelphia). July 16, 1814.
May 27	Moralist. (New York). November 7, 1814.
July 5	The Weekly Recorder. (Chillicothe, Mo.). October 6, 1821?
July 27	The Beau. (New York). July 27, 1814//?
September	The Columbia Magazine. (Hudson, N.Y.). August 1815.
November 19	Intellectual Regale; or, Ladies' Tea Tray. (Philadelphia). December 30, 1815.
December 27?	The Christian's Weekly Monitor. (Sangerfield, N.Y.). May 1818.

1815

February	Academic Recreations. (New Haven). July 1815.
February 21	General Shipping and Commercial List. (New York). June 30, 1894.
March	*The Monthly Preceptor. (Colchester, Conn.). March 1815//?
March 31	*Youth's Cabinet. (Utica, N.Y.). April 21, 1815.
April 15	*L'Abeille Américaine. (Philadelphia). July 9, 1818.

May	North American Review. (Boston). Winter 1939/40.
June	The American Magazine. (Albany). May 1816.
June 3	Christian Visitant. (Albany). May 25, 1816.
July	Corrector; or, Independent American. (New York). no month 1817?
July	The Friend. (Albany). June 1816.
July	*Luncheon. (Philadelphia). January 1816.
July 8	The Christian Monitor. (Richmond, Va.). August 30, 1817.
November	The Christian Messenger. (Pittsford, N.Y.). March 1816.
November 16	Layman's Magazine. (Martinsburgh, Va.). November 7, 1816.
no month	Friend of Peace. (Boston). no month 1827.
no month	*Monitor. (Utica, N.Y.). no month 1815//?
no month	New England Missionary Magazine. (Concord, N.H.). no month 1816.

1816

January	Evangelical Repository. (Philadelphia). December 1816.
January	The New York City Hall Recorder. (New York). January 1822.
January	The Portico. (Baltimore). April/June 1818.
January	The Western Christian Monitor. (Chillicothe, Mo.). December 1816.
January 3	Congregationalist and Herald of Gospel Liberty. (Boston). March 29, 1934.
January 6	Cobbett's American Political Register. (New York). January 10, 1818.
March 2	The National Register. (Washington, D.C.). February 5, 1820.

March 30   The Christian Herald and Seaman's Maga-
                  zine. (New York). November 20, 1824.

May 18   The Aeronaut. (New York). September 30,
                  1822.

June 1   The Religious Intelligencer. (New Haven).
                  October 7, 1927.

June 3   The Country Courrier. (New York). March
                  24, 1817.

June 15   The Parterre. (Philadelphia). June 28,
                  1817.

July   The Christian Register and Moral Theological
                  Review. (New York). July 1817.

July   The Monthly Visitant. (Alexandria, D.C.).
                  December 1816.

July   Olla Podrida. (Providence, R.I.). August
                  1816.

July 4   Alleghany Magazine. (Meadville, Penn.).
                  November 1817.

October   The Sunday School Repository. (New York).
                  February 1819.

October 12   The Boston Weekly Magazine. (Boston).
                  December 25, 1824.

November 18   Civil and Religious Intelligencer. (Sanger-
                  field, N.Y.). no month 1835.

no month   *Wanderer, A Literary Magazine. (Baltimore).
                  no month 1816?

1817

January   American Baptist Magazine. (Boston).
                  November 1824.

January   Atheneum. (Boston). March 1833.

January   New Jerusalem Church Repository. (Phila-
                  delphia). December 1818.

January 4   *The Parlour Companion. (Philadelphia).
                  August 21, 1819.

January 22   Christian Journal and Literary Register.
                    (New York). December 1830.

March 20   Independent Balance. (Philadelphia). Decem-
                    ber 22, 1832.

April 16   Spirit of the Forum. (Hudson, N.Y.).
                    April 16, 1817 //?

May   American Monthly Magazine and Critical
                    View. (New York). April 1819.

May   Evangelical Guardian and Review. (New
                    York). April 1819.

May 10   Christian Messenger. (Baltimore). May 1,
                    1819.

May 21   Star of Freedom. (Newtown, Penn.). March
                    25, 1818.

June 4   *Weekly Monitor. (Boston). September 20,
                    1817.

June 28   Nantucket Weekly Magazine. (Nantucket,
                    Mass.). January 3, 1818.

July 5   Literary and Musical Magazine. (Phila-
                    delphia). July 1820 //?

August 29   Philanthropist. (Mount Pleasant, Ohio).
                    May 15, 1822.

October 10   New England Galaxy and Masonic Magazine.
                    (Boston). March 29, 1839.

November 1   Weekly Visitor, and Ladies' Museum. (New
                    York). October 18, 1823.

no month   American Register. (Philadelphia). no
                    month 1817.

no month   *Swallow. (Pittsburgh). no month 1817.

1818

January   The American Medical Recorder. (Phila-
                    delphia). July 1829.

January   The Literary and Evangelical Magazine.
                    (Richmond, Va.). December 1828.

January   The Methodist Review. (New York). May/
                 June 1931.

January   Philadelphia Magazine and Weekly Repertory.
                 (Philadelphia). November 7, 1818.

January   Quarterly Theological Review. (Philadelphia).
                 October 1819.

January 3   *The Sunday Visitant. (Charleston, S.C.).
                 December 25, 1819//?

January 7   The Academician. (New York). January 29,
                 1820.

January 10   Idiot; or, Invisible Rambler. (Boston).
                 January 2, 1819.

January 31   Evangelical Recorder. (Auburn, N.Y.).
                 September 8, 1821.

February   The Latter Day Luminary. (Philadelphia).
                 December 1825.

February   The Scientific Journal. (New York). Janu-
                 ary 1820.

February 7   Christian Chronicle. (Bennington, Vt.).
                 December 26, 1818.

May   The Christian Herald. (Portsmouth, N.H.).
                 March? 1835.

May 2   Baltimore Weekly Magazine, and Ladies'
                 Miscellany. (Baltimore). October 24, 1818.

May 15   Farrier's Magazine. (Philadelphia). August
                 5, 1818.

July   The American Journal of Science. (New
                 Haven). still published.

July 15   The Religious Museum. (Northumberland,
                 Penn.). July 21, 1819.

July 18   Robinson's Magazine. (Baltimore). June 26,
                 1819.

July 31   Western Monitor and Religious Journal.
                 (Knoxville, Tenn.). May 12, 1820.

September   New York Judicial Repository. (New York).
                 February/March 1819.

September 12	Journal of the Times. (Baltimore). March 6, 1819.
November	The Castigator. (Lexington, Ky.). January 22, 1820.
November 28	Boston Kaleidoscope and Literary Rambler. (Boston). November 27? 1819.
December 30	The Inquisitor. (Philadelphia). January 19, 1820.
no month	The Medical and Surgical Register. (New York). no month 1820
no month	*The Union Magazine. (Arlington, Vt.). no month 1818?

1819

January	The Collegian. (New York). February 1819.
January	The Globe. (New York). June 1819.
January	*The Guardian and Monitor. (New Haven). December 1828.
January	The Herald of Life and Immortality. (Boston). October 1820.
January	New England Missionary Intelligencer. (Concord, N.H.). October 1819.
January	The Quarterly Christian Spectator. (New Haven). November 1838.
January 2	The Saturday Magazine. (Philadelphia). June 29, 1822.
February	The Rural Magazine. (Hartford). July 1819.
February 13	The Ladies' Magazine. (Savannah, Ga.). August 7, 1819.
March 27	The Southern Evangelical Intelligencer. (Charleston, S.C.). December 29, 1821.
April	The Villager. (Greenwich Village, N.Y.). June 1819.
April 2	The American Farmer. (Baltimore). February 1897.

May	The New York Literary Journal. (New York). April 1821.
May 15	The Ladies' Literary Cabinet. (New York). December 14, 1822.
May 24	Ladies' Visitor. (Marietta, Penn.). April 18, 1820.
May 29	Watchman-Examiner. (Boston). May 11, 1848.
June 5	The Plough Boy. (Albany). June 17, 1823.
June 9	The True Briton. (Boston). December 8, 1819.
June 16	Columbian Telescope and Literary Compiler. (Alexandria, D.C.). May 20, 1820.
July 3	Universalist. (Boston). December 28, 1879.
July 20	Religious Informer. (Andover, N.H.). December 1825.
August	The Theological Repertory. (Washington, D.C.). December 1830.
August	The Village Museum. (York, Penn.). July 1823.
August	Western Review and Miscellaneous Magazine. (Lexington, Ky.). July 1821.
August 7	The Christian Messenger. (Philadelphia). July 12, 1821.
October 23	Red Book. (Baltimore). March 1820.
November	*Juvenile Gazette. (Providence, R.I.). January 1820?
November 20	Journal of Belles Lettres. (Lexington, Ky.). February 26, 1820.
November 22	Literary Cadet. (Cincinnati). April 27, 1820.
December 18	Honey Bee. (Philadelphia). January 22, 1820.
no month	*Southern Intelligencer. (Charleston, S.C.). no month 1822.

REGISTER OF PRINTERS, PUBLISHERS, EDITORS AND ENGRAVERS

This is a list of all printers, publishers, editors, and engravers connected with American magazines from 1810 to 1820. The basic names and addresses are those appearing in the magazines themselves, but outside information has been used to compile this list.

Many of the magazines were edited anonymously, and the printers did not always include their own names. Many gaps thus exist in this list, but it is as complete as reasonable searching will allow. No doubt other names can be located, and no doubt errors have crept in; but it is hoped they are at a minimum.

Five other registers, those by Rollo Silver, Harry Brown, and George McKay, have already been cited and are fully listed in the bibliography. These were valuable in filling in first names and in verifying spelling.

All names are here given as fully as possible, rather than as they appeared in the magazines. Cross references are made under firm names and from pseudonyms when possible.

Under each name the magazines that person was associated with are listed chronologically. Obviously many magazines had many people connected with them and there are many repititions of title. For this reason the titles are as brief as possible, and the full information will be found with the annotations.

THE REGISTER

A. A. <u>see</u> Anderson, Alexander.

Abbey, D. & S. A.   Printer, Publisher; Albany.
    The Friend; April-May 1816.

Abercrombie, James.   Editor; Christ Church, Philadelphia.
    The Quarterly Theological Magazine; 1814.

Adams, Thomas G.   see   Riley, Isaac and Adams, Thomas G.

Adrian, Robert.   Editor; Philadelphia.
    The Analyst; 1808-1814.

Akin, James.   Engraver; Philadelphia.
    Freemason's Magazine; 1811.

Alburtis, John.   Printer; Martinsburgh, Va.
    Layman's Magazine; 1815-1816.

Alden, Timothy.   Editor; Meadville, Penn.
    Alleghany Magazine; 1816-1817.

Alexander and Phillips.   Printers; Carlisle, Penn.
    Emporium of Arts and Sciences; June 1813-October 1814.

Allen, Francis D.   Editor; 182 Water Street, then 78 John Street,
    then 57 Liberty Street, New York.
    Christian Monitor and Religious Intelligencer; 1812-1813.

Allen, Paul.   Editor; Baltimore.
    Journal of the Times; 1818-1819.

Allinson, David.   Editor, Printer, Publisher; Burlington, N.J.
    The Rural Visiter; July 30, 1810-February 11, 1811.

Allinson, John C.   see   Allinson & Co.

Allinson, Samuel.   Publisher; Burlington, N.J.
    The Quarterly Theological Magazine; 1813.

Allinson and Company.   Editors, Printers, Publishers; Burlington,
    N.J.
    The Rural Visiter; February 11-July 22, 1811.

The American Society for the Dissemination of the Doctrines of the
    New Jerusalem Church.   Editors; Philadelphia.
    New Jerusalem Church Repository; 1817-1818.

Anderson, Alexander.   Engraver; New York.
    American Medical and Philosophical Register; 1810, 1812.
    American Mineralogical Journal; 1810.
    Medical Repository; 1810, 1811, 1815, 1818, 1819.
    Theophilanthropist; 1810.
    Emporium of the Arts and Sciences; 1814.

The Analectic; 1815.
The Medical and Surgical Register; 1818.

Anderson, Robert and Meehan, John S.   Printers, Publishers; 59
    Locust Street, Philadelphia.
    The Latter Day Luminary; 1818-   .

Andrews, John.   Editor, Printer, Publisher; Water Street, then
    Main Street, Chillicothe, Ohio.
    The Weekly Recorder; 1814-1821.

Annin, William B.   Engraver; Boston.
    *The Monthly Preceptor; 1815.
    New England Journal of Medicine; 1815-1816.
    Massachusetts Agricultural Repository and Journal; 1817.

Annin, William B. and Smith, George Girdler.   Engravers; Boston.
    Massachusetts Agricultural Repository and Journal; 1817,
        1819.
    New England Journal of Medicine; 1819.

Armstrong, Samuel T.   Printer; Charlestown, Mass., then 50
    Cornhill, Boston.
    The New England Literary Herald; 1809-1810.
    Missionary Herald; 1810-1820.

Asbridge, George.   Editor, Publisher; 35 Nassau Street, New York.
    Independent Mechanic; January 4-March 28, 1812.
    see also: Harmer, Joseph & Co.

An Association of Clergymen in New York.   Editors; New York.
    The Evangelical Guardian and Review; 1817-1819.

An Association of Gentlemen.   Editors; Hudson, N.Y.
    Spirit of the Forum; 1817.

An Association of Gentlemen.   Editors; New Haven, Conn.
    The Quarterly Christian Spectator; 1819-   .

An Association of Gentlemen.   Editors; New York, N.Y.
    The Aeronaut; May 18-July 26, 1816.

An Association of Young Men.   Editors; York, Penn.
    The Village Museum; 1819-1823.

Atkinson, Thomas.   Printer; Meadville, Penn.
    Alleghany Magazine; 1816-1817.

Austin, John B.   Printer, Publisher; N.W. Corner of Third and
    Lombard Streets, then 55 Lombard Street, Philadelphia.
    Literary Register; 1813-1814.

Bachelor, Origen.   Editor? Publisher?   Providence, R.I.
    *Juvenile Gazette; 1819-1820.

Bacon, D____.   Editor; New York.
    The New York Judicial Repository; 1818-1819.

Bager, Thomas, Jr.   see   Farnham, Robert and Bager, Thomas, Jr.

Bailey, Isaac.   Editor; Providence, R.I.
    Rhode Island Literary Repository; 1814-1815.

Bailey, Lydia R.   Printer; 10 North Street, Philadelphia.
    New Jerusalem Church Repository; 1817-1818.

Bailhache, J____.   Printer; The Fredonian Press, Chillicothe,
    Ohio.
    The Western Christian Monitor; 1816.

Baldwin, Charles N.   Editor, Printer, Publisher; 49 Division
    Street, then 1 Chamber Street, New York.
    Literary Miscellany; 1811.   (Editor)
    The New York City Hall Recorder; 1816.   (Printer)
    The War; February 24, 1817.   (Publisher)
    The Academician; September 25, 1819-January 29, 1820.
    (Printer)

Baldwin, Thomas.   Editor; Boston.
    Massachusetts Baptist Missionary Magazine; 1803-1816.
    American Baptist Magazine; 1817-1824.

Ball, William.   Engraver; Winchester, Va.?
    The Monthly Magazine; 1813.

Ballou, Hosea.   Editor; Charlestown, then Boston, Mass.
    Gospel Visitant; June 1811-March 1818.
    The Universalist; 1819-   .

Bangs, Thomas G.   Printer; Boston.
    Herald of Gospel Liberty; 1816-1817.

Banks, David.   see   Gould, Stephen and Banks, David.

Baptist Missionary Society in Massachusetts.   see   Massachusetts
    Baptist Convention.

Barton, William C. and Edes, Richard W.   Editors, Printers,
    Publishers; Corner of Bull Street and Bay Lane, Savannah, Ga.
    The Ladies' Magazine; February 13-May 8, 1819.

Beauchamp, William.   Editor; Chillicothe, Ohio.
    The Western Christian Monitor; 1816.

Beck, Gideon and Foster, Daniel C.   Printers, Publishers; At the
  Office of The [New Hampshire] Gazette, Portsmouth, N. H.
  The Christian Herald; 1818-   .

Belcher, Joshua.   Printer; Congress Street, Boston.
  New England Journal of Medicine; 1814.
  Massachusetts Agricultural Repository; January 1815.

Bement, Caleb N.   Editor, Printer, Publisher; 221 Warren Street,
  Hudson, N. Y.
  The Casket; 1811-1812.   (Printer, Publisher)
  *The Lounger; between June 1812 and April 1817?   (Editor?)

The Berean Society.   Editors, Publishers; Boston.
  The Berean; 1802-1810.

Biddle, Nicholas.   Editor; Philadelphia.
  Port Folio; 1812-1814.

Biglow, H____.   Editor; New York.
  The American Monthly Magazine; May 1817-October 1818.

Bioren, John.   Printer; 88 Chestnut Street, Philadelphia.
  *The Juvenile Port Folio; 1812-1816.
  The Whim; 1814.
  *The Parlour Companion; 1817-1819.

Birch, George L. and Co.   Printers; New York.
  The New York Literary Journal; May-July 1819.

Blake, George E.   Publisher; South 5th Street, Philadelphia.
  The Trangram; 1809-1810.

Blocquerst, Andrew J.   Printer; 130 South 5th Street, Philadelphia.
  *L'Abeille Américaine; 1815-1818.
  *Le Médiateur; July 23-August 8, 1814.

Booker, Arthur G. and Co.   Printers; Four Doors Below the Bell
  Tower, Richmond, Va.
  The Christian Monitor; July 8-December 2, 1815.

Booth, George.   Editor; Philadelphia.
  Literary Register; 1813-1814.

Boston Bard, pseud.   see   Coffin, R. S.

Bowen, Henry.   Printer, Publisher; Devonshire Street, then Con-
  gress Street, Boston.
  The Boston Weekly Magazine; May 16, 1818-   .   (Publisher)
  The Universalist; 1819-   .   (Printer)

Boyd, John.   Engraver; Philadelphia.

Select Reviews of Literature; 1811.
Port Folio; 1812, 1815.
see also: Edwin, David and Boyd, John.

Bradford, Alden and Reed, Ezra.   Publisher; 58 Cornhill, Boston.
New England Journal of Medicine; 1813-1816.

Bradford, Samuel and Inskeep, John, Jr.   Publishers; 4 South Third
Street, Philadelphia.
The Mirror of Taste; January-December 1810.
Port Folio; 1810-June 1815.

Bradford, T. G.   Editor; Nashville, Tenn.
*Museum; 1810?

Bridport, Hugh.   Engraver; Philadelphia.
Port Folio; 1817.

Broderick, Joseph and Ritter, Frederick W.   Printers; New York.
The Ladies' Literary Cabinet; December 4, 1819-   .

Bronson, Enos.   Printer; Lorenzo Press, Corner of Chestnut and
Fourth Streets, Philadelphia.
Select Reviews; January 1809-December 1810.

Brown, H____.   see   Heiskell, F. S. & Brown, H.

Brown, S. R.   Publisher; 72 State Street, Albany, N.Y.
Geographical and Military Museum; 1814.

Brown, William.   Printer, Publisher; 24 Church Alley, then 42
Prune Street, Philadelphia.
The Beacon; 1811.   (Publisher)
The Emporium of Arts and Sciences; May 1812-April 1813.
(Printer)
The American Medical Recorder; January 1818-   .
(Printer)

Bruce, Archibald.   Editor; New York.
American Mineralogical Journal; 1810-1814.

Buchanan, Joseph.   Editor; Cincinnati, Ohio.
Literary Cadet; 1819-1820.

Buckingham, Joseph Tinker.   Editor, Printer, Publisher; Winter
Street, then 17 Cornhill, Boston.
The Polyanthos; 1805-1814.   (Publisher)
*Bibliothèque Portative; 1810?   (Editor?)
The Comet; 1811-1812.   (Printer)
Friend of Peace; 1815-1819.   (Printer)
The Christian Disciple; 1817-1818.   (Publisher)
New England Galaxy; 1817-1839.   (Publisher)

Buell, William S. Publisher; Schenectady, N.Y.
    Floriad; 1811.

Burke, ____. see DuVal and Burke.

Burr, ____. see Roberts and Burr.

Burr, David J. Publisher; 50 Cornhill, Boston.
    Congregationalist; April 10-June 12, 1816.

Burton, Asa. Editor; Middlebury, Vt.
    The Advisor; January 1809-December 1814.

Butler, Merrill. Editor, Publisher; Devonshire Street, then 79
    State Street, Boston.
    The Scourge; 1811.

Butler, Steuben. Publisher; Wilkesbarre, Penn.
    Literary Visitor; 1813-1815.

Buzzell, John. Editor; Portland, Vt.
    Religious Magazine; 1811-1822.

Caldwell, Charles. Editor; Philadelphia.
    Port Folio; 1814-1816.

Caldwell, John Edwards. Editor, Publisher; 279 Broadway, New
    York.
    The Christian Herald; March 30, 1816-March 21, 1818
        (Publisher); March 30, 1816-March 6, 1819 (Editor).

Camp, ____. see Merrell and Camp.

Campbell, John Page. Editor; Lexington, Ky.
    Evangelical Record and Western Review; named in December
        1813, but no further issues appeared?

Canan, Moses. Editor; Huntingdon, Penn.
    Huntingdon Literary Museum; 1810.

Candid, Charles, pseud. Editor; Hudson, N.Y.
    The Casket; 1811-1812.

Carpenter, Stephen Cullen. Editor; Philadelphia.
    The Mirror of Taste; 1810-1811.
    The Bureau; 1812.

Carr, Joseph. Editor; Baltimore.
    *Carr's Musical Miscellany; 1813.

Carr, Mrs. Mary. Editor, Printer, Publisher; 98 Race Street,
    then 8 South Fifth Street; then 5 Hartung's Alley, then 133 1/2

South Sixth Street, Philadelphia.
Intellectual Regale; 1814-1815.   April 8-December 30, 1815.
    (Printer)

Carver, John.   Editor; Philadelphia
    Farrier's Magazine; 1818.

Chaigneau, Benjamin.   Editor; 56 Chapel Street, New York.
    *Journal des Dames; January-March 1810.

Chandler, Cara and Chandler, Charles.   Editors; 108 Race Street,
    Philadelphia.
    The Parterre; 1816-1817.

Chandler, Joseph R.   Editor; Philadelphia.
    The Philadelphia Magazine; 1818.

Channing, Edward Tyrrel.   Editor; Boston.
    North American Review; 1818-1819.

Chase, Ebenezer.   Editor, Publisher; Andover, N.H.
    Religious Informer; 1819-1825.

Chaudron, Jean-Simon.   Editor; Philadelphia.
    *L'Abeille Américaine; 1815-1818.

Childs, Cephas G.   Engraver; Philadelphia.
    The Analectic; 1816-1818.
    Port Folio; 1817-1818.

Churchill and Abbey.   Printer, Publisher; 95 State Street, Albany,
    New York.
    The Friend; July 1815-March 1816.

Clark, Ambrose.   Editor; Cooperstown, N.Y.
    The Religious Inquirer; 1811.

Clark, Darius.   Printer; Bennington, Vt.
    Christian Chronicle; 1818.

Clark, John C. and Raser, Matthias.   Printers; 78 North Fifth
    Street, Philadelphia.
    The Saturday Magazine; 1819-1822.

Clayton, Edward B. and Kingsland, Joseph.   Printers: 15 Cedar
    Street, then 84 Maiden Lane, then 64 Pine Street, New York.
    The New York City Hall Recorder; 1817-1819.

Clayton, Henry and Fanshaw, Daniel.   Printers; 62 Pine Street,
    New York.
    The Shamrock; July 20-August 3, 1816; January 4-16,
    1817.

Coale, Edward J.   Publisher; 176 Market Street, Baltimore.
    The Literary Visitor; 1812-1813.
    The American Law Journal; 1814.
    The Portico; 1817.

Cobbett, Henry.   Printer, Publisher; 19 Wall Street, then John
    and Cliff Streets, New York.
    Cobbett's American Political Register; May 1817-January 10,
        1818.

Cobbett, Henry and Oldfield, G. S.   Publishers; 19 Wall Street,
    New York.
    Cobbett's American Political Register; January 6-September
        17, 1816.

Cobbett, William.   Editor; New York.
    Cobbett's American Political Register; 1816-1817.

Coburn, _____.   see Ward and Coburn.

Cochran, James.   Publisher; Washington, D.C.
    The National Register; July 25-October 31, 1818.

Coffin, R. S.   Editor; Philadelphia.
    Honey Bee; 1819-1820.

Cohen, Joseph I.   Editor; 110 Market Street, Baltimore.
    Cohen's Gazette; 1814-1830.

Colcord, John P.   Printer; Portland, Vt.
    Herald of Gospel Liberty; 1811.
    Religious Magazine; January-April 1811.

Cole, John. see Neal, Abner; Wills, Francis M.; and Cole John.

Cole, John O.   Printer; Albany.
    The Plough Boy; 1819-   .

Coleman, E. B.   Editor; New Haven, Conn.
    *The Guardian and Monitor; January 1819-   .

Colhoun, W. B.   Editor; New Haven, Conn.
    Atheneum; 1814.

Collins, Thomas and Co.   Printers; 189 Pearl Street, New York.
    American Mineralogical Journal; 1810-1814.
    The Medical and Surgical Register; 1818-1820.

Collins, Thomas and Perkins.   Publishers; New York.
    Medical Repository; 1808-1812.

The Columbian Peitho-Logian Society.   Editors; New York.
    Academic Recreations; 1815.

A Committee of Congregational and Presbyterian Clergymen.
Editors; Utica, N.Y.
The Utica Christian Magazine; 1813-1816.

A Committee of the Baptist Board of Froeign Missions for the
United States. Editors; Philadelphia.
The Latter Day Luminary; 1818-	.

Condie, Thomas G., Jr. Editor; 22 Carter's Alley, Philadelphia.
*The Juvenile Port Folio; 1812-1816.
*The Parlour Companion; 1817-1819.

Conrad, Cornelius and A. Publishers; Philadelphia.
The American Register; 1810.

Conrad, John. Editor, Publisher; 30 Chestnut Street, Philadelphia.
American Weekly Messenger; 1813-1814.

Converse, S. Printer; New Haven.
The Quarterly Christian Spectator; 1819-	.

Cook, John. Editor; Albany, N.Y.
Stranger; 1813-1814.

Cooke, George. Engraver; Philadelphia.
Port Folio; 1810.

Cooke, Oliver D. Publisher; Hartford, Conn.
Connecticut Evangelical Magazine; 1813-1814.

Cooper, Thomas. Editor; Philadelphia.
The Emporium of Arts and Sciences; June 1813-October 1814.

Cooper, W. Printer; 11th near Pennsylvania, Washington, D.C.
Hive; March 30-June 15, 1811.

Corss, Mr. Printer; Hudson, N.Y.
Spirit of the Forum; 1817.

Coverly, Nathaniel. Printer; Milk Street, Boston.
The Idiot; 1818-1819.

Coxe, Alexander F. Editor; Philadelphia.
The Trangram; 1809-1810.

Coxe, John Redman. Editor; Philadelphia.
The Philadelphia Medical Museum; 1804-1811.
The Emporium of Arts and Sciences; May 1812-April 1813.

Crabtree, Christopher, pseud. Editor; Bardstown, Ky.
The Garden; 1810.

Crag, Christopher, Esq., his Grandmother, and Uncle, pseuds.
see Coxe, Alexander F.; and Noah, Mordecai.

Cramer; Spear and Eichbaum; Franklin Mead.   Publishers; Market
Street, Pittsburgh.
The Western Gleaner; 1813-1814.

Cranston, Barzillai. see Jones, Josiah and Company.

Crissy, James. see Elliot, William and Crissy, James.

Croswell, Henry.   Publisher; 62 Pearl Street, then 80 Pearl Street,
Albany.
Balance and State Journal; July 1810-1811.

Croswell, Henry and Frary, Jonathan.   Publishers; Albany.
Balance and State Journal; January 5, 1802-July 3, 1810.

Cummings, Jacob A. and Hilliard, William.   Publishers; 1 Cornhill,
Boston.
The Christian Disciple; 1813-1815.
North American Review; 1817-1820.

Cummins, Ebenezer Harlow.   Editor, Publisher; Philadelphia.
Evangelical Repository; 1816.

Cunningham, John H.   Printer; 70 South Third, between Chestnut
and Walnut, Philadelphia.
Honey Bee; 1819-1820.

Cutler, James. see Russell, John and Cutler, James and Co.

Dana, Richard Henry.   Editor; Boston.
North American Review; 1819-1820.

Davis, Cornelius.   Publisher; Utica, and Auburn, New York.
The Utica Christian Magazine; 1813-1816.   (Utica)
Evangelical Recorder; June 5, 1819-   .   (Auburn)

Davis, Samuel H.   Printer, Publisher; The Apollo Press, Printers
Alley, Alexandria, D.C.
Columbian Telescope; 1819-1820.

Davis and Force.   Printers; Pennsylvania Avenue, Washington City.
The Theological Repertory; 1819-1830.

Day, Mahlon and Turner, Charles.   Printers, Publishers; 55-58
Beaver Street, then 84 Water Street, New York.
General Shipping and Commercial List; February 21, 1815-
September 7, 1819.

Deare, Lewis.   Printer; Elizabethtown, N.J.
The Churchman's Magazine; 1813-1815.

Delaplaine, Joseph.   Publisher; Philadelphia.
The Emporium of Arts and Sciences; May 1812-April 1813.

Democritus, The Younger, pseud.   see   Helmbold, George.

Dennie, Joseph.   Editor; Philadelphia.
Port Folio; 1801-1812.

DeSilver, Thomas.   Publisher; Philadelphia.
Port Folio; July-December 1815.

Desnoues, Joseph.   Printer, Publisher; 6 Church Street, Rear of
St. Paul's Church Yard, then 61 Church Street, then 69 Chapel
Street, then 7 Murray Street, New York.
*Journal des Dames; 1810.
Military Monitor and American Register; 1812-1813.
*Le Médiateur; April 2-July 16, 1814.

DeWitt, Benjamin.   Editor; New York.
New York Medical and Philosophical Register; 1809-1811.

Dobbin, George and Murphy, Thomas.   Printers; Baltimore.
National Museum; November 13-December 4, 1813.

Dobson, Thomas.   Printer, Publisher; At the Stone House, 41
South Second Street, Philadelphia.
Journal of Foreign Medical Science; 1811-1813.

Dobson, Thomas and Son.   Publishers; At the Stone House, 41
South Second Street, Philadelphia.
Journal of Foreign Medical Science; 1814-1820.
American Register; 1817.

Donaldson, Arthur.   Editor; 88 North Front Street, Philadelphia.
*The Juvenile Magazine; 1811-1813.

Doolittle, Amos.   Engraver; New Haven, Conn.
The American Journal of Science; 1819.

Dorsey, John Syng.   Engraver; Philadelphia.
Journal of Foreign Medical Science; 1811.
New York Medical and Philosophical Journal; 1811.

Drayton, J____.   Engraver; Philadelphia.
The Analectic; 1819.

Dromgoogle, William, pseud.   Publisher; Bardstown, Ky.
The Garden; 1810.

Dunning, ____.   see   Prior and Dunning.

Dupuy, Starke.   Editor; Frankfort, Ky.
Kentucky Missionary and Theological Magazine; 1812-1814?

Durand, Francis.   Editor; 131 William Street, then 6 Carlille (!)
    Street, New York.
    *Journal des Dames; April-December 1810.

DuVal, Philip.   Publisher; Richmond, Va.
    The Christian Monitor; July 8-December 2, 1815.

DuVal, Philip and Burke.   Publishers; Four Doors Below the Bell
    Tower, Richmond, Va.
    The Christian Monitor; December 9, 1815-June 6, 1816.

Dwight, Theodore.   Editor, Publisher; 87 Pearl Street, New York.
    The Country Courrier; February 20-March 24, 1817.

Earle, Edward.   Publisher; Philadelphia.
    Journal of Foreign Medical Science; name announced as pub-
        lisher, but does not appear on the title page.
    Select Reviews; January-December 1810.

Eastburn, James and Co.   Publishers; The Literary Rooms, Corner
    of Broadway and Pine Street, New York.
    The Evangelical Guardian and Review; 1817-1819.
    The American Journal of Science; July 1818-   .

Eastburn, James and Kirk, Thomas and Co.   Publishers; Corner of
    Wall and Nassau Streets, New York.
    Academic Recreations; 1815.

Eberle, John.   Editor, Philadelphia.
    The American Medical Recorder; 1819-   .

Economical School.   Printers; 56 Chapel Street, New York.
    *Journal des Dames; 1810.

Eddy, Henry.   Editor; Pittsburgh.
    *Swallow; 1817?

Edes, Benjamin.   Printer, Publisher; Corner of Market and South
    Streets, Philadelphia, then Baltimore.
    Emerald; 1810-1811 (Publisher)
    Baltimore Medical and Philosophical Lycaeum; 1811.   (Printer)
    The Portico; 1817-   .

Edes, Richard W.   see   Barton, William C. and Edes, Richard W.
    Russell, Henry P. and Edes, Richard W.

Edmands, Thomas Jr.   see   Lincoln, Ensign and Edmands, Thomas,
    Jr.

Edwards, James L.   Printer, Publisher; 70 State Street, Boston.
    The Satirist; 1812.

Edwin, David. Engraver; Philadelphia.
  The Mirror of Taste; 1810-1811.
  Port Folio; 1810-1815.
  Select Reviews of Literature; 1810-1811.
  Freemason's Magazine; 1811.
  Emporium of Arts and Sciences; 1812-1813.
  New England Journal of Medicine; 1812.
  The Polyanthos; 1812-1814.
  The Analectic; 1813-1814.
  Rhode Island Literary Repository; 1814.

Edwin, David and Boyd, John. Engravers; Philadelphia.
  The Polyanthos; 1812.

Edwin, David and Lawson, Alexander. Engravers; Philadelphia.
  Port Folio; 1810.

Eichbaum, _____. see Carmer; Spear and Eichbaum; Franklin Mead.

Elliott, John M. see Harmer, Joseph and Elliott, John.

Elliott, Jonathan. Publisher; Washington.
  The National Register; May 15, 1819-February 5, 1820.

Elliott, William and Crissy, James. Printers; At the Sign of the
  Ledger, 114 Water Street, New York.
  The Observer; 1810-1811.

Ely, Ezra Stiles. Editor; Philadelphia.
  Quarterly Theological Review; 1818-1819.

Engles, S. and Co. Printers, Publishers; Pittsburgh.
  The Pioneer; 1812.

Evarts, Jeremiah. Editor; Boston.
  Missionary Herald; 1810-1820.

Everett, _____. Editor; Lexington, Ky.
  Journal of Belles Lettres; 1819-1820.

Everett, Edward. Editor; Cambridge, Mass.
  Harvard Lyceum; 1810-1811.

Ewing, Samuel. Editor; Philadelphia.
  Select Reviews; 1809-1812.

Exilious, John G. Engraver; Philadelphia.
  Port Folio; 1813.

Fairman, Gideon. Engraver; Philadelphia.
  The Analectic; 1813, 1815, 1818.
  The Portico; 1816.
  Port Folio; 1817-1818.

Fanshaw, Daniel. Printer; 241 Pearl Street, New York.
     The American Monthly Magazine; November 1817-April 1818.
     see also: Clayton, Henry and Fanshaw, Daniel.

Farnham, Robert and Bager, Thomas, Jr. Editors, Publishers;
     4 Suffolk Building, Congress Street, Boston.
     *The Weekly Monitor; 1817.

Farrand, _____. see McDuffee and Farrand.

Farrand, William P. and Co. Publishers; Philadelphia.
     The Analyst; 1808-1811.

Farrand, William P., Mallory, Daniel and Co. Publishers; Suffolk
     Building, Boston.
     The New England Literary Herald; 1809-1810.
     Something; 1809-1810.

Farrand, William P. and Nicholas, Charles F. Publishers; Corner
     of Chestnut and Sicth Streets, Philadelphia.
     The American Law Journal; 1810.
     American Review of History and Politics; January 1811-
          October 1812.

Fay, W_____. Publisher; Rutland, Vt.
     The Vermont Baptist Missionary Magazine; 1811-1812.

Fennell, James. Editor; Boston, then Philadelphia.
     Something; 1809-1810. (Boston)
     The Whim; 1814. (Philadelphia)

Fenton, D_____ Co. Publisher; Trenton, N.J.
     The Quarterly Theological Magazine; July-October 1813.

Ferguson, Robert. Printer; Pittsburgh.
     The Western Gleaner; 1813-1814.

Finley, Anthony. Publisher; Northeast Corner of Fourth and Chest-
     nut Streets, Philadelphia.
     Journal of Foreign Medical Science; 1810.
     Quarterly Theological Review; January-December 1818.

Flagg, J. F. Engraver; Boston?
     New England Journal of Medicine; 1813.

Forbes, John. Publisher; 61 Fair Street, New York.
     Medical Repository; 1813-1814.

Forbes, John and Co. Printers; 78 Gold Street, New York.
     Academic Recreations; 1815.

Force, _____. see Davis and Force.

Forman, ____. see Smith and Forman.

Foster, Daniel C. see Beck, Gideon and Foster, Daniel C.

Foster, F____. Engraver; Philadelphia?
Journal of Musick; 1810.

Foster, Robert. Editor; Portsmouth, N. H.
The Christian Herald; 1818-

Fowler, Andrew. Editor; Charleston, S. C.
*The Sunday Visitant; 1818-1819.

Francis, David. see Munroe, Edmund and Francis, David.
                    Munroe, Edmund; Francis, David; and Parker,
                    Samuel H.

Francis, John Wakefield. Editor; New York.
American Medical and Philosophical Register; 1810-1814.

Franks, Lewis P. Editor; Philadelphia.
*Luncheon; 1815-1816.

Frary, Jonathan. see Crosswell, Henry and Frary, Jonathan.

French, Ebenezer. Printer; Southwest Corner of Market and
Seventh Streets, Baltimore.
The American Farmer; April 2-September 10, 1819.

Frick, Henry. Printer; At the Office of the Miltonian; Milltown, Pa.
The Religious Museum; 1818-1819.

Fry, William. Printer; 52 Prune Street, then Walnut near Fifth,
Philadelphia.
Journal of Foreign Medical Science; 1812-1813.
The American Law Journal; 1814.
Evangelical Repository; 1816.
American Register; 1817.
Quarterly Theological Review; January-December 1818.

Fry, William and Krammerer, Joseph. Printers; Philadelphia.
The Analyst; 1808-1811.
The American Law Journal; 1810.
Journal of Foreign Medical Science; 1810-1811.
The Mirror of Taste; January-December 1811.
American Review of History and Politics; 1811-1812.

Gaines, Xenophon J. Publisher; Lexington, Ky.
The Castigator; 1818-1820.

Gales, Joseph. Printer, Publisher; Raleigh, N. C.
Carolina Law Repository; 1813-1816.

Gardenier, Barent.   Editor, Printer, Publisher; 34 Cedar Street,
    then 87 Pearl Street, New York.
        Examiner; 1813-1816.
        The Country Courrier; 1816-1817.

Gardner, Jonathan.   Editor, Philadelphia.
        The Christian Messenger; August-September 4, 1819.

Gardner, Simon.   see   Russell, John; Cutler, James, and Co.

Gemmill, William and Lewis, James.   Printers; At the Office of
    the York Recorder, York, Penn.
        The Village Museum; October 1819-

A Gentleman of Education and Talents.   Editor; Boston.
        The Boston Mirror; 1808-1810.

Gerard, Mrs. William.   Public Printer, Frankfort, Ky.
        Kentucky Missionary and Theological Magazine; 1812-1814?

German Evangelical Lutheran Synod.   Publisher; Philadelphia.
        *Evangelisches Magazin; 1811-1817.

Gillespy, Edward.   Editor, Publisher; 104 Water Street, then 24
    William Street, New York.
        The Shamrock; 1810-1817.   Editor only December 15, 1810-
            June 5, 1813.

Gillespy, Edward and O'Connor, Thomas.   Publishers; 69 William
    Street, New York.
        The Shamrock; June 25, 1814-January 28, 1815.

Gilley, William B.   Publisher; 92 Broadway, New York.
        The Christian Herald; April 4, 1818-March 6, 1819.

Gimbrede, Thomas.   Engraver; New York.
        The Monthly Recorder; 1813.
        The Analectic; 1814-1816.
        Port Folio; 1815-1816, 1819.
        Medical Repository; 1817.
        The Methodist Review; 1818.
        The Rural Magazine; 1819.

Gleason, Peter B.   Printer, Publisher; Hartford, Conn.
        Connecticut Evangelical Magazine; 1809-1815.

Gobrecht, Christian.   Engraver; Philadelphia.
        Port Folio; 1816.
        The Baptist Missionary Magazine; 1819.

Goodman, Charles.   Engraver; Philadelphia.
        The Analectic; 1815-1816.

Goodman, Charles and Piggot, Robert. Engravers; Philadelphia.
    The Analectic; 1815, 1819.
    Port Folio; 1816-1819.

Goodman, George. Publisher; 32 South Seventh Street, then 108
    Race Street, Philadelphia.
    The Philadelphia Magazine; January 14-August 8, 1818.

Goodrich, A. T. and Co. Publishers; 124 Broadway, New York.
    The New York Literary Journal; 1819-1821.

Goss, Sylvester T. Publisher; Boston.
    Boston Kaleidoscope; July 17-November 27, 1819.
    see also: Hews, Abraham, Jr. and Goss, Sylvester T.

Gould, Stephen. see Peluse, William L. and Gould, Stephen.

Gould, Stephen and Banks, David. Publishers; Corner of Nassau
    and Spruce Streets, New York.
    The New York Judicial Repository; 1818-1819.

Graham, David. Editor; Pittsburgh.
    The Pioneer; 1812.

Gratton, William. Printer; New York.
    The New York Judicial Repository; 1818-1819.

Gray, John. Publisher; 8 Murray Street, New York.
    The Christian Herald; April 17, 1819-   .

Gray, John and Co. Printer; Dover Street, New York.
    The Christian Herald; April 17, 1819-   .

Gray, William W. Editor; Lynchburg, Va.
    *Lynchburg Evangelical Magazine; 1810?

Gray, William W. Printer; The Franklin Press, Richmond, Va.
    The Literary and Evangelical Magazine; 1818-   .

Gready, Andrew P. Publisher; Charleston, S.C.
    Christian Mirror; 1814.

Green, P. N. Editor, Printer; Haverhill, Mass.
    The Gospel Visitant; April-July 1818.

Greer, William. Printer; Lancaster, Penn.
    The Hive; May 19-June 23, 1810.

Gridley, Enoch G. Engraver; New York.
    Port Folio; 1810.

Gruff, Growler, pseud. Editor; Philadelphia.
    The Cynick; 1811.

Hall, Harrison. Publisher; 133 Chestnut Street, near Fourth,
Philadelphia.
Port Folio; January-February 1816.
The American Law Journal; 1817.

Hall, John Elihu. Editor, Publisher; Philadelphia.
The American Law Journal; 1808-1817. (Editor)
Port Folio; March 1816-1827.

Hall Sergeant. Printer; Philadelphia.
The American Law Journal; 1813.

Hamilton, William. Editor, Printer, Publisher; Lancaster, Penn.
The Hive; July 24-December 11, 1810.

Hamilton Baptist Missionary Society. Editors; Morrisville, N.Y.
Western New York Baptist Magazine; 1814-1825.

Hamlin, William. Engraver; Providence, R.I.
New England Journal of Medicine; 1814.
Rhode Island Literary Repository; 1814.

Hardcastle, John and VanPelt, Peter. Printers, Publishers; 63
Pine Street, New York.
Military Monitor and American Register; September 14-
October 5, 1812.

Hardie, James. Editor; 58 Murray Street, New York.
The New York Magazine; 1814.

Hardt, Peter. Publisher; At the Office of the York Recorder,
York, Penn.
The Village Museum; August-September 1819.

Harmer, Joseph. Editor, Publisher; 7 Counties Slip, then 19
William Street, New York.
Independent Mechanic; April 6-July 27, 1811.

Harmer, Joseph and Co. Editors, Publishers; 35 Nassau Street,
New York.
Independent Mechanic; August 17-December 28, 1811.

Harmer, Joseph and Elliott, John M. Editors and Publishers;
New York.
Independent Mechanic; August 3-10, 1811.

Harper, John and John, Jr. Printers; 136 Fulton Street, New York.
The Medical and Surgical Register; 1818-1820.

Harrison, Charles. Printer, Publisher; 3 Peck Slip, New York.
The Ladies' Weekly Museum; April 2, 1808-May 2, 1812.

Harrison, John. Printer, Publisher; 3 Peck Slip, New York.
The Ladies' Weekly Museum; May 14, 1791-February 8,
1806.

Harrison, John and Purdy, Stephen, Jr. Printers, Publishers;
3 Peck Slip, New York.
The Ladies' Weekly Museum; May 17, 1788-May 7, 1791.

Harrison, Margaret. Publisher; 3 Peck Slip, New York.
The Ladies' Weekly Museum; February 15, 1806-March 26,
1808.

Harrison, Richard G. Engraver; Philadelphia.
Port Folio; 1815.
The Analectic; 1818-1819.

Hart, Henry. Printer; 117 Chatham Street, New York.
Theophilanthropist; 1810.

Haswell, Anthony T. Publisher; Bennington, Vt.
Christian Chronicle; 1818.

Heartt, Dennis. Editor, Printer, Publisher; 17 Arch Street, then
Marshall's Alley, between Fourth and Fifth Streets near St.
Mary's Church, then 318 Market Street, Philadelphia.
Philadelphia Repertory; 1810-1812.
The Bureau; 1812. (Printer)
American Weekly Messenger; 1813-1814. (Printer)
Intellectual Regale; November 19, 1813-April 1, 1815.
(Printer)
The Philadelphia Magazine; August 15-November 7, 1818.
(Printer, Publisher)

Heiskell, F. S. Editor; Knoxville, Tenn.
The Western Monitor and Religious Journal, 1818-

Heiskell, F. S. and Brown, H. Printers, Publishers; Knoxville,
Tenn.
The Western Monitor and Religious Journal; 1818-

Heiskell, John. Editor, Publisher; Winchester, Va.
The Monthly Magazine and Literary Journal; 1812-1813.

Helmbold, George. Editor, Publisher; 13 Fromberger's Court,
back of No. 34 North Second Street, Philadelphia.
Independent Balance; 1817-1832.

Helmbold, George, Jr. Editor, Publisher; 131 South Front Street,
Philadelphia.
Tickler; September 16, 1807-July 21, 1812.

Helmbold, Henry K. Publisher; 131 South Front Street, then
37 Walnut Street, Philadelphia.
Tickler; July 28, 1812-November 17, 1813.

Helmuth, Julius Heinrich Christian.   Editor; Philadelphia.
   *Evangelisches Magazin; 1811-1817.

Henry, R. Norris.   see   Littell, Eliakim and Henry, R. Norris.

Heustis, Samuel.   Publisher; 235 Broadway, New York.
   The Ladies' Literary Cabinet; December 4, 1819-   .
   see also: Woodworth, Samuel and Heustis, Samuel.

Hewitt, ____.   Engraver; Philadelphia?
   Port Folio; 1812-1814.

Hews, Abraham, Jr. and Goss, Sylvester T.   Publishers; 6 Merchant's Hall, Congress Street, Boston.
   Boston Kaleidoscope; November 28, 1818-July 17, 1819.

Hill, George.   Publisher; Baltimore.
   Baltimore Medical and Philosophical Lycaeum; 1811.

Hill, Isaac.   Printer; Concord, N.H.
   New England Missionary Magazine; 1815.

Hill, John.   Engraver and aquatinter; Philadelphia.
   The Analectic; 1817, 1819.
   Port Folio; 1819.

Hill and Moore.   Printers; Concord, N.H.
   The New England Missionary Intelligencer; 1819.

Hilliard, William.   Publisher; Boston.
   General Repository and Review; 1812-1813.
   see also: Cummings, Jacob A. and Hilliard, William
             Hilliard, William and Metcalf, Charles.

Hilliard, William and Metcalf, Charles.   Publishers; Cambridge,
   then Boston, Mass.
   Harvard Lyceum; 1810-1811.
   General Repository and Review; 1812-1813.
   The Christian Disciple; 1813-1815.
   Massachusetts Agricultural Repository; May 1814.
   North American Review; 1815-   .   (Boston)

Hobart, John Henry.   Editor; New York.
   The Churchman's Magazine; May/June 1808-November/
      December 1811.
   The Christian Journal; 1817-1819.

Hogan, David.   Printer, Publisher; Philadelphia.
   *Literary Reporter; 1810?   (Printer?)
   Archives of Useful Knowledge; 1810-1813.

Holley, Orville Luther.   Editor; New York.
   The American Monthly Magazine; November 1817-April 1819.

Homespun, Henry, Jr., pseud. see Southwick, Solomon.

Honeycomb, Will, pseud. Editor; Lancaster, Penn.
    The Hive; May 19-June 23, 1810.

Hoogland, William. Engraver, New York.
    The American Journal of Science; 1819.

Hooker, William. Engraver; Philadelphia.
    Port Folio; 1813-1817.
    American Medical and Philosophical Register; 1814.

Hooker, William G. Publisher; Middlebury, Vt.
    The Advisor; January 1809-December 1810.

Hosack, David. Editor; New York.
    American Medical and Philosophical Register; 1810-1814.

Hosford, E. and E. Printers; Albany, N.Y.
    Stranger; 1813-1814.
    The American Magazine; 1815-1816.

Hough, John. Editor; Middlebury, Vt.
    The Advisor; January-December 1815.

How, Thomas Y. Editor; New York.
    The Christian Register; 1816-1817.

Howe and Spaulding. Publishers; New Haven, Conn.
    The American Journal of Science; July 1818-   .
    The Quarterly Christian Spectator; 1819-1820.

Howland, Benjamin R. see Robinson, Martin and Howland, Ben-
    jamin R.

Humphreys, James and A. Y. Printers, Publishers; Change Walk,
    Corner of Second and Walnut Street, Philadelphia.
    The Philadelphia Medical Museum; 1810-1811.

Hunt, William Gibbs. Editor, Publisher; Lexington, Ky.
    The Western Review and Miscellaneous Magazine; 1819-1821.

Huntington, Joseph D. Printer; Middlebury, Vt.
    The Advisor; January 1809-December 1810.

Hutchens, John. see Miller, John and Hutchens, John.

Hyde de Neuville, Guillaume. Editor; New York.
    *Journal des Dames; 1810.

Inskeep, John, Jr. see Bradford, Samuel and Inskeep, John, Jr.

Irving, Washington. Editor; Philadelphia.
  The Analectic Magazine; 1813-1815.

Jackson, J____. Editor, Printer, Publisher; Bridge Street,
  Boston.
  The True Briton; 1819.

Jansen, Benjamin G. Printer; 8 Warren Street, then 20 James
  Street, New York.
  The American Monthly Magazine; May 1818-April 1819.

Johnson, John B. Printer; Morrisville, N.Y.
  The Western New York Baptist Magazine; 1814-1825.

Johnston, John. see Turner, Charles and Co.

Jones, Josiah and Co. Printers; Office of the Providence Patriot,
  Providence, R.I. (Firm consisted of: Josiah Jones, Bennett
  H. Wheeler, and Barzillai Cranston.)
  *Juvenile Gazette; 1819-1820.

Jones, William R. Engraver; Philadelphia.
  Philadelphia Medical Museum; 1810.
  Port Folio; 1815.

Justice, J. P. see Probasco, Simon and Justice, J. P.

K., T. V. and Co. see Tanner, Benjamin; Vallance, John;
  Kearny, Francis and Company.

Kearny, Francis. Engraver; Philadelphia.
  The Casket; 1811.
  Select Reviews of Literature; 1811-1812.
  The Emporium of Arts and Sciences; 1812.
  The Analectic; 1813-1814, 1817.
  Port Folio; 1815.
  see also: Tanner, Benjamin; Vallance, John; Kearny, Francis
              and Company.
            Tiebout, Cornelius and Kearny, Francis.

Keen, William C. Printer; 181 South Fifth Street, Philadelphia.
  *L'Hémisphère; 1809-1811.

Kennard, Timothy. Printer, Publisher; 73 State Street, Boston.
  Omnium Gatherum; 1809-1810.

Kennedy, James. Engraver; New York.
  New York Medical and Philosophical Journal; 1811.

Kidder, J.   Engraver; Boston.
   The Polyanthos; 1813.

Kimber, Thomas and Richardson, John.   Publishers; 237 Market
   Street, Philadelphia.
   The Emporium of Arts and Sciences; June 1813-October 1814.

Kingsland, Joseph.   see   Clayton, Edward B.   and Kingsland,
   Joseph.

Kirk, Thomas.   see   Eastburn, James and Kirk, Thomas.
                        Kirk, Thomas and Mercein, William A.

Kirk, Thomas and Mercein, William A.   Publishers; 22 Wall
   Street, New York.
   The American Monthly Magazine; May 1817-April 1818.

Knap, Luscomb.   Editor, Printer; Pittsford, New York.
   The Christian Messenger; 1815-1816.

Knapp, Samuel L.   Editor; Boston.
   New England Galaxy; October 10, 1817-Summer 1818.

Kneass, William.   Engraver; Philadelphia.
   Archives of Useful Knowledge; 1811-1813.
   Baltimore Medical and Philosophical Lyceum; 1811.
   Journal of Foreign Medical Science; 1811.
   The Emporium of Arts and Sciences; 1812, 1814.
   The Monthly Magazine; 1812.
   Port Folio; 1813, 1815.
   The Analectic; 1816.
   Portico; 1816.

Kneass, William and Young, James H.   Engravers; Philadelphia.
   The American Medical Recorder; 1818.
   The Analectic; 1818-1819.
   Farrier's Magazine; 1818.
   The American Journal of Science; 1819.

Kneeland, Abner.   Editor; Philadelphia.
   The Christian Messenger; November 6, 1819-July 21, 1821.

Krammer, Joseph.   see   Fry, William and Krammer, Joseph.

Lansing, Dirck C.   Publisher; Auburn, N.Y.
   Evangelical Recorder; January 31-September 5, 1818.

Largin, George and Thompson, Thomas.   Printers; 189 Water
   Street, between Beakman and Burling Slip, then 5 Burling Slip,
   New York.
   The Shamrock; December 15, 1810-September 12, 1812.

Lash'em, Lodowick, pseud.   Editor; Boston.
    The Satirist; 1812.

Lavigne, _____   Engraver; Boston.
    Polyanthos; 1814.

Lawrence and Wilson.   Printers; Washington, D.C.
    The National Register; July 25, 1818-May 8, 1819.

Lawson, Alexander.   Engraver; Philadelphia.
    The Emporium of Arts and Sciences; 1812.
    Journal of Foreign Medical Science; 1813.
    Port Folio; 1817.
    see also: Edwin, David and Lawson, Alexander.
                Tiebout, Cornelius and Lawson, Alexander.

A Layman, pseud.   see   Southwick, Solomon.

Lemmon, George.   Editor, Publisher; Baltimore.
    A Magazine; 1810.

Leney, William Satchwell.   Engraver; New York.
    American Medical and Philosophical Register; 1810-1813.
    The Mirror of Taste; 1810.
    Port Folio; 1810-1811, 1813, 1819.
    The Monthly Recorder; 1813.
    The Analectic; 1814-1817.

Le Pelletier, Madame.   Editor, Publisher; Baltimore.
    *Journal de Musique; 1809-1810?   (Editor?)
    Journal of Musick; 1810-1811?   (Publisher)

Levavasseur, C. A. F.   Editor; New York, later Philadelphia.
    *Le Médiateur; 1814.

Levis, Isaac and Weaver, William.   Publishers; Philadelphia.
    Freemason's Magazine; 1811-1812.

Lewis, Henry C.   Editor, Printer, Publisher; Pine Street, Phila-
    delphia; then G Street, Washington; then 157 South Eleventh
    Street, then 164 South Eleventh Street, then 272 Market Street,
    Philadelphia.
    Hive; 1811.
    Literary and Musical Magazine; 1817-1820.

Lewis, James.   see   Gemmill, William and Lewis, James.

Lilly, Robert.   see   Wells, William and Lilly, Robert.

Lincoln, Ensign and Edmands, Thomas, Jr.   Printers; Boston.
    Massachusetts Baptist Missionary Magazine; March 1811-

December 1813.
Baptist Missionary Magazine; 1817-1824.

Lincoln, Ezra.   Printer, Publisher; Devonshire and State Streets,
    Boston.
    Congregationalist; January 31-April 3, 1816 (Publisher);
        April 10-April 24, 1816 (Printer).

A Literary Association.   Editors; New York.
    The Aeronaut; August 1, 1816-September 30, 1822.

Littell, Eliakim.   Editor; Philadelphia.
    The Saturday Magazine; 1819-1822.

Littell, Eliakim and Henry, R. Norris.   Publishers; 74 South Second
    Street, Philadelphia.
    The Saturday Magazine; 1819-1822.

Long, George.   Printer, Publisher; 71 Pearl Street, New York.
    The Analyst; 1814.

Longacre, James Barton.   Engraver; New York.
    The Analectic; 1819.
    The Methodist Review; 1819.
    Port Folio; 1819.

Longworth, David.   Publisher; New York.
    The Rambler's Magazine; 1809-1810.
    The Monthly Recorder; 1813.

Looker, Reynolds and Co.   Printers; 108 Main Street, Cincinnati.
    Literary Cadet; 1819-1820.

Loring, James.   Publisher; Boston.
    American Baptist Magazine; 1817-1824.
    see also: Manning, William and Loring, James.

Loudon, Archibald.   Printer, Publisher; Carlisle, Penn.
    Religious Instructor; 1810-1811.

Lucidantus, pseud.   Editor; Philadelphia.
    The Beacon; 1811.

Lynch and Southgate.   Publishers; Corner of Harris' Building,
    Richmond, Va.
    The Visitor; 1809-1810.

M_____.   Engraver; Philadelphia?
    Port Folio; 1812.

McCahan, John.   Printer; Huntingdon, Penn.
    Huntingdon Literary Museum; 1810.

McCarty, William and White, Samuel B. Publishers; 46 Fair
Street, New York.
The Lady's Miscellany; December 2, 1809-October 20, 1810.

McDuffee and Farrand. Printers; 1 Murray Street, New York.
The Globe; January-May 1819.

M'Kenzie, _____. see Smith and M'Kenzie.

M'Kown, J_____. Printer; Portland, Vt.
Religious Magazine; January-April 1812.

M'Minn, James. Publisher; 136 North Fifth Street, then 37 Walnut
Street, Philadelphia.
The Inquisitor; 1818-1820.

Magill, Robert. Printer; 6 Liberty Street, New York.
The Ladies' Weekly Museum; May 3, 1817.

Magill, Samuel. Printer, Publisher; 224 Baltimore Street, Baltimore.
Scourge; 1810.

Mallory, Daniel. see Farrand, William P. and Mallory, Daniel.

Mann, Camill M. Editor, Publisher; 13 Baltimore Street, Baltimore.
National Museum; 1813-1814.

Mann, Herman B. Printer; Providence, R.I.
Rhode Island Literary Repository; 1814-1815.

Manning, William and Loring, James. Printers; Boston.
Massachusetts Baptist Missionary Magazine; 1803-1816.

Mariano, _____. Editor; Lexington, Ky.
Journal of Belles Lettres; 1819-1820.

Marks, Samuel. Printer, Publisher; Corner of Church and
Anthony Streets, New York.
The Olio; 1813-1814.
The Academician; January 7, 1818-July 10, 1819. (Printer)

Marrat, W_____. Editor, Publisher; Between 1 Murray Street and
Broadway, New York.
The Scientific Journal; 1818-1820. (Publisher, February-
August 1818 only)

Mason, John Mitchell. Editor; New York.
The Christian's Magazine; 1806-1811.

Mason, Thomas. Editor; New York.
The Methodist Review; 1818-1820.
see also: Soule, Joshua and Mason, Thomas.

Massachusetts Baptist Convention. Publishers; Boston.
The Massachusetts Baptist Missionary Magazine; 1803-1816.

Massachusetts Baptist Missionary Society. see Massachusetts
Baptist Convention.

Massachusetts Society for Promoting Agriculture. Editors, Publishers; Boston.
Massachusetts Agricultural Repository; 1813-1832.

Matchett, Richard J. Printer, Publisher; Corner of South Gay and
Water Streets, Baltimore.
*Wanderer, A Literary Magazine; 1816?

Maund, Thomas. see Schaeffer, Frederick G. and Maund, Thomas.

Maverick, Peter Rushton. Engraver; Newark, N. J.
Port Folio; 1810.
The Emporium of Arts and Sciences; 1813.
The Analectic; 1814-1815.
The American Magazine; 1815.

Maxwell, James. Printer; Philadelphia.
The Mirror of Taste; July-December 1810.
Port Folio; July 1810-
The Quarterly Theological Magazine; 1814.
The American Law Journal; 1817.
see also: Smith, Thomas and Maxwell, James.

Mead, Franklin. see Carmer; Spear and Eichbaum; Franklin Mead.

Mead, Joel K. Editor, Publisher; Washington, D. C.
The National Register; March 2, 1816-July 18, 1818.

Meadows, R. M. Engraver; Philadelphia.
The Analectic; 1817.

Mease, James. Editor; Philadelphia.
Archives of Useful Knowledge; 1810-1813.

Meehan, John S. see Anderson, Robert and Meehan, John S.

Mein, John. Editor, Publisher; 179 Water Street, Corner of
Burling Slip, New York.
The Beau; 1814.

Mercein, T. and W. Printers; 93 Gold Street, New York.
The American Monthly Magazine; May-October 1817.

Mercein, William A. Publisher; 93 Gold Street, New York.
Medical Repository; 1819-1820.
see also: Kirk, Thomas and Mercein, William A.

Merrell and Camp. Printers; Utica, New York.
The Utica Christian Magazine; 1813-1816.

Metcalf, Charles. see Hilliard, William and Metcalf, Charles.

Meyer, H____. Engraver; Philadelphia?
The Analectic; 1816.

Miller, John. Publisher; 25 Bow Street, Covent Garden, London.
Port Folio; January 1819-   .

Miller, John and Hutchens, John. Printers; 4th Door West of the
Bridge, Providence, R.I.
Olla Podrida; 1816.

Miner, Asher. Editor; Newton, Penn.
The Star of Freedom; 1817-1818.

Ming, Alexander. Editor, Printer, Publisher; 86 Front Street,
then 84 Front Street, New York.
The Weekly Visitor, and Ladies' Museum; 1817-1822.

Mitchell, Samuel Latham. Editor; New York.
Medical Repository; 1797-1820.

Moore, ____. see Hill and Moore.

Morse, Jedidiah. Editor; Boston.
Missionary Herald; 1805-1810.

Morton, Alexander C. Editor, Printer, Publisher; 3 Dutch Street,
New York.
Weekly Visitor; 1810-1811.

Mott, Valentine. Editor; New York.
The New York Medical Magazine; 1814-1815.
The Medical and Surgical Register; 1818-1820.

Munroe, Alvan. Editor, Publisher; 54 South Street, Baltimore.
Baltimore Weekly Magazine; 1818.

Munroe, Edmund and Francis, David. Printers, Publishers; The
Shakespeare Bookstore, No. 4 Cornhill, Corner of Water Street,
Boston.
The Berean; 1802-1810. (Printers)
The Christian Monitor; 1810-1811. (Publisher)
The Atheneum; 1817-   (Publisher)

Munroe, Edmund; Francis, David; and Parker, Samuel H.
Printers; 4 Cornhill, Boston.
The Boston Spectator; 1814-1815.

Murden, Joseph T.   Printer; Perth Amboy, N.J.
    The Scientific Journal; July 1819-January 1820.

Murphy, Thomas.   see   Dobbin, George and Murphy, Thomas.

Murray, George.   Engraver; Philadelphia.
    Archives of Useful Knowledge; 1810.
    Port Folio; 1810-1812, 1819.
    Portico; 1817.

Neagle, James.   Engraver; Philadelphia.
    The Analectic; 1819.

Neal, Abner; Wills, Francis M.; and Cole, John.   Publishers;
    Baltimore.
    The Portico; 1816.

Negrin, Jean Jacques.   Editor; Philadelphia.
    *L'Hémisphère; 1809-1811.

Newman, G____.   Engraver; Philadelphia?
    Freemason's Magazine; 1811.

Nicholas, Charles F.   see   Farrand, William P. and Nicholas,
    Charles F.

Niles, Hezekiah.   Editor, Publisher; The Franklin Press, South
    Street.   Next Door to the Merchants' Coffee House, Baltimore.
    Niles' Weekly Register; 1811-1837.

Noah, Mordecai.   Editor; Philadelphia.
    The Trangram; 1809-1810.

Nobody, Nemo, Esq., pseud.   see   Fennell, James.

Noel, Silas M.   Editor; Frankfort, Ky.
    *The Gospel Herald; 1813-1814.

Norton, Andrews.   Editor; Cambridge.
    General Repository and Review; January 1812-April 1813.

Norton, Jacob P.   see   Parmenter, James and Norton, Jacob P.

A Number of Gentlemen.   Editors; Middlebury, Vt.
    The Literary and Philosophical Repertory; 1812-1817.

O'Connor, Thomas.   Editor, Publisher; 2 Varick Street, then 53
    Barclay Street, then Orange Street, then 4 Nassau Street, New
    York.
    Military Monitor and American Register; 1812-1814.   (Editor)
    The War; 1812-1817.   (Editor)
    The Shamrock; September 7, 1815-August 17, 1816; then
        January 4-August 16, 1817.   (Publisher)

The Globe; 1819. (Editor)
see also: Gillespy, Edward and O'Connor, Thomas.

Oded, Obadiah, pseud. see Heartt, Dennis.

Oldfield, G. S. see Cobbett, Henry and Oldfield, G. S.

Oldschool, Oliver, Esq., pseud. see Dennie, Joseph.

Oliver, Edward. Printer; 70 State Street, Boston.
The Boston Mirror; 1810.

Onderdonk, Benjamin T. Editor, New York.
The Christian Journal; 1817-1819.

Onderdonk, Henry U. Editor; New York.
The New York Medical Magazine; 1814-1815.

Oram, James. Printer, Publisher; 241 Pearl Street and 70 John
Street, then 13 Fair Street, then 102 Water Street, then 68
William Street, then 5 Burling Slip, New York.
The Ladies' Weekly Museum; May 9, 1812-October 25, 1817.
The New York Magazine; 1814.
The Globe; June 1819. (Printer only)

Osborn, Charles. Editor; Mt. Pleasant, Ohio.
The Philanthropist; 1817-1822.

Otis, Bass. Engraver; Philadelphia.
The Analectic; 1819.

Pacificus, Philo, pseud. see Worcester, Noah.

Palfrey, Warwick. Printer; Charleston, Mass.
The Gospel Visitant; April 1817-January 1818.

Palmer, George. Printer, Publisher; 201 Chestnut, Philadelphia.
Historical Register of the United States; 1812-1814/15.

Palmer, Thomas and Palmer, George. Printers; Philadelphia.
The Trangram; 1809-1810.

Pantagruel, pseud. Editor; Baltimore.
Red Book; 1819-1820.

Park, John. Editor; Boston.
The Boston Spectator; 1814-1815.

Parker, Samuel H. see Munroe, Edmund; Francis, David; and
Parker, Samuel H.

Parmenter, James. Editor; Roger's Building, Congress Street,
Rear of No. 12 State Street, Boston.

The Boston Weekly Magazine; October 12, 1816-April 4,
    1818.
see also: Parmenter, James and Norton, Jacob P.
          Tileston, Ezra B. and Parmenter, James.

Parmenter, James and Norton, Jacob P.   Publisher; Roger's
    Building, Congress Street, Rear of No. 12 State Street, Boston.
    The Boston Weekly Magazine; October 12, 1816-April 4,
    1818.

Paul, Abraham.   Printer; New York, New Haven.
    The Evangelical Guardian and Review; 1817-1819.
    The American Journal of Science; July 1818-

Paul, Abraham and Thomas, William.   Printers; 182 Water Street,
    Corner of Burling Slip, New York.
    Christian Monitor and Religious Intelligencer; 1812-1813.

Peirce (!), William.   Publisher; Market Street, Marietta, Penn.
    Ladies' Visitor; 1819-1820.

Pelissier, Victor.   Editor; 46 South Fifth Street, Philadelphia.
    Pelissier's Columbian Melodies; 1812.

Peluse, William L. and Gould, Stephen.   Printers; 3 New Street,
    New York.
    The Shamrock; September 12-November 14, 1812.

Perkins, ____.   see   Collins, Thomas and Perkins.

Phillips, ____.   see   Alexander and Phillips.

Philolagos, Euphronius, pseud.   Editor; Providence, R.I.
    Olla Podrida; 1816.

Picket, Albert.   Editor; New York.
    *Juvenile Mirror; 1810?-1812?
    The Academician; 1818-1820.

Picket, John W.   Editor; New York.
    *Juvenile Mirror; 1810?-1812?
    The Academician; 1818-1820.

Piggot, Robert.   see   Goodman, Charles and Piggot, Robert.

Pleasant, Peter, pseud.   Editor; Baltimore.
    Emerald; 1810-1811.

Plocher, Jacob J.   Engraver; Philadelphia.
    The Monthly Magazine; 1812.
    The American Medical Recorder; 1818-1819.

Pomeroy, Ralph W. and Toy, John D.   Printers; Baltimore.
    The Christian Messenger; May 10-August 16, 1817.

Potter, Nathaniel.   Editor; Baltimore.
    Baltimore Medical and Philosophical Lycaeum; 1811.

Prentis, J. H. and H.   Printers; Cooperstown, N.Y.
    The Religious Inquirer; 1811.

Prior and Dunning.   Printers; 111 Water Street, New York.
    The Villager; 1819.

Probasco, Simon and Justice, J. P.   Printers; 350 North Second
    Street, Philadelphia.
    The Parterre; 1816-1817.

Purdy, Stephen, Jr.   see   Harrison, John and Purdy, Stephen, Jr.

Quiz, Peter, pseud.   Editor; Alexandria, D.C.
    Columbian Telescope; 1819-1820.

Ramsey, David.   Printer; Auburn, N.Y.
    Evangelical Recorder; 1819-

Raser, Matthias.   see   Clark, John C. and Raser, Matthias.

Rawdon, Ralph.   see   Willard, Asaph and Rawdon, Ralph.

Reed, Abner.   Engraver; Boston?
    Polyanthos; 1814.

Reed, Ezra.   see   Bradford, Alden and Reed, Ezra.

(Salem, Mass.) Register Office.   Printer; Salem, Mass.
    The Gospel Visitant; June-September 1811.

Reinagle, H____.   Engraver; Philadelphia?
    Port Folio; 1818.

Reynolds, ____.   see   Looker, Reynolds and Co.

Rice, John Holt.   Editor; Richmond, Va.
    The Christian Monitor; 1815-1817.
    The Literary and Evangelical Magazine; 1818-

Richards, George.   Editor; Philadelphia.
    Freemason's Magazine; 1811-1812.

Richardson, John.   see   Kimber, Thomas and Richardson, John.

Riley, Benjamin.   see   VanPelt, Peter and Riley, Benjamin.

Riley, E____. Music engraver, Publisher; 17 Chatham Street,
    New York.
    Halcyon Luminary; 1812-1813.

Riley, Isaac and Adams, Thomas G.   Publishers; 23 Chatham
    Street, Next Door to the American Museum, New York.
    Literary Miscellany; 1811.

Rind, W. A. Printer, Publisher; Georgetown, D.C.
    Agricultural Museum; 1810-1811.

Ritchie, Trueheary and DuVal, Philip. Printers; E Street,
    Richmond, Va.
    The Christian Monitor; June 15-29, 1816.

Ritter, Frederick W. see Broderick, Joseph and Ritter,
    Frederick W.

Roberts and Burr. Printers; Hartford, Conn.
    The Rural Magazine; 1819.

Robinson, J____. Engraver; Philadelphia.
    The Analectic; 1817.

Robinson, Joseph. Printer, Publisher; At the Circulating Library,
    then 94 Baltimore Street, then Corner of Market and Belvidere
    Streets, Baltimore.
    Baltimore Repertory of Papers; 1811.
    National Museum; December 11, 1813-January 1, 1814.
        (Printer)
    Cohen's Gazette; 1817-   . (Publisher)
    Robinson's Magazine; 1818-1819.
    The American Farmer; 1819-   . (Printer)
    Red Book, 2d ed.; 1819-1820. (Publisher)

Robinson, Martin and Howland, Benjamin R. Publisher; Providence,
    R.I.
    Rhode Island Literary Repository; 1814-1815.

Rogers, Daniel. Editor; New York.
    The New York City Hall Recorder; 1816-1822.

Rollinson, William. Engraver; New York.
    New York Medical and Philosophical Journal; 1811.
    The Analectic; 1813.
    Port Folio; 1813.

Rudd, John C. Editor; Elizabethtown, N.J.
    The Churchman's Magazine; 1813-1815.

Russell, Henry P. and Edes, Richard W. Editors, Printers,

Publishers; Corner of Bull Street and Bay Lane, Savannah, Ga.
The Ladies' Magazine; May 15-August 7, 1819.

Russell, J. and W.   Publishers; Hartford, Conn.
The Rural Magazine; 1819.

Russell, John; Cutler, James; and Co.   Printers; Boston.   (Firm
included: Simon Gardner.)
Massachusetts Agricultural Repository; November 1813.

Russell, Joshua T.   Editor, Publisher; North Eutaw Street, Baltimore, Md.
The Christian Messenger; 1817-1819.

Ruter, Martin.   Editor; Concord, N.H.
New England Missionary Magazine; 1816.

Sargeant, Ezra.   Publishers; Corner of Wall Street and Broadway,
New York.
American Medical and Philosophical Register; 1810-1813.

Savage, James.   Editor; Boston.
The Monthly Anthology; 1806-1811.

Schaeffer, Frederick G. and Maund, Thomas.   Publishers; 214
Market Street, Baltimore.
Journal of the Times; 1818-1819.

Schoolcraft, Henry Rowe.   Editor; Hamilton Village, N.Y., etc.
The Cricket; 1809-1818.

Scratch'em, Toby, pseud.   see   Helmbold, George.

Seymour, James.   Printer; New York.
The Christian Herald; March 30, 1816-March 21, 1818.

Seymour, Jonathan.   Printer; New York.
The Christian's Magazine; 1806-1811.

Seymour, Samuel.   Engraver; Philadelphia.
Port Folio; 1813.

The Shamrock Press.   Printers; New York.
The Shamrock; November 14, 1812-June 5, 1813.

Sharp, Daniel.   Editor; Boston.
American Baptist Magazine; 1817.

Shaw, William Smith.   Editor; Boston.
The Monthly Anthology; 1806-1811.

Shirley, Arthur.   Printer; Portland, Vt.
Religious Magazine; July-October 1812.

Sidrophel, pseud. Editor; Baltimore, Md.
Red Book; 1819-1820.

Siegfried, Simeon. Printer; Newtown, Penn.
The Star of Freedom; 1817-1818.

Silliman, Benjamin. Editor; New Haven.
The American Journal of Science; July 1818-April 1838.

Simpleton, Samuel, pseud. Editor; Boston.
The Idiot; 1818-1819.

Simpson, Stephen. Editor; Boston.
The Portico; January 1816-June 1817.

Skillman, Thomas T. Editor, Printer, Publisher; Lexington, Ky.
Evangelical Record and Western Review; 1812-1813.
The Almoner; 1814-1815.

Skinner, John S. Editor; 8 North Calvert Street, Baltimore, Md.
The American Farmer; 1819-

Skinner, T. M. Printer; Auburn, N.Y.
Evangelical Recorder; January 31-September 5, 1818.

Skinner, T. M. and Co. Printers; Colchester, Conn.
*The Monthly Preceptor; March 1815.

Small, Abraham. Printer; Philadelphia.
The American Register; 1810.

Smith, Elias. Editor, Publisher; Buck Street, later Jeffrey Street,
    Portsmouth, N.H.; then Head of Fish Street, Portland, Maine;
    then 186 South Fifth Street, Philadelphia; then 2 Ladd Street,
    Portsmouth, N.H.; then Boston, Mass.
    Herald of Gospel Liberty; 1808-1817.
    The Herald of Life and Immortality; 1819-1820.

Smith, F. N. Editor; Northumberland, Penn.
The Religious Museum; 1818-1819.

Smith, George Girdler. see Annin, William B. and Smith, George
Girdler.

Smith, J. Augustine. Editor; New York.
New York Medical and Philosophical Journal; 1809-1811.

Smith, John Rubens. Engraver; New York.
Polyanthos; 1812-1814.

Smith, Thomas. Publisher; At the Office of the [Kentucky] Reporter, Lexington, Ky.
Journal of Belles Lettres; 1819-1820.

Smith, Thomas and Maxwell, James. Printers; Philadelphia.
    Port Folio; 1807-June 1810.

Smith, William H. Editor; Providence, R.I.
    *Juvenile Gazette; 1819-1820.

Smith, William R. Editor; Huntingdon, Penn.
    Huntingdon Literary Museum; 1810.

Smith and Forman. Printers; 195 and 213 Greenwich Street, New
    York.
    *Juvenile Mirror; 1810?-1812?

Smith and M'Kenzie. Printers; Philadelphia.
    The Mirror of Taste; January-June 1810.

Snelling, Samuel G. Printer; Boston.
    The Berean; 1810.

Snowden, S____. Printer; Alexandria, Va.
    The Monthly Visitant; 1816.

Snowdon, Thomas. see Tunison, Grant C. and Snowdon, Thomas.

A Society. Editors; New York.
    Theophilanthropist; 1810.

A Society for Promoting Christian Knowledge, Piety, and Charity.
    Boston.
    The Christian Monitor; 1806-1811.

A Society of Gentlemen. Editors; Baltimore.
    Baltimore Repertory of Papers; 1811.

A Society of Gentlemen. Editors; Cambridge, Mass.
    General Repository and Review; 1812-1813.

A Society of Gentlemen. Editors; New York.
    American Medical and Philosophical Register; 1810-1814.

A Society of Gentlemen. Editors; New York.
    Halcyon Luminary; 1812-1813.

A Society of Gentlemen Connected with the New Market Weslyan
    Academy. Editors; Concord, N.H.
    The New England Missionary Intelligencer; 1819.

A Society of Physicians. Editors; Philadelphia.
    Journal of Foreign Medical Science; 1810-1824.

Soule, Joshua. Editor; New York.
    The Methodist Review; 1818-1820.

Soule, Joshua and Mason, Thomas.   Publishers; New York.
   The Methodist Review; 1818-   .

Souter, John.   Publisher; No. 2 Paternoster Row, London.
   Port Folio; February 1817-December 1818.

Southgate, _____.   see   Lynch and Southgate.

Southwick, Henry C.   Printer, Publisher; Faust's Statue, 94 State
   Street, Albany, N.Y.
   Christian Visitant; 1815-1816.

Southwick, Solomon.   Editor; Albany, N.Y.
   Christian Visitant; 1815-1816.
   The Plough Boy; 1819-   .

Spafford, Horatio Gates.   Editor; Albany, N.Y.
   The American Magazine; 1815-1816.

Sparks, Jared.   Editor; Boston.
   North American Review; May 1817-1818.

Spaulding, _____.   see   Howe and Spaulding.

Spear and Eichbaum.   see   Carmer; Spear and Eichbaum; Franklin
   Mead.

Spear, William S. and Henry.   Printers; Charlestown, Mass.
   Gospel Visitant; March 1812.

Stalker, E_____.   Engraver; Philadelphia.
   The Analectic; 1815.

Steele, Oliver.   Printer, Publisher; New Haven, Conn.
   *Youth's Repository of Christian Knowledge; 1813.
   Atheneum; 1814.

Stephens, T. B.   Printer; 266 E. Bay Street, then 8 Tradd Street,
   Georgetown, S.C.
   *The Sunday Visitant; 1819.

Stevens, Alexander Hodgdon.   Editor; New York.
   The Medical and Surgical Register; 1818-1820.

Stiles, Thomas T.   Printer; Philadelphia.
   Archives of Useful Knowledge; 1810-1813.
   Select Reviews; January 1811-December 1812.

Stoddard, Ashbel.   Printer, Publisher; 135, Corner of Warren
   and Third Streets, Hudson, N.Y.
   The Columbia Magazine; 1814-1815.

Storer, E. Gilman. Printer, Publisher; Arlington, Vt.
     *The Union Magazine; 1818?

Strickland, William. Engraver; Philadelphia.
     The Emporium of Arts and Sciences; 1812.
     Port Folio; 1814-1817.
     The Analectic; 1816.
     The Portico; 1816.
     New Jerusalem Church Repository; 1818.

Strong, Thomas C. Printer, Publisher; Middlebury, Vt.
     The Advisor; January 1811-December 1815.
     The Literary and Philosophical Repertory; 1812-1817.

Studiosus, Solomon, pseud. Editor; Alexandria, D.C.
     Columbian Telescope; 1819-1820.

Sullivan, J. L. Engraver, New Haven, Conn.
     The American Journal of Science; 1818.

Swift, Samuel. Publisher; Middlebury, Vt.
     The Advisor; January 1811-December 1814.
     The Literary and Philosophical Repertory; 1812-1817.

Swords, Thomas and James. Printers, Publishers; 160 Pearl
     Street, New York.
     The Churchman's Magazine; 1808-1811. (Printers)
     New York Medical and Philosophical Journal; 1809-1811.
        (Printers)
     Medical Repository; 1815-1817. (Publishers)
     The Christian Register; 1816-1817. (Printers, Publishers)
     The Christian Journal; 1817-1830. (Publishers; also listed
        as editors, 1819-1830).

T. V. K. and Co. see Tanner, Benjamin; Vallance, John;
     Kearny, Francis and Co.

Tannatt, A. G. Editor, Publisher; Main Street, Nantucket, Mass.
     Nantucket Weekly Magazine; 1817-1818.

Tanner, Benjamin. Engraver; Philadelphia.
     Journal of Musick; 1810-1811.
     Philadelphia Medical Museum; 1810.
     Port Folio; 1810-1812, 1816, 1819.
     Journal of Foreign Medical Science; 1811.

Tanner, Benjamin; Vallance, John; Kearny, Francis and Co. En-
     gravers; Philadelphia.
     Port Folio; 1819.

Taws, John. Publisher; 61 South Third Street, Philadelphia.
     Pelissier's Columbian Melodies; July-December 1812.

Tenny, Joseph.   Editor, Publisher; Sangerfield, N.Y.
    The Christian's Monitor; 1814-1818.   (Publisher)
    Civil and Religious Intelligencer; 1816-1817.   (Editor)

Terry, Ezekiel.   Editor, Publisher; Palmer, Mass.
    The Massachusetts Watchman; 1809-1810.

Thomas, Moses.   Printer, Publisher; 52 Chestnut Street, Phila-
    delphia.
    The American Law Journal; 1813.   (Publisher)
    The Analectic Magazine; 1813-1819.   (Printer)
    The Quarterly Theological Magazine; 1814.   (Publisher)

Thomas, William.   see   Paul, Abraham and Thomas, William.

Thompson, Thomas.   see   Largin, George and Thompson, Thomas.

Tickler, Titus, Esq. and Co., pseud.   Editor; Baltimore.
    Scourge; 1810.

Tiebout, Cornelius.   Engraver; Philadelphia.
    Port Folio; 1810-1812.
    The Monthly Magazine; 1812.
    The Emporium of Arts and Sciences; 1812-1814.
    Journal of Foreign Medical Science; 1815.

Tiebout, Cornelius and Kearny, Francis.   Engravers; Philadelphia.
    The Emporium of Arts and Sciences; 1812.

Tiebout, Cornelius and Lawson, Alexander.   Engravers; Phila-
    delphia.
    The Emporium of Arts and Sciences; 1813.

Tileston, Ezra B.   Editor, Printer; Boston.
    Massachusetts Agricultural Repository; June 1815.   (Printer)
    New England Journal of Medicine; 1815.   (Printer)
    The Boston Weekly Magazine; October 12, 1816-April 4,
        1818.   (Editor)

Tileston, Ezra B. and Parmenter, James.   Printers; No. 4
    Rogers Building, Congress Street, Boston.
    New England Journal of Medicine; 1816.
    Massachusetts Agricultural Repository; January 1817.

Tileston, Ezra B. and Weld, Giles E.   Printers; Boston.
    Massachusetts Agricultural Repository; January-June 1816.

Timrod, William Henry.   Editor; Charleston, S.C.
    *The Evening Spy; 1813?

Titcomb, ____ .   Printer?   Boston.
    *Bibliothèque Portative; 1810?

Totten, John C.   Printer; New York.
The Methodist Review; 1818-

Touchstone, Tim, pseud.   see   Butler, Merrill.

Toy, John D.   Printer; Baltimore.
The Christian Messenger; August 23, 1817-May 1, 1819.
see also: Pomeroy and Toy.

A Trio, pseud.   (Alexandria, D.C.)   see
Whimsical, Geoffrey
Studiosus, Solomon
Quiz, Peter

A Trio, pseud.   see   Chandler, Cora and Chandler, Charles.

True, Benjamin.   Printer; Boston.
*Bibliothèque Portative; 1810?

True, Benjamin and Weston, Equality.   Printers; 78 State Street,
Boston.
Watchman-Examiner; 1819-

Trueheary, _____.   see   Ritchie, Trueheary, and DuVal.

Trumbull, Henry.   Publisher; Washington Street, Boston.
The Idiot; 1818-1819.

The Trustees of the Massachusetts Society for Promoting Agriculture.   Publishers; Boston.
Massachusetts Agricultural Repository; 1813-1832.

Tuckfield, W. H. P.   Publisher? Philadelphia.
Literary and Musical Magazine; 1819?

Tudor, William.   Editor; Boston.
North American Review; May 1815-March 1817.

Tunison, Garnt C. and Snowdon, Thomas.   Editors, Printers;
100 Church Street, New York.
Moralist; 1814.

Turner, Charles.   see   Day, Mahlon and Turner, Charles.

Turner, Charles and Co.   Printer, Publisher; New York.   (Firm
consisted of: Charles Turner and John Johnston)
General Shipping and Commercial List; September 10, 1819-
April 28, 1820.

Turner, Edward.   Editor; Charlestown, Mass.
Gospel Visitant; 1811-1818.

Two Men of Padua, pseud. see
    Watkins, Tobias
    Simpson, Stephen

Union College Literary Societies. Editors; Schenectady, N.Y.
    Floriad; 1811.

Vallance, John. see Tanner, Benjamin; Vallance, John; Kearny,
    Francis and Co.

VanPelt, Peter. see Hardcastle, John and VanPelt, Peter.

VanPelt, Peter and Riley, Benjamin. Printers; 9 Wall Street,
    Corner of Broad, New York.
    The Shamrock; January 25-August 16, 1817.

VanRiper, Nicholas. Printer; 194 Greenwich Street, Corner of
    Vesey, New York.
    The New York Medical Magazine; 1814-1815.
    The Shamrock; June 25, 1814-January 1, 1815.

VanWinkle, Cornelius S. Printer, Publisher; 101 Greenwich Street,
    New York.
    American Medical and Philosophical Register; July 1810-
        April 1811. (Publisher)
    Medical Repository; 1818. (Publisher)
    The Ladies' Literary Cabinet; May 15-November 27, 1819.
        (Printer)
    The New York Literary Journal; August 1819-   . (Printer)

VanWinkle, Cornelius S. and Wiley, Charles. Printers, Publishers;
    3 Wall Street, New York.
    American Medical and Philosophical Register; July 1813-
        April 1814. (Publisher)
    Cobbett's American Political Register; 1816-1818. (Printers)

Vosburgh, Abraham. Printer, Publisher, 87 Pearl Street, New
    York.
    The Country Courrier; July 4, 1816-January 23, 1817.
    The New York City Hall Recorder; 1818.

Wait, Thomas B. and Co. Printers, Publishers; Court Street,
    Boston.
    The Monthly Anthology; 1810-1811.
    New England Journal of Medicine; 1812.

Waldie, Adam. Printer; Back of 74 South Second Street, Phila-
    delphia.
    Quarterly Theological Review; January-October 1819.
    The Christian Messenger; September 11, 1819-   .

Waldo, Samuel Putnam. Editor; Hartford, Conn.
    The Rural Magazine; 1819.

Wall, S____. Editor; New York.
  Military Monitor and American Register; August 17-November 23, 1812.

Walsh, Robert.   Editor; Philadelphia.
  The American Register; 1809-1810.
  American Review of History and Politics; 1811-1812.
  American Register; 1817.

Ward and Coburn.   Printers; North Street, Salem, Mass.
  The Gospel Visitant; December 1811.

Ware, Henry, Jr.   Editor; Boston.
  The Christian Disciple; 1819-1823.

Warren, John C.   Editor; Boston.
  New England Journal of Medicine; 1812-   .

Warren, Obed.   Editor; Rutland, Vt.
  The Vermont Baptist Missionary Magazine; 1811.

Warrock, John.   Printer, Publisher; Richmond, Va.
  The Christian Monitor; September 14, 1816-August 30, 1817.

Watchful, Will, Esq., pseud. see Mein, John.

Waterman, Eleazer.   Printer; At the Office of the Winya Intelligencer, Georgetown, S.C.
  *The Sunday Visitant; 1818.

Watkins, Tobias.   Editor; Baltimore.
  The Portico; 1816-1818.

Watson, Ebenezer. see Whiting, Samuel and Watson, Ebenezer.

Watson, John F.   Publisher; Southwest Corner of Third and Chestnut Streets, Philadelphia.
  Select Reviews; January 1811-December 1812.

Watts, John.   Editor; New York.
  The Medical and Surgical Register; 1818-1820.

Weaver, William. see Levis, Isaac and Weaver, William.

Webster, James.   Publisher; 10 South 8th Street, then 24 South 8th
  Street, Philadelphia.
  The American Medical Recorder; January 1818-   .

Weld, Giles E. see Tileston, Ezra B. and Weld, Giles E.

Wells, William and Lilly, Robert.   Printers, Publishers; 97 Court
  Street, Boston.
  North American Review; 1815-1816.

The Christian Disciple; 1816, new series 1819-
Massachusetts Agricultural Repository; July 1817-June 1823.
New England Journal of Medicine; 1817-

West, I. E. Engraver; New York.
American Medical and Philosophical Register; 1813.

Weston, Equality. see True, Benjamin and Weston, Equality.

Wharton, Charles H. Editor; St. Mary's Church, Burlington, N.J.
The Quarterly Theological Magazine; 1814.

Wharton, Thomas Isaac. Editor; Philadelphia.
The Analectic Magazine; 1815-1821.

Wheeler, Bennett H. see Jones, Josiah and Co.

Whimsical, Geoffrey, pseud. Editor; Alexandria, D.C.
Columbian Telescope; 1819-1820.

Whimsical, Will. see Lemmon, George.

White, George S. Editor; Freetown, Mass.
Spiritual Magazine; 1813-1814.

White, Samuel B. Publisher; 317 Water Street, then 28 Frankfort
Street, New York.
The Lady's Miscellany; October 27, 1810-October 17, 1812.
see also: McCarty, William and White, Samuel B.

Whiting, Nathan. Editor, Publisher; At the Sign of Franklin's
Head, Corner of Chapel and College Streets, then At the Office
of the Religious Intelligencer, New Haven, Conn.
The Religious Intelligencer; 1816-1837.
*The Guardian and Monitor; January 1819-

Whiting, Samuel. see Whiting, Samuel and Co.
Whiting, Samuel a nd Watson, Ebenezer.
Williams, _____ and Whiting, Samuel.

Whiting, Samuel and Co. Publishers; 118 Pearl Street, New York.
The Christian's Magazine; May 1811.

Whiting, Samuel and Watson, Ebenezer. Publishers; 96 Broadway,
New York.
The Christian's Magazine; June-December 1811.

Whitlock, Henry. Editor; New Haven, Conn.
*Youth's Repository of Christian Knowledge; 1813.

Wildfire, Walter, pseud. Editor; Boston.
The Comet; 1811-1812.

Wiley, Charles. see VanWinkle, Cornelius S. and Wiley, Charles.

Wiley, David. Editor; Georgetown, D. C.
    Agricultural Museum; 1810-1812.

Willard, Asaph and Rawdon, Ralph. Engravers; Albany, N.Y.
    The American Magazine; 1816.

Williams, _____ and Whiting, Samuel. Publishers; 118 Pearl
    Street, New York.
    The Christian's Magazine; January 1810-May 1811.

Williams, Nathan. Editor; Hartford, Conn.
    Connecticut Evangelical Magazine; 1808-1810.

Willig, George. Printer, Publisher; 24 South Fourth Street,
    Philadelphia.
    Journal of Musick; 1810-1811? (Printer)
    Pelissier's Columbian Melodies; January-June 1812.

Willis, Nathaniel. Printer, Publisher; 76 State Street, then No. 3
    Suffolk Building, Congress Street, Boston.
    New England Journal of Medicine; 1813. (Printer)
    Congregationalist; 1816-

Wills, Francis M. see Neal, Abner; Wills, Francis M. and
    Cole, John.

Wilson, _____. see Lawrence and Wilson.

Winchell, James M. Editor; Boston.
    American Baptist Magazine; 1817-

Woodworth, Samuel. Editor, Printer, Publisher; 473 Pearl Street,
    then 60 Vesey Street, then 26 Chatham Street, New York.
    The War; 1812-1814. (Editor of single issue in 1817)
    Halcyon Luminary; 1812-1813.
    The Ladies' Literary Cabinet; 1819-1822.

Woodworth, Samuel and Heustis, Samuel. Publishers; Corner of
    Duane and Chatham Streets, New York.
    The Ladies' Literary Cabinet; May 15-November 27, 1819.

Worcester, Noah. Editor; Boston.
    The Christian Disciple; 1813-1818.
    Friend of Peace; 1815-1827.

Wright, Nathaniel H. Editor; Boston.
    Boston Kaleidoscope; 1818-1819.

Wrightman, Thomas. Engraver; Devonshire Street, Boston.
    Omnium Gatherum; 1810.

Young, James H. see Kneass, William and Young, James H.
    and Co.

Young, William Cox. Printer; 44 Broad Street, Charleston, S.C.
    The Southern Evangelical Intelligencer; 1819-1821.

Zantzinger, Thomas Barton and Co. Publishers; Shakespeare
    Buildings, South Sixth near Chestnut Street, Philadelphia.
    The Mirror of Taste; January-December 1811.

Zentler, Conrad. Printer; Philadelphia.
    *Evangelisches Magazin; 1811-1817.

SELECTED BIBLIOGRAPHY

The titles in this list represent some of the better historical material about early American magazines. The full citations for items referred to only by the author's last name are in this list, as are many items used as background but not necessarily cited directly in the study. The most important sources are the magazines themselves.

BOOKS

Adams, Herbert Baxter. The Life and Writings of Jared Sparks. Boston: Houghton, Mifflin, 1893. 2 vols.

Alden, Henry Mills. Magazine Writing and the New Literature. New York: Harper, 1908.

Anthology Society, Boston. Journal of the Proceedings of the Society which Conducts the Monthly Anthology and Boston Review, October 3, 1805 to July 2, 1811. Boston: The Boston Athenaeum, 1910.

Arndt, Karl J. R. and May E. Olson. German-American Newspapers and Periodicals, 1732-1955. (Deutsche Presseforschung, Bd. 3) Heidelberg: Quelle & Meyer, 1961.

Bardeen, Charles William. History of Educational Journalism in the State of New York. Syracuse: C. W. Bardeen, 1893.

Barrett, John Pressley. The Centennial of Religious Journalism. 2d ed. Dayton, Ohio: Christian Publishing Association, 1908.

Baumgartner, Apollinaris William. Catholic Journalism; a Study of its Development in the United States, 1798-1930. New York: Columbia University Press, 1931.

Bolton, Henry Carrington. Catalogue of Scientific and Technical Periodicals, 1665-1895. 2d ed. (Smithsonian Institution. "Miscellaneous Collections," vol. 40) Washington: Smithsonian Institution, 1897.

Brigham, Clarence Saunders. History and Bibliography of American Newspapers, 1690-1820. Worcester: American Antiquarian Society, 1947. 2 vols.

Brown, Harry Glenn and Maude O. Brown. A Directory of Printing,
Publishing, Bookselling, and Allied Trades in Rhode Island to
1865. New York: The New York Public Library, 1958.

_____. A Directory of the Book-Arts and Book Trade in Phila-
delphia to 1820, Including Printers and Engravers. New York:
The New York Public Library, 1950.

Brown, Herbert Ross. The Sentimental Novel in America, 1789-
1860. New York: Pageant Books, 1959.

Buckingham, Joseph Tinker. Personal Memoirs and Recollections
of Editorial Life. Boston: Ticknor, Reed, and Fields, 1852.
2 vols.

Butler, Nicholas Murray. The Effect of the War of 1812 Upon the
Consolidation of the Union. (Johns Hopkins University.
"Studies," series 5, no. 7) Baltimore: Johns Hopkins, 1887.

Cairns, William B. British Criticism of American Writings,
1783-1815. (Wisconsin University. "Studies in Language and
Literature," no. 1) Madison: Wisconsin University, 1918.

_____. On the Development of American Literature from 1815
to 1833; with especial Reference to Periodicals. Madison:
Published by the University, 1898.

Caldwell, Charles. Autobiography of Charles Caldwell ...
Philadelphia: Lippincott and Grambo, 1855.

Calverton, Victor Francis. The Liberation of American Literature.
New York: Scribners, 1932.

Chamberlain, John. The Enterprising Americans: A Business
History of the United States. New York: Harper and Row,
1963.

Charvat, William. Literary Publishing in America, 1790-1850.
Philadelphia: University of Pennsylvania, 1959.

_____. The Origins of American Cultural Thought, 1810-1835.
Philadelphia: University of Pennsylvania Press, 1936.

Chu, Pao Hsun. The Post Office of the United States. 2d ed.
New York: Columbia University Press, 1932.

Clark, Harry Hayden. Transitions in American Literary History.
Durham: Duke University Press, 1954.

Craigie, William Alexander, ed. A Dictionary of American English.
     Chicago: University of Chicago Press, 1938-44. 4 vols.

Curti, Merle. The Growth of American Thought. 2d ed. New
     York: Harper, 1951.

Dangerfield, George. The Era of Good Feelings. New York:
     Harcourt, Brace, 1952.

Davis, Sheldon Emmor. Educational Periodicals During the Nine-
     teenth Century. (U.S. Department of the Interior. Bureau of
     Education. "Bulletin," 1919, no. 28) Washington: Government
     Printing Office, 1919.

Demaree, Albert Lowther. The American Agricultural Press,
     1819-1860. New York: Columbia University Press, 1941.

DeVinne, Theodore Low. Printing in the Nineteenth Century.
     New York: Lead Mould Electrotype Foundry, 1924.

Dictionary of American Biography. New York: Scribner's, 1928-
     1936. 20 vols.

Drake, Milton. Almanacs of the United States. New York: Scare-
     crow Press, 1962. 2 vols.

Drewry, John Eldridge. Some Magazines and Magazine Makers.
     Boston: Stradford, 1924.

Earle, Alice Morse. Stage-coach and Tavern Days. New York:
     Macmillan, 1922.

Ellis, Harold Milton. Joseph Dennie and His Circle: A Study in
     American Literature from 1792-1812. (University of Texas.
     "Studies in English," no. 3) Austin: University of Texas, 1915.

Ellison, Rhoda Coleman. Early Alabama Publications: A Study in
     Literary Interests. University, Ala.: University of Alabama
     Press, 1947.

Fielding, Mantle. American Engravers Upon Copper and Steel:
     A Supplement to David McNeely Stauffer's American Engravers.
     Philadelphia: Wickersham Press, 1917.

_____. Dictionary of American Painters, Sculptors, and En-
     gravers. New York: Paul A. Struck, 1945.

Flanders, Bertram Holland. Early Georgia Magazines; Literary
     Periodicals to 1865. Athens: University of Georgia Press,
     1944.

Foik, Paul Joseph. Pioneer Catholic Journalism. New York:
     United States Catholic Historical Society, 1930.

Ford, Edwin Hopkins. History of Journalism in the United States:
     A Bibliography of Books and Annotated Articles. Minneapolis:
     Burgess Publishing Company, 1938.

Forsyth, David P. The Business Press in America, 1750-1865.
     Philadelphia: Chilton Books, 1964.

Gage, Thomas Hovey. An Artist Index to Stauffer's "American
     Engravers." Worcester, Mass. Published by the Society,
     1921.

Gilmer, Gertrude Cordelia. Checklist of Southern Periodicals to
     1861. Boston: Faxon, 1934.

Goodnight, Scott Holland. German Literature in American Maga-
     zines Prior to 1846. Madison: The University of Wisconsin,
     1907.

Graham, Walter James. English Literary Periodicals. New York:
     Thomas Nelson, 1930.

Hammond, Otis Grant. Bibliography of the Newspapers and Periodi-
     cals of Concord, New Hampshire, 1790-1898. Concord: Ira C.
     Evans, 1902.

Holland, Dorothy Garesche. An Annotated Checklist of Magazines
     Published in St. Louis Before 1900. (Washington University
     Library Studies, no. 2) St. Louis: Washington University Press,
     1951.

Hoole, William Stanley. A Checklist and Finding List of Charleston
     Periodicals, 1732-1864. Durham: Duke University Press,
     1936.

Hounchell, Saul. The Principal Literary Magazines of the Ohio
     Valley to 1840. (George Peabody College for Teachers. "Con-
     tributions to Education," no. 144) Nashville: George Peabody
     College for Teachers, 1934.

Hudson, Frederick. Journalism in the United States from 1690 to
     1872. New York: Harper, 1873.

Index to Early American Periodical Literature, 1728-1870. Part I.
     The List of Periodicals Indexed. New York: Pamphlet Dis-
     tributing Company, 1941.

Ingersoll, Charles Jared. A Discourse Concerning the Influence of
     America on the Mind. Philadelphia: A. Small, 1823.

Jillson, Willard Rouse. The Newspapers and Periodicals of Frank-
     fort, Kentucky, 1795-1945. Frankfort: The Kentucky State
     Historical Society, 1945.

Jones, Howard Mumford. Ideas in America. Cambridge, Mass.:
Harvard University Press, 1944.

Karpinski, Louis Charles. Bibliography of Mathematical Works
Printed in America Through 1850. Ann Arbor: University of
Michigan Press, 1940.

Knapp, Samuel Lorenze. American Cultural History, 1607-1829.
Gainsville, Fla.: Scholars' Facsimilies and Reprints, 1961.

Krout, John Allen and Dixon Ryan Fox. The Completion of Independence, 1790-1830. New York: Macmillan, 1944.

Layer, Robert G. Earnings of Cotton Mill Operatives, 1825-1914.
Cambridge: Committee on Research in Economic History, 1955.

Lewis, Benjamin Morgan. A Register of Editors, Printers and
Publishers of American Magazines, 1741-1810. New York:
New York Public Library, 1957.

Luxon, Norval Neil. Niles' Weekly Register: News Magazine of
the Nineteenth Century. Baton Rouge: Louisiana State University Press, 1947.

McCorison, Marcus A. Vermont Imprints, 1778-1820. Worcester.
American Antiquarian Society, 1963.

McKay, George Leslie. A Register of Artists, Engravers, Book-
binders, Printers, and Publishers in New York City, 1633-
1820. New York: New York Public Library, 1942.

McMaster, John Bach. A History of the People of the United
States from the Revolution to the Civil War. New York:
Appleton, 1883-1913. 8 vols.

Miller, James McDonald. The Genesis of Western Culture: The
Ohio Valley, 1800-1825. Columbus, Ohio: Ohio State Archaeo-
logical and Historical Society, 1938.

Mitchell, Samuel L. A Discourse on the State and Prospects of
American Literature. Albany: Websters and Skinners, 1821.

The Monthly Anthology and Boston Review. The Federalist Literary
Mind ... Lewis P. Simpson, ed. Baton Rouge: Louisiana
State University Press, 1962.

Mott, Frank Luther. American Journalism; A History 1690-1960.
3d ed. New York: Macmillan, 1962.

_____. A History of American Magazines, Vol. I: 1741-1850;
Vol. II: 1850-1865. 2d printing. Cambridge, Mass.: Harvard
University Press, 1939, 1957.

Murray, James Augustus Henry, ed. The Oxford English Dictionary.
     Oxford: Clarendon Press, 1933. 13 vols.

Oberholtzer, Ellis Paxton. The Literary History of Philadelphia.
     Philadelphia: George W. Jacobs, 1906.

Orians, George Harrison. A Short History of American Literature,
     Analyzed by Decades. New York: F. S. Crofts, 1940.

Osborn, Chase Salmon. Schoolcraft, Longfellow, Hiawatha.
     Lancaster, Penn.: The Jaques Cattell Press, 1942.

Pattee, Fred L. The First Century of American Literature, 1770-
     1870. New York: Appleton-Century, 1935.

Peck, Louis F. A Life of Matthew G. Lewis. Cambridge:
     Harvard University Press, 1961.

Perkins, Bradford. Prologue to War; England and the United States,
     1805-1812. Berkeley: University of California Press, 1961.

Perrin, William Henry. The Pioneer Press of Kentucky. (Filson
     Club. "Publications," no. 3) Louisville. J. P. Morton
     Company, 1888.

Poole's Index to Periodical Literature. By William Frederick
     Poole. Boston: Houghton, Mifflin, 1893.

Quinn, Arthur Hobson. The Literature of the American People.
     New York: Appleton-Century-Crofts, 1951.

Rich, Wesley Everett. The History of the United States Post Office
     to the Year 1829. Cambridge: Harvard University Press, 1924.

Richardson, Lyon Norman. A History of American Magazines,
     1741-1789. New York: Thomas Nelson, 1931.

Riegel, Robert E. American Feminists. Lawrence: University
     of Kansas Press, 1963.

Robertson, Ross M. History of the American Economy. 2d ed.
     New York: Harcourt, 1964.

Rusk, Ralph Leslie. The Literature of the Middle Western Frontier.
     New York: Columbia University Press, 1925. 2 vols.

Sabin, Joseph. Dictionary of Books Relating to America, from its
     Discovery to the Present Time. New York: Bibliographical
     Society of America, 1928-36. 29 vols.

Schlesinger, Arthur Meyer, Jr. Paths of American Thought.
     Boston: Houghton, Mifflin, 1963.

Schneider, Herbert Wallace. A History of American Philosophy. 2d ed. New York: Columbia University Press, 1963.

Shaw, Ralph Robert. American Bibliography; A Preliminary Checklist for 1801-1819. New York: Scarecrow Press, 1958-1963. 19 vols.

Silver, Rollo Gabriel. The Baltimore Book Trade, 1800-1825. New York: New York Public Library, 1953.

_____. The Boston Book Trade, 1800-1825. New York: New York Public Library, 1949.

Smyth, Albert Henry. The Philadelphia Magazines and Their Contributors, 1741-1850. Philadelphia: Robert M. Lindsay, 1892.

Sparks, Herbert B. The Life and Writings of Jared Sparks. Boston: Houghton, Mifflin, 1893. 2 vols.

Spencer, Benjamin T. The Quest for Nationality. Syracuse: University of Syracuse, 1957.

Stauffer, David McNeely. American Engravers Upon Copper and Steel. New York: The Grolier Club, 1907. 2 vols.

Steiner, Bernard C. One Hundred and Ten Years of Bible Society Work in Maryland, 1810-1920. n.p.: The Maryland Bible Society, 1921.

Stevens, Daniel Gurden. The First Hundred Years of the American Baptist Publishing Society. Philadelphia: The American Baptist Publishing Company, 1925.

Stuntz, Stephen Conrad. List of Agricultural Periodicals of the United States and Canada Published During the Century July 1810 to July 1910. (U.S. Department of Agriculture. "Miscellaneous Publication, " no. 398, 1941) Washington: Government Printing Office, 1941.

Sutton, Walter. The Western Book Trade: Cincinnati as a Nineteenth-Century Publishing and Book-Trade Center. Columbus: Ohio State University Press, 1961.

Sweet, William Warren. Religion in the Development of American Culture, 1765-1840. Gloucester, Mass.: Peter Smith, 1963.

_____. Religion on the American Frontier: The Baptists, 1783-1830. New York: Cooper Square Publishers, 1964.

Taft, Phillip. Organized Labor in American History. New York: Harper & Row, 1954.

Tapley, Harriet Silvester. Salem Imprints, 1768-1825. Salem, Mass.: The Essex Institute, 1927.

Tassin, Algernon de Vivier. The Magazine in America. New York: Dodd, Mead, 1916.

Thomas, Isaiah. History of Printing in America. 2d ed. Albany: Joel Munsell, 1874.

Tucker, Gilbert Milligan. American Agricultural Periodicals: An Historical Sketch. Albany; Privately printed, 1909.

Tudor, William. Miscellanies. Boston: Wells and Lilly, 1821.

Union List of Serials in Libraries of the United States and Canada. 2d ed. Edited by Winifred Gregory. New York: The H. W. Wilson Company, 1943.

_____. Supplement, 1941-43. New York: Wilson, 1945.

_____. Second Supplement, 1944-49. New York: Wilson, 1953.

U.S. Census Office. 3d Census, 1810. Aggregate Amount of Each Description of Persons Within the U.S.A., and the Territories Thereof ... in the Year 1810. Washington: 1811.

_____. _____. 4th Census, 1820. Census for 1820. Washington: Gales and Seaton, 1821.

Williams, Stanley T. The Life of Washington Irving. New York: Oxford University Press, 1935. 2 vols.

Wish, Harvey. Society and Thought in Early America. New York: Longmans, Green, 1950.

Wood, James Plysted. Magazines in the United States; Their Social and Economic Influence. New York: Ronald Press, 1949.

PERIODICALS AND ARTICLES

Albaugh, Gaylord P. "American Presbyterian Periodicals and Newspapers, 1752-1830, with Library Locations," Journal of Presbyterian History, XLI (September 1963), 165-87; (December 1963), 243-62; XLII (March 1964), 54-67; (June 1964), 124-44.

Allen, Frederick Lewis, et al. "American Magazines, 1741-1941; with List," New York Public Library. Bulletin, XLV (June 1941), 439-60.

Barnard, Henry. "Educational Periodicals and Reports," American Journal of Education, XXXII (1882), 942-5.

Barnett, Claribel R. "The Agricultural Museum: An Early Ameri-
    can Agricultural Periodical, " Agricultural History, II (April
    1928), 99-102.

"Biography--For the Port Folio, " The Port Folio, 5th Series, II
    (October 1816), 273-7.

Booth, Robert Edmund. "American Periodicals, 1800-1825; Uni-
    versity Microfilms Commences a New Series, " Library Journal,
    LXXI (February 1, 1946), 156-63.

Brainerd, Marion. "Historical Sketch of American Legal Periodi-
    cals, " Law Library Journal, XIV (October 1921), 63-9.

"Centennial of Religious Journalism, " Independent, LXV (October 1,
    1908), 800-1.

Clark, Charles Hopkins. "Newspapers and Periodicals of Connecti-
    cut, " in Norris Galpin Osborn, ed. History of Connecticut in
    Monographic Form. New York: The States History Company,
    1925. II, 57-188.

Clark, Harry Hayden. "Literary Criticism in the North American
    Review, 1815-1835, " Wisconsin Academy of Sciences, Arts and
    Letters, Transactions, XXXII (1940), 299-350.

_____. "Nationalism in American Literature, " University of
    Toronto Quarterly, II (July 1933), 492-519.

Connecticut Historical Society. Bulletin. VII (October 1940), 2-4.

Ditzion, Sidney. "History of Periodical Literature in the United
    States, " Bulletin of Bibliography, XV (January/April 1935),
    110; (May/August 1935), 129-33.

Ebert, Myrl L. "Rise and Development of the American Medical
    Periodical, 1797-1850, " Medical Library Association, Bulletin,
    XL (July 1953), 243-76.

Elsbree, Oliver Wendell. "The Rise of the Missionary Spirit in
    New England, 1790-1815, " The New England Quarterly, I (July
    1928), 295-322.

Fishwick, Marshall W. "The Portico and Literary Nationalism
    After the War of 1812, " The William and Mary Quarterly, 3d
    Series, VIII (April 1951), 238-45.

Garnsey, Caroline John. "Ladies' Magazines to 1850; the Beginnings
    of an Industry, " New York Public Library, Bulletin, LVIII
    (February 1954), 74-88.

Gilmer, Gertrude Cordelia. "Maryland Magazines - Antebellum,
    1793-1861, " Maryland Historical Magazine, XXIX (June 1934),
    120-31.

Hale, Will T. "Early American Journalism," Methodist Quarterly Review, LII (January 1903), 42-8.

Hall, Hiland. "Country Items," The Vermont Historical Gazetteer, I (1867), 252.

Hewett, Daniel. "Daniel Hewett's List of Newspapers and Periodicals in the United States in 1828," American Antiquarian Society, Proceedings, n. s., XLIV (1935), 365-98.

Kinietz, Vernon. "Schoolcraft's Manuscript Magazines," Bibliographical Society of America, Papers, XXXV (Second Quarter 1941), 151-4.

Luxon, Norval Neil. "H. Niles, the Man and the Editor," Mississippi Valley Historical Review, XXVII (June 1941), 27-40.

_____. "Niles' Weekly Register--Nineteenth Century News Magazine," Journalism Quarterly, XVIII (September 1941), 273-91.

McCloskey, John C. "The Campaign of Periodicals after the War of 1812 for National American Literature," PMLA, L (March 1935), 262-73.

_____. "A Note on the Portico," American Literature, VIII (November 1936), 300-4.

McDowell, Tremaine. "Bryant and The North American Review," American Literature, I (March 1929), 14-26.

McMurtrie, Douglas Crawford. "The Westward Migration of the Printing Press in the United States, 1786-1836," Gutenberg Jahrbuch, V (1930), 269-88.

Matthews, Albert. "A Projected Harvard Magazine, 1814," Harvard Graduate Magazine, XXXVII (June 1929), 445-7.

Matthews, Brander. "American Magazines," Bookman, XLIX (July 1919), 533-41.

Mendenhall, Lawrence. "Early Literature of the Miami Valley," Midland Monthly, VIII (August 1897), 144-51.

Middleton, Thomas Cooke. "Catholic Periodicals Published in the United States From the Earliest in 1809 to the Close of the Year 1892," American Catholic Historical Society of Philadelphia, Records, XIX (1908), 18-41.

_____. "A List of Catholic and Semi-Catholic Periodicals Published in the United States from the Earliest Date Down to the Close of the Year 1892," American Catholic Historical Society of Philadelphia, Records, IV (1893), 213-42.

Morrison, Alfred J. "Presbyterian Periodicals of Richmond, 1815-
1860," Tyler's Quarterly Historical and Genealogical Magazine,
I (January 1920), 174-6.

_____. "The Virginia Literary and Evangelical Magazine, Rich-
mond, 1818-1828," William and Mary Quarterly, First Series,
XIX (April 1911), 266-72.

Mott, Frank Luther. "The Christian Disciple and the Christian
Examiner," New England Quarterly, I (April 1928), 197-207.

Paine, Gregory. "Cooper and The North American Review,"
Studies in Philology, XXVIII (October 1931), 799-809.

Peabody, Andrew P. "The Farmer's Weekly Museum," American
Antiquarian Society, Proceedings, n. s., VI (October 23, 1889),
106-29.

Postal, Bernard. "The Early American Jewish Press," Reflex, II
(April 1928), 68-77.

Randall, Randolph C. "Authors of the Port Folio Revealed by the
Hall Files," American Literature, XI (January 1940), 379-416.

Rawings, Kenneth W. "Trial List of Titles of Kentucky Newspapers and Periodicals Before 1860," Kentucky Historical Society, Register, XXXVI (July 1938), 263-87.

Seilhamer, George. "Weekly Magazines and Newspapers," in John
Russell Young, ed. Memorial History of the City of Phila-
delphia, from Its First Settlement to the Year 1895. New York:
New York History Company, 1895-98. II, 268-84.

Severance, Frank Hayward. "The Periodical Press of Buffalo,
1811-1915," Buffalo Historical Society, Publications, XI X (1915),
177-280.

Shafer, Henry Burnell. "Early Medical Magazines in America,"
Annals of Medical History, n. s., VII (1935), 480-91.

Shearer, Augustus H. "American Historical Magazines," Mississippi
Valley Historical Review, IV (March 1918), 484-91.

Sheerin, John B. "The Development of the Catholic Magazine in the
History of American Journalism," United States Catholic Historical Society, Historical Records and Studies, XLI (1953),
5-13.

Shrell, Darwin. "Nationalism and Aesthetics in the North American
Review, 1815-1850," in Waldo McNeir and Leo B. Levy, eds.
Studies in American Literature. (Louisiana State University
Studies, "Humanities Series," no. 8) Baton Rouge, La.:
Louisiana State University Press, 1960. pp. 11-21.

Silver, Rollo Gabriel. "Problems in Nineteenth Century American Bibliography," Bibliographical Society of America, Papers, XXXV (First Quarter 1941), 35-47.

Simpson, Louis P. "A Literary Adventure of the Early Republic: The Anthology Society and the Monthly Anthology," New England Quarterly, XXVII (June 1954), 168-90.

_____. "The Literary Miscellany and The General Repository," The Library Chronicle of the University of Texas, III (Spring 1950), 177-90.

Smith, David Eugene. "Early American Mathematical Periodicals," Scripta Mathematica, I (June 1933), 277-85.

Stearns, Bertha Monica. "Before Godey's," American Literature, II (November 1930), 248-55.

_____. "Early New England Magazines for Ladies," New England Quarterly, II (July 1929), 420-57.

_____. "Early Philadelphia Magazines for Ladies," Pennsylvania Magazine of History and Biography, LXIV (October 1940), 479-91.

_____. "Southern Magazines for Ladies, 1819-1860," South Atlantic Quarterly, XXXI (January 1932), 70-87.

Stephens, Ethel. "American Popular Magazines: A Bibliography," Bulletin of Bibliography, IX (1916), 7-10, 41-3, 69-70, 95-8.

Streeter, Gilbert Lewis. "Account of the Newspapers and Other Periodicals Published in Salem, From 1768 to 1856," Essex Institute, Proceedings, I (1848-1856), 157-87.

Thursfield, Richard Emmons. "Henry Barnard's American Journal of Education," Johns Hopkins University, Studies in Historical and Political Science, LXIII (1945), 1-359.

Thwaites, Reuben Gold. "The Ohio Valley Press Before the War of 1812-15," American Antiquarian Society, Proceedings, n.s., XIX (1909), 309-68.

Venable, William Henry. "Early Periodical Literature of the Ohio Valley," Magazine of Western History, VIII (June 1888), 101-110; (July 1888), 197-203.

Watson, Sereno. "The American Journal of Education," The New Englander, XXIV (July 1865), 513-30.

Weiss, Harry B. "The Growth of the Graphic Arts in Philadelphia, 1663-1820," New York Public Library, Bulletin, LVI (February 1952), 76-83; (March 1952), 139-45.

_____. "The Number of Persons and Firms Connected with the Graphic Arts in New York City, 1663-1820," New York Public Library, Bulletin, L (October 1946), 775-86.

Willging, Eugene P. and Herta Hatzfeld. "Catholic Serials in the Nineteenth Century in the United States; A Bibliographical Survey and a Union List," American Catholic Historical Society of Philadelphia, Records, LXV (September 1954), 158-75; LXVI (September 1955), 156-73; LXVI (December 1955), 222-38.

UNPUBLISHED MATERIAL

Birnbaum, Henry. American Literary Nationalism After the War of 1812: 1815-1825. Unpublished Ph.D. dissertation. George Washington University, 1954.

Cardwell, Guy Adams, Jr. Charleston Periodicals, 1795-1860. Unpublished Ph.D. dissertation. North Carolina, 1936.

Coberly, James H. The Growth of Nationalism in American Literature, 1800-1815. Unpublished Ph.D. dissertation. George Washington University, 1950.

Dickson, Algernon Smith. The Western Review and Miscellaneous Magazine. Unpublished Master's thesis. Columbia, 1954.

Farrior, John Edward. A Study of the North American Review: The First Twenty Years. Unpublished Ph.D. dissertation. North Carolina, 1954.

Flewelling, H. Lloyd. Literary Criticism in American Magazines, 1783-1820. Unpublished Ph.D. dissertation. The University of Michigan, 1931.

Hudson, Laura Thermo. The North American Review and Atlantic Monthly: Their Places in the History of American Literature. Unpublished Master's thesis. John B. Stetson, 1927.

Jones, Arthur Edwin. Early American Literary Criticism; A Study of American Literary Opinions and Attitudes, 1741-1820. Unpublished Ph.D. dissertation. Syracuse, 1950.

Kerr, Willis Holmes. Periodical Literature in America From the Revolution to 1815. Unpublished Master's thesis. Columbia, 1902.

Lewis, Benjamin Morgan. A History and Bibliography of American Magazines, 1800-1810. Unpublished Ph.D. dissertation. The University of Michigan, 1955.

Lyon, Betty Longenecker. A History of Children's Secular Magazines

Published in the United States from 1789-1899.   Unpublished
Ph.D. dissertation. Johns Hopkins, 1942.

Mahan, Howard F.   Joseph Gales, the National Intelligencer and
the War of 1812. Unpublished Ph.D. dissertation. Columbia,
1958.

Marino, Samuel Joseph. The French Refugee Newspapers and
Periodicals in the United States, 1789-1825. Unpublished Ph.D.
dissertation. The University of Michigan, 1962.

Mason, Julian Dewey. The Critical Reception of American Negro
Authors in American Magazines, 1800-1900. Unpublished Ph.D.
dissertation. North Carolina, 1962.

Merrill, Goldie Platner. The Development of American Secular
Juvenile Magazines. Unpublished Ph.D. dissertation. The University of Washington, 1939.

Pfennig, Hazel Tesh. Periodical Literary Criticism 1800-1865.
Unpublished Ph.D. dissertation. New York University, 1932.

Pierce, William S. A Directory of Newspapers and Periodicals
Published in Pittsburgh Before 1900. Unpublished Master's
thesis. Carnegie Institute of Technology, 1954.

Queenan, John. The Portfolio: A Study of the History and Significance of an Early American Magazine. Unpublished Ph.D.
dissertation. Pennsylvania, 1954.

Scott, Franklin William. Newspapers and Periodicals of Illinois,
1814-1879. Unpublished Ph.D. dissertation. The University
of Illinois, 1911.

Snodgrass, Isabelle S. American Musical Periodicals of New
England and New York, 1786-1850. Unpublished Master's
thesis. Columbia, 1947.

Streeter, Robert E. Critical Thought in the North American Review, 1815-1865. Unpublished Ph.D. dissertation. North-
western, 1943.

Wheeler, Effie Jane. Narrative Art in the Prose Fiction of
Eighteenth-Century Magazines. Unpublished Ph.D. dissertation.
The University of Michigan, 1942.

White, Maxwell Otis. A History of American Historical Periodicals
to the Founding of the American Historical Review 1741-1895.
Unpublished Ph.D. dissertation. Iowa State University, 1946.

Windle, John Taylor. Wood Engraving and Magazine Publishing in
America. Unpublished Master's thesis. Chicago, 1942.

Wunderlich, Charles Edward. <u>A History and Bibliography of Early</u>
    <u>American Musical Periodicals, 1782-1852.</u> Unpublished Ph. D.
    dissertation. The University of Michigan, 1962.

                        OTHER SOURCES

The American Antiquarian Society.   Access to the stack collections
    and to the serials shelf list.

The Cincinnati Historical Society.   Correspondence with the Acting
    Librarian, Mrs. Andrew N. Jergens, Jr.

The Connecticut Historical Society.   Interview with the Librarian,
    Mr. Thompson R. Harlow.

The Filson Club, Louisville, Ky.   Correspondence with the Curator
    and Librarian, Mrs. Dorothy Thomas Cullen.

Harvard University.   Widener Library.   Access to the general
    stacks and to the serials shelf list.

The Library Company of Philadelphia.   Access to the general
    stacks and to the serials shelf list.

Philadelphia College of Pharmacy and Science.   Correspondence
    with the Acting Librarian, Mrs. Theodora Jackson.

Southern Baptist Theological Seminary.   Correspondence with the
    Librarian, Mr. Leo T. Crismon.

The Union Theological Seminary.   Correspondence with the Assistant
    to the Librarian, Mr. Hugh H. Tidwell.

Yale University.   Beinecke Library.   Correspondence with Miss
    Marjorie Wynne.

Yale University.   Sterling Library.   Correspondence with Mr. John
    A. Braswell.

INDEX

The number of individuals associated with American magazines is remarkably large. Not only were many individuals, both men and women, producers of the magazines; but many were also contributors. Some of these names are listed in Appendix C. To list all the others would be to index the magazines in detail, and that is not a purpose of this book. But there are some names associated with the magazines and otherwise mentioned in the Introduction which should have some access. These names are listed in this Index. Along with them are the names of a few literary clubs and other things which might be of interest.

Some few of the magazines themselves are also mentioned in the Introduction. These are listed here by title. The basic source of information about the magazines in each case is its annotation, and since these are alphabetical in the main body of the work, reference can easily be made there as well.

One exception involves alternative names for the magazines. Some of them are quite different; and, in fact, some magazines are incorrectly known by one of these different titles. As an aid in finding information about these titles, the Index contains a number of cross-references to the magazine titles used in this book. In each case, the user should refer to the main annotation. No page numbers are given to differentiate these references from references to the Introduction. In a few cases, there will also be a reference to the Introduction, but this will be under the name used for the annotation title.

One other type of reference is used in this Index. A few broad terms and phrases are used as subjects, and these are in all capital letters.

This book then has three index approaches. This short index will lead mainly to the Introduction. It should be used in conjunction with Appendix C and with the annotations themselves. All three should provide the fullest possible range of information about the magazines covered in this study.